COMMENTARIES

ON

THE BOOK OF JOSHUA

THE CALVIN TRANSLATION SOCIETY,

INSTITUTED IN MAY M.DCCC.XLIII.

FOR THE PUBLICATION OF TRANSLATIONS OF THE WORKS OF JOHN CALVIN.

COMMENTARIES

ON

THE BOOK OF JOSHUA

BY JOHN CALVIN

TRANSLATED FROM THE ORIGINAL LATIN, AND COLLATED WITH THE FRENCH EDITION,

BY HENRY BEVERIDGE, ESQ

WIPF & STOCK · Eugene, Oregon

Wipf and Stock Publishers
199 W 8th Ave, Suite 3
Eugene, OR 97401

Commentaries on the Book of Joshua
By Calvin, John and Beveridge, Henry
Softcover ISBN-13: 979-8-3852-1492-1
Hardcover ISBN-13: 979-8-3852-1493-8
eBook ISBN-13: 979-8-3852-1494-5
Publication date 1/26/2024
Previously published by Baker Book House, 2005

This edition is a scanned facsimile of the original edition published in 2005.

TRANSLATOR'S PREFACE.

The Commentary on Joshua was the last literary labour of its venerable Author. When he engaged in it, his constitution, which had never been strong, was completely worn out by excessive exertion, and almost every line of it must have been dictated to his amanuensis during momentary intervals of relief from severe bodily pain. On this point we possess authentic documents which leave no room for doubt.

In a letter dated 30th November 1563, not quite six months before his death, after alluding to the difficulty he felt in continuing his studies, while both mind and body were exhausted by sickness, he states that he had undertaken a Commentary on Joshua, in compliance with the wishes of his friends, but had not then been able to advance beyond the third Chapter, though he had endeavoured to be as brief as possible.

Little more than two months after this letter was written, on 6th February 1564, he made his appearance in the pulpit for the last time ; and on 10th March following, the complication of diseases which too plainly indicated that his earthly career was about to close, had become so alarming as to cause an entry in the Register of Geneva in the following terms :—" Arrêté que chacun prie Dieu pour la santé de M. Calvin, qui est indisposé depuis longtemps, et même en danger de mort :"—" Decreed that every one pray to God for the health of Mr. Calvin, who has been indisposed for a long time, and even in danger of death."

Such are the circumstances in which this Commentary was composed, and it is impossible, in reflecting on them, not to admire the indomitable energy which CALVIN displayed in proceeding with his task, and in meeting the remonstrances of those who would have withdrawn him from it, with the heroic exclamation, "Would you that the Lord, when He comes, should find me idle!"

A Work written at such a time, and in such a spirit, might justly claim exemption from criticism; but it has no need of indulgence, and can well afford to be judged by its own intrinsic merits. Viewed merely as an intellectual effort, it displays all the excellencies which characterize the other Commentaries of its distinguished Author: viewed in a higher and better light, it is his dying bequest to the Church—a solemn ratification of the whole System of Doctrine which he had so long, so earnestly, and so successfully promulgated.

H. B.

December 30, 1854.

CONTENTS.

CALVIN'S

ARGUMENT OF THE BOOK OF JOSHUA.

As to the AUTHOR of this Book, it is better to suspend our judgment than to make random assertions. Those who think that it was JOSHUA, because his name stands on the title page, rest on weak and insufficient grounds. The name of SAMUEL is inscribed on a part of the Sacred History containing a narrative of events which happened after his death; and there cannot be a doubt that the book which immediately follows the present is called JUDGES, not because it was written by them, but because it recounts their exploits. JOSHUA died before the taking of Hebron and Debir, and yet an account of it is given in the 15th chapter of the present Book. The probability is, that a summary of events was framed by the high priest ELEAZAR, and furnished the materials out of which the Book of JOSHUA was composed. It was a proper part of the high priest's duty not only to give oral instruction to the people of his own time, but to furnish posterity with a record of the goodness of God in preserving the Church, and thus provide for the advancement of true religion. And before the Levites became degenerate, their order included a class of scribes or notaries who embodied in a perpetual register everything in the history of the Church which was worthy of being recorded. Let us not hesitate, therefore, to pass over a matter which we are unable to determine, or the knowledge of which is not very necessary, while we are in no doubt as to the essential point —that the doctrine herein contained was dictated by the Holy Spirit for our use, and confers benefits of no ordinary kind on those who attentively peruse it.[1]

Although the people had already gained signal victories, and become the occupants of a commodious and tolerably fertile tract of country, the Divine promise as to the land of Canaan still remained suspended. Nay, the leading article in the Covenant was unaccomplished, as if God, after cooping up his people in a corner, had left his work in a shapeless

[1] This practical conclusion, which is indeed the only one of real importance, is founded partly on the general consent of the Church, evinced by the place which the Book of Joshua has always held in the Sacred Canon, and partly on the strong sanction given to it by the direct or indirect references and quotations of the other inspired writers both of the Old and the New Testament, *e.g.*, 1 Kings xvi. 34; Psalms xliv.; lxviii. 12-14; lxxviii. 54, 55; cxiv. 4, 5; Hab. iii. 11; Acts vii. 45; Heb. iv. 8; xi. 30, 31; xiii. 5; and James ii. 25. The authorship, however, is so uncertain, that there is scarcely a writer of eminence from the period of the history itself down to the time of Ezra, for whom the honour has not been claimed. Among others may be mentioned Phinehas, Samuel, and Isaiah. The obvious inference is, that the question of authorship is one of those destined only to be agitated but never satisfactorily determined. The opinion above stated by Calvin is perhaps as plausible as any other, though he scarcely appreciates the claims which may be urged in favour of Joshua himself. It is, of course, impossible to attribute to him either the narrative of his own death, or the references to one or two events which happened subsequent to it. Such anachronisms, if they may be so called, only prove what has never been denied, that some insertions or interpolations have been made in the original work. But as the account of the death of Moses in the last book of the Pentateuch is not allowed to cast any doubt on the claim of Moses to have been the true author, it is not easy to see why similar insertions should be supposed to have any stronger effect in regard to the claim of Joshua. In addition to the evidence furnished by those passages in which the writer speaks as an eye-witness, and an actor in the events recorded, those who attribute the Book to Joshua find a strong argument in the position which Joshua occupied. He was not only the divinely appointed successor, but the ardent admirer and diligent imitator of Moses. Is it reasonable to suppose, that while imitating him in the general principles of his government, he forgot to imitate him in the use of his pen, or that he was not as careful as Moses had been to draw up a written narrative of the wonderful events which the Lord performed by his hand? The important fact that Joshua did *write* is distinctly stated in chapter xxiv. 26; and though the writing there referred to seems to have been confined to the narrative of a special event, analogy goes far to justify the inference, that what he did on this occasion was in accordance with his usual practice, and that the record which we now possess of his eventful life, is, in substance at least, the production of his pen.—*Ed.*

and mutilated form. This Book, then, shews how, when the intolerable impiety of the people had interrupted the course of deliverance, God, while inflicting punishment, so tempered the severity of justice as ultimately to perform what he had promised concerning the inheritance of Canaan.

This suggests the very useful reflection, that while men are cut off by death, and fail in the middle of their career, the faithfulness of God never fails. On the death of Moses a sad change seemed impending; the people were left like a body with its head lopped off. While thus in danger of dispersion, not only did the truth of God prove itself to be immortal, but it was shewn in the person of Joshua as in a bright mirror, that when God takes away those whom he has adorned with special gifts, he has others in readiness to supply their place, and that though he is pleased for a time to give excellent gifts to some, his mighty power is not tied down to them, but he is able, as often as seemeth to him good, to find fit successors, nay, to raise up from the very stones persons qualified to perform illustrious deeds.

First, we see how, when the wandering of forty years in the wilderness had almost effaced the remembrance of the passage of the Red Sea, the course of deliverance was proved to have been uninterrupted by the repetition of the same miracle in the passage of the Jordan. The renewal of circumcision was equivalent to a re-establishment of the Covenant which had been buried in oblivion by the carelessness of the people, or abandoned by them from despair. Next, we see how they were conducted by the hand of God into possession of the promised land. The taking of the first city was an earnest of the perpetual aid which they might hope for from heaven, since the walls of Jericho fell of their own accord, shaken merely by the sound of trumpets. The nations, however, were not completely routed by a single battle, nor in one short campaign, but were gradually worn out and destroyed by many laborious contests.

Here, it is to be observed, that arduous difficulties were thrown in the way of the people when the kings entered into a league, and came forth to meet them with united forces, because it became necessary not only to war with single nations, but with an immense body which threatened to overwhelm them by one great onset. Ultimately, however, all these violent attempts had no other effect than to make the power of God more manifest, and give brighter displays of mercy and faithfulness in the defence of his chosen people. In fact, their uninterrupted course of success, and their many unparalleled victories, shewed the hand of God as it were visibly stretched forth from heaven.

More especially, a signal proof that they were warring under divine auspices was given when the sun was checked in his course at the mere prayer of Joshua, as if the elements had been armed for his assistance, and were waiting ready to obey him. Again, while the delays which occurred in the progress of the war were useful trials of the constancy of the people, we must not lose sight of another admirable use of which Moses, to prevent them from fainting in their minds, had at an earlier period forewarned them, viz., that God was unwilling to destroy the nations at once, lest the country, from being converted into a kind of desert, might be overrun by wild beasts.

But the provision which God had thus most graciously made for their security, they wickedly perverted to their own destruction: for having obtained what they deemed a large enough space for commodious habitation, they turned backwards to indulge in sloth and cowardice. This one crime brought others along with it. For after they had been enrolled under the banners of the Lord, they treacherously and disobediently refused to fulfil their period of service, in the very same way as deserters, regardless of the military oath, basely quit their standards.[1] The dominion of the land, which had been divinely offered, they, with

[1] The French here is,—"Car tout ainsi comme des gendarmes fuyars, qui laissent vilainement leur enseigne, oublians le serment par lequel ils se sont obligez, ils furent traitres et perjures à Dieu, sous lequel ils estoyent enrollez pour servir tout le temps par luy ordonné;" "For just like fugitive soldiers, who villanously desert their standards, forgetting the oath by which they have bound themselves, they became perjured traitors to God under whom they were enlisted to serve for the whole period ordained by him."—*Ed.*

flagrant ingratitude, rejected, by taking possession of only a part.

Moreover, though they had been ordered to purge the sacred territory of all pollutions, in order that no profanation of the pure and legitimate worship might remain, they allowed the impious superstitions which God abhorred to be practised as before; and though they also knew that the order had been partly given as a security for their own safety, lest, through intermixture with the nations, they might be ensnared by their impostures and insidious arts, yet, as if they had determined to court danger, they left them to furnish the fuel of a dire conflagration.

Their obstinate incredulity betrays itself in their disregard of the penalty denounced against such transgression. But they at length learned by experience that God had not threatened in vain, that those nations whom they had wickedly[1] spared, would prove to them thorns and stings. For they were harassed by constant incursions, pillaged by rapine, and at length almost oppressed by tyrannical violence. In short, it was not owing to any merit of theirs that the truth of God did not utterly fail.[2]

On this point, indeed, a question may be raised: for if the promise given to Abraham was founded on the mere good pleasure of God,[3] then, be the character of the people what it might, it is absurd to say that it could be defeated by their fault. How are we to reconcile the two things,—that the people did not obtain the full and complete inheritance promised to them, and that yet God was true? I answer, that so far was the faithfulness of God[4] from being overthrown, or shaken, or in any way impaired, that we

[1] "Wickedly." Latin, "Male." French, "Contre leur devoir;" "Contrary to their duty."—*Ed.*

[2] "Did not utterly fail." Latin, "Irrita caderet." French, "Ne tombast tout à plat sans avoir son effet;" "Did not fall quite flat without producing its effect."—*Ed.*

[3] "Was founded on the mere good pleasure of God." French, "A esté purement et simplement fondée au bon plaisir de Dieu, et non ailleurs;" "Was founded purely and simply on the good pleasure of God, and not on anything else."—*Ed.*

[4] "Faithfulness of God." Latin, "Dei fides." French, "La certitude de la promesse de Dieu;" "The certainty of the promise of God."—*Ed.*

here perceive more clearly how wonderful are His workings, who, in unsearchable wisdom, knows how to bring light out of darkness.

It had been said to Abraham, (Gen. xv. 18,) To thy seed will I give this land, from the river of Egypt to the great river Euphrates. Joshua affirms that the event drew near, and was actually at hand. But the Israelites, overcome by sloth, do not reach those boundaries; nay, in settling down of their own accord within narrow limits, they in a manner oppose barriers to the divine liberality. In this way the covenant of God seemed to suffer a kind of eclipse.

And there is no doubt that pious minds were often filled with anxiety when they saw His work cut short. But the punishment inflicted on the people for their wickedness was so tempered, that what might otherwise have been a grievous and perilous trial of faith, was converted into a powerful support. The apparent failure reminded the children of God that they were to look forward to a more excellent state, where the divine favour would be more clearly displayed, nay, would be freed from every obstruction, and shine forth in full splendour. Hence their thoughts were raised to Christ, and it was made known to them that the complete felicity of the Church depended on its Head. In arriving at this conclusion, they were assisted by new prophecies. For the rehearsal which Joshua here makes of the ancient covenant is applied in the Psalms (Ps. lxxii. and lxxxix.) to the Messiah's reign, unto which time, the Lord had, for the purpose of rendering it more glorious, deferred the full fruition of the promised land. The same thing was exemplified in David, who bore a typical resemblance to Christ, and in whom it was shewn that the divine promises were only established and confirmed in the hand of a Mediator.

No longer, therefore, does it seem strange that the result promised, after being retarded by the wickedness of the people, was not fully accomplished till the state of the Church was rightly arranged, seeing that in the person of David the image of the Mediator, on whom the perfect felicity of the Church depended, was visibly held forth to view. Meanwhile the moderate foretaste which believers received of the divine favour, must have sufficed to sustain[1] them, preparatory to the more complete realization.

Nor, indeed, was the partition made by Joshua and the heads of the tribes, to whom that duty was intrusted, elusory or fallacious; but the inheritance, in possession of which God had placed them by His own hand, was truly and distinctly divided by His orders. In this respect, too, the sacred observance of the covenant made with Abraham was conspicuous. Jacob, when about to die, had destined certain settlements to some of his children. Had each tribe received its portion simply by the determination and suffrages of men, it might have been thought that they had merely followed the directions of the Patriarch. But when the lot, than which nothing is deemed more fortuitous, confirmed the prophecy, the stability of the donation[2] was as clearly ratified as if God had visibly appeared. Accordingly, after the sluggishness of the people put an end to the war, Joshua sent back the tribes of Reuben and Gad, with the half tribe of Manasseh, as if their period of service had expired.

Next follows a remarkable narrative, clearly shewing how zealous the Israelites who dwelt in the land of Canaan were to maintain the pure worship of God. For when these two tribes and half tribe had erected a monument of fraternal alliance, the others, thinking that it was an altar intended for sacrifice, and consequently an abomination, immediately determine to declare war, and prepare sooner to destroy their kindred[3] than allow religion to be torn asunder by a bastard worship. At the same time they are commended for their moderation, in being so easily appeased on obtaining satisfaction, after a sacred zeal had suddenly roused them to arms.

[1] "Sustain." French, "Consoler et soustenir;" "Comfort and sustain." —*Ed.*

[2] "Stability of the donation." Latin, "Donationis stabilitas." French, "La verité de la prophetie;" "The truth of the prophecy."—*Ed.*

[3] "Sooner to destroy their kindred." Latin, "Suos consanguineos potius delere." French, "De plutost exterminer leur cousins, c'est à dire ces lignées-la qui estoyent de leur sang;" "Sooner to exterminate their cousins, (kindred,) that is to say, lineage which was of their own blood."—*Ed.*

In the end of the book it is shewn how anxious Joshua was to advance the glory of God,[1] and how diligently he endeavoured to obviate the fickleness and treachery of the people. With this view, not only the most impressive exhortations, but protestations, were employed, and more especially the covenant was renewed in regular form with the solemnity of an oath.[2]

[1] Latin, "Quantopere solicitus fuerit Josue de propaganda Dei gloria." French, "Combien Josué a eté songneux de procurer qu'apres sa mort Dieu fust glorifié;" "How careful Joshua was to provide that God should be glorified after his death."—*Ed.*

[2] In addition to the above excellent summary, it may be proper to mention that the Book of Joshua extends over a period, estimated by Josephus at twenty-five, and by other Jewish chronologists at twenty-seven, though others attempt to reduce it to only seventeen years, and that its contents are naturally divided into three great sections,—the *first* extending from chapter i.-xii. inclusive, and giving a continuous narrative of Joshua's conquests; the *second* from chapter xiii.-xxiii. inclusive, consisting chiefly of a description more or less detailed of the division of the country among the different tribes; and the *third* occupying the remainder of the book, principally with an account of the great convention of the tribes held at Shechem, on Joshua's summons, and of the interesting and important proceedings which then took place.—*Ed.*

A BRIEF COMMENTARY

ON

THE BOOK OF JOSHUA

BY JOHN CALVIN,

A SHORT TIME BEFORE HIS DEATH.

CHAPTER I.

1. Now, after the death of Moses, the servant of the Lord, it came to pass, that the Lord spake unto Joshua the son of Nun, Moses' minister, saying,

2. Moses my servant is dead: now therefore arise, go over this Jordan, thou, and all this people, unto the land which I do give to them, *even* to the children of Israel.

3. Every place that the sole of your foot shall tread upon, that have I given unto you, as I said unto Moses.

4. From the wilderness and this Lebanon, even unto the great river, the river Euphrates, all the land of the Hittites, and unto the great sea, toward the going down of the sun, shall be your coast.

1. Fuit autem post mortem Mosis, ut Jehova alloqueretur Josue, dicendo,[1]

2. Moses servus meus mortuus est: nunc ergo surge, trajice Jordanem istum tu, et omnis hic populus, ad terram quam ego do illis, nempe filiis Israel.

3. Omnem locum quem calcaverit planta pedis vestri vobis dedi; quemadmodum locutus sum Mosi.

4. A deserto et Libano isto usque ad flumen magnum, flumen Euphraten, tota terra Hittæorum usque ad mare magnum ad occasum solis, erit terminus vester.

1. *Now, after*, &c. Here, first, we see the steadfastness of God in watching over his people, and providing for their

[1] The copulative particle which commences the Book, and is usually translated *and*, or, as in our English version, *now*, evidently connects it with some previous writing, and seems to vindicate the place which it holds in the Canon as a continuation of the Book of Deuteronomy. In this first verse, Calvin's Latin version omits the epithets, "Servant of the Lord," and "Moses' minister," applied respectively to Joshua and Moses. The Hebrew contains both, but the former is omitted by the ordinary text of the Septuagint, though placed among its various readings.—*Ed.*

safety. The sanction given to Joshua's appointment, as new leader by a renewed commission,[1] was intended to indicate the continuance of his favour, and prevent the people from thinking themselves forsaken in consequence of the death of Moses. Joshua, indeed, had already been chosen to rule the people; and not only invested with the office, but also endowed with spiritual gifts. But as the most valiant, however well provided, are apt to halt or waver when the period for action arrives, the exhortation to Joshua to make ready forthwith for the expedition was by no means superfluous. Still, however, the call thus formally given was not so much on his own account, as to inspire the people with full confidence in following a leader whom they saw advancing step by step in the path divinely marked out for him.[2]

2. *Moses my servant*, &c. A twofold meaning may be extracted—the one, since Moses is dead, the whole burden has now devolved upon thee, take the place of him to whom thou hast been appointed successor; the other, although Moses is dead, do not desist, but go forward. I prefer the former, as containing the inference that he should, by right of succession, take up the office which Moses had left vacant.[3] The epithet or surname of *servant* applied to Moses, has respect to his government of the people and his exploits; for it ought to be accommodated to actual circumstances.[4] The allusion here is not to the Law but to the leadership, which had passed to Joshua by the decease of Moses, and God thus acknowledges his servant, not so much with the view of praising him, as of strengthening the authority of Joshua, who had been substituted in his place. And as the people might not have acquiesced sufficiently in a bare command, he promises, while ordering them to pass the Jordan,

[1] "A renewed commission." Latin, "Repetitis mandatis." French, "En reiterant les articles de sa commission;" "By reiterating the articles of his commission."—*Ed.*

[2] Or rather, "Who they saw, did not advance a single step till the Lord had preceded him."—*Ed.*

[3] "Which Moses had left vacant." Latin, "Ex qua decesserat Moses." French, "De laquelle Moyse estoit sorti ayant fait son temps;" "Which Moses had left, having held his own time of it."—*Ed.*

[4] "To actual circumstances." Latin, "Ad circumstantiam loci." French, "A la circonstance du passage;" "To the circumstance of the passage."—*Ed.*

to give them peaceable possession of the whole country, and of every spot of it on which they should plant their foot. For as nothing tends more than distrust to make us sluggish and useless, so when God holds forth a happy issue, confidence inspires us with vigour for any attempt.

It may be added, that he does now begin for the first time to give them good hopes, by making a promise of which they had not previously heard, but recalls to their remembrance what Moses had formerly testified. He says, therefore, that the time had now come for exhibiting and performing that which he had promised to Moses. Should any one object that the same thing had been said to Abraham long before Moses was born, nay, that the perpetual covenant deposited with Abraham included everything which was heard by Moses four hundred years after;[1] I answer, that here no notice is taken of the ancient promise which was everywhere known and celebrated, and that Moses is produced as a witness whose memory was more recent, and by whose death the confidence of the people might have been shaken, had not God declared that the accomplishment of all which he had said was at hand.

4. *From the wilderness and this Lebanon, &c.* How the truth and fulfilment of this promise surmounted all the obstacles interposed by the wickedness of the people, though they did not obtain immediate possession of the whole territory, I have explained in the Argument. For although God had unfolded the inestimable treasures of his beneficence by constituting them lords of the country, it did not follow that their misconduct was not to be chastised. Nay, there behoved to be a fulfilment of the threatening which Moses had denounced, viz., that if the nations doomed to destruction were not destroyed, they would prove thorns and stings in their eyes and sides. But as the promise was by no means

[1] The French here gives the same meaning in a paraphrastic form, "Ou mesmes qu'a parler proprement, tout ce qui a este dit a Moyse dependoit de l'alliance perpetuelle que Dieu avoit mise en garde entre les mains d'Abraham quatre cens ans auparavant." "Or even, to speak properly, all that was said to Moses depended on the perpetual covenant which God had deposited in the hands of Abraham four hundred years before."—*Ed.*

broken or rendered void by the delay of forty years, during which they were led wandering through the desert, so the entire possession, though long suspended, proved the faithfulness of the decree by which it had been adjudged.

The people had it in their power to obtain possession of the prescribed boundaries in due time; they declined to do so. For this they deserved to have been expelled altogether.[1] But the divine indulgence granted them an extent of territory sufficient for their commodious habitation ; and although it had been foretold that, in just punishment, the residue of the nations whom they spared would prove pernicious to them, still, they suffered no molestation, unless when they provoked the Divine anger by their perfidy and almost continual defection : for as often as their affairs became prosperous, they turned aside to wantonness. Still, owing to the wonderful goodness of God, when oppressed by the violence of the enemy, and, as it were, thrust down to the grave, they continued to live in death ; and not only so, but every now and then deliverers arose, and, contrary to all hope, retrieved them from ruin.[2]

The *Great Sea* means the Mediterranean, and to it the land of the Hittites forms the opposite boundary; in the same way Lebanon is opposed to the Euphrates; but it must be observed that under Lebanon the desert is comprehended, as appears from another passage.[3]

[1] The two last sentences form only one in the French, which is as follows, "Le peuple pouuoit du premier coup, et des l'entree s'estendre jusqu'aux bornes que Dieu lui mesme auoit marquees ; il n'a pas voulu : il estoit bien digne d'en estre mis dehors, et du tout forclos." "The people might at the first blow, and immediately on their entrance, have extended themselves to the limits which God himself had marked ; they would not : they well deserved to be put out and wholly foreclosed."—*Ed.*

[2] Latin, "Qui præter spem rebus perditis succurrerent ;" French, "Qui outre toute esperance venoyent a remedier aux affaires si fort deplorez, et redresser aucunement l'estat du peuple ;" "Who, beyond all hope, came to remedy the very deplorable affairs, and, in some degree, restore the condition of the people."—*Ed.*

[3] Calvin's language here is not very clear, and seems to convey an erroneous impression. The *desert* or *wilderness*, instead of being comprehended under Lebanon, is obviously contrasted with it, and forms the south, while Lebanon forms the north frontier. We have thus three great natural boundaries—Lebanon on the north, the desert of Sin on the south, and the Mediterranean on the west. The eastern boundary occasions more difficulty. According to some, the Euphrates is expressly mentioned as this

5. There shall not any man be able to stand before thee all the days of thy life: as I was with Moses, *so* I will be with thee; I will not fail thee, nor forsake thee.

6. Be strong, and of a good courage; for unto this people shalt thou divide for an inheritance the land which I sware unto their fathers to give them.

7. Only be thou strong, and very courageous, that thou mayest observe to do according to all the law which Moses my servant commanded thee: turn not from it *to* the right hand or *to* the left, that thou mayest prosper whithersoever thou goest.

8. This book of the law shall not depart out of thy mouth; but thou shalt meditate therein day and night, that thou mayest observe to do according to all that is written therein: for then thou shalt make thy way prosperous, and then thou shalt have good success.

9. Have not I commanded thee? Be strong, and of a good courage; be not afraid, neither be thou dismayed: for the Lord thy God *is* with thee whithersoever thou goest.

5. Non consistet quisquam contra te cunctis diebus vitæ tuæ; quia sicuti fui cum Mose, ita ero tecum; non te deseram, neque derelinquam.

6. Confirmare, ergo, et roborare; quia tu in hæreditatem divides populo huic terram, de qua juravi patribus eorum me daturum illis.

7. Tantum confirmare et roborare vehementer: ut custodias et facias secundum totam legem quam præcepit tibi Moses servus meus; non recedes ad dextram vel ad sinistram ut prudenter (*vel* prospere) agas in omnibus.

8. Non recedat liber legis hujus ab ore tuo; sed mediteris in eo, die et nocte, ut custodias et facias, secundum id totum quod scriptum est in eo. Tunc enim secundas reddes vias tuas, et tunc prudenter ages.

9. Nonne præcepi tibi, ut te confirmes, et te robores? Ne formides, neque animo frangaris; quoniam tecum sum Jehova Deus tuus in omnibus ad quæ tu pergis.

5. *There shall not any man*, &c. As a contest was about to be waged with numerous and warlike enemies, it was necessary thus to inspire Joshua with special confidence. But for this, the promise of delivering over the land which God

boundary, and an attempt is made to reconcile the vast difference between the actual possession of the Israelites, even in the most prosperous period of their history, and the tract of country thus bounded, by having recourse to the explanation of St. Augustine, who, in his Commentary on Jos. xxi., gives it as his opinion that the country extending eastward beyond the proper limits of Canaan was intended to be given not so much for possession as for tribute. This view receives some confirmation from the extensive conquests which were made by David and Solomon. According to other expositors, the Euphrates is intended to be taken in connection with Lebanon so as to form, by one of its windings or branches, part of the north boundary, while the east boundary is left indefinite, or rather, was so well defined by the Jordan that it did not require to be separately mentioned. In this general uncertainty, there is much practical wisdom in Calvin's suggestion in his Argument, that the indefiniteness of the boundaries assigned to the promised land, contrasted with its actual limits, tended to elevate the minds of Old Testament believers, and carry them beyond the present to a period when, under a new and more glorious dispensation, the promise would be completely fulfilled.—*Ed.*

had given, would ever and anon have become darkened; for how vast the enterprise to overthrow so many nations! This objection therefore is removed. And the better to free him from all doubt, he is reminded of the victories of Moses, by which God had made it manifest that nothing was easier for him than utterly to discomfit any host however great and powerful. Joshua, therefore, is ordered to behold in the assistance given to Moses the future issue of the wars which he was to undertake under the same guidance and protection. For the series of favours is continued without interruption to the successor.

What follows is to the same effect, though it is more fully expressed by the words, *I will not fail thee*, &c. Hence the Apostle, (Heb. xiii. 5,) when wishing to draw off believers from avarice, makes an application of these words for the purpose of calming down all anxieties, and suppressing all excessive fears. And in fact, the distrust which arises from anxiety kindles in us such tumultuous feelings that on the least appearance of danger, we turmoil and miserably torment ourselves until we feel assured that God both will be with us and more than suffice for our protection. And, indeed, while he prescribes no other cure for our timidity, he reminds us that we ought to be satisfied with his present aid.

6. *Be strong*, &c. An exhortation to fortitude is added, and indeed repeated, that it may make the deeper impression. At the same time the promise is introduced in different words, in which Joshua is assured of his divine call, that he might have no hesitation in undertaking the office which had been divinely committed to him, nor begin to waver midway on being obliged to contend with obstacles. It would not have been enough for him diligently to begirt himself at the outset without being well prepared to persevere in the struggle.

Although it is the property of faith to animate us to strenuous exertion, in the same way as unbelief manifests itself by cowardice or cessation of effort, still we may infer from this passage, that bare promises are not sufficiently energetic without the additional stimulus of exhortation. For if Joshua, who was always remarkable for alacrity, required to be incited to the performance of duty, how much more necessary must it be that we who labour under so much sluggishness should be spurred forward.

We may add, that not once only or by one single expression are strength and constancy required of Joshua, but he is confirmed repeatedly and in various terms, because he was to be engaged in many and various contests. He is told to be of strong and invincible courage. Although these two epithets make it obvious that God was giving commandment concerning a most serious matter, still not contented with this reduplication, he immediately after repeats the sentence, and even amplifies it by the addition of the adverb *very*.

From this passage, therefore, let us learn that we can never be fit for executing difficult and arduous matters unless we exert our utmost endeavours, both because our abilities are weak, and Satan rudely assails us, and there is nothing we are more inclined to than to relax our efforts.[1] But, as many exert their strength to no purpose in making erroneous or desultory attempts, it is added as a true source of fortitude that Joshua shall make it his constant study to observe the Law. By this we are taught that the only way in which we can become truly invincible is by striving to yield a faithful obedience to God. Otherwise it were better to lie indolent and effeminate than to be hurried on by headlong audacity.

Moreover, God would not only have his servant to be strong in keeping the Law, but enjoins him to contend manfully, so as not to faint under the burden of his laborious office. But as he might become involved in doubt as to the mode of disentangling himself in matters of perplexity, or as to the course which he ought to adopt, he refers him to the teaching of the Law, because by following it as a guide he will be sufficiently fitted for all things. He says, You shall act prudently in all things, provided you make the Law your master; although the Hebrew word שכל, means to act not

[1] French, "Et il ne faut qu'un rien pour nous faire perdre courage;" "And a mere nothing is all that is necessary to make us lose courage."—*Ed.*

only *prudently* but *successfully*, because temerity usually pays the penalty of failure.

Be this as it may, by submitting entirely to the teaching of the Law he is more surely animated to hope for divine assistance. For it is of great consequence, when our fears are excited by impending dangers, to feel assured that we have the approbation of God in whatever we do, inasmuch as we have no other object in view than to obey his commands. Moreover, as it would not be enough to obey God in any kind of way,[1] Joshua is exhorted to practise a modesty and sobriety which may keep him within the bounds of a simple obedience.

Many, while possessed of right intention, sometimes imagine themselves to be wiser than they ought, and hence either overlook many things through carelessness, or mix up their own counsels with the divine commands. The general prohibition, therefore, contained in the Law, forbidding all men to add to it or detract from it, God now specially enforces on Joshua. For if private individuals in forming their plan of life behove to submit themselves to God, much more necessary must this be for those who hold rule among the people. But if this great man needed this curb of modesty that he might not overstep his limits, how intolerable the audacity if we, who fall so far short of him, arrogate to ourselves greater license? More especially, however, did God prescribe the rule to his servant, in order that those who excel in honour might know that they are as much bound to obey it as the meanest of the people.

8. *This book of the Law*, &c. Assiduous meditation on the Law is also commanded; because, whenever it is intermitted, even for a short time, many errors readily creep in, and the memory becomes rusted, so that many, after ceasing from the continuous study of it, engage in practical business, as if they were mere ignorant tyros. God therefore enjoins his servant to make daily progress, and never cease, during the whole course of his life, to profit in the Law. Hence it fol-

[1] The French adds, "Ou en quelques points;" "Or in some points."—*Ed.*

lows that those who hold this study in disdain, are blinded by intolerable arrogance.

But why does he forbid him to allow the Law to depart from his mouth rather than from his eyes? Some interpreters understand that the *mouth* is here used by synecdoche for *face;* but this is frigid. I have no doubt that the word used is peculiarly applicable to a person who was bound to prosecute the study in question, not only for himself individually, but for the whole people placed under his rule. He is enjoined, therefore, to attend to the teaching of the Law, that in accordance with the office committed to him, he may bring forward what he has learned for the common benefit of the people. At the same time he is ordered to make his own docility a pattern of obedience to others. For many, by talking and discoursing, have the Law in their mouth, but are very bad keepers of it. Both things, therefore, are commanded, that by teaching others, he may make his own conduct and whole character conformable to the same rule.

What follows in the second clause of the verse shews, that everything which profane men endeavour to accomplish in contempt of the word of God, must ultimately fail of success, and that however prosperous the commencement may sometimes seem to be, the issue will be disastrous; because prosperous results can be hoped for only from the divine favour, which is justly withheld from counsels rashly adopted, and from all arrogance of which contempt of God himself is the usual accompaniment. Let believers, therefore, in order that their affairs may turn out as they wish, conciliate the divine blessing alike by diligence in learning and by fidelity in obeying.

In the end of the verse, because the term used is ambiguous, as I have already observed, the sentence is repeated, or a second promise is added. The latter is the view I take. For it was most suitable, that after the promised success, Joshua should be reminded that men never act skilfully and regularly except in so far as they allow themselves to be ruled by the word of God. Accordingly, the prudence which believers learn from the word of God, is opposed to the confidence of those who deem their own sense sufficient to guide them aright.[1]

9. *Have not I commanded*, &c. Although in Hebrew a simple affirmation is often made in the form of a question, and this phraseology is of very frequent occurrence, here, however, the question is emphatic, to give an attestation to what had previously been taught, while the Lord, by bringing his own authority distinctly forward, relieves his servant from care and hesitancy. He asks, Is it not I who have commanded thee? I too will be present with thee. Observe the emphasis: inasmuch as it is not lawful to resist his command.[2] This passage also teaches that nothing is more effectual to produce confidence than when trusting to the call and the command of God, and feeling fully assured of it in our own conscience, we follow whithersoever he is pleased to lead.

10. Then Joshua commanded the officers of the people, saying,

11. Pass through the host, and command the people, saying, Prepare you victuals; for within three days ye shall pass over this Jordan, to go in to possess the land, which the Lord your God giveth you to possess it.

12. And to the Reubenites, and to the Gadites, and to half the tribe of Manasseh, spake Joshua, saying,

13. Remember the word which Moses, the servant of the Lord, commanded you, saying, The Lord your God hath given you rest, and hath given you this land.

14. Your wives, your little ones, and your cattle, shall remain in the

10. Tunc præcepit Josue præfectis populi dicendo,

11. Transite per medium castrorum et præcipite populo, dicendo, Parate vobis annonam: quia post tres dies transibitis Jordanem hunc, ut intretis et possideatis terram, quam Jehova Deus vester dat vobis possidendam.

12. Ad Reubenitas vero et Gaditas et dimidiam tribum Manasse locutus est Josue, dicendo,

13. Recordamini verbi quod præcepit vobis Moses servus Jehovæ, dicendo, Jehova Deus vester reddidit vos quietos et dedit vobis terram hanc:

14. Uxores vestræ, parvuli vestri, et pecora vestra residebunt in

[1] The French paraphrases the whole sentence thus: " Ainsi la prudence et sagesse que les fideles apprennent de la parole de Dieu, est opposee à l'assurance de ceux auxquels il semble bien qu'ils se gouvernent assez discretement et sagement, quand ils besongnent selon leur propre sens;" " Thus the prudence and wisdom which believers learn from the word of God, is opposed to the assurance of those who think they govern themselves discreetly and wisely enough, when they manage according to their own sense."—*Ed.*

[2] French, " C'est bien pour certain avec grande signifiance que ceci se dit d'autant qu'il n'est pas question de resister à son commandement;" " It is certainly with great significancy that this is said, inasmuch as there is no question of resisting his command."—*Ed.*

land which Moses gave you on this side Jordan; but ye shall pass before your brethren armed, all the mighty men of valour, and help them;

15. Until the Lord have given your brethren rest, as *he hath given* you, and they also have possessed the land which the Lord your God giveth them; then ye shall return unto the land of your possession, and enjoy it, which Moses, the Lord's servant, gave you on this side Jordan, toward the sun-rising.

16. And they answered Joshua, saying, All that thou commandest us we will do, and whithersoever thou sendest us we will go.

17. According as we hearkened unto Moses in all things, so will we hearken unto thee: only the Lord thy God be with thee, as he was with Moses.

18. Whosoever *he be* that doth rebel against thy commandment, and will not hearken unto thy words, in all that thou commandest him, he shall be put to death: only be strong, and of a good courage.

terra quam dedit vobis Moses trans Jordanem; vos autem transibitis armati ante fratres vestros, quicunque erunt viri bellicosi, juvabitisque eos,

15. Donec quietem præstiterit Jehova fratribus vestris sicut vobis, et possideant ipsi quoque terram quam Jehova Deus vester dat eis: et tunc redibitis ad terram hæreditatis vestræ, possidebitisque eam quam dedit vobis Moses servus Jehovæ ultra Jordanem ad exortum solis.

16. Tunc responderunt, dicendo, Omnia quæ præcepisti nobis faciemus, et ad omnia ad quæ miseris nos, ibimus.

17. Sicut in omnibus obedivimus Mosi, sic obediemus tibi: tantum sit Jehova Deus tuus tecum sicut fuit cum Mose.

18. Quisquis fuerit qui rebellaverit ore tuo, nec verbis tuis acquieverit in omnibus quæ ei mandaveris, interficiatur. Tantum confirmare et roborare.

10. *Then Joshua commanded,*[1] &c. It may be doubted whether or not this proclamation was made after the spies

[1] It is almost impossible to doubt that the view here taken is correct, and in confirmation of it, it may be observed, that it receives more countenance from the original than appears either from Calvin's or our English version. They have both rendered the first word of the tenth verse by "Then," as if meaning, "At that precise time;" whereas the Hebrew is simply the copulative ו, which only means "And," and is accordingly here rendered in the Septuagint by καὶ. It implies, indeed, that the order issued to the prefects by Joshua was given *subsequently* to the gracious and encouraging message which he had received, but not that it was given *immediately* or at that particular instant, and it thus leaves it open for us to infer, that a period of less or greater length intervened during which the spies were sent on their mission, and the proceedings detailed in the second chapter took place. The sacred writer in thus omitting to follow the order of time in his narrative, has only adopted a method which is often convenient in itself, and which has been repeatedly followed by the most celebrated historians, both of ancient and modern times, and nothing can be more absurd than the inference attempted to be drawn chiefly by some German Rationalists, from this and a few similar apparent anachronisms, that the Book of Joshua is not so much a continuous history as a patchwork of distinct or even contradictory narratives by different writers.—*Ed.*

were sent, and of course on their return. And certainly I think it not only probable, but I am fully convinced that it was only after their report furnished him with the knowledge he required, that he resolved to move his camp. It would have been preposterous haste to hurry on an unknown path, while he considered it expedient to be informed on many points before setting foot on a hostile territory. Nor is there anything novel in neglecting the order of time, and afterwards interweaving what had been omitted. The second chapter must therefore be regarded as a kind of interposed parenthesis, explaining to the reader more fully what had happened, when Joshua at length commanded the people to collect their vessels.

After all necessary matters had been ascertained, he saw it was high time to proceed, and issued a proclamation, ordering the people to make ready for the campaign. With the utmost confidence he declares that they will pass the Jordan after the lapse of three days: this he never would have ventured to do, without the suggestion of the Spirit. No one had attempted the ford, nor did there seem to be any hope that it could be done.[1] There was no means of crossing either by a bridge or by boats: and nothing could be easier for the enemy than to prevent the passage. The only thing, therefore, that remained was for God to transport them miraculously. This Joshua hoped for not at random, nor at his own hand, but as a matter which had been divinely revealed. The faith of the people also was conspicuous in the promptitude of their obedience: for, in the view of the great difficulties which presented themselves, they never would have complied so readily had they not cast their

[1] This must be taken with some qualification, since, according to the view taken by Calvin himself, the river must, before this, have been forded by the spies, both in going and returning; and it is also obvious, from the direction which their pursuers took, in endeavouring to overtake them, that what are called "the fords," must have been understood to be practicable, even during the season of overflow. Still a spot or two where an individual might manage to cross was altogether unavailable for such a body as the Israelites, and therefore Calvin's subsequent statement cannot be disputed, that if they were to cross at all, human agency was unavailing, and the only thing which remained was for God himself to transport them miraculously.—*Ed.*

care upon God. It cannot be doubted that He inspired their minds with this alacrity, in order to remove all the obstacles which might delay the fulfilment of the promise.

12. *And to the Reubenites,* &c. An inheritance had been granted them beyond the Jordan, on the condition that they should continue to perform military service with their brethren in expelling the nations of Canaan. Joshua therefore now exhorts them to fulfil their promise, to leave their wives, their children, and all their effects behind, to cross the Jordan, and not desist from carrying on the war till they had placed their brethren in peaceable possession. In urging them so to act, he employs two arguments, the one drawn from authority and the other from equity. He therefore reminds them of the command given them by Moses, from whose decision it was not lawful to deviate, since it was well known to all that he uttered nothing of himself, but only what God had dictated by his mouth. At the same time, without actually asserting, Joshua indirectly insinuates, that they are bound, by compact, inasmuch as they had engaged to act in this manner.[1] He next moves them by motives of equity, that there might be no inequality in the condition of those to whom the same inheritance had been destined in common. It would be very incongruous, he says, that your brethren should be incurring danger, or, at least, toiling in carrying on war, and that you should be enjoying all the comforts of a peaceful settlement.

When he orders them to precede or pass before, the meaning is, not that they were to be the first to enter into conflict with the enemy, and in all emergencies which might befall them, were to bear more than their own share of the burden; he only in this way urges them to move with alacrity, as it would have been a kind of tergiversation to keep in the rear and follow slowly in the track of others. The expression,

[1] The agreement made with Moses was very explicit. As recorded in the thirty-second chapter of Numbers, he distinctly stipulates that they shall "go armed before the Lord to war," "armed over Jordan before the Lord, until he hath driven out his enemies from before him, and the land be subdued before the Lord;" and they answer, "As the Lord hath said unto thy servants so will we do: we will pass over armed before the Lord, into the land of Canaan, that the possession of our inheritance on this side Jordan may be ours."—*Ed.*

pass before your brethren, therefore, does not mean to stand in the front of the battle, but simply to observe their ranks, and thereby give proof of ready zeal. For it is certain that as they were arranged in four divisions they advanced in the same order. As he calls them men of war, we may infer, as will elsewhere more clearly appear, that the aged, and others not robust, were permitted to remain at home in charge of the common welfare, or altogether relieved from public duty, if in any way disabled from performing it.

16. *And they answered*, &c. They not only acquiesce, but freely admit and explicitly detail the obedience which they owe. Our obligations are duly discharged only when we perform them cheerfully, and not in sadness, as Paul expresses it. (2 Cor. ix. 7.) If it is objected that there is little modesty in their boast of having been obedient to Moses whom they had often contradicted, I answer, that though they did not always follow with becoming ardour, yet they were so much disposed to obey, that their moderation was not only tolerable, but worthy of the highest praise, when it is considered how proudly their fathers rebelled, and how perversely they endeavoured to shake off a yoke divinely imposed upon them. For the persons who speak here were not those rebellious spirits of whom God complains (Psalm xcv. 8-11) that he was provoked by them, but persons who, subdued by the examples of punishment, had learned quietly to submit.[1]

Indeed, it is not so much to herald their own virtues as to extol the authority of Joshua, when they declare that they will regard him in the same light in which they regarded Moses. The groundwork of their confidence is at the same time expressed in their wish or prayer, that God may be present to assist his servant Joshua as he assisted his ser-

[1] The objection taken to the modesty of the answer seems to be founded on a misinterpretation of its true meaning. For the original, literally interpreted, does not contain any assertion that they had obeyed Moses in all things, as implied both in Calvin's Latin and in our English version, but simply means, that "in everything," or, "according to everything," (ככל, *kekol*,) in which they had hearkened to Moses they would hearken to him: in other words, that they would hold his authority to be in every respect equal to that of Moses. This meaning is retained by the Septuagint, which renders Κατὰ πάντα ὅσα ἠκούσαμεν Μωυσῇ, ἀκουσόμεθά σου.—*Ed.*

vant Moses. They intimate that they will be ready to war under the auspices of their new leader, because they are persuaded that he is armed with the power and hope that he will be victorious by the assistance of God, as they had learned by experience how wonderfully God assisted them by the hand of Moses. We may infer, moreover, that they actually felt this confidence, both because they call to mind their experiences of God's favour to animate themselves, and because they regard Joshua as the successor of Moses in regard to prosperous results.

The epithet *thy God*[1] is not without weight, as it evidently points to a continued course of divine favour. The form of expression also is intermediate between the confidence of faith and prayer.[2] Accordingly, while they intimate that they cherish good hope in their minds, they at the same time have recourse to prayer, under a conviction of the arduousness of the work. Immediately after, when they of their own accord exhort him to constancy, they shew that they are ready to follow and to imitate him in his confidence. Here, it is to be observed, that though Joshua was a model of courage, and animated all, both by deed and precept, he was in his turn stimulated onwards, that his own alacrity might be more effectual in arousing that of the people.

CHAPTER II.

1. And Joshua the son of Nun	1. Miserat[3] autem Josue filius Nun

[1] This emphasis is lost by the Septuagint, which renders not ὁ Θεός σου, "thy God," but, "ὁ Θεὸς ἡμῶν," "our God."—*Ed.*

[2] French, "Toutefois la maniere de parler qui est ici mise, est moyenne, et peut estre prise ou pour un glorifiement de la foy, ou pour un souhait;" "However, the manner of speaking which is here used is of a middle kind, and may be taken either for a glorying of faith, or for a wish."—*Ed.*

[3] Calvin's "miserat," "had sent," is in accordance with his opinion, that the spies had been sent some time before the transactions with which the first chapter concludes actually took place, but is not justified either by the Hebrew or by the Septuagint, which has simply ἀπέστειλεν. It is worthy of remark, however, that Luther's German agrees with Calvin, and renders "hatte zween kundschafter heimlich ausgesandt von Sittim;" "had sent out two spies secretly from Sittim." The mention of the place, Sittim or Shittim, occurs in the French version, but is omitted without explanation in Calvin's Latin. It was situated in the plains of Moab near the left bank of the Jordan, and is particularly mentioned in Numbers xxv. as the abode of the Israelites, when they allowed themselves to be seduced

sent out of Shittim two men to spy secretly, saying, Go view the land, even Jericho. And they went, and came into an harlot's house, named Rahab, and lodged there.

viros duos exploratores clam,[1] dicendo: Ite, considerate terram et Jericho. Profecti sunt igitur et ingressi sunt domum mulieris meretricis, cujus nomen erat Rahab, et dormierunt illic.

2. And it was told the king of Jericho, saying, Behold, there came men in hither to-night of the children of Israel to search out the country.

2. Dictum autem fuit regi Jericho, Ecce venerunt huc viri nocte hac e filiis Israel ad explorandum terram.

3. And the king of Jericho sent unto Rahab, saying, Bring forth the men that are come to thee, which are entered into thine house: for they be come to search out all the country.

3. Tunc misit rex Jericho ad Rahab, dicendo; Educ viros qui ingressi sunt ad te, qui venerunt domum tuam; quia ad explorandam totam terram venerunt.

4. And the woman took the two men, and hid them, and said thus, There came men unto me, but I wist not whence they *were:*

4. Sumpserat autem mulier duos viros, et absconderat eos: Tunc ait, Venerunt quidem ad me viri, sed non noveram undenam essent.

5. And it came to pass, *about the time* of shutting of the gate, when it was dark, that the men went out; whither the men went, I wot not: pursue after them quickly; for ye shall overtake them.

5. Fuit autem dum porta clauderetur in tenebris, egressi sunt viri; nec cognovi quo abierint. Sequimini cito eos, quia comprehendetis eos.

6. But she had brought them up to the roof of the house, and hid them with the stalks of flax, which she had laid in order upon the roof.

6. Ipsa autem ascendere fecerat eos in tectum, et absconderat eos sub culmis lini ab ea ordinatis super tectum.

7. And the men pursued after them the way to Jordan unto the fords: and as soon as they which pursued after them were gone out, they shut the gate.

7. Viri autem persequuti sunt eos itinere Jordanis usque ad vada: portam vero clauserunt, simul ac egressi sunt qui eos persequebantur.

8. And, before they were laid down, she came up unto them upon the roof;

8. Antequam vero dormirent, ipsa ascendit super tectum ad eos.

9. And she said unto the men, I know that the Lord hath given you the land, and that your terror is fallen upon us, and that all the inhabitants of the land faint because of you.

9. Et ait ad viros: Novi quod Jehova dederit vobis terram, eo quod cecidit terror vester super nos, et quod defluxerunt omnes habitatores terræ a facie vestra.

10. For we have heard how the

10. Audivimus enim quomodo are-

into gross idolatry by the daughters of Moab, and were in consequence signally punished.—*Ed.*

[1] This word "clam" may refer either to the secrecy of Joshua in sending the spies, or to the secrecy which they were to employ in making their inquiries. Either meaning seems good. The latter is countenanced by the Septuagint, which unites the secrecy and the spying in the single compound word κατασκοπεῦσαι; but it is evident, both from the version and the Commentary, that Calvin prefers the former.—*Ed.*

Lord dried up the water of the Red sea for you, when ye came out of Egypt; and what ye did unto the two kings of the Amorites, that *were* on the other side Jordan, Sihon and Og, whom ye utterly destroyed.

11. And as soon as we had heard *these things*, our hearts did melt, neither did there remain any more courage in any man, because of you; for the Lord your God, he *is* God in heaven above, and in earth beneath.

12. Now therefore, I pray you, swear unto me by the Lord, since I have shewed you kindness, that ye will also shew kindness unto my father's house, and give me a true token:

13. And *that* ye will save alive my father, and my mother, and my brethren, and my sisters, and all that they have, and deliver our lives from death.

14. And the men answered her, Our life for yours, if ye utter not this our business. And it shall be, when the Lord hath given us the land, that we will deal kindly and truly with thee.

15. Then she let them down by a cord through the window; for her house *was* upon the town wall, and she dwelt upon the wall.

16. And she said unto them, Get you to the mountain, lest the pursuers meet you; and hide yourselves there three days, until the pursuers be returned: and afterward may ye go your way.

17. And the men said unto her, We *will be* blameless of this thine oath which thou hast made us swear:

18. Behold, *when* we come into the land, thou shalt bind this line of scarlet thread in the window which thou didst let us down by: and thou shalt bring thy father, and thy mother, and thy brethren, and all thy father's household, home unto thee.

19. And it shall be, *that* whosoever shall go out of the doors of thy house into the street, his blood *shall be* upon his head, and we *will be* guiltless; and whosoever shall be with

fecerit Jehova aquas maris Suph a facie vestra dum exiistis ex Ægypto; et quae fecistis duobus regibus Æmorrhæi, qui erant trans Jordanem: Sihon et Og quos interemistis.

11. Audivimus, et dissolutum est cor nostrum, neque constitit ultra spiritus a facie vestra. Jehova enim Deus vester Deus est in cœlo sursum et super terram deorsum.

12. Nunc ergo jurate mihi, quaeso, per Jehovam (feci enim vobiscum misericordiam) quod facietis etiam vos cum domo patris mei misericordiam, et dabitis mihi signum verum,

13. Quod vivos servabitis fratrem meum, et matrem meam, et fratres meos, et sorores meas, et omnes qui sunt eorum, eruetisque animas nostras a morte.

14. Dixerunt ei viri: Anima nostra pro vobis ad moriendum: modo non prodideris sermonem nostrum hunc: tunc erit, ubi tradiderit Jehova nobis terram, faciemus tecum misericordiam et veritatem.

15. Demisit itaque eos fune per fenestram: domus enim ejus erat in pariete muri, et in muro ipsa habitabat.

16. Dixit autem eis: Ad montem pergite, ne forte occurrant vobis qui insequuntur, et latitate illic tribus diebus, donec redeant qui insequuntur, et postea ibitis per viam vestram.

17. Tunc dixerunt ei viri, Innoxii erimus a juramento tuo hoc quo nos adjurasti.

18. Ecce, quum ingrediemur terram, funiculum hunc fili coccinei ligabis in fenestra, per quam demiseris nos: patrem vero tuum et matrem tuam congregabis ad te in domum, et omnem familiam patris tui.

19. Erit autem, quicunque egressus fuerit e valvis domus tuæ foras, sanguis ejus erit in caput ejus, nos vero innoxii: quicunque vero tecum fuerit in domo, sanguis illius in caput

thee in the house, his blood *shall be* on our head, if *any* hand be upon him.

nostrum, si manus injecta fuerit in eum.

20. And if thou utter this our business, then we will be quit of thine oath which thou hast made us to swear.

20. Si vero prodideris sermonem hunc nostrum, erimus innoxii a juramento quo adjurasti nos.

21. And she said, According unto your words, so *be* it. And she sent them away, and they departed: and she bound the scarlet line in the window.

21. Respondit illa: Ut loquuti estis, ita sit. Tunc dimisit eos, et abierunt, ligavitque filum coccineum in fenestra.

22. And they went, and came unto the mountain, and abode there three days, until the pursuers were returned. And the pursuers sought *them* throughout all the way, but found *them* not.

22. Profecti venerunt ad montem, et manserunt ibi tribus diebus, donec reverterentur qui insequuti fuerant, qui quæsierunt per omnem viam, nec invenerunt.

23. So the two men returned, and descended from the mountain, and passed over, and came to Joshua the son of Nun, and told him all *things* that befell them:

23. Reversi ergo duo illi, postquam descenderunt e monte, transierunt, veneruntque ad Josue filium Nun, et narraverunt ei quæcunque acciderant sibi.

24. And they said unto Joshua, Truly the Lord hath delivered into our hands all the land: for even all the inhabitants of the country do faint because of us.

24. Dixeruntque ad Josue, Tradidit Jehova in manus nostras totam terram. Dissoluti enim sunt omnes habitatores terræ a facie nostra.

1. *And Joshua the son of Nun sent,* &c. The object of the exploration now in question was different from the former one, when Joshua was sent with other eleven to survey all the districts of the land, and bring back information to the whole people concerning its position, nature, fertility, and other properties, the magnitude and number of the cities, the inhabitants, and their manners. The present object was to dispose those who might be inclined to be sluggish, to engage with more alacrity in the campaign. And though it appears from the first chapter of Deuteronomy, (Deut. i. 22,) that Moses, at the request of the people, sent chosen men to spy out the land, he elsewhere relates (Numb. xiii. 4) that he did it by command from God. Those twelve, therefore, set out divinely commissioned, and for a somewhat different purpose, viz., to make a thorough survey of the land, and be the heralds of its excellence to stir up the courage of the people.

Now Joshua secretly sends two persons to ascertain whether

or not a free passage may be had over the Jordan, whether the citizens of Jericho were indulging in security, or whether they were on the alert and prepared to resist. In short, he sends spies on whose report he may provide against all dangers. Wherefore a twofold question may be here raised —Are we to approve of his prudence? or are we to condemn him for excessive anxiety, especially as he seems to have trusted more than was right to his own prudence, when, without consulting God, he was so careful in taking precautions against danger? But, inasmuch as it is not expressly said that he received a message from heaven to order the people to collect their vessels and to publish his proclamation concerning the passage of the Jordan, although it is perfectly obvious that he never would have thought of moving the camp unless God had ordered it, it is also probable that in sending the spies he consulted God as to his pleasure in the matter, or that God himself, knowing how much need there was of this additional confirmation, had spontaneously suggested it to the mind of his servant. Be this as it may, while Joshua commands his messengers to spy out Jericho, he is preparing to besiege it, and accordingly is desirous to ascertain in what direction it may be most easily and safely approached.

They came into a harlot's house, &c. Why some try to avoid the name *harlot,* and interpret זונה as meaning *one who keeps an inn,* I see not, unless it be that they think it disgraceful to be the guests of a courtezan, or wish to wipe off a stigma from a woman who not only received the messengers kindly, but secured their safety by singular courage and prudence. It is indeed a regular practice with the Rabbins, when they would consult for the honour of their nation, presumptuously to wrest Scripture and give a different turn by their fictions to anything that seems not quite reputable.[1] But the probability is, that while the messengers were courting secrecy, and shunning observation and all places of public intercourse, they came to a woman who

[1] In the present instance they set no limits to their extravagance, and gravely tell us, that instead of leading a life of infamy, she was merely an innkeeper or "hostess," and was afterwards honoured to be the wife of Joshua.—*Ed.*

dwelt in a retired spot. Her house was contiguous to the wall of the city, nay, its outer side was actually situated in the wall. From this we may infer that it was some obscure corner remote from the public thoroughfare; just as persons of her description usually live in narrow lanes and secret places. It cannot be supposed with any consistency to have been a common inn which was open to all indiscriminately, because they could not have felt at liberty to indulge in familiar intercourse, and it must have been difficult in such circumstances to obtain concealment.

My conclusion therefore is, that they obtained admission privily, and immediately betook themselves to a hiding-place. Moreover, in the fact that a woman who had gained a shameful livelihood by prostitution was shortly after admitted into the body of the chosen people, and became a member of the Church, we are furnished with a striking display of divine grace which could thus penetrate into a place of shame, and draw forth from it not only Rahab, but her father and the other members of her family. Most assuredly while the term זונה, almost invariably means *harlot*, there is nothing here to oblige us to depart from the received meaning.

2. *And it was told the king*, &c. It is probable that watchmen had been appointed to take notice of suspicious strangers, as is wont to be done in doubtful emergencies, or during an apprehension of war. The Israelites were nigh at hand; they had openly declared to the Edomites and Moabites that they were seeking a settlement in the land of Canaan; they were formidable for their number; they had already made a large conquest after slaying two neighbouring kings; and as we shall shortly perceive, their famous passage of the Red Sea had been noised abroad. It would therefore have argued extreme supineness in such manifest danger to allow any strangers whatever to pass freely through the city of Jericho, situated as it was on the frontiers.

It is not wonderful, therefore, that men who were unknown and who appeared from many circumstances to have come with a hostile intention, were denounced to the king. At the same time, however, we may infer that they were supernaturally blinded in not guarding their gates more carefully; for with the use of moderate diligence the messengers after they had once entered might easily have been detained. Nay, a search ought forthwith to have been instituted, and thus they would to a certainty have been caught. The citizens of Jericho were in such trepidation and so struck with judicial amazement, that they acted in everything without method or counsel. Meanwhile the two messengers were reduced to such extremities that they seemed on the eve of being delivered up to punishment. The king sends for them; they are lurking in the house; their life hangs upon the tongue of a woman, just as if it were hanging by a thread. Some have thought that there was in this a punishment of the distrust of Joshua, who ought to have boldly passed the Jordan, trusting to the divine guidance. But the result would rather lead us to conclude differently, that God by rescuing the messengers from extreme danger gave new courage to the people; for in that manifestation of his power he plainly shewed that he was watching over their safety, and providing for their happy entrance into the promised land.

4. *And the woman took the two men*, &c. We may presume that before Rahab was ordered to bring them forth the rumour of their arrival had been spread, and that thus some little time had been given for concealing them.[1] And indeed on receiving the king's command, had not measures for concealment been well taken, there would have been no room for denial; much less would she have dared to lie so coolly. But after she had thus hidden her guests, as the search would have been difficult, she comes boldly forward and escapes by a crafty answer.

[1] Had the season of the year when these transactions took place not been known from other sources, the mode of concealment to which Rahab resorted would have gone far to fix it. The "stalks of flax" with which she covered them, was evidently the crop of flax as it had been taken from the ground after attaining maturity, and laid out in the open air to dry, agreeably to a custom still practised, before it was subjected to the process of *skutching*, for the purpose of being deprived of its woody fibre. The flax sown about the end of September was pulled in the end of March or beginning of April, which accordingly was the period when the Israelites began to move their camp.—*Ed.*

Now, the questions which here arise are, first, Was treachery to her country excusable? Secondly, Could her lie be free from fault? We know that the love of our country, which is as it were our common mother, has been implanted in us by nature. When, therefore, Rahab knew that the object intended was the overthrow of the city in which she had been born and brought up, it seems a detestable act of inhumanity to give her aid and counsel to the spies. It is a puerile evasion to say, that they were not yet avowed enemies, inasmuch as war had not been declared; since it is plain enough that they had conspired the destruction of her fellow-citizens.[1] It was therefore only the knowledge communicated to her mind by God which exempted her from fault, as having been set free from the common rule. Her faith is commended by two Apostles, who at the same time declare, (Heb. xi. 31; James ii. 25,) that the service which she rendered to the spies was acceptable to God.

It is not wonderful, then, that when the Lord condescended to transfer a foreign female to his people, and to ingraft her into the body of the Church, he separated her from a profane and accursed nation. Therefore, although she had been bound to her countrymen up to that very day, yet when she was adopted into the body of the Church, her new condition was a kind of manumission from the common law by which citizens are bound toward each other. In short, in order to pass by faith to a new people, she behoved to renounce her countrymen. And as in this she only acquiesced in the judgment of God, there was no criminality in abandoning them.[2]

[1] It may either mean that "they" (the Israelites) "had conspired," as here translated, or as the French has it, that "Rahab had conspired."—*Ed.*

[2] Latin, "Nullum in proditione fuit crimen;" literally, "there was no crime in the treachery." French, "Il n'y a point eu de crime de trahison en ce faict;" "There was no crime of treachery in the act." Neither of these properly conveys Calvin's meaning. From what follows it is evident that he held all treachery to be criminal as implying a deviation from truth; while he also held, that under the special circumstances Rahab was justified in withdrawing her allegiance from her countrymen and transferring it to the Israelites. He therefore only justifies the *act* without approving of the *mode* of it. This view appears to be accurately expressed

As to the falsehood, we must admit that though it was done for a good purpose, it was not free from fault. For those who hold what is called a dutiful lie[1] to be altogether excusable, do not sufficiently consider how precious truth is in the sight of God. Therefore, although our purpose be to assist our brethren, to consult for their safety and relieve them, it never can be lawful to lie, because that cannot be right which is contrary to the nature of God. And God is truth. And still the act of Rahab is not devoid of the praise of virtue, although it was not spotlessly pure. For it often happens that while the saints study to hold the right path, they deviate into circuitous courses.

Rebecca (Gen. xxviii.) in procuring the blessing to her son Jacob, follows the prediction. In obedience of this description a pious and praiseworthy zeal is perceived. But it cannot be doubted that in substituting her son Jacob in the place of Esau, she deviated from the path of duty. The crafty proceeding, therefore, so far taints an act which was laudable in itself. And yet the particular fault does not wholly deprive the deed of the merit of holy zeal; for by the kindness of God the fault is suppressed and not taken into account. Rahab also does wrong when she falsely declares that the messengers were gone, and yet the principal action was agreeable to God, because the bad mixed up with the

by the term "abandoning," which has accordingly been substituted in the translation.—*Ed.*

[1] Latin, "Mendacium officiosum." French, "Le mensonge qui tend au profit du prochain;" "The lie which tends to our neighbour's profit." The *mendacium officiosum* is an expression of frequent use among the Casuists, and properly means, "a lie which it may be an act of duty to tell." One of the most common instances given is the case in which a simple statement of the truth might essentially endanger the interest, or, it may be, the life of an individual whom we are under a natural or conventional obligation to defend from all injury. A son, for example, is pursued by murderers; he takes shelter under the paternal roof; his mother has just succeeded in concealing him when the murderers arrive. Is she entitled to give a false answer to their interrogatories? The question is one of the most difficult and delicate that can be raised; but Calvin has undoubtedly given the right decision when he lays down the broad principle, that those who hold any lie to be excusable, "do not sufficiently consider how precious truth is in the sight of God." Were anything necessary to reconcile us to this decision, we may easily find it in the havoc which has been made of all morality by acting on its opposite, as evinced particularly in the case of Jesuit and other Romish casuists.—*Ed.*

good was not imputed. On the whole, it was the will of God that the spies should be delivered, but he did not approve of saving their life by falsehood.

7. *And the men pursued*, &c. Their great credulity shews that God had blinded them. Although Rahab had gained much by deluding them, a new course of anxiety intervenes; for the gates being shut, the city like a prison excluded the hope of escape. They were therefore again aroused by a serious trial to call upon God. For seeing that this history was written on their report, it is impossible they could have been ignorant of what was then going on, especially as God, for the purpose of magnifying his grace, purposely exposed them to a succession of dangers. And now when they were informed that search was made for them, we infer from the fact of their being still awake, that they were in anxiety and alarm. Their trepidation must have been in no small degree increased when it was told them that their exit was precluded.

It appears, however, that Rahab was not at all dismayed, since she bargains with so much presence of mind, and so calmly, for her own safety and that of her family. And in this composure and firmness her faith, which is elsewhere commended, appears conspicuous. For on human principles she never would have braved the fury of the king and people, and become a suppliant to guests half dead with terror. Many, indeed, think there is something ridiculous in the eulogium bestowed upon her both by St. James and the author of the Epistle to the Hebrews, (James ii. 25; Heb. xi. 31,) when they place her in the catalogue of the faithful. But any one who will carefully weigh all the circumstances will easily perceive that she was endowed with a lively faith.

First, If the tree is known by its fruits, we here see no ordinary effects, which are just so many evidences of faith. *Secondly,* A principle of piety must have given origin to her conviction that the neighbouring nations were already in a manner vanquished and laid prostrate, since terror sent from above had filled all minds with dismay. It is true that in profane writers also we meet with similar expressions, which

God has extorted from them that he might assert his power to rule and turn the hearts of men in whatever way he pleases. But while these writers prate like parrots, Rahab declaring in sincerity of heart that God has destined the land for the children of Israel, because all the inhabitants have fainted away before them, claims for him a supreme rule over the hearts of men, a rule which the pride of the world denies.

For although the experience of all times has shewn that more armies have fallen or been routed by sudden and unlooked for terror than by the force and prowess of the enemy, the impression of this truth has forthwith vanished away, and hence conquerors have always extolled their own valour, and on any prosperous result gloried in their own exertions and talents for war. They have felt, I admit, that daring and courage are occasionally bestowed or withheld by some extraneous cause, and accordingly men confess that in war fortune does much or even reigns supreme. Hence their common proverb with regard to panic terrors, and their vows made as well to Pavor (*Dread*) as to Jupiter Stator.[1] But it never became a serious and deep-seated impression in their minds, that every man is brave according as God has inspired him with present courage, or cowardly according as he has suppressed his daring. Rahab, however, recognises the operation of a divine hand in striking the nations of Canaan with dismay, and thus making them as it were by anticipation pronounce their own doom ; and she infers that the terror which the children of Israel have inspired is a presage of victory, because they fight under God as their Leader.

[1] French, "Et y a eu un proverbe commun entre eux, pour signifier les frayeurs soudaines dont le cause n'apparoit point ; (car ils les appeloyent Epouvantemens Paniques ;) aussi ils faisoyent voeus à un Juppiter qu'ils appeloyent Stator, c'est à dire Arrestant ; et à une deesse qu'ils nommoyent Pavor, c'est à dire Peur afin que les armees tinssent bon, et ne s'en fuissent de peur ;" "And there was a common proverb among them to denote the sudden alarms of which the cause does not appear ; for they called them Panic Terrors ; in like manner they made vows to a Jupiter, whom they called Stator, that is, Staying ; and to a goddess whom they named *Pavor*, that is Fear, in order that armies might stand good, and not flee from fear."—*Ed.*

In the fact, that while the courage of all had thus melted away, they however prepared to resist with the obstinacy of despair; we see that when the wicked are broken and crushed by the hand of God, they are not so subdued as to receive the yoke, but in their terror and anxiety become incapable of being tamed. Here, too, we have to observe how in a common fear believers differ from unbelievers, and how the faith of Rahab displays itself. She herself was afraid like any other of the people; but when she reflects that she has to do with God, she concludes that her only remedy is to eschew evil by yielding humbly and placidly, as resistance would be altogether unavailing. But what is the course taken by all the wretched inhabitants of the country? Although terror-struck, so far is their perverseness from being overcome that they stimulate each other to the conflict.

10. *For we have heard how,* &c. She mentions, as the special cause of consternation, that the wide-spread rumour of miracles, hitherto without example, had impressed it on the minds of all that God was warring for the Israelites. For it was impossible to doubt that the way through the Red Sea had been miraculously opened up, as the water would never have changed its nature and become piled up in solid heaps, had not God, the author of nature, so ordered. The transmutation of the element, therefore, plainly shewed that God was on the side of the people, to whom he had given a dry passage through the depths of the sea.

The signal victories also gained over Og and Bashan, were justly regarded as testimonies of the divine favour towards the Israelites. This latter conclusion, indeed, rested only on conjecture, whereas the passage of the sea was a full and irrefragable proof, as much so as if God had stretched forth his hand from heaven. All minds, therefore, were seized with a conviction that in the expedition of the Israelitish people God was principal leader;[1] hence their terror and consternation. At the same time, it is probable that they were

[1] French, "Que Dieu estoit le principal conducteur de l'entreprise du peuple d'Israel, et qu'il marchoit avec iceluy;" "That God was the principal conductor of the enterprise of the people of Israel, and that he was marching along with them."—*Ed.*

deceived by some vain imagination that the God of Israel had proved superior in the contest to the gods of Egypt; just as the poets feign that every god has taken some nation or other under his protection, and wars with others, and that thus conflicts take place among the gods themselves while they are protecting their favourites.

But the faith of Rahab takes a higher flight, while to the God of Israel alone she ascribes supreme power and eternity. These are the true attributes of Jehovah. She does not dream, according to the vulgar notion, that some one, out of a crowd of deities, is giving his assistance to the Israelites, but she acknowledges that He whose favour they were known to possess is the true and only God. We see, then, how in a case where all received the same intelligence, she, in the application of it, went far beyond her countrymen.

11. *The Lord your God, he is God*, &c. Here the image of Rahab's faith appears, as if reflected in a mirror, when casting down all idols she ascribes the government of heaven and earth to the God of Israel alone. For it is perfectly clear that when heaven and earth are declared subject to the God of Israel, there is a repudiation of all the pagan fictions by which the majesty, and power, and glory of God are portioned out among different deities; and hence we see that it is not without cause that two Apostles have honoured Rahab's conduct with the title of *faith*. This is sneered at by some proud and disdainful men, but I wish they would consider what it is to distinguish the one true God from all fictitious deities, and at the same time so to extol his power as to declare that the whole world is governed at his pleasure. Rahab does not speak hesitatingly, but declares, in absolute terms, that whatever power exists resides in the God of Israel alone, that he commands all the elements, that he orders all things above and below, and determines human affairs. Still I deny not that her faith was not fully developed, nay, I readily admit, that it was only a germ of piety which, as yet, would have been insufficient for her eternal salvation. We must hold, nevertheless, that however feeble and slender the knowledge of God which the woman possessed may have been, still in surrendering herself to his

power, she gives a proof of her election, and that from that seed a faith was germinating which afterwards attained its full growth.

12. *Now, therefore, I pray you, swear*, &c. It is another manifestation of faith that she places the sons of Abraham in sure possession of the land of Canaan, founding on no other argument than her having heard that it was divinely promised to them. For she did not suppose that God was favouring lawless intruders who were forcing their way into the territories of others with unjust violence and uncurbed licentiousness, but rather concluded that they were coming into the land of Canaan, because God had assigned them the dominion of it. It cannot be believed that when they sought a passage from the Edomites and others, they said nothing as to whither they were going. Nay, those nations were acquainted with the promise which was made to Abraham, and the memory of which had been again renewed by the rejection of Esau.

Moreover, in the language of Rahab, we behold that characteristic property of faith described by the author of the Epistle to the Hebrews, when he calls it a vision, or sight of things not appearing. (Heb. xi. 1.) Rahab is dwelling with her people in a fortified city : and yet she commits her life to her terrified guests, just as if they had already gained possession of the land, and had full power to save or destroy as they pleased. This voluntary surrender was, in fact, the very same as embracing the promise of God, and casting herself on his protection. She, moreover, exacts an oath, because often, in the storming of cities, the heat and tumult of the struggle shook off the remembrance of duty. In the same way she mentions the kindness she had shewn to them, that gratitude might stimulate them the more to perform their promise. For although the obligation of the oath ought of itself to have been effectual, it would have been doubly base and inhumane not to shew gratitude to a hostess to whom they owed deliverance. Rahab shews the kindliness of her disposition, in her anxiety about her parents and kindred. This is, indeed, natural; but many are so devoted to themselves, that children hesitate not to ransom their own lives by the death of their parents, instead of exerting courage and zeal to save them.

14. *Our life for yours*, &c. They imprecate death upon themselves, if they do not faithfully make it their business to save Rahab. For the interpretation adopted by some, We will pledge our lives, seems far-fetched, or too restricted, since their intention was simply to bind themselves before God. They constitute themselves, therefore, a kind of expiatory victims, if any evil befalls Rahab through their negligence. The expression, *for yours*, ought, doubtless, to be extended to the parents, brothers, and sisters. They therefore render their own lives liable in such a sense, that blood may be required of them, if the family of Rahab do not remain safe. And herein consists the sanctity of an oath, that though its violation may escape with impunity, so far as men are concerned, yet God having been interposed as a witness, will take account of the perfidy. In Hebrew, to do mercy and truth, is equivalent to performing the office of humanity faithfully, sincerely, and firmly.

A condition, however, is inserted,—provided Rahab do not divulge what they have said. This was inserted, not on account of distrust, as is usually expounded, but only to put Rahab more upon her guard, on her own account. The warning, therefore, was given in good faith, and flowed from pure good will: for there was a danger that Rahab might betray herself by a disclosure. In one word, they shew how important it is that the matter should remain, as it were, buried, lest the woman, by inconsiderately talking of the compact, might expose herself to capital punishment. In this they shew that they were sincerely anxious for her safety, since they thus early caution her against doing anything which might put it out of their power to render her a service. In further distinctly stipulating, that no one should go out of the house, or otherwise they should be held blameless, we may draw the important inference, that in making oaths soberness should be carefully attended to, that we may not profane the name of God by making futile promises on any subject.

The advice of Rahab, to turn aside into the mountain,

and there remain quiet for three days, shews that there is no repugnance between faith and the precautions which provide against manifest dangers. There is no doubt that the messengers crept off to the mountain in great fear, and yet that confidence which they had conceived, from the remarkable interference of God in their behalf, directed their steps, and did not allow them to lose their presence of mind.

Some have raised the question, whether, seeing it is criminal to overleap walls, it could be lawful to get out of the city by a window? But it ought to be observed, *first*, that the walls of cities were not everywhere sacred, because every city had not a Romulus, who could make the overleaping a pretext for slaying his brother;[1] and *secondly*, That law, as Cicero reminds us, was to be tempered by equity, inasmuch as he who should climb a wall for the purpose of repelling an enemy, would be more deserving of reward than punishment. The end of the law is to make the citizens secure by the protection of the walls. He, therefore, who should climb over the walls, neither from contempt nor petulance, nor fraud, nor in a tumultuous manner, but under the pressure of necessity, could not justly on that account be charged with a capital offence. Should it be objected that the thing was of bad example, I admit it: but when the object is to rescue one's life from injury, violence, or robbery, provided it be done without offence or harm to any one, necessity excuses it. It cannot be charged upon Paul as a crime, that when in danger of his life at Damascus, he was let down by a basket, seeing he was divinely permitted to escape, without tumult, from the violence and cruelty of wicked men.[2]

[1] This is an instance of the quiet and almost sly humour which occasionally betrays itself in Calvin's other writings, and shews, that had it comported with the general gravity of his character, he might easily have added wit to the other weapons with which he fought the battles of the faith. In private life, when greater freedom was allowable, it appears, according to Beza's statement, to have not unfrequently contributed to the charm of his conversation.—*Ed.*

[2] The whole objection, as to the overleaping of walls, is so ridiculous in itself, and so very inapplicable to the circumstances of all parties at the time, that it is difficult to understand why Calvin should have condescended to notice it at all, or, at least, given himself so much trouble to refute it. If one might hazard a conjecture, it would be that some question

24. *And they said unto Joshua*, &c. This passage shews that Joshua was not mistaken in selecting his spies; for their language proves them to have been right-hearted men possessed of rare integrity. Others, perhaps, not recovered from the terror into which they had once been thrown, would have disturbed the whole camp, but these, while they reflect on the wonderful kindness of God, displayed in their escape from danger, and the happy issue of their expedition, exhort Joshua and the people to go boldly forward. And although the mere promise of possessing the land ought to have been sufficient, yet the Lord is so very indulgent to their weakness, that, for the sake of removing all doubt, he confirms what he had promised by experience. That the Lord had not spoken in vain, was proved by the consternation of the nations, when it began already to put them to flight, and to drive them out, as if hornets had been sent in upon them. For they argue in the same way as Rahab had done, that the land was given to them, as the inhabitants had almost fainted away from fear. I have therefore used the illative particle *for*, though the literal meaning is, *and also*. But it is sufficiently plain, that in the other way there is a confirmation of what they had said. And, indeed, the courage of all melted away, as if they felt themselves routed by the hand of God.

CHAPTER III.

1. And Joshua rose early in the morning; and they removed from Shittim, and came to Jordan, he and all the children of Israel, and lodged there before they passed over.

1. Surrexit autem Josue summo mane, et profecti sunt e Sittim, veneruntque usque ad Jordanem ipse et omnes filii Israel, pernoctaveruntque illic antequam transirent.

2. And it came to pass after three days, that the officers went through the host;

2. Et fuit a fine trium dierum, ut præfecti transirent per medium castrorum.

3. And they commanded the people, saying, When ye see the ark of the covenant of the Lord your God, and the priests the Levites bearing it, then ye shall remove from your place, and go after it:

3. Præciperentque populo, dicendo, Quum videritis arcam fœderis Jehovæ Dei vestri, et sacerdotes Levitas portantes eam, proficiscemini e loco vestro, ibitisque post illam.

of a similar nature had been raised in regard to the walls of Geneva, and given a local interest to a discussion which otherwise seems somewhat out of place.—*Ed.*

4. Yet there shall be a space between you and it, about two thousand cubits by measure: come not near unto it; that ye may know the way by which ye must go: for ye have not passed *this* way heretofore.

5. And Joshua said unto the people, Sanctify yourselves: for to-morrow the Lord will do wonders among you.

6. And Joshua spake unto the priests, saying, Take up the ark of the covenant, and pass over before the people. And they took up the ark of the covenant, and went before the people.

7. And the Lord said unto Joshua, This day will I begin to magnify thee in the sight of all Israel, that they may know that, as I was with Moses, *so* I will be with thee.

8. And thou shalt command the priests that bear the ark of the covenant, saying, When ye are come to the brink of the water of Jordan, ye shall stand still in Jordan.

9. And Joshua said unto the children of Israel, Come hither, and hear the words of the Lord your God.

10. And Joshua said, Hereby ye shall know that the living God *is* among you, and *that* he will without fail drive out from before you the Canaanites, and the Hittites, and the Hivites, and the Perizzites, and the Girgashites, and the Amorites, and the Jebusites.

11. Behold, the ark of the covenant of the Lord of all the earth passeth over before you into Jordan.

12. Now therefore take you twelve men out of the tribes of Israel, out of every tribe a man.

13. And it shall come to pass, as soon as the soles of the feet of the priests that bear the ark of the Lord, the Lord of all the earth, shall rest in the waters of Jordan, *that* the waters of Jordan shall be cut off *from* the waters that come down from above; and they shall stand upon an heap.

4. Veruntamen interstitium erit inter vos et ipsam fere duorum milium cubitorum in mensura: ne appropinquetis ei, ut cognoscatis viam per quam ambulaturi estis. Non enim transiistis per viam illam heri vel nudius tertius.

5. Dixerat autem Josue ad populum, sanctificate (*præparate*) vos. Cras enim faciet Jehova in medio vestri mirabilia.

6. Loquutus autem est Josue ad sacerdotes, dicendo, Tollite arcam fœderis, et transite ante populum. Tulerunt itaque arcam fœderis, et ambularunt ante populum.

7. Dixerat autem Jehova ad Josuam, Hodie incipiam magnificare te in oculis totius Israel, ut, sciant, quomodo fui cum Mose, sic me fore tecum.

8. Tu ergo præcipies sacerdotibus portantibus arcam fœderis, dicendo, Quum ingressi fueritis usque ad extremum aquæ Jordanis, in Jordane stabitis.

9. Dixitque Josue ad filios Israel, Accedite huc, et audite verba Jehovæ Dei vestri.

10. Dixit item Josue, In hoc cognoscetis quod Deus vivens est in medio vestri, et quod expellendo expellet a facie vestra Chananæum, Hitthæum, et Hivæum, et Pherisæum, et Gergesæum, et Amorrhæum, et Jebusæum.

11. Ecce arca fœderis Dominatoris universæ terræ transibit ante vos per Jordanem.

12. Nunc ergo tollite vobis duodecim viros e tribubus Israel, singulos per singulas tribus.

13. Quum autem quieverint plantæ pedum sacerdotum portantium arcam Jehovæ Dominatoris universæ terræ in aquis Jordanis, aquæ Jordanis intercidentur, et aquæ superne (*vel* desuper, *vel* desursum) fluentes, consistent in acervo uno.

1. *And Joshua rose early*, &c. We must remember, as I formerly explained, that Joshua did not move his camp till the day after the spies had returned, but that after hearing their report, he gave orders by the prefects that they should collect their vessels, as three days after they were to cross the Jordan.[1] His rising in the morning, therefore, does not

[1] This seems to be the proper place to insert a short account of the Jordan, and more especially of that part of it in the neighbourhood of which the Israelites were now encamped. This becomes necessary, because Calvin has altogether omitted it, partly, as some expressions in his Commentary would seem to indicate, from having unfortunately attached little comparative importance to geographical details, and partly, as he very modestly expresses it, from not having been very well acquainted with them. Indeed, at the period when he wrote, the geography of the Holy Land was very imperfectly known, but we have not the same excuse, as numerous well-qualified travellers have since traversed it in all directions, and published careful descriptions both of its general features and of almost all the localities possessed of much historical interest. In a single note, only a few leading points can be adverted to, but it seems not impossible, in this way, to give a distinct idea of the nature of the passage which the Israelites were now preparing to make, and of the wonderful interposition by which they were enabled to accomplish it.

The Jordan, then, by far the most important river of Palestine, is formed, near its northern frontiers, by several streams which descend from the mountains of Lebanon, and after flowing nearly due south, for a direct distance of about 175 miles, discharges its waters into the north side of the Dead Sea. In the upper part of its course, before it reaches the lake of Tiberius, more familiarly known by its usual scriptural name of the Sea of Galilee, it has much of the character of an impetuous torrent, and is hemmed closely in on both sides by lofty mountains, but on issuing from the south side of the lake, it begins to flow in a valley, the most remarkable circumstance connected with which, is its great depth beneath the level of the ocean. Even the Sea of Galilee is 84 feet, and the Dead Sea, where the Jordan falls into it, is 1337 feet beneath this level. The intervening space between the two seas, forms what is properly called the valley of the Jordan, and consists of a plain, about six miles across in its northern, but much wider in its southern half, where it spreads out, on its east or left bank, into the plains of Moab, and on its west or right bank, into the plains of Jericho. This valley, throughout its whole length, is terminated on either side by a mountain chain, which in many parts rises so rapidly as soon to attain a height exceeding 2500. Within the valley thus terminated, a minor valley is enclosed. It is about three quarters of a mile in breadth, and consists, for the most part, of a low flat, bounded by sandy slopes, and covered by trees or brushwood. Nearly in the centre of this flat the river, almost concealed beneath its overhanging banks, pursues its course, with few large windings, but with such a multiplicity of minute tortuosities, that though the direct distance is not more than sixty-five, the indirect distance or total length of the stream is estimated at not less than two hundred miles. The river, in its ordinary state, within its banks, has a width of from twenty to thirty yards, and a depth, varying from nine to fifteen feet. The banks are there from twelve to fourteen feet high, and immediately beyond them, the flat bears evident marks of being fre-

refer simply to their return, but rather to the issuing of his proclamation. When the three days were completed, the prefects were again sent through the camp to acquaint the people with the mode of passage. Although these things are mentioned separately, it is easy to take up the thread of the narrative. But before it was publicly intimated, by what means he was to open a way for the people, the multitude spread out on the bank of the river were exposed to some degree of confusion.

It is true, there were fords by which the Jordan could be passed. But the waters were then swollen, and had overflowed, so that they might easily prevent even men altogether without baggage from passing. There was therefore no hope, that women and children, with the animals, and the rest of the baggage, could be transported to the further bank. That, in such apparently desperate circumstances, they calmly wait the issue, though doubtful, and to them incomprehensible, is an example of faithful obedience, proving how unlike they were to their fathers, who, on the slightest occasions, gave way to turbulence, and inveighed against the Lord and against Moses. This change was not produced without the special agency of the Holy Spirit.

2. *And it came to pass after three days*, &c. That is, three days after their departure had been intimated. For they did not halt at the bank longer than one night. But as the period of three days had previously been fixed for crossing, and they had no hope of being able to accomplish it, Joshua now exhorts them to pay no more regard to obstacles and

quently inundated. These inundations take place in spring, and are caused by the melted snow brought down, partly by the three principal tributaries of the Jordan, the Jarmuch, or Shurat-el-Mandour, the Jabbok, or Zerka, and the Arnon, or Wady Modjet, which all join it from the east, but chiefly by the main stream, which is then copiously supplied from the snowy heights of Lebanon. This rising of the waters, of course, begins as soon as the thawing influence of the returning heat begins to be felt, but does not attain its maximum till the impression has been fully made, or, in the first weeks of April. Such was the state of the stream as the Israelites now approached it, at a spot which cannot be exactly ascertained, but may be safely assumed to have been from seven to twelve miles north of the Dead Sea, and not far from the Bethabarah, where our Saviour, after condescending to receive baptism at the hands of his forerunner, went up from the banks, while the heavens opened, and the Spirit of God descended like a dove, and lighted upon him.—*Ed.*

difficulties, and to attend to the power of God. For although the form of the miracle is not yet explained, yet when the ark of the covenant is brought forward like a banner to guide the way, it was natural to infer that the Lord was preparing something unusual. And while they are kept in suspense, their faith is again proved by a serious trial; for it was an example of rare virtue to give implicit obedience to the command, and thus follow the ark, while they were obviously uninformed as to the result. This, indeed, is the special characteristic of faith, not to inquire curiously what the Lord is to do, nor to dispute subtlely as to how that which he declares can possibly be done, but to cast all our anxious cares upon his providence, and knowing that his power, on which we may rest, is boundless, to raise our thoughts above the world, and embrace by faith that which we cannot comprehend by reason.

4. *Yet there shall be a space,* &c. As the younger Levites, whose province it was to carry the ark, (Numb. iv. 15,) were strictly forbidden to touch it, or even to look at it, when uncovered, it is not wonderful that the common people were not allowed to approach within a considerable distance of it. The dignity of the ark, therefore, is declared, when the people are ordered to attest their veneration by leaving a long interval between themselves and it. And we know what happened to Uzzah, (2 Sam. vi.,) when seeing it shaken by restive oxen, he with inconsiderate zeal put forth his hand to support it. For although God invites us familiarly to himself, yet faithful trust so far from begetting security and boldness, is, on the contrary, always coupled with fear. In this way the ark of the covenant was, indeed, a strong and pleasant pledge of the divine favour, but, at the same time, had an awful majesty, well fitted to subdue carnal pride. This humility and modesty, moreover, had the effect of exercising their faith by preventing them from confining the grace of God within too narrow limits, and reminding them, that though they were far distant from the ark, the divine power was ever near.

In the end of the verse it is shewn how necessary it was for them to be divinely guided by an unknown way; that anxiety and fear might keep them under the protection of the ark.

5. *And Joshua said*, &c. Some unwonted manifestation of divine power in bringing assistance behoved to be held forth, lest the backwardness arising from hesitancy might produce delay; and yet, in order that the Israelites might depend on the mere counsel of God, Joshua does not yet plainly point out the special nature of the miracle, unless, indeed, we choose to read what follows shortly after, as forming part of one context. Herein lies the true test of faith, to lean so on the counsel of God, as not to keep inquiring too anxiously concerning the mode of action or the event. As the word קדש means sometimes to *prepare*, and sometimes to *sanctify*, and either meaning is not inappropriate, I thought it best to leave a free choice. For faith prepares us to perceive the operation of God; and in those times, when God manifested himself to men more nearly, they consecrated themselves by a solemn rite; thus we see how Moses, on the promulgation of the Law, sanctified the people as God had commanded. The view taken by some expositors, that the people were thus commanded to purge themselves from defilements, merely in order that nothing might impede the passage of the Jordan, seems to be too confined.

6. *And Joshua spake unto the priests*, &c. It is probable that the priests were informed why God wished the ark to precede, that they might be more ready to execute the command, for the whole people are immediately after made acquainted with the intended division of the waters. As the prefects had formerly published in the camp, that the people were to follow the ark of the covenant, the priests could not possibly be ignorant as to the office which they were to perform. For it had been distinctly declared that they were to be leaders or standard-bearers. But when all were in readiness, Joshua publicly unfolded the divine message which he had received. For it would have been incongruous to make the divine favour more clearly manifest to the common people than to them. It is added, however, immediately after, that the people were made acquainted with the miracle.

I conclude, therefore, that after the priests had for some time been kept in suspense, along with the multitude, the Lord, on ascertaining the obedience of all, publicly declared what he was to do. First, then, it is related that the priests were enjoined by Joshua to bear the ark before the people; and secondly, lest any one might think that he was making the attempt at random, or at his own hand, mention is at the same time made of the promise with which he had been furnished as a means of ensuring his command. But although it is not then distinctly said that the course of the Jordan would be interrupted, yet, from the language which Joshua used to the people, we may infer that the Lord spoke more in detail, and explained more distinctly what he had determined to do. For Joshua did not mention anything which he had not previously learned from the mouth of God himself. Nay, before he makes any mention of the matter at all, he tells them to hear the words of the Lord, and thus premises that he has the authority of God for what he is about to say.

10. *Hereby ye shall know*, &c. He makes the power of the miracle extend further than to the entrance of the land, and deservedly; for merely to open up a passage into a hostile territory, from which there was afterwards no retreat, would have been nothing else than exposure to death. For either entangled among straits, and in an unknown region, they would easily have been destroyed, or they would have perished, worn out by hunger and the absolute want of all things. Joshua therefore declares before hand, that when God would restore the river to its course, it would just be as if he were stretching forth his hand to rout all the inhabitants of the land; and that the manifestation of his power given in the passage of the Jordan, would be a sure presage of the victory which they would obtain over all the nations.

He says, Hence shall you know that the Lord is present with you; to what end? Not only to plant your feet in the land of Canaan, but also to give you full possession of it. For surely when mention is made of the overthrow of the nations, an ultimate, free, and peaceful possession is implied. Therefore, as the Lord by dividing the river clearly shewed that his power resided with the Israelites, so the people must on their part have conceived hopes of perpetual assistance, as much as if they had already seen their enemies worsted and lying prostrate before them.

For God does not abandon the work of his hands midway, leaving it maimed and unfinished. (Ps. cxxxviii. 8.) When he leads his people unto the promised inheritance, he makes a dry passage for them by cutting off the course of the Jordan. How perverse then would it have been for the Israelites to stop short at that momentary act, instead of feeling confident in all time to come, until quiet possession of the land were actually obtained! Let us learn then from this example, prudently to combine the different acts of divine goodness relating to our final salvation, so that a happy commencement may cherish and keep alive in our minds the hope of an equally happy termination.

When Joshua says that the people will know the presence of God from the miracle, he indirectly upbraids them with their distrust, as the mere promise of God ought to have sufficed for a full assurance, and our faith, unless founded solely on this promise, must be continually wavering. But although faith ought properly to recline on the truth of God alone, it does not follow that experimental knowledge may not act as a secondary support to its weakness, and give subsidiary aid to its confirmation. For that which God promises to us in word he seals by act, and as often as he exhibits to us manifestations of his grace and might, he intends them to be so many confirmations of what he has spoken, and so many helps tending to suppress all our doubts.

11. *Behold the ark of the covenant*, &c. First he says that the ark of God will go before; and secondly, he explains for what purpose, namely, that Jordan may retire from its place, trembling, so to speak, at the presence of the Lord, as is said in the Psalms. (Ps. cxiv.) The narrative introduced concerning the twelve men is parenthetical, as it only briefly alludes to what it will afterwards deliver more fully and clearly. At present let us merely understand, that while the

ark went before, God displayed his power in guiding the people. And in this way there was a confirmation of the sanctity of the worship appointed by the Law, when the Israelites perceived that it was no empty symbol of his presence that God had deposited with them. For Jordan was compelled to yield obedience to God just as if it had beheld his majesty.

Let us however remember, that the only reason which induced the Lord to display his grace in the ark was because he had placed the tables of his covenant within it. Moreover, as the thing could not be easily credited, Joshua directs the mind of the people to the contemplation of the divine power, which surmounts all difficulties. The title of Ruler of the whole earth here applied to God is not insignificant, but extols his power above all the elements of nature, in order that the Israelites, considering how seas and rivers are subject to his dominion, might have no doubt that the waters, though naturally liquid, would become stable in obedience to his word.

14. And it came to pass, when the people removed from their tents, to pass over Jordan, and the priests bearing the ark of the covenant before the people;

15. And as they that bare the ark were come unto Jordan, and the feet of the priests that bare the ark were dipped in the brim of the water, (for Jordan overfloweth all his banks all the time of harvest,)

16. That the waters, which came down from above, stood, *and* rose up upon an heap, very far from the city Adam, that *is* beside Zaretan: and those that came down toward the sea of the plain, *even* the salt sea, failed, *and* were cut off; and the people passed over right against Jericho.

17. And the priests, that bare the ark of the covenant of the Lord, stood firm on dry ground in the midst of Jordan, and all the Israelites passed over on dry ground, until all the people were passed clean over Jordan.

14. Et fuit, quum proficisceretur populus ad transeundum Jordanem, sacerdotes qui portabant arcam fœderis erant ante populum.

15. Postquam autem venerunt qui portabant arcam usque ad Jordanem, et pedes sacerdotum portantium arcam intincti fuerunt in extremo aquarum (Jordanes autem erat plenus ultra omnes suas ripas toto tempore messis,)

16. Constiterunt aquæ quæ descendebant desuper, et assurexerunt in acervum unum procul valde, ab Adam urbe quæ est ad latus Sarthan, et quæ descendebant ad mare solitudinis, mare salis, consumptæ sunt, interciderunt: populus autem transierunt è regione Jericho.

17. Stabant autem sacerdotes portantes arcam fœderis Jehovæ in sicco in medio Jordanis expediti, (*vel* præparati,) totus vero Israel transibant per siccum donec finem facerent universa gens transeundi Jordanis.

15. *And as they that bare the ark*, &c. The valour of the priests in proceeding boldly beyond the bed into the water itself, was deserving of no mean praise, since they might have been afraid of being instantly drowned. For what could they expect on putting in their feet, but immediately to find a deep pool in which they would be ingulfed? In not being afraid on reaching the stream, and in continuing to move firmly forward to the appointed place, they gave a specimen of rare alacrity, founded on confidence.

To the general danger was added the special one, that the Jordan had then overflowed its banks, as it is wont to do at the commencement of every summer. As the plain was covered, it was impossible to observe the line of the banks or the ford, and the slime spread far and wide, increased their fear and anxiety.[1] God was pleased that his people, and especially the priests, should contend with these obstacles, in order that the victory of their faith and constancy might be more illustrious. At the same time, the difficulty thus presented tended to magnify the glory of the miracle when the waters, which had overflowed their banks, retired at the divine command, and were gathered together into a solid heap. First, Joshua explains the nature of the miracle for the purpose of removing doubt, and preventing profane men from denying the divine interposition by a subtle searching

[1] These remarks are made on the assumption that the waters had risen so as not only to reach the highest edge of the banks, and make the usual channel what may be called brim-full, but had spread themselves to some distance over the plain. It may have been so, but there is no distinct statement to this effect, and the concluding clause of the fifteenth verse does not literally bear the meaning which Calvin and our English translators have assigned to it. His rendering is, "Jordanes autem erat plenus ultra omnes suas ripas;" literally, "Now Jordan was full beyond all his banks." The English rendering is, "For Jordan overfloweth all his banks." The original only says that "Jordan fills up to (completely fills) all his banks." The Septuagint, in like manner, says, "Ὁ δὲ Ἰορδάνης ἐπληροῦτο καθ᾽ ὅλην τὴν κρηπῖδα αὐτοῦ;" "Now the Jordan was filled as to all his embankment." The same meaning is very exactly given by Luther, whose version is "Der Jordan aber war voll an allen seinen ufern;" "Now Jordan was full on all his banks." The difference between the renderings is slight, but it is of importance not to overlook it, because even such slight differences have sometimes furnished the infidel with plausible grounds for assailing the credit of the sacred narrative. In the present instance it has been insinuated that the historian has exaggerated the extent of the inundation in order to heighten the importance of the miracle.—*Ed.*

for other causes. It is not, indeed, impossible that the flowing of the water might have been restrained for a short time, and that some portion of the channel might thus have appeared dry, or that the course might have changed and taken some other direction. But it was certainly neither a natural nor fortuitous event, when the waters stood gathered up into a heap. It is therefore said that the waters which previously flowed from the higher ground, seeking in their descent a continuous outlet, stood still.

There cannot be a doubt that this wonderful sight must have been received with feelings of fear, leading the Israelites more distinctly to acknowledge that they were saved in the midst of death. For what was that collected heap but a grave in which the whole multitude would have been buried, had the waters resumed their naturally liquid state?[1] Had they walked upon the waters their faith might have served them as a kind of bridge. But now, while mountains of water hung over their heads, it is just as if they had found an open and level path beneath them. The locality is marked out as situated between two cities,[2] that the remembrance of it might never be lost; and, in like manner, God ordered stones to be set up as a perpetual memorial, that this distinguished mercy might be celebrated by posterity in all ages.

[1] French, "Si les eaux, selon leur nature, eussent alors recommencé a couler;" "Had the waters then according to their nature begun again to flow."—*Ed.*

[2] This is not very explicit, and may have been left vague on purpose, because the original itself, as it now stands, is obscure, and both translators and commentators, instead of throwing any light upon it, have rather increased the darkness. For Adam, the Vulgate substitutes Edom, and the Septuagint, the district of Kirjath-jearim (μέρους Καριαθιαρίμ.) Two towns near each other, and bearing the respective names of Adam and Zarethan, are mentioned in Scripture as situated in the tribe of Manasseh, the one on the right and the other on the left bank of the Jordan. Their distance above the place at which the Israelites are presumed to have crossed is about forty miles; and the most natural meaning of the passage seems to be, that when the waters stood, as it were, congealed in a heap, they remained so long in that state, as to cause a kind of reflux tide, which was perceptible as far back as Adam on the one hand, and Zareptan on the other.—*Ed.*

CHAPTER IV.

1. And it came to pass, when all the people were clean passed over Jordan, that the Lord spake unto Joshua, saying,

2. Take you twelve men out of the people, out of every tribe a man;

3. And command ye them, saying, Take you hence out of the midst of Jordan, out of the place where the priests' feet stood firm, twelve stones; and ye shall carry them over with you, and leave them in the lodging-place where ye shall lodge this night.

4. Then Joshua called the twelve men, whom he had prepared of the children of Israel, out of every tribe a man;

5. And Joshua said unto them, Pass over before the ark of the Lord your God into the midst of Jordan, and take you up every man of you a stone upon his shoulder, according unto the number of the tribes of the children of Israel:

6. That this may be a sign among you, *that* when your children ask *their fathers* in time to come, saying, What *mean* ye by these stones?

7. Then ye shall answer them, That the waters of Jordan were cut off before the ark of the covenant of the Lord; when it passed over Jordan, the waters of Jordan were cut off: and these stones shall be for a memorial unto the children of Israel for ever.

8. And the children of Israel did so as Joshua commanded, and took up twelve stones out of the midst of Jordan, as the Lord spake unto Joshua, according to the number of the tribes of the children of Israel, and carried them over with them unto the place where they lodged, and laid them down there.

9. And Joshua set up twelve stones in the midst of Jordan, in the place where the feet of the priests which bare the ark of the covenant stood: and they are there unto this day.

1. Et fuit, postquam finem fecit tota gens trajiciendi Jordanis; quia loquutus erat Jehova ad Josuam, dicendo.

2. Tollite vobis e populo duodecim viros virum unum ex quaque tribu.

3. Et præcipite illis dicendo: Tollite vobis hinc e medio Jordanis a loco ubi stant pedes sacerdotum expeditorum, duodecim lapides quos feretis vobiscum, et deponetis in loco ubi hac nocte manebitis.

4. Tunc vocavit Josue duodecim viros quos ordinaverat e filiis Israel, singulos ex quaque tribu.

5. Et dixit illis Josue, Transite ante arcam Jehovæ Dei vestri per medium Jordanis, et tollat quisque ex vobis lapidem unum super humerum suum pro numero tribuum filiorum Israel.

6. Ut sit hoc inter vos (*vel,* in medio vestri) signum quum interrogaverint filii vestri cras patres suos, quid sunt lapides isti apud vos?

7. Tunc respondeatis eis, quod intercisæ fuerunt aquæ Jordanis ante arcam fœderis Jehovæ, quum, inquam, transiret Jordanem, intercisæ fuerunt aquæ Jordanis, tunc facti fuerunt lapides isti in monumentum filiis Israel perpetuo.

8. Fecerunt itaque filii Israel sicut præceperat Josue, et sustulerunt duodecim lapides e medio Jordanis sicut loquutus fuerat Jehova ad Josuam pro numero tribuum filiorum Israel, tuleruntque eos secum ad locum ubi pernoctaverunt, et reposuerunt illic.

9. Duodecim quoque lapides erexit Josue in medio Jordanis sub statione pedum sacerdotum qui portabant arcam fœderis, manseruntque ibi usque in hunc diem.

1. *And it came to pass*, &c. The brief and obscure allusion previously made with regard to the twelve men he now explains more at length. He had said that they were chosen by the order of God, one each from his own tribe; but breaking off his discourse, he had not mentioned for what purpose. He now says, that by command of Joshua[1] they took up twelve stones and placed them in Gilgal, that a well marked memorial might exist among posterity. Moreover, as he only relates what was done after the passage of the people, what is interposed should be interpreted as in the pluperfect tense.[2] It is also very obvious that the copula is used instead of the rational particle.[3] The substance is, that before the priests moved their foot from the middle of the river where they stood, the stones at their feet were taken and placed in Gilgal, to be perpetual witnesses of the miracle, and that Joshua thus faithfully executed what God had commanded. Joshua, therefore, called the men whom he had previously chosen, but not without the command of God, that through it he might have a stronger attestation to his authority. For had Joshua raised up a trophy of that kind of his own accord, the piety which dictated it might indeed have been laudable, but the admonition founded only on the will of man might perhaps have been despised. But now when God himself raises the sign, it is impious to pass it carelessly by. He intimates, accordingly, that it was a monument deserving of the greatest attention when he introduces the children asking, what mean these stones?

7. *Then ye shall answer them*, &c. Although the stones themselves cannot speak, yet the monument furnished the parents with materials for speaking, and for making the kindness of God known to their children. And here zealous

[1] "Joshua." Apparently a misprint for "Jehovah;" as the French says more accurately, "Le commandement de Dieu;" "The command of God." —*Ed.*

[2] French, "Par un temps passé plus que parfait (comme parlent les Latins;)" "By a past time more than perfect, (as the Latins speak.)"—*Ed.*

[3] French, "Et quant a ce mot *Et*, on peut aisement juger qu'il se prend pour *Car*;" "And as to this word *And*, we may easily judge that it is taken for *For*."—*Ed.*

endeavours to propagate piety are required of the aged,[1] and they are enjoined to exert themselves in instructing their children. For it was the will of God that this doctrine should be handed down through every age; that those who were not then born being afterwards instructed by their parents might become witnesses to it from hearing, though they had not seen it with their eyes.

The stones were placed according to the number of the tribes, that each might be incited to gratitude by its own symbol. It is true that two tribes and a half tribe who had obtained their inheritance beyond the Jordan, had not, when considered apart from the others, any occasion for making that passage. But as the land of Canaan was possessed by the others for the common good of the whole race of Abraham, so it behoved those who were all engaged in the same or a common cause not to be separated from each other. And although as yet mention had been made only of twelve men, it is obvious from a short clause, that the divine command had been declared to the whole people; for it is said that the children of Israel obeyed the words of Joshua. Nay, it is even probable that deputies were elected by suffrage to carry the stones in the name of the whole people.

9. *And Joshua set up twelve stones*, &c. Apparently there was no use of stones under the water, and it may therefore seem to have been absurd to bury stones at a depth. The others which were placed in Gilgal being publicly visible, furnished occasion for inquiry; but stones hidden from the eyes of men at the bottom of the water could have no effect in inciting their minds. I admit that a monument altogether buried in silence would have been useless.[2] But when they talked among themselves of the evidence of the passage left there, the hearing even of what they did not see, strongly tended to confirm their faith. The ark of the

[1] French, " Or ce passage est pour monstrer, que les gens anciens doivent etre affectionnez a la pieté;" " Now this passage is to shew that the aged ought to be attached to piety."—*Ed.*

[2] French, " Or je confesse bien que c'eust esté un tesmoignage du tout inutile, si on l'eust laissé là comme enseveli sans en parler;" " Now, I confess, that it would have been an entirely useless testimony had they left it there, as it were, buried without speaking of it."—*Ed.*

covenant was shut up in the sanctuary and covered by a veil placed over against it, and yet its hidden splendour was not without benefit, when they learned from the Law that the covenant of God was deposited in it. It might also happen, that when the river was low, the tops of the heap would sometimes appear. But what I have already said is more probable, that though Joshua buried the stones in the middle of the stream, he did a useful act by establishing a testimony in presence of the people, which would afterwards become the subject of general conversation.

10. For the priests which bare the ark stood in the midst of Jordan, until every thing was finished that the Lord commanded Joshua to speak unto the people, according to all that Moses commanded Joshua: and the people hasted and passed over.

11. And it came to pass, when all the people were clean passed over, that the ark of the Lord passed over, and the priests, in the presence of the people.

12. And the children of Reuben, and the children of Gad, and half the tribe of Manasseh, passed over armed before the children of Israel, as Moses spake unto them.

13. About forty thousand, prepared for war, passed over before the Lord unto battle, to the plains of Jericho.

14. On that day the Lord magnified Joshua in the sight of all Israel: and they feared him, as they feared Moses, all the days of his life.

15. And the Lord spake unto Joshua, saying,

16. Command the priests that bear the ark of the testimony, that they come up out of Jordan.

17. Joshua therefore commanded the priests, saying, Come ye up out of Jordan.

18. And it came to pass, when the priests that bare the ark of the covenant of the Lord were come up out of the midst of Jordan, *and* the soles of the priests' feet were lifted up unto the dry land, that the waters of Jor-

10. Sacerdotes autem portantes arcam stabant in medio Jordanis donec compleretur omnis sermo quem præceperat Jehova ad Josuam, ut diceret populo: prorsus ut præceperat Moses ipsi Josue: festinavit autem populus transeundo.

11. Quum vero transeundi finem fecisset universus populus, transivit arca Jehovæ, et sacerdotes coram populo.

12. Transierunt quoque filii Reuben, et filii Gad, et dimidia tribus Manasse armati ante filios Israel: quemadmodum loquutus fuerat ad eos Moses.

13. Quadraginta millia armatorum transierunt coram Jehova ad prælium ad campestria Jericho.

14. Eo die magnificavit Jehova Josuam in oculis totius Israelis: et timuerunt eum quemadmodum timuerant Mosen omnibus diebus vitæ ejus.

15. Loquutus est autem Jehova ad Josuam, dicendo,

16. Præcipe sacerdotibus portantibus arcam testimonii ut ascendant e Jordane.

17. Et præcepit Josue sacerdotibus, dicendo, Ascendite ex Jordane.

18. Porro quum ascendissent sacerdotes portantes arcam foederis Jehovæ e medio Jordane, et translatæ essent plantæ pedum sacerdotum in siccum, reversæ sunt aquæ Jordanis ad locum suum, et fluxe-

dan returned unto their place, and flowed over all his banks, as *they did* before.

runt sicut heri et nudius tertius, super omnes ripas ejus.

10. *For the priests which bare*, &c. If we are ordered to halt while others are hastening, we know how easily a feeling of irksomeness is produced, because we seem to be occupying an inferior position. The priests, therefore, are justly praised for their patience in calmly remaining alone at their post, while the whole people were swiftly hurrying on to the further bank. For they might have begun to feel doubtful lest the heaps of water which were suspended over their heads might suddenly melt away and ingulf them. They therefore evinced their piety no less by remaining there than by venturing to proceed into the opposing current. Thus, in the first place, they displayed their ready obedience, and in the second their constancy, making it manifest that they had not obeyed from mere impulse. For their firmness of purpose, which is praised, must have had its origin in a living principle. It was a proof of modesty that they attempted nothing rashly, but regulated their whole procedure as it were in strict conformity to the word of God.

Although it is probable that Joshua was instructed by a new message from heaven as to what was necessary to be done, he is, however, said to have followed what Moses had commanded. By this I understand that Moses had carefully enjoined him to hang on the lips of God, that he was thoroughly obedient to the injunction, and accordingly was always observant of what was pleasing to God. In short, the command of Moses here mentioned was general, but God gave special injunctions to Joshua as each circumstance arose.

12. *And the children of Reuben*, &c. He makes mention of the expedition of the two tribes and half tribe, as they did not set out to engage in warfare on their own private account, but to assist their brethren, by whose valour their own possession had been obtained in seizing the land of Canaan. Moses had laid them under this obligation, and they had bound themselves by oath that they would accompany the rest of the people till all should have obtained a

quiet settlement. They again made the same promise when the camp was about to be moved as we saw in chapter i. But from the narrative here we gather that only a part was selected, for the number amounts only to forty thousand, that is, a third, or about a third of the number ascertained by the census taken shortly before. Now, as they are everywhere said to have performed their promise, it may be probably conjectured that it was not the intention of Moses strictly to insist that all who had assented should leave their wives and children, and do military service in the land of Canaan till it was wholly subdued. And certainly it would have been harsh and cruel to leave an unwarlike multitude unprotected in the midst of many hostile nations. Nor would the remains of the enemy, assisted by neighbouring nations, have long failed to take advantage of such an opportunity to avenge themselves by massacring the women and children. It was necessary, therefore, in a country not yet sufficiently pacified, permanently to retain a force sufficient to prevent incursions. Moses was not of so stern a nature as not to consult for the helpless. Nay, his prudence and equity would never have allowed him to leave a territory lately seized by arms unoccupied by a body of troops.

We may add, that such an immense concourse would have impeded rather than assisted the acquisition of the land of Canaan. All which Moses required, therefore, was simply that the Reubenites and Gadites should not, while their brethren were engaged in carrying on the war, remain indolently at home and eat their food at ease without giving any assistance to those to whom they were indebted for having obtained the inheritance. And the good faith of the forty thousand was approved by their not declining the burdens, toils, and perils of warfare, while the remainder of their own tribes were enjoying quiet. They might readily have alleged that they were as well entitled as the others to exemption, but in proceeding with alacrity after the levy was made, to obey the orders given them, without envying the immunity given to their brethren, they show that they were voluntarily and heartily disposed to do their duty. At the same time, it is not doubtful that by accepting the flower of their tribes, the handle for complaint and quarrel was cut off. For it could not justly have been maintained that not even the aged and worn out, or the young and feeble, were to be spared. Some, perhaps, may be inclined to conjecture that the army was raised not by choice but by lot, though it rather seems to me that all who were most robust and best able to bear fatigue were enrolled.

14. *On that day the Lord magnified*, &c. It was not indeed the principal end of the miracle to proclaim Joshua's pre-eminence in power and authority, but as it greatly concerned the public interest, that the government of Joshua should be firmly established, it is justly set down as an additional instance of the divine favour, that he was, so to speak, adorned with sacred insignia to render him venerable in the eyes of the people, and prevent any one from presuming to despise him. For a promiscuous multitude, not ruled by a head, breaks up and falls away of its own accord. The Lord, therefore, to provide for the safety of his people, distinguished Joshua by a special mark declaratory of his vocation.

From this passage we may learn that God specially recommends to us all those through whose hands he displays his excellent working, and requires us to give them due honour and reverence. When it is said that the people feared Joshua as they had feared Moses, should any one object that the statement is refuted by the many seditions and tumults which they stirred up against him, not only wantonly but furiously, it is easy to answer, that it does not apply to the whole period from their departure out of Egypt, but only refers to that when subdued by plagues and softened down, they began to be duly obedient to Moses. For what is now described is a tranquil government, as if they had laid aside their ancient perverseness, more especially when the turbulent parents were dead and a better race had succeeded. Accordingly, we do not read that there was any difficulty in ruling and turning them. I now only briefly advert to what I have already explained. For when Joshua at the outset exhorted them to obedience, they said that they would be obedient as they had been to Moses.

16. *Command the priests,* &c. Here it is shewn more clearly how meekly and calmly the priests yielded implicit obedience to the divine command, for they did not move a foot until Joshua ordered the signal to retire. But as it was an instance of rare virtue to be thus modest and obedient, so the fatherly kindness of God is conspicuous in this, that he condescended to direct and govern almost every step in their progress by his own voice, lest any perplexity might occur to retard them.

Next follows a more conspicuous confirmation of the miracle; for as soon as they climbed the opposite bank, the Jordan began again to flow as usual. Had it not returned to its former state, and indeed, suddenly, many would have imagined the cause of the change to be hidden but fortuitous. But when God displays his power and favour at minute intervals of time all doubt is removed. The moment the feet of the priests were made wet the Jordan retired; now on their departure he recovers his free course, and that at the very instant when they reached the bank. For the term *dry* here means that part which was not covered by the overflow.[1] Thus the river, though dumb,[2] was the best of heralds, proclaiming with a loud voice that heaven and earth are subject to the God of Israel.

19. And the people came up out of Jordan on the tenth *day* of the first month, and encamped in Gilgal, in the east border of Jericho.	19. Populus autem ascendit e Jordane decima die primi mensis, et castrametati sunt in Gilgal ad plagam orientalem Jericho.
20. And those twelve stones, which they took out of Jordan, did Joshua pitch in Gilgal.	20. Ac duodecim lapides quos tulerant ex Jordane statuit Josue in Gilgal.

[1] Calvin, still adhering to the view that part of the plain beyond the immediate bank was overflowed, seems to think that the priests, after climbing up the steep bank, continued to walk for some time among the shallow water. The other view which supposes that the banks were only filled and not overflowed, besides being more in accordance with the original, as was formerly shewn, appears to derive additional confirmation from the language here used. It is said the waters returned the moment the priests touched the dry ground with the *soles* of their feet; in other words, so long as they were climbing up the steep bank, and, of course, had no firm footing, the heap of waters continued, but it was immediately dissolved as soon as they could set down their foot firmly in consequence of having reached the flat.—*Ed.*

[2] "Dumb." Latin, "mutus." French, "une creature insensible et sans voix;" "An inanimate creature without voice."—*Ed.*

21. And he spake unto the children of Israel, saying, When your children shall ask their fathers in time to come, saying, What *mean* these stones?

22. Then ye shall let your children know, saying, Israel came over this Jordan on dry land.

23. For the Lord your God dried up the waters of Jordan from before you, until ye were passed over, as the Lord your God did to the Red sea, which he dried up from before us, until we were gone over;

24. That all the people of the earth might know the hand of the Lord, that it *is* mighty; that ye might fear the Lord your God for ever.

21. Et loquutus est ad filios Israel, dicendo: Quum interrogaverint cras filii vestri patres suos dicendo, Quid lapides isti?

22. Indicabitis filiis vestris dicendo, Per aridam transivit Israel Jordanem istum:

23. Quoniam siccavit Jehova Deus vester aquas Jordanis a facie vestra donec transiretis: quemadmodum fecit Jehova Deus vester mari Suph, quod siccavit a facie nostra donec transiremus.

24. Ut cognoscant omnes populi terræ manum Jehovæ, quod fortis sit: ut timeatis Jehovam Deum vestrum cunctis diebus.

19. *And the people came up*, &c. Why the day on which they entered the land, and first encamped in it, is marked, we shall see in next chapter. But the name of Gilgal is given to the first station by anticipation, for this new name was afterwards given to it by Joshua on the renewal of circumcision; its etymology will be explained in its own place. Moreover, the thing here principally treated of is the monument of twelve stones; for though it was formerly mentioned, a kind of solemn dedication is now related, namely, that Joshua not only erected a mound, but called the attention of the people to its use in enabling fathers to keep the memory of the divine goodness alive among their children. From his introducing the children asking, What mean these stones? we infer that they were arranged so as to attract the notice of spectators. For had they been heaped together at random without any order, it would never have come into the mind of posterity to inquire concerning their meaning. There must therefore have been something so remarkable in their position as not to allow the sight to be overlooked.

Moreover, because the covenant by which God had adopted the race of Abraham was firm in an uninterrupted succession for a thousand generations, the benefit which God had bestowed on the deceased fathers is, on account of the unity of the body, transferred in common to their children who were born long after. And the continuation must have more strongly awakened their attention, inasmuch as posterity were in this way reminded that what had long ago been given to their ancestors belonged to them also. The answer of the parents would have been coldly listened to had the divine favour been confined to a single day. But when the sons' sons hear that the waters of Jordan were dried up many ages before they were born, they acknowledge themselves to be the very people towards whom that wonderful act of divine favour had been manifested. The same account is to be given of the drying up of the Red Sea, though the event was not very ancient. It is certain that of those who had come out of Egypt, Caleb and Joshua were the only survivors, and yet he addresses the whole people as if they had been eye-witnesses of the miracle. God dried up the Red Sea before our face; in other words, it was done in virtue of the adoption which passed without interruption from the fathers to the children. Moreover, it was worth while to call the passage of the Red Sea to remembrance, not only that the similarity of the miracle might cause belief, but that on hearing the story of the Jordan, that former miracle might be at the same time renewed, although no visible symbol of it was present to the eye.

24. *That all people of the earth might know*, &c. He states that God had put forth that manifestation of his power that it might not only be proclaimed among his own people, but that the form of it might spread far and wide among the nations. For although it pleased him that his praise should dwell in Zion, it pleased him also that his works should so far be made known to strangers that they might be forced to confess that he is the true God, and compelled unwillingly to fear him whom they had willingly contemned, as it is said in the song of Moses, (Deut. xxxii. 31,) "Our enemies are judges." For he means that unbelievers, whether they will or not, have this confession extorted from them by a knowledge of the works of God. But as it did not at all profit them to know how great the might of God was, Joshua distinguishes them from the Israelites, to whom he attributes a special knowledge, namely, that which begets serious fear of God. That the nations may know, he says; but that thou

mayest fear thy God. Therefore while unbelievers extinguish the light by their darkness, let us learn from considering the works of God to advance in his fear. He says *all days*, because the favour here spoken of was diffused over several generations.

CHAPTER V.

1. And it came to pass, when all the kings of the Amorites, which *were* on the side of Jordan westward, and all the kings of the Canaanites, which *were* by the sea, heard that the Lord had dried up the waters of Jordan from before the children of Israel, until we were passed over, that their heart melted; neither was there spirit in them any more, because of the children of Israel.

1. Fuit autem quum audissent omnes reges Æmorrhaci qui erant trans Jordanem ad Occidentem, et omnes reges Chananæi, qui juxta mare, quod siccasset Jehova aquas Jordanis a facie filiorum Israel donec transirent, liquefactum fuit cor eorum, neque fuit amplius in eis, Spiritus a facie filiorum Israel.

2. At that time the Lord said unto Joshua, Make thee sharp knives, and circumcise again the children of Israel the second time.

2. Eo tempore dixit Jehova ad Josuam, Fac tibi cultros acutos, et iterum circuncide filios Israel secundo.

3. And Joshua made him sharp knives, and circumcised the children of Israel at the hill of the foreskins.

3. Et fecit sibi Josue cultros acutos, circunciditque filios Israel in colle præputiorum.

4. And this *is* the cause why Joshua did circumcise: All the people that came out of Egypt, *that were* males, *even* all the men of war, died in the wilderness by the way, after they came out of Egypt.

4. Hæc autem est causa cur circunciderit Josue: Universus populus qui egressus fuerat ex Ægypto, masculi omnes viri bellatores mortui erant in deserto in itinere posteaquam egressi erant ex Ægypto.

5. Now all the people that came out were circumcised; but all the people *that were* born in the wilderness by the way as they came forth out of Egypt, *them* they had not circumcised.

5. Nam circuncisus fuerat totus populus qui egressus est, at totum populum, qui natus fuerat in deserto in itinere, postquam egressi erant ex Ægypto, non circunciderant.

6. For the children of Israel walked forty years in the wilderness, till all the people *that were* men of war, which came out of Egypt, were consumed, because they obeyed not the voice of the Lord: unto whom the Lord sware that he would not shew them the land which the Lord sware unto their fathers that he would give us, a land that floweth with milk and honey.

6. Nam quadraginta annis ambulaverunt filii Israel per desertum, donec consumeretur universa gens virorum bellatorum, qui egressi fuerant ex Ægypto, qui non audierant vocem Jehovæ, quibus juraverat Jehova quod non ostenderet terram de qua juraverat Jehova patribus eorum, se daturum illis terram fluentem lacte et melle.

7. And their children, *whom* he raised up in their stead, them Joshua circumcised: for they were uncircumcised, because they had not circumcised them by the way.	7. Filios itaque eorum quos substituit in locum ipsorum circuncidit Josue, quia incircuncisi erant: neque enim eos circunciderat in itinere.
8. And it came to pass, when they had done circumcising all the people, that they abode in their places in the camp till they were whole.	8. Quum autem fuit circuncisus universus populus, manserunt in loco suo in castris donec sanarentur.
9. And the Lord said unto Joshua, This day have I rolled away the reproach of Egypt from off you: wherefore the name of the place is called Gilgal unto this day.	9. Dixit Jehova ad Josuam, Hodie devolvi opprobrium Ægypti a vobis. Et vocavit nomen loci illius Gilgal, usque in hunc diem.

1. *And it came to pass when*, &c. The recognition of the fearful power of God had such an effect upon them that they were astonished and fainted with terror, but it did not incline their minds to seek a remedy for the evil. Their heart was melted inasmuch as destitute of counsel and strength they did not bestir themselves, but in regard to contumacy they remained as hard-hearted as before. We have already seen elsewhere how unbelievers, when smitten with fear, cease not to wrestle with God, and even when they fall, continue fiercely to assail heaven. Hence the dread which ought to have urged them to caution had no other effect than to hurry them on headlong. They were, however, terrified from above for the sake of the people, that victory might be more easily obtained, and the Israelites might be emboldened when they saw they had to do with an enemy already broken and stricken with dismay. Thus God spared their weakness, as if he had opened up the way by removing obstacles, because they had already proved themselves to be otherwise more sluggish and cowardly than was meet. The substance then is, that before the conflict commenced, the enemy were already routed by the terror which the fame of the miracle had inspired.

2. *At that time the Lord said*, &c. It seems very strange and almost monstrous, that circumcision had so long been laid aside, especially as it became those who were receiving daily admonitions to be more than usually careful to cultivate the exercises of piety. It was the symbol of the adoption to which they owed their freedom. And it is certain

that when they were reduced to extremity and groaning under tyranny, they always circumcised their children. We know also how sternly God threatened to be an avenger against any one who should allow the eighth day to pass. Had the observance been neglected in Egypt their carelessness might have admitted of excuse, as at that time the covenant of God appeared to have become in a manner obsolete. But now when the divine faithfulness in establishing the covenant is once more refulgent, what excuse could there be for not testifying on their part that they are the people of God?

The apology which commentators offer is altogether frivolous. I admit that they were constantly under arms, and always uncertain when they would require to move. But I hold it erroneous to infer from this that they had not a day's leisure, and that it would have been cruel to circumcise tender infants when the camp must shortly after have been moved. Nothing ought to have weighed so much with them as to produce a contemptuous disregard of what had been said to Abraham, (Gen. xvii. 14,) The soul that is not circumcised shall be cut off from the people. But if there was risk of life in the circumcision, the best and only method was to trust to the paternal providence of God, who certainly would not have allowed his own precept to become fatal to infants. In short, the omission from a fear of danger, could not originate in any other cause than distrust. But even had it been certain that infants would be brought into danger, God ought nevertheless to have been obeyed, inasmuch as the seal of the covenant by which they were received into the Church was more precious than a hundred lives. Nor would Moses have suffered such cowardly procedure had he not been influenced by some different motive. Moreover, though the point is doubtful, I presume that they did not desist from circumcising their children, the very first day after their departure, but only after they had been obliged to retrace their steps through their own perverseness. And in this way both the defection and the punishment are accurately expressed. For it is not said that circumcision was resumed, because the constant change of place during their wanderings made it previously impossible, but because forty years behoved to elapse until those wicked apostates who had cut themselves off from the promised inheritance were consumed.

Attention should be paid to the reason here given, namely, that the children of Israel wandered through the desert till the whole of the generation which had refused to follow God was extinct; from this we may, in my opinion, infer, that the use of circumcision ceased during the whole of that period as a sign of malediction or rejection. It is true, indeed, that the penalty was inflicted on the innocent, but it was expedient that the fathers should be chastised in their person, as if God were repudiating them for the time to come. When they saw that their offspring differed in no respect from profane persons and strangers, they had a plain demonstration of what they themselves deserved.

Here, however, an inconsistency seems to arise in respect, *first*, that while they were condemned, their offspring were immediately received into favour; and *secondly*, that to themselves also was left a hope of pardon; and more especially, that they were not deprived of the other sacraments of which they could not be partakers, except on the ground of their being separated from profane nations.

The Lord, I admit, in rejecting them, declares at the same time that he will be propitious to their children, but to behold in their offspring a sign of repudiation till they themselves all perished, was salutary chastisement. For God withdrew the pledge of his favour only for a time, and kept it, as it were, locked up until their death. This punishment, therefore, was not properly inflicted on the children who were afterwards born, but had the same effect as a suspension, just as if God were making it manifest that he had put off circumcision for a time lest it should be profaned, but was waiting for an opportunity of renewing it.

Should any one object that it was absurd to celebrate the Passover in uncircumcision, I admit that it was so according to the usual order. For none were admitted to the Passover and the sacrifices save those who were initiated into the worship of God; just as in the present day the ordinance of the Supper is common only to those who have been admitted into the Church by baptism. But the Lord might choose for a time to alter the ordinary rule, and allow those from whom he had taken away circumcision to be partakers of other sacred rites. Thus the people were excommunicated in one matter, and yet, in the meanwhile, furnished with fit aids to prevent them from falling into despair; just as if a father, offended with his son, were to raise his fist, apparently to drive him away, and were at the same time to detain him by his other hand,—were to frighten him by threats and blows, and yet be unwilling to part with him. This seems to me to have been the reason why God, while depriving the people of the special pledge of adoption, was, however, unwilling to deprive them of other ordinances.

Should it be objected that there is a distinct assertion that none were circumcised on the way after they had set out, I answer, that, with a view to brevity, all things are not stated exactly, and yet that it may be gathered from the context that none remained uncircumcised but those who were born after the sedition. For it is said that their sons, whom God substituted for them, were circumcised by Joshua. From this it appears that a new people were then created to supply the place of perverse rebels. It was, moreover, a sad and severe trial that God did not choose to have the people circumcised till they were hemmed in by enemies on every side. It would, certainly, have been safer and more convenient to perform the rite before crossing the Jordan, in the land of Bashan, which had been reduced to peace by the overthrow of the inhabitants. The Lord waits till they are shut up in the midst of enemies, and exposed to their lust and violence, as if he were purposely exposing them to death; since all weakened by their wound must have given way at once, and been slaughtered almost without resistance. For if in similar circumstances (Gen. xxxiv.) two sons of Jacob were able to force their way into the town of Sichem and plunder it, after slaying its citizens, how much more easy would it have been for the neighbouring nations to attack the Israelites while thus wounded, and make a general massacre of them.

This was, therefore, as I have said, a very harsh trial, and hence the readiness with which it was submitted to is deserving of the greater praise. The place itself, however, appears to have been purposely selected by the divine wisdom, that they might be more disposed to obey. Had the same command been given on the other side of the Jordan, there was reason to fear that they might be cast into despondency, and from the delay thus interposed might again decline to enter the land. But now, when they had been brought into possession under happy auspices, as if by the hand of God, and conceived from the removal of this one obstacle a sure hope of warring with success, it is not wonderful if they obey more willingly than they might have done if they had not been so singularly strengthened. The very sight of the promised land must have furnished additional incentives, when they understood that they were again consecrated to God, in order that their uncircumcision might not pollute the holy land.

9. *And the Lord said unto Joshua,* &c. The disgrace of Egypt is expounded by some as meaning that the want of circumcision rendered them similar to the Egyptians, in other words, profane and marked with a stigma; as if it had been said that they were again made the peculiar property of God when they were anew stamped with this mark, to distinguish them from the nations that were unclean. Others understand it actively, as meaning that they would no longer be scorned by the Egyptians, as if God had deceived them. This I have no hesitation in rejecting as too far fetched. Others understand that they would no longer lie under the false imputation of worshipping the gods of that nation. I rather understand the meaning to be, that they were freed from an invidious charge, by which they were otherwise overborne. It was disreputable to have shaken off the yoke and revolted from the king under whose government they lived. Moreover, as they gave out that God was the avenger of unjust tyranny, it was easy to upbraid them with using the name of God as a mere colour for their conduct. They might, therefore, have been regarded as deserters, had not the disgrace been wiped off by the appeal to circumcision, by which the divine election was

sealed in their flesh before they went down into Egypt. It was accordingly made plain by the renewal of the ancient covenant that they were not rebels against legitimate authority, nor had rashly gone off at their own hand, but that their liberty was restored by God, who had long ago taken them under his special protection.

From the removal of disgrace the place obtained its name. For those who think that the prepuce cut off was called Gilgal, because it was a kind of circle, abandon the literal meaning, and have recourse to a very unnecessary fiction; while it is perfectly obvious that the place was called *Rolling Off*, because God there rolled off from his people the disgrace which unjustly attached to them. The interpretation of *liberty*, adopted by Josephus, is vain and ridiculous, and makes it apparent that he was as ignorant of the Hebrew tongue as of jurisprudence.

10. And the children of Israel encamped in Gilgal, and kept the passover on the fourteenth day of the month at even, in the plains of Jericho.	10. Itaque castrametati sunt filii Israel in Gilgal, et fecerunt Pæsah quartadecima die mensis ad vesperum in campestribus Jericho.
11. And they did eat of the old corn of the land on the morrow after the passover, unleavened cakes, and parched *corn* in the self-same day.	11. Et comederunt e fructu terræ postridie Pæsah infermentata, et polentam ipsomet die.
12. And the manna ceased on the morrow after they had eaten of the old corn of the land; neither had the children of Israel manna any more; but they did eat of the fruit of the land of Canaan that year.	12. Et cessavit man postridie postquam comederunt e frumento terræ: neque fuit ultra filiis Israel man, sed comederunt e fructu terræ Chanaan eo anno.
13. And it came to pass, when Joshua was by Jericho, that he lifted up his eyes and looked, and, behold, there stood a man over against him, with his sword drawn in his hand: and Joshua went unto him, and said unto him, *Art* thou for us, or for our adversaries?	13. Contigit autem quum esset Josue apud Jericho, ut levaret oculos suos ac aspiceret: et ecce vir stabat contra eum, in cujus manu erat gladius evaginatus: et ivit Josue ad eum, dixitque illi, Ex nostris es? an ex adversariis nostris?
14. And he said, Nay; but *as* captain of the host of the Lord am I now come. And Joshua fell on his face to the earth, and did worship, and said unto him, What saith my Lord unto his servant?	14. Et dixit, Non: sed sum princeps exercitus Jehovæ: nunc veni. Et cecidit Josue in faciem suam ad terram, et adoravit, dixitque ei: Quid Dominus meus loquitur ad servum suum?
15. And the captain of the Lord's host said unto Joshua, Loose thy	15. Et dixit princeps exercitus Jehovæ ad Josuam: Solve calcea-

shoe from off thy foot; for the place whereon thou standest *is* holy. And Joshua did so.

mentum tuum e pedibus tuis: quia locus super quem stas, sanctitas est. Et ita fecit Josue.

10. *And the children of Israel . . . kept the Passover*, &c. Here it is stated that the Passover was celebrated on the regular day, although there are some who think that the words used imply that the practice was unusual. They hence infer that, like circumcision, it had been interrupted for a period of forty years, as it would have been absurd for persons uncircumcised to take part in a sacred feast. To confirm this view, they observe that we do not read of the Passover having been observed after the beginning of the second year. But it is not probable that that which God had lately ordered to be perpetual, (Exod. xii. 42,) was suddenly cast aside. For it had been said to them, It is a night to be observed by the children of Israel in all their generations. How inconsistent, then, would it have been had this practice, which was to be observed throughout all ages, become obsolete in the course of two years! And again, how heartless it would have been to bury the memory of a recent favour within so short a period!

But it is said that the want of circumcision must have kept back a large proportion, that the mystery might not be profaned; for at its institution it had been declared, No uncircumcised person shall eat of it. To this I have already answered, that it was an extraordinary privilege; as the children of Israel were freed from the law.[1] For it is certain that they continued to use sacrifices, and to observe the other parts of legal worship, although this was unlawful, unless something of the form prescribed by the law had been remitted by divine authority. It is certain that unclean persons were prohibited from entering the court of the tabernacle, and yet the children of Israel, while uncircumcised, offered sacrifices there, thus doing what was equivalent to the slaying of the Passover. They were therefore

[1] "Freed from the law." Latin, "Lege soluti." French, "Ont esté exemptez et dispensez de ce a quoy la Loy les assujettissoit;" "Have been exempted and dispensed from that to which the law subjected them."—*Ed.*

permitted, by sufferance, to do that which it was not lawful to do according to the rule of the law.

The mention made by Moses of the second celebration of the Passover (Numb. ix.) is for a different purpose, namely, for the purpose of indirectly censuring the carelessness and sluggishness of the people, who would not have observed the sacred anniversary at the end of the first year if they had not been reminded of it. For although God had proclaimed that they should through all ages annually renew the memory of their deliverance, yet they had grown so oblivious before the end of the year, that they had become remiss in the discharge of the duty. It is not without cause they are urged by a new intimation, as they were not sufficiently attentive of their own accord. That passage, therefore, does not prove that the use of the Passover was afterwards interrupted; on the contrary, it may, with some probability, be inferred from it that it was annually observed; as the Lord, towards the end of the year, anticipates the observance, telling them to make careful provision for it in future, and never deviate from the command which had been given them.[1]

11. *And they did eat of the old corn,* &c. Whether they then began first to eat wheaten bread is not very clear. For they had dwelt in a country that was not uncultivated, and was tolerably fertile. At least in the territories of the two kings there was enough of corn to supply the inhabitants. It does not seem reasonable to suppose that the children of Israel allowed the corn which they found there to rot and

[1] These remarks place the view which Calvin takes in its most favourable light; but, on the other hand, it is strongly argued, 1. That the eating of the Passover by an uncircumcised person was expressly prohibited, (Exod. xii. 48.) 2. That the observance of it during the wandering in the desert is, by implication at least, dispensed with in the words, "And it shall come to pass, when ye be come to the land which the Lord will give you, according as he hath promised, that ye shall keep this service," (Exod. xii. 25.) 3. That the observance of the Passover at Mount Sinai was in compliance with a special mandate, and would not have taken place without it. 4. The assumption that sacrifices were offered in the desert is questioned as inconsistent with Amos v. 25. It may be added, that the order to circumcise, evidently intended as a preparation for the celebration of the approaching Passover, seems to imply that there had previously been a similar omission of both ordinances. It must also have been difficult, if not impossible, while in the wilderness, to obtain flour in sufficient quantity to make unleavened Passover bread for a whole people.—*Ed.*

perish by mere waste. And I have no doubt that they ate the flesh which remained over of the sacrifices. It is quite possible, therefore, that they did not wholly abstain from wheaten bread, and yet did not abandon their accustomed food. For a country which was assigned to a tenth part could not have furnished food sufficient for the whole multitude, as there cannot be a doubt that a just estimate was made when Moses settled in it only two tribes and a half tribe. As yet, therefore, the twelve tribes had not found sufficient food, more especially as the country had been devastated by war, and the Israelites, who were not in safety to leave the camp, could not devote their attention to agriculture. The manna was thus necessary to feed them until a more abundant supply was obtained. This took place in the land of Canaan, and then, accordingly, they returned to common food. But why they deferred it till that day is not known, unless it be that after their wound was cured, some days behoved to be spent in collecting corn, while religion did not permit them to bake bread lest they should break the Sabbath. But although that rest was sacred, we gather from the circumstances that they made haste, as the flour must have been previously prepared, seeing they could not grind it and bake it in a single day.

Be this as it may, the Lord furnished them with provision as long as their want required to be supplied. The failure of the manna on a sudden, and at the very moment, must have furnished an additional attestation to the kindness of God, inasmuch as it was thence apparent that the manna was a temporary resource, which had descended not so much from the clouds as from a paternal providence. It is moreover plain, that this is to be understood of the produce of the former year, and it is needless to raise any question in regard to it; for it would have implied too much precipitation to rush upon the produce of the present year when not yet properly matured, and a whole month would scarcely have sufficed to collect enough for the supply of so great a multitude. I cannot see why expounders should give themselves so much trouble with so clear a matter.

13. *And it came to pass when Joshua,* &c. Here we have

the narrative of a remarkable vision, by which Joshua was greatly encouraged and emboldened. For though he was strenuously discharging his office, the application of an additional stimulus was not without its use. The angel, however, did not appear solely on his private account, but for the confirmation of the whole people: nay, the Lord looked further forward, that he might furnish posterity with stronger proofs of a kindness which was never duly considered. For although they boasted in lofty terms of having been planted by the hand of God in a holy land, they were scarcely induced by all the miracles to acknowledge in good earnest that they were placed there as God's vassals. This vision, therefore, must have been beneficial to all ages, by leaving no doubt as to the divine kindness bestowed. Its being said that he lifted his eyes, tends to confirm the certainty of the vision, lest any one might suppose that his eyesight had merely been dazzled by some evanescent phantom.

The spectacle, when first presented, must have inspired fear; for it is probable that Joshua was then alone, whether he had withdrawn from public view to engage in prayer, or for the purpose of reconnoitring the city. I am rather inclined to think it was the latter, and that he had gone aside to examine where the city ought to be attacked, lest the difficulty might deter others. It appears certain that he was without attendants, as he alone perceives the vision; and there can be no doubt that he was prepared to fight had he fallen in with an enemy. But he puts his question as if addressing a man, because it is only from the answer he learns that it is an angel. This doubt gives more credibility to the vision, while he is gradually led from the view of the man whom he addresses to the recognition of an angel. The words, at the same time, imply that it was not an ordinary angel, but one of special excellence. For he calls himself captain of the Lord's host, a term which may be understood to comprehend not merely his chosen people, but angels also.

The former view, however, is the more correct, as God does not produce anything of an unwonted nature, but continues that which we previously read that he performed to Moses. And we know that Moses himself preferred this favour to all others; and justly, for God there manifested his own glory in an open and familiar manner. Accordingly, he is indiscriminately called an angel, and distinguished by the title of the eternal God. Of this fact Paul is a competent witness, who distinctly declares that it was Christ. (1 Cor. x. 4.) And Moses himself embraced God as present in the person of the Mediator. For when God declares, after the making of the calf, (Ex. xxxii. 37,) that he would no longer be the Leader of the people, he at the same time promises that he will give one of his angels, but only one, as it were taken out of the general body of the angelic host.[1] This Moses earnestly deprecates, obviously because he could have no hope that God would be propitious if the Mediator were removed. It was thus a special pledge of the divine favour that the Captain and Head of the Church, to whom Moses had been accustomed, was now present to assist. And indeed the divine adoption could not be ratified in any other way than in the hand of the Mediator.

14. *And he said, Nay; but as captain,* &c. Although the denial applies equally to both parts of the question, namely, that he was neither an Israelite nor a Canaanite, and was thus equivalent to a denial of his being a mortal man, yet it seems to be more properly applicable to the second, or to that part of the question in which Joshua asked if he were one of the enemy. This, however, is a matter of little moment; the essential thing is to understand that he had come to preside over the chosen people whom he honourably styles the Lord's host. In his representing himself as different from God, a personal distinction is denoted, but unity of essence is not destroyed.

We have said that in the books of Moses the name of Jehovah[2] is often attributed to the presiding Angel, who was undoubtedly the only-begotten Son of God. He is indeed

[1] French, "Mais comme le premier qui se rencontrera;" "But as it were the first who may happen to present himself."—*Ed.*

[2] The French adds, " C'est à dire d'Eternel;" " That is to say of Eternal."—*Ed.*

very God, and yet in the person of Mediator by dispensation, he is inferior to God. I willingly receive what ancient writers teach on this subject,—that when Christ anciently appeared in human form, it was a prelude to the mystery which was afterwards exhibited when God was manifested in the flesh. We must beware, however, of imagining that Christ at that time became incarnate, since, *first*, we nowhere read that God sent his Son in the flesh before the fulness of the times; and, *secondly*, Christ, in so far as he was a man, behoved to be the Son of David. But as is said in Ezekiel, (chap. i.,) it was only a likeness of man. Whether it was a substantial body or an outward form, it is needless to discuss, as it seems wrong to insist on any particular view of the subject.[1]

The only remaining question is, how the Captain of the Lord's host can speak of having *now* come, seeing he had not deserted the people committed to his trust, and had lately given a matchless display of his presence in the passage of the Jordan. But according to the common usage of Scripture, God is said to come to us when we are actually made sensible of his assistance, which seems remote when not manifested by experience. It is therefore just as if he were offering his assistance in the combats which were about to be waged, and promising by his arrival that the war would have a happy issue. It cannot be inferred with certainty from the worship which he offered, whether

[1] Several modern commentators, among others Grotius, have maintained that the personage who thus appeared was merely a created angel. In this they have only followed in the steps of the Jewish Rabbins, who not satisfied with holding that he was an angel, have gone the farther length of fixing what particular angel it was. With almost unanimous consent they declare it to have been Michael, though they are unable to support their opinion by anything stronger than the first verse of the twelfth chapter of Daniel, in which it is said, that " at that time shall Michael stand up, the great prince which standeth for the children of thy people." The sounder view here advocated by Calvin, and generally adopted by the early Christian Fathers, is well expressed by Origen, who says, in his Sixth Homily on this Book, " Joshua knew not only that he was of God, but that he was God. For he would not have worshipped, had he not recognised him to be God. For who else is the Captain of the Lord's host but our Lord Jesus Christ?" It would make sad havoc with our ideas of divine worship to admit that the homage which Joshua here pays could be lawfully received, or rather could, so to speak, be imperiously demanded by one creature from another.—*Ed.*

Joshua paid divine honour to Christ distinctly recognised as such; but by asking, What command does my Lord give to his servant? he attributes to him a power and authority which belong to God alone.

15. *Loose thy shoe from off thy foot*, &c. To give additional sanctity to the vision, the great Angel requires as a sign of reverence and fear that Joshua put off his shoes. Moses relates, (Exod. iii. 5,) that the same command was given to him on Mount Sinai, and for no other reason than that the Lord there manifested his glory. For one place cannot have a greater sanctity than another, except God deigns specially to make it so. Thus Jacob exclaims, (Gen. xxvi. 17,) that the place where he had known God more nearly is the house of God, a dreadful place, and the gate of heaven. Here, therefore, when God orders his holy servant to take off his shoes, he by this ceremony attests the reality of his presence, and adds more weight to the vision; not that nakedness of feet is of itself of any value in the worship of God, but because the weakness of men requires to be aided by helps of this kind, that they may the better excite and prepare themselves for veneration. Moreover, as God by his presence sanctifies the places in which he appears, I think it probable that the expression, holy ground, is in part commendatory of the excellence of the land of Canaan, which God had chosen for his own habitation and the seat of his pure worship. Hence in various passages it is called "his rest." (Ps. xcv. 11, and cxxxii. 11.) In the end of the verse Joshua is praised for his obedience, that posterity might learn by his example to cultivate pure piety in that land. There seems thus to be a kind of tacit comparison or antithesis, by which the land of Canaan is extolled above all other countries.[1]

CHAPTER VI.

1. Now Jericho was straitly shut up because of the children of Israel: none went out, and none came in.	1. Jericho autem erat clausa, et claudebatur propter filios Israel, nec poterat quisquam egredi, vel ingredi.

[1] The incident here recorded is one of the principal reasons for the designation of the Holy Land usually applied to Palestine.—*Ed.*

2. And the Lord said unto Joshua, See, I have given into thine hand Jericho, and the king thereof, *and* the mighty men of valour.

3. And ye shall compass the city, all *ye* men of war, *and* go round about the city once. Thus shalt thou do six days.

4. And seven priests shall bear before the ark seven trumpets of rams' horns; and the seventh day ye shall compass the city seven times, and the priests shall blow with the trumpets.

5. And it shall come to pass, that when they make a long *blast* with the rams' horn, *and* when ye hear the sound of the trumpet, all the people shall shout with a great shout; and the wall of the city shall fall down flat, and the people shall ascend up, every man straight before him.

6. And Joshua the son of Nun called the priests, and said unto them, Take up the ark of the covenant, and let seven priests bear seven trumpets of rams' horns before the ark of the Lord.

7. And he said unto the people, Pass on, and compass the city, and let him that is armed pass on before the ark of the Lord.

8. And it came to pass, when Joshua had spoken unto the people, that the seven priests, bearing the seven trumpets of rams' horns, passed on before the Lord, and blew with the trumpets; and the ark of the covenant of the Lord followed them.

9. And the armed men went before the priests that blew with the trumpets, and the rere-ward came after the ark, *the priests* going on, and blowing with the trumpets.

10. And Joshua had commanded the people, saying, Ye shall not shout, nor make any noise with your voice, neither shall *any* word proceed out of your mouth, until the day I bid you shout; then shall ye shout.

11. So the ark of the Lord compassed the city, going about *it* once:

2. Dixitque Jehova ad Josuam, Ecce tradidi in manum tuam Jericho, et regem ejus, et virtute præstantes.

3. Circuibitis itaque urbem, omnes viri bellatores, circundando eam semel: sic facies sex diebus.

4. Porro septem sacerdotes ferent septem cornua arietina ante arcam: Die autem septima circuibitis urbem septem vicibus, et sacerdotes ipsi clangent tubis.

5. Quum vero protraxerint sonitum cornu arietino: ubi primum audieritis vocem tubae, vociferabitur universus populus vociferatione magna, et concidet murus urbis sub se: populus vero ascendet quisque e regione sua.

6. Vocavit ergo Josue filius Nun sacerdotes, et dixit eis, Tollite arcam fœderis, et septem sacerdotes accipient septem tubas arietinas coram arca Jehovæ.

7. Dixit quoque ad populum, Transite, et circuite urbem, et armatus quisque præcedat arcam Jehovæ.

8. Et fuit postquam loquutus est Josue ad populum, tulerunt septem sacerdotes septem tubas arietinas, et transeuntes ante arcam Jehovæ clanxerunt tubis. Arca autem fœderis Jehovæ sequebatur ipsos.

9. Et armatus quisque præcedebat sacerdotes clangentes tubis, Et qui cogebat agmen sequebatur arcam eundo et clangendo tubis.

10. Populo autem præceperat Josue, dicendo, Non vociferabimini, nec facietis audire vocem vestram, neque egredietur ex ore vestro verbum, usque ad diem quo dixero vobis, vociferamini: tunc vociferabimini.

11. Circuivit itaque arca Jehovæ urbem, circundando semel, et re-

and they came into the camp, and lodged in the camp.

12. And Joshua rose early in the morning, and the priests took up the ark of the Lord.

13. And seven priests, bearing seven trumpets of rams' horns before the ark of the Lord, went on continually, and blew with the trumpets: and the armed men went before them; but the rere-ward came after the ark of the Lord, *the priests* going on, and blowing with the trumpets.

14. And the second day they compassed the city once, and returned into the camp: so they did six days.

15. And it came to pass on the seventh day, that they rose early, about the dawning of the day, and compassed the city after the same manner seven times: only on that day they compassed the city seven times.

16. And it came to pass at the seventh time, when the priests blew with the trumpets, Joshua said unto the people, Shout; for the Lord hath given you the city.

17. And the city shall be accursed, *even* it, and all that *are* therein, to the Lord: only Rahab the harlot shall live, she and all that *are* with her in the house, because she hid the messengers that we sent.

18. And ye, in any wise keep *yourselves* from the accursed thing, lest ye make *yourselves* accursed, when ye take of the accursed thing, and make the camp of Israel a curse, and trouble it.

19. But all the silver, and gold, and vessels of brass and iron, *are* consecrated unto the Lord: they shall come into the treasury of the Lord.

versi sunt in castra: manseruntque illic.

12. Rursum surrexit Josue mane, tuleruntque sacerdotes arcam Jehovæ.

13. Septem autem sacerdotes ferentes septem tubas arietinas præcedebant arcam Jehovæ, eundo: et clangebant tubis. Armatus vero præcedebat eos, et qui cogebat agmen sequebatur arcam Jehovæ, eundo, et clangendo tubis.

14. Circuiverunt ergo urbem die secundo vice alia, reversique sunt ad castra: sic fecerunt sex diebus.

15. Ubi autem advenit septimus dies, surrexerunt simul ac ascendit aurora, et circuiverunt urbem secundum eundem morem septem vicibus: tantum die illa circuiverunt urbem septem vicibus.

16. Septima autem vice quum clangerent sacerdotes tubis, dixit Josue ad populum, vociferamini, tradidit Jehova vobis urbem.

17. Erit autem urbs anathema, ipsa et quæcunque in ea sunt, Jehovæ: tantum Rahab meretrix vivet, ipsa et quicunque fuerint cum ea domi, quia abscondidit nuncios quos misimus.

18. Veruntamen vos cavete ab anathemate, ne forte contingatis aliquid de anathemate, tollatisque de anathemate, et ponatis castra Israel anathema, et turbetis ea.

19. Omne autem argentum, et aurum, et vasa ærea et ferrea, sanctitas erunt Jehovæ: thesaurum Jehovæ ingredientur.

1. *Now Jericho was straitly shut up*, &c. Jericho is said to be shut up, because the gates were not opened: as in time of war cities are guarded with more than usual care. It is added, by way of emphasis, that they were sealed, or

locked up,[1] as if it were said that the inhabitants were attentive in watching, so as not to be taken by surprise. Hence, as it could not be taken by stratagem, the only hope of taking it was by open force. This tends to display the goodness of God to the children of Israel, who would have been worn out by a long and difficult siege, had not a substitute been early provided from heaven. Meanwhile there was a danger, lest being forced into a corner, they might be consumed by want and famine, as there was no means of obtaining food and provender in a hostile region. The Lord, therefore, that they might not sit down despondingly before one city, assisted them by an extraordinary miracle, and opened up an entrance to them by throwing down the walls, that they might thereafter have the greater confidence in attacking other cities.

We now see the connection between the two first verses, in the one of which it is said, that Jericho was shut up, and the children of Israel thus prevented from approaching it, while in the other God promises that he will take it for them. He makes this promise with the view of preventing them from tormenting themselves with anxious thoughts. In one word, God, by this easy victory at the outset, provides against their giving way to despondency in future. We, at the same time, perceive the stupidity of the inhabitants, who place their walls and gates as obstacles to the divine omnipotence ; as if it were more difficult to break up or dissolve a few bars and beams than to dry up the Jordan.

3. *And ye shall compass the city,* &c. The promise was, indeed, fit and sufficient of itself to give hope of victory, but the method of acting was so strange, as almost to destroy its credibility. God orders them to make one circuit round the city daily until the seventh day, on which they are told to go round it seven times, sounding trumpets, and shouting. The whole looked like nothing else than child's play, and yet was no improper test for trying their faith, as it proved their acquiescence in the divine message, even when they

[1] The Septuagint has συγκεκλεισμένη καὶ ὠχυρωμένη, "completely closed and made sure, by being barred or barricaded."—*Ed.*

saw in the act itself nothing but mere disappointment. With the same intention, the Lord often, for a time, conceals his own might under weakness, and seems to sport with mere trifles, that his weakness may at length appear stronger than all might, and his folly superior to all wisdom.

While the Israelites thus abandon their own reason, and depend implicitly on his words, they gain much more by trifling than they could have done by making a forcible assault, and shaking the walls by numbers of the most powerful engines. Only it behoved them to play the fool for a short time, and not display too much acuteness in making anxious and subtle inquiries concerning the event: for that would have been, in a manner, to obstruct the course of the divine omnipotence. Meanwhile, though the circulatory movement round the walls might have excited derision, it was afterwards known, by its prosperous result, that God commands nothing in vain.

There was another subject of care and doubt, which might have crept into their minds. Should the inhabitants of the city suddenly sally forth, the army would, without difficulty, be put to the rout, while, in long straggling lines, it was proceeding round the city, without any regular arrangement that might have enabled it to repel a hostile assault. But here, also, whatever anxiety they might have felt, they behoved to cast it upon God; for sacred is the security which reclines on his providence. There was an additional trial of their faith, in the repetition of the circuit of the city during seven days. For what could seem less congruous than to fatigue themselves with six unavailing circuits? Then, of what use was their silence,[1] unless to betray their timidity, and tempt the enemy to come out and attack besiegers who seemed not to have spirit enough to meet them? But as profane men often, by rash intermeddling fervour, throw everything into confusion, the only part which God here assigns to his people, is to remain calm and silent, that thus they may the better accustom themselves simply to execute his commands.

[1] French, "De ne dire mot, ne faire aucun bruit;" "Not to speak a word, not to make any noise."—*Ed.*

Here, too, it is worthy of remark, that the instruments given to the priests to blow with, are not the silver trumpets deposited in the sanctuary, but merely rams' horns. The sound of the sacred trumpets would certainly have inspired more confidence, but a better proof of obedience was given, when they were contented with the vulgar symbol. Moreover, their movements were so arranged, that the greater number, by which is understood the armed, went before the ark, while those who usually accompanied the baggage followed. It was their part to take care that the rear did not fall into confusion. As the term *congregating*, applied to them, was obscure, I have rendered it by the corresponding term usually employed by the Latins.[1] Some think that the tribe of Dan were thus employed, but this is uncertain, as they were not then arranged in the manner usual on other expeditions.

15. *And it came to pass on the seventh day*, &c. Here, also, God seemed, by leading the people so often round the city, not only to keep the matter in suspense, but purposely to sport with the miseries of the people, who were fatiguing themselves to no purpose. For why does he not order them suddenly to attack the city? Why does he keep them in their former silence, even to weariness, and not open their mouths to shout? But the happy fruit of this endurance teaches us, that there is nothing better than to leave the decisive moments and opportunities of acting at his disposal, and not, by our haste, anticipate his providence, in which, if we acquiesce not, we obstruct the course of his agency. Therefore, while the priests were sounding, God ordered a corresponding shout to be raised by the people, that in this way he might prove that he is not pleased with any impetuosity which men manifest at their own hands, but above all things requires a regulated zeal, of which the only rule is not to move either tongue, or feet, or hands, till he order. Here the rams' horns undoubtedly represented his authority.

17. *And the city shall be accursed*, &c. Although God

[1] French, "Mais je l'ay traduit par un terme plus accoustumé à la langue Françoise;" "But here I have translated it by a term more commonly used in the French language."—*Ed.*

had determined not only to enrich his people with spoil and plunder, but also to settle them in cities which they had not built, yet there was a peculiarity in the case of the first city; for it was right that it should be consecrated as a kind of first fruits. Accordingly, he claims the buildings, as well as all the moveable property, as his own, and prohibits the application of any part of it to private uses. It may have been an irksome and grievous task for the people voluntarily to pull down houses in which they might have commodiously dwelt, and to destroy articles which might have been important for use. But as they had not been required to fight, it behoved them to refrain, without grudging, from touching the prey, and willingly yield up the rewards of the victory to God, as it was solely by his nod that the walls of the city had fallen, and the courage of the citizens had fallen along with them. God was contented with this pledge of gratitude, provided the people thereby quickly learned that everything they called their own was the gift of his free liberality. For with equal right all the other cities might have been doomed to destruction, had not God granted them to his people for habitations.

As to the Hebrew word חרם, I will now only briefly repeat from other passages. When it refers to sacred oblations, it becomes, in respect of men, equivalent to *abolition,* since things devoted in this manner are renounced by them as completely as if they were annihilated. The equivalent Greek term is *ἀνάθημα,* or *ἀνάθεμα,* meaning *set apart,* or as it is properly expressed in French, *interdicted.* Hence the exhortation to beware of what was under anathema, inasmuch as that which had been set apart for God alone had perished, in so far as men were concerned. It is used in a different sense in the following verse, where caution is given not to place the camp of Israel in anathema. Here its simple meaning is, excision, perdition, or death. Moreover, God destined vessels made of metals for the use of the sanctuary; all other things he ordered to be consumed by fire, or destroyed in other manners.

20. So the people shouted when *the priests* blew with the trumpets: and it came to pass, when the people

20. Itaque vociferatus est populus postquam clanxerunt tubis. Quum enim audisset populus vocem

heard the sound of the trumpet, and the people shouted with a great shout, that the wall fell down flat, so that the people went up into the city, every man straight before him, and they took the city.

tubarum, vociferatus est vociferatione maxima, et cecidit murus subtus, tum ascendit populus in urbem quisque e regione sua, et ceperunt eam.

21. And they utterly destroyed all that *was* in the city, both man and woman, young and old, and ox, and sheep, and ass, with the edge of the sword.

21. Et perdiderunt omnia quæ erant in urbe, a viro usque ad mulierem, a puero usque ad senem, ad bovem, et ovem, et asinum, acie gladii.

22. But Joshua had said unto the two men that had spied out the country, Go into the harlot's house, and bring out thence the woman, and all that she hath, as ye sware unto her.

22. Duobus autem viris qui exploraverant terram dixit Josue, Ingredimini domum mulieris meretricis, et inde educite eam, et quæcunque habet, quemadmodum jurastis ei.

23. And the young men that were spies went in, and brought out Rahab, and her father, and her mother, and her brethren, and all that she had; and they brought out all her kindred, and left them without the camp of Israel.

23. Ingressi itaque exploratores eduxerunt Rahab, et patrem ejus, et matrem ejus, et fratres ejus, et quæcunque habebat, et totam cognationem ejus eduxerunt, ac locarunt extra castra Israel.

24. And they burnt the city with fire, and all that *was* therein: only the silver, and the gold, and the vessels of brass and of iron, they put into the treasury of the house of the Lord.

24. Urbem vero succenderunt igni, et quæcunque erant in ea: tantummodo aurum et argentum, vasa ærea et ferrea posuerunt in thesauro domus Jehovæ.

25. And Joshua saved Rahab the harlot alive, and her father's household, and all that she had; and she dwelleth in Israel *even* unto this day; because she hid the messengers which Joshua sent to spy out Jericho.

25. Itaque Rahab meretricem, et domum patris ejus, et quæcunque habebat vivere fecit Josue: habitavitque in medio Israel usque ad hunc diem, quia absconderat nuntios quos miserat Josue ad explorandum Jericho.

26. And Joshua adjured *them* at that time, saying, Cursed *be* the man before the Lord that riseth up and buildeth this city Jericho: he shall lay the foundation thereof in his first-born, and in his youngest *son* shall he set up the gates of it.

26. Adjuravit autem Josue tempore illo, dicendo, Maledictus vir coram Jehova qui surget ut edificet urbem istam Jericho. In primogenito suo fundabit eam et in minore suo statuet portas ejus.

27. So the Lord was with Joshua; and his fame was *noised* throughout all the country.

27. Fuit autem Jehova cum Josue, et fama ejus fuit in tota terra.

20. *So the people shouted*, &c. Here the people are praised for obedience, and the faithfulness of God is, at the same time, celebrated. They testified their fidelity by shouting, because they were persuaded, that what God had commanded would not be in vain, and he, in not allowing them

to lose their labour, vindicated the truth of what he had said. Another virtue of not inferior value was displayed by the people, in despising unlawful gain, and cheerfully suffering the loss of all the plunder. For there cannot be a doubt, that in the minds of many the thought must have risen, For what end does God please to destroy all the wealth? Why does he envy us that which he has given into our hand? Why does he not rather gladden us by furnishing us with the materials of thanksgiving? Dismissing these considerations, which might have interfered with their duty, it was a proof of rare and excellent self-denial, voluntarily to cast away the spoils which were in their hands, and the wealth of a whole city.

The indiscriminate and promiscuous slaughter, making no distinction of age or sex, but including alike women and children, the aged and decrepit, might seem an inhuman massacre, had it not been executed by the command of God. But as he, in whose hands are life and death, had justly doomed those nations to destruction, this puts an end to all discussion. We may add, that they had been borne with for four hundred years, until their iniquity was complete. Who will now presume to complain of excessive rigour, after God had so long delayed to execute judgment? If any one object that children, at least, were still free from fault, it is easy to answer, that they perished justly, as the race was accursed and reprobated. Here then it ought always to be remembered, that it would have been barbarous and atrocious cruelty had the Israelites gratified their own lust and rage, in slaughtering mothers and their children, but that they are justly praised for their active piety and holy zeal, in executing the command of God, who was pleased in this way to purge the land of Canaan of the foul and loathsome defilements by which it had long been polluted.[1]

[1] In confirmation of the views thus admirably expressed, it is not out of place to add those of the profoundest and most philosophical of English theologians on the same subject. Bishop Butler, in his Analogy, Part ii., chap. iii., after saying that " it is that province of reason to judge of the morality of Scripture; *i.e.*, not whether it contains things different from what we should have expected from a wise, just, and good Being—but

22. *But Joshua had said unto the two men,* &c. The good faith of Joshua in keeping promises, and his general integrity, are apparent in the anxious care here taken. But as the whole city had been placed under anathema, a question might be raised as to this exception of one family. No mortal man was at liberty to make any change on the decision of God. Still as it was only by the suggestion of the Spirit that Rahab had bargained for her impunity, I conclude that Joshua, in preserving her, did only what was considerate and prudent.

We may add, that the messengers were not yet under any contrary obligation, as the complete destruction of the city had not been declared. It is true, they had heard in general, that all those nations were to be destroyed, but they were still at liberty to make a compact with a single woman,

whether it contains things plainly contradictory to wisdom, justice, or goodness; to what the light of nature teaches us of God," continues thus: "I know nothing of this sort objected against Scripture, excepting such objections as are formed upon suppositions which would equally conclude, that the constitution of nature is contradictory to wisdom, justice, or goodness: which most certainly it is not. Indeed there are some particular precepts in Scripture, given to particular persons, requiring actions, which would be immoral and vicious, were it not for such precepts. But it is easy to see, that all these are of such a kind, as that the precept changes the whole nature of the case and of the action: and both constitutes and shews that not to be unjust or immoral, which, prior to the precept, must have appeared, and really have been so: which well may be, since none of these precepts are contrary to immutable morality. If it were commanded to cultivate the principles, and act from the spirit of treachery, ingratitude, cruelty; the command would not alter the nature of the case, or of the action, in any of these instances. But it is quite otherwise in precepts, which require only the doing an external action: for instance, taking away the property or life of any. For men have no right to either life or property, but what arises solely from the grant of God. When this grant is revoked, they cease to have any right at all in either: and when this revocation is made known, as surely it is possible it may be, it must cease to be unjust to deprive them of either. And though a course of external acts, which, without command, would be immoral, must make an immoral habit, yet a few detached commands have no such natural tendency. I thought proper to say thus much of the few Scripture precepts which require, not vicious actions, but actions which would have been vicious had it not been for such precepts: because they are sometimes weakly urged as immoral, and great weight is laid upon objections drawn from them. But to me there seems no difficulty at all in these precepts, but what arises from their being offences; *i.e.*, from their being liable to be perverted, as, indeed, they are, by wicked designing men, to serve the most horrid purposes, and, perhaps, to mislead the weak and enthusiastic." —*Ed.*

who had voluntarily abandoned her countrymen. But we shall afterwards meet with a far easier solution, namely, that while the Israelites, by the divine command, exhorted all whom they attacked, to surrender, by holding out the hope of pardon, the blinded nations obstinately refused the peace thus offered, because God had decreed to destroy all of them. But while all, in general, were hardened to their destruction, it follows that Rahab was exempted by special privilege, and might escape in safety, while the others perished. Joshua, therefore, judged wisely, that a woman who had voluntarily gone over to the Church, was rescued thus early, not without the special grace of God. The case of the father and the whole family is, indeed, different, but seeing they all spontaneously abjure their former state, they confirm the stipulation which Rahab had made for their safety, by the promptitude of their obedience.

Moreover, let us learn from the example of Joshua, that we do not sufficiently attest our probity, by refraining from violating our promise intentionally and of set purpose, unless we also diligently exert ourselves to secure its performance. He not only allows Rahab to be delivered by her guests, but is careful to guard against her sustaining any injury in the first tumult; and to make the messengers more diligent in performing their office, he reminds them that they had promised with the intervention of an oath.

23. *And the young men that were spies went in*, &c. God, doubtless, wished those to be safe, whose minds he thus inclined to embrace deliverance. Had it been otherwise, they would have rejected it not less proudly, and with no less scorn than the two sons-in-law of Lot. But a still better provision is made for them, when, by being placed without the camp, they receive a strict injunction to abandon their former course of life.[1] For had they been immediately admitted and allowed to mix indiscriminately with the people, the thought of their impurity might never, perhaps, have

[1] French, « Car combien qu'il y ait en cela de la severité, toutes fois c'est un bon moyen par lequel ils sont appelez a renoncer à leur vie precedente ;" " For though there is severity in this, it is, however, a good method of calling upon them to renounce their previous life."—*Ed.*

occurred to them, and they might thus have continued to indulge in it. Now when they are placed apart, that they may not, by their infection, taint the flock, they are impressed with a feeling of shame, which may urge them to serious conversion.

It cannot be meant that they were thus set apart for safety, lest any one in the crowd might have risen up violently against them: for they would have been received by all with the greatest favour and gladness, whereas they might have been attacked in a solitary place more easily, and even with impunity. Their impurity, therefore, was brought visibly before them, that they might not while polluted come rashly forward into the holy meeting, but rather might be accustomed by this rudimentary training to change their mode of life. For it is added shortly after, that they dwelt in the midst of the people; in other words, having been purged from their defilements, they began to be regarded in the very same light as if they had originally belonged to the race of Abraham. In short, the meaning is, that after they had made a confession of their previous impurity, they were admitted indiscriminately along with others. By this admission, Rahab gained one of the noblest fruits of her faith.

26. *And Joshua adjured them*, &c. This adjuration, then, was not merely to have effect for one day, but to warn posterity through all ages that that city had been taken only by divine power. He wished, therefore, that the ruins and devastation should exist for ever as a kind of trophy; because the rebuilding of it would have been equivalent to an erasure effacing the miracle. In order, therefore, that the desolate appearance of the place might keep the remembrance of the divine power and favour alive among posterity, Joshua pronounces a heavy curse upon any one who should again build the ruined city. From this passage we gather that the natural torpidity of men requires the aid of stimulants to prevent them from burying the divine favours in oblivion; and hence this spectacle, wherein the divine agency was made conspicuous to the people, was a kind of indirect censure of their ingratitude.

The substance of the imprecation is, that if any one ever attempt to rebuild Jericho he may be made sensible by the unpropitious and mournful result that he had done a cursed and abominable work. For to lay the foundations in his first-born, were just as if he were to cast forth his son to perish, crushed and buried beneath the mass of stones; and to set up the gates in his younger son, is the same thing as to plan an edifice which could not be erected without causing the death of a son. Thus he who should dare to make the insane attempt is condemned in his own offspring. Nor did Joshua utter this curse at his own suggestion; he was only the herald of celestial vengeance.

This makes it the more monstrous that among the people of God a man should have been found, whom that fearful curse, couched in formal terms, could not restrain from sacrilegious temerity. In the time of Ahab (1 Kings xvi. 34) arose Hiel, a citizen of Bethel, who dared, as it were avowedly, to challenge God in this matter; but the Sacred History at the same time testifies, that the denunciation which God had pronounced by the mouth of Joshua did not fail of its effect; for Hiel founded the new Jericho in Abiram his first-born, and set up its gates in his younger son Segub, and thus learned in the destruction of his offspring what it is to attempt anything against the will and in opposition to the command of God.[1]

[1] This rebuilding by Hiel on the very site of the ancient city, took place, according to the ordinary chronology, 520 years after Joshua pronounced the curse. It would seem, however, that another Jericho had been built at a much earlier period, not actually on the former site which, while the memory of the curse remained, was probably avoided, but at no great distance from it. Of this fact, the mention made of Jericho in Joshua xviii. 21, as one of the cities of Benjamin, is not decisive, because it may have been intended to indicate merely a locality, and not an actually existing city, nor is it absolutely certain that the "city of palm trees" which Eglor captured, (Judges iii. 14,) was a rebuilt Jericho, though by that name Jericho was generally known. Its existence, however, at least a century before Hiel, is clearly established by the directions given to David's ambassadors, after their insulting treatment by the king of Ammon, "to tarry at Jericho." (Sam. x. 5.) It may be worth while briefly to glance at the subsequent history of Hiel's sacrilegious city. As if the penalty of rebuilding had been fully paid by the exemplary punishment inflicted on the founder, the curse appears to have been withdrawn, and in the course of about twenty years we learn that it had not only been selected as a school of the prophets, (2 Kings ii. 5,) but received a very important addition to

CHAPTER VII.

1. But the children of Israel committed a trespass in the accursed thing: for Achan, the son of Carmi, the son of Zabdi, the son of Zerah, of the tribe of Judah, took of the accursed thing: and the anger of the Lord was kindled against the children of Israel.

1. Transgressi autem sunt transgressione filii Israel in anathemate: quia Achan, filius Chermi filii Zabdi, filii Zerah de tribu Jehudæ abstulit de anathemate: et accensa est excandescentia Jehovæ contra filios Israel.

2. And Joshua sent men from Jericho to Ai, which *is* beside Beth-aven, on the east side of Beth-el, and spake unto them, saying, Go up and view the country. And the men went up and viewed Ai.

2. Porro misit Josue viros e Jericho contra Hai, quæ erat juxta Bethaven ad orientem Bethel, et loquutus est cum illis, dicendo, Ascendite et explorate terram. Ascenderunt itaque viri, et exploraverunt Hai.

3. And they returned to Joshua, and said unto him, Let not all the people go up; but let about two or three thousand men go up and smite Ai; *and* make not all the people to labour thither; for they *are but* few.

3. Qui reversi ad Josuam, dixerunt ei, Ne ascendat totus populus; circiter duo millia virorum aut circiter tria millia virorum ascendant, et percutient Hai.[1]

4. So there went up thither of the people about three thousand men; and they fled before the men of Ai.

4. Ascenderunt ergo illuc e populo fere tria millia virorum, et fugerunt coram viris Hai.

its other attractions as a residence by the miraculous cure of its waters by Elisha. (2 Kings ii. 19-22.) Its inhabitants, on the return from the Babylonish captivity, are mentioned as having assisted in rebuilding the walls of Jerusalem. (Neh. iii. 2.) At a later period Jericho was fortified by the Syrian general Bacchides, or rather received from him additions to its previously existing fortifications, (1 Maccabees ix. 50,) but does not seem to have acquired very much importance till the time of Herod the Great, who, after capturing and sacking it, rebuilt it in a much more magnificent form, and erected in it a splendid palace, where he often resided and ultimately died. It also became a favourite residence of his son Archelaus. Our Saviour himself not only honoured it by his presence, but by the display of his miraculous agency. It appears in the latter period of the Roman empire to have ranked as one of the chief cities of Palestine. The general devastation of the country on the dissolution of that empire effected its final ruin, and its site is now only doubtfully represented by a miserable village called Riha, containing from 200 to 300 souls.—*Ed.*

[1] Calvin's Latin as well as the French version omit the concluding clause of this verse, "Make not the whole people to labour thither: for they are few." The omission, for which no reason is assigned, is the more remarkable, as there appears to be no doubt as to the genuineness of the original clause, and its meaning is very exactly given not only in the Septuagint but other versions, such as Luther's, with which Calvin was well acquainted.—*Ed.*

5. And the men of Ai smote of them about thirty and six men: for they chased them *from* before the gate *even* unto Shebarim, and smote them in the going down; wherefore the hearts of the people melted, and became as water.

6. And Joshua rent his clothes, and fell to the earth upon his face before the ark of the Lord until the even-tide, he and the elders of Israel, and put dust upon their heads.

7. And Joshua said, Alas, O Lord God, wherefore hast thou at all brought this people over Jordan, to deliver us into the hand of the Amorites, to destroy us? would to God we had been content, and dwelt on the other side Jordan!

8. O Lord, what shall I say, when Israel turneth their backs before their enemies?

9. For the Canaanites, and all the inhabitants of the land, shall hear *of it*, and shall environ us round, and cut off our name from the earth: and what wilt thou do unto thy great name?

5. Percusseruntque ex eis circiter triginta et sex viros, et persequuti sunt eos a porta usque ad Sebarim, et percusserunt eos in descensu: atque ita liquefactum est cor populi, fuitque velut aqua.

6. Porro Josue scidit vestimenta sua, prociditque in faciem suam in terram coram arca Jehovæ usque ad vesperam, ipse et seniores Israel, et posuerunt pulverem super caput suum.

7. Dixitque Josue, Ah, ah, Dominator Jehova, ut quid traduxisti populum hunc trans Jordanem, ut traderes nos in manum Amorrhaei qui perdat nos? Atque utinam libuisset nobis manere in deserto trans Jordanem!

8. O Domine quid dicam postquam vertit Israel cervicem coram inimicis suis?

9. Audientque Chananæus et omnes incolæ terræ, et vertent se contra nos, disperdentque nomen nostrum e terra: quid vero facies nomini tuo magno?

1. *But the children of Israel committed*, &c. Reference is made to the crime, and indeed the secret crime, of one individual, whose guilt is transferred to the whole people; and not only so, but punishment is at the same time executed against several who were innocent. But it seems very unaccountable that a whole people should be condemned for a private and hidden crime of which they had no knowledge. I answer, that it is not new for the sin of one member to be visited on the whole body. Should we be unable to discover the reason, it ought to be more than enough for us that transgression is imputed to the children of Israel, while the guilt is confined to one individual. But as it very often happens that those who are not wicked foster the sins of their brethren by conniving at them, a part of the blame is justly laid upon all those who by disguising become implicated in it as partners. For this reason Paul, (1 Cor. v. 4-6,) upbraids all the Corinthians with the private enormity of one individual, and inveighs against their pride in presum-

ing to glory while such a stigma attached to them. But here it is easy to object that all were ignorant of the theft, and that therefore there is no room for the maxim, that he who allows a crime to be committed when he can prevent it is its perpetrator. I certainly admit it not to be clear why a private crime is imputed to the whole people, unless it be that they had not previously been sufficiently careful to punish misdeeds, and that possibly owing to this, the person actually guilty in the present instance had sinned with greater boldness. It is well known that weeds creep in stealthily, grow apace and produce noxious fruits, if not speedily torn up. The reason, however, why God charges a whole people with a secret theft is deeper and more abstruse. He wished by an extraordinary manifestation to remind posterity that they might all be criminated by the act of an individual, and thus induce them to give more diligent heed to the prevention of crimes.

Nothing, therefore, is better than to keep our minds in suspense until the books are opened, when the divine judgments which are now obscured by our darkness will be made perfectly clear. Let it suffice us that the whole people were infected by a private stain ; for so it has been declared by the Supreme Judge, before whom it becomes us to stand dumb, as having one day to appear at his tribunal. The stock from which Achan was descended is narrated for the sake of increasing, and, as it were, propagating the ignominy ; just as if it were said, that he was the disgrace of his family and all his race. For the writer of the history goes up as far as the tribe of Judah. By this we are taught that when any one connected with us behaves himself basely and wickedly, a stigma is in a manner impressed upon us in his person that we may be humbled—not that it can be just to insult over all the kindred of a wicked man, but *first,* that all kindred may be more careful in applying mutual correction to each other, and *secondly,* that they may be led to recognise that either their connivance or their own faults are punished.

A greater occasion of scandal, fitted to produce general alarm, was offered by the fact of the crime having been detected in the tribe of Judah, which was the flower and glory of the whole nation. It was certainly owing to the admirable counsel of God, that a pre-eminence which fostered the hope of future dominion resided in that tribe. But when near the very outset this honour was foully stained by the act of an individual, the circumstance might have occasioned no small disturbance to weak minds. The severe punishment, however, wiped away the scandal which might otherwise have existed; and hence we gather that when occasion has been given to the wicked to blaspheme, the Church has no fitter means of removing the opprobrium than that of visiting offences with exemplary punishment.

2. *And Joshua sent men from Jericho,* &c. To examine the site of the city and reconnoitre all its approaches was an act of prudence, that they might not, by hurrying on at random through unknown places, fall into an ambuscade. But when it would be necessary shortly after to advance with all the forces, to send forward a small band with the view of taking the city, seems to betray a want of military skill. Hence it would not have been strange that two or three thousand men, on a sudden sally were panic-struck and turned their backs. And it was certainly expedient for the whole body that twenty or thirty thousand should have spread in all directions in foraging parties. We may add, that even the act of slaying, though no resistance were offered, was of itself sufficient to wear out a small body of troops. Therefore, when the three thousand or thereabouts were repulsed, it was only a just recompense for their confidence and sloth. The Holy Spirit, however, declares that fewness of numbers was not the cause of the discomfiture, and ought not to bear the blame of it. The true cause was the secret counsel of God, who meant to shew a sign of his anger, but allowed the number to be small in order that the loss might be less serious. And it was certainly a rare display of mercy to chastise the people gently and without any great overthrow, with the view of arousing them to seek an instant remedy for the evil. Perhaps, too, the inhabitants of Ai would not have dared to make an attack upon the

Israelites had they advanced against the city in full force. The Lord therefore opened a way for his judgment, and yet modified it so as only to detect the hidden crime under which the people might otherwise have been consumed as by a lingering disease.

But although there is nothing wonderful in the defeat of the Israelites, who fought on disadvantageous terms on lower ground, it was, however, perfectly obvious that they were vanquished by fear and the failure of their courage before they came to close quarters; for by turning their backs they gave up the higher ground and retired to the slope of a valley. The enemy, on the other hand, shewed how thoroughly they despised them by the confidence and boldness with which they ventured to pursue the fugitives at full speed in the direction of their camp. In the camp itself, such was the trepidation that all hearts melted. I admit, indeed, that there was cause for fear when, after having gained so many victories as it were in sport, they saw themselves so disgracefully defeated. In unwonted circumstances we are more easily disturbed. But it was a terror from heaven which dismayed them more than the death of thirty men and the flight of three thousand.

6. *And Joshua rent his clothes,* &c. Although it was easy to throw the blame of the overthrow or disgrace which had been sustained on others, and it was by no means becoming in a courageous leader to be so much cast down by the loss of thirty men, especially when by increasing his force a hundred-fold it would not have been difficult to drive back the enemy now weary with their exertions, it was not, however, without cause that Joshua felt the deepest sorrow, and gave way to feelings bordering on despair. The thought that the events of war are doubtful—a thought which sustains and reanimates the defeated—could not be entertained by him, because God had promised that they would always be victorious. Therefore when the success did not correspond to his hopes, the only conclusion he could draw was, that they had fought unsuccessfully merely because they had been deprived of the promised assistance of God.

Accordingly, both he and the elders not only gave themselves up to sorrow and sadness, but engage in solemn mourning, as used in the most calamitous circumstances, by tearing their garments and throwing dust on their heads. That mode of expressing grief was used also by the heathen, but was specially appropriate in the pious worshippers of God in suppliantly deprecating his wrath. The rending of the garments and other accompanying acts contained a profession of repentance, as may also be inferred from the annexed prayer, which, however, is of a mixed nature, dictated partly by faith and the pure spirit of piety, and partly by excessive perturbation. In turning straightway to God and acknowledging that in his hand, by which the wound was inflicted, the cure was prepared, they are influenced by faith; but their excessive grief is evidently carried beyond all proper bounds. Hence the freedom with which they expostulate, and hence the preposterous wish, Would God we had remained in the desert![1]

It is not a new thing, however, for pious minds, when they aspire to seek God with holy zeal, to obscure the light of faith by the vehemence and impetuosity of their affections. And in this way all prayers would be vitiated did not the Lord in his boundless indulgence pardon them, and wiping away all their stains receive them as if they were pure. And yet while in thus freely expostulating, they cast their cares upon God, though this blunt simplicity needs pardon, it is far more acceptable than the feigned modesty of hypocrites, who, while carefully restraining themselves to prevent any confident expression from escaping their lips, inwardly swell and almost burst with contumacy.

Joshua oversteps the bounds of moderation when he challenges God for having brought the people out of the desert; but he proceeds to much greater intemperance when, in opposition to the divine promise and decree, he utters the turbulent wish, Would that we had never come out of the desert! That was to abrogate the divine covenant altogether. But as his object was to maintain and assert the

[1] French, "O que je voudroye que nous eussions prins à plaisir de demeurer au dela du Jordain;" "O how I wish that we had been pleased to remain beyond the Jordan."—*Ed.*

divine glory, the vehemence which otherwise might have justly provoked God was excused.

We are hence taught that saints, while they aim at the right mark, often stumble and fall, and that this sometimes happens even in their prayers, in which purity of faith and affections framed to obedience ought to be especially manifested. That Joshua felt particularly concerned for the divine glory, is apparent from the next verse, where he undertakes the maintenance of it, which had been in a manner assigned to him. What shall I say, he asks, when it will be objected that the people turned their backs? And he justly complains that he is left without an answer, as God had made him the witness and herald of his favour, whence there was ground to hope for an uninterrupted series of victories. Accordingly, after having in the loftiest terms extolled the divine omnipotence in fulfilment of the office committed to him, it had now become necessary for him, from the adverse course of events, to remain ignominiously silent. We thus see that nothing vexes him more than the disgrace brought upon his calling. He is not concerned for his own reputation, but fears lest the truth of God might be endangered in the eyes of the world.[1] In short, as it was only by the order of God that he had brought the people into the land of Canaan, he now in adversity calls upon him as author and avenger, just as if he had said, Since thou hast brought me into these straits, and I am in danger of seeming to be a deceiver, it is for thee to interfere and supply me with the means of defence.

9. *For the Canaanites and all the inhabitants,* &c. He mentions another ground of fear. All the neighbouring nations, who, either subdued by calamities or terrified by miracles, were quiet, will now resume their confidence and make a sudden attack upon the people. It was indeed probable, that as the divine power had crushed their spirit and filled them with dismay, they would come boldly forward to battle as soon as they knew that God had become hostile to the Israelites. He therefore appeals to God in regard to

[1] French, "Soit revoquee en doute, ou moins estimee devant le monde;" "Be called in question, or less esteemed before the world."—*Ed.*

the future danger, entreating him to make speedy provision against it, as the occasion would be seized by the Canaanites, who, though hitherto benumbed with terror, will now assume the aggressive, and easily succeed in destroying a panic-struck people.

It is manifest, however, from the last clause, that he is not merely thinking of the safety of the people, but is concerned above all for the honour of the divine name, that it may remain inviolable, and not be trampled under foot by the petulance of the wicked, as it would be if the people were ejected from the inheritance so often promised. We know the language which God himself employed, as recorded in the song of Moses, (Deut. xxxii. 26, 27,) "I would scatter them into corners, I would make the remembrance of them cease among men ; were it not that I feared the wrath (pride) of the enemy, lest their adversaries should behave themselves strangely, and lest they should say, Our hand is high, and the Lord hath not done all this." The very thing, then, which God declares that he was, humanly speaking, afraid of, Joshua wishes now to be timeously prevented ; otherwise the enemy, elated by the defeat of the people, will grow insolent and boast of triumphing over God himself.

10. And the Lord said unto Joshua, Get thee up ; wherefore liest thou thus upon thy face ?

11. Israel hath sinned, and they have also transgressed my covenant which I commanded them : for they have even taken of the accursed thing, and have also stolen, and dissembled also, and they have put *it* even among their own stuff.

12. Therefore the children of Israel could not stand before their enemies, *but* turned *their* backs before their enemies, because they were

10. Tunc dixit Jehova ad Josuam, Surge. Ut quid tu ita procidis super faciem tuam?

11. Peccavit Israel, atque adeo transgressi sunt pactum meum quod præcepi illis, atque etiam tulerunt de anathemate, atque etiam furati sunt, atque etiam mentiti, atque etiam reposuerunt in vasa sua.

12. Itaque non potuerunt filii Israel stare coram inimicis suis : cervicem vertent coram inimicis suis :[1] quia sunt in anathema,

[1] The English version puts the verb in the past tense, and translates "turned their backs;" Calvin's, "vertent cervicem," "will turn their neck ;" making the expression not a declaration of what had taken place, but a denunciation of what was still to take place, is truer to the original, and has also the sanction of the Septuagint, which has αὐχένα ὑποστρέψουσιν. Luther even adds to the force of the expression by saying, "müssen ihren Feinden den Rücken kehren ;" "must turn the back on their enemies." Calvin's punctuation of the same verse is peculiar. By making a colon at

accursed; neither will I be with you any more, except you destroy the accursed from among you.	non perseverabo esse vobiscum, nisi deleatis anathema e medio vestri.
13. Up, sanctify the people, and say, Sanctify yourselves against to-morrow; for thus saith the Lord God of Israel, *There is* an accursed thing in the midst of thee, O Israel: thou canst not stand before thine enemies, until ye take away the accursed thing from among you.	13. Surge, sanctifica populum et dicas, Sanctificate vos in crastinum: sic enim dicit Jehova Deus Israel, Anathema est in medio tui Israel: non poteris stare coram inimicis tuis, donec abstuleris anathema e medio vestri.
14. In the morning therefore ye shall be brought according to your tribes; and it shall be, *that* the tribe which the Lord taketh shall come according to the families *thereof:* and the family which the Lord shall take shall come by households; and the household which the Lord shall take shall come man by man.	14. Accedetis ergo mane per tribus vestras, et tribus quam deprehendet Jehova accedet per domos: et domus quam deprehendet Jehova accedet per viros.
15. And it shall be, *that* he that is taken with the accursed thing shall be burnt with fire, he and all that he hath: because he hath transgressed the covenant of the Lord, and because he hath wrought folly in Israel.	15. Qui autem deprehensus fuerit in anathemate, comburetur igni, ipse, et omnia quæ ejus sunt: quod transgressus fuerit pactum Jehovæ, et quod fecerit nefas in Israel.
16. So Joshua rose up early in the morning, and brought Israel by their tribes; and the tribe of Judah was taken:	16. Surrexit igitur Josue mane, et accedere fecit Israelem per tribus suas, et deprehensa est tribus Juda.
17. And he brought the family of Judah; and he took the family of the Zarhites: and he brought the family of the Zarhites man by man; and Zabdi was taken:	17. Tunc applicuit cognationes Juda, et deprehendit cognationem Zari, applicuit deinde familiam Zari per viros, et deprehensa est familia Zabdi.
18. And he brought his household man by man; and Achan, the son of Carmi, the son of Zabdi, the son of Zerah, of the tribe of Judah, was taken.	18. Et applicuit domum ejus per viros, et deprehensus est Achan filius Carmi, filii Zabdi, filii Zera, de tribu Juda.

10. *And the Lord said unto Joshua,* &c. God does not reprimand Joshua absolutely for lying prostrate on the ground and lamenting the overthrow of the people, since the true method of obtaining pardon from God was to fall down suppliantly before him; but for giving himself up to excessive sorrow. The censure, however, ought to be referred to

enemies, he separates the words "quia sunt in anathema," from the end of the first, and makes it the beginning of the second clause, which accordingly reads thus: "Because they are in anathema, (have taken of the accursed thing,) I will not continue to go with you," &c.—*Ed.*

the future rather than to the past; for he tells him to put an end to his wailing, just as if he had said, that he had already lain too long prostrate, and that all sloth must now be abandoned, as there was need of a different remedy. But he first shews the cause of the evil, and then prescribes the mode of removing it. He therefore informs him that the issue of the battle was disastrous, because he was offended with the wickedness of the people, and had cast off their defence.

We formerly explained why the punishment of a private sacrilege is transferred to all; because although they were not held guilty in their own judgment or that of others, yet the judgment of God, which involved them in the same condemnation, had hidden reasons into which, though it may perhaps be lawful to inquire soberly, it is not lawful to search with prying curiosity. At the same time we have a rare example of clemency in the fact, that while the condemnation verbally extends to all, punishment is inflicted only on a single family actually polluted by the crime. What follows tends to shew how enormous the crime was, and accordingly the particle גם is not repeated without emphasis; as they might otherwise have extenuated its atrocity. Hence, when it is said that they have *also* transgressed the covenant, the meaning is, that they had not sinned slightly. The name of covenant is applied to the prohibition which, as we saw, had been given; because a mutual stipulation had been made, assigning the spoils of the whole land to the Israelites, provided He received the first fruits. Here, then, he does not allude to the general covenant, but complains that he was defrauded of what had been specially set apart; and he accordingly adds immediately after, by way of explanation, that they had taken of the devoted thing, and that not without sacrilege, inasmuch as they had stolen that which he claimed as his own. The term *lying* is here used, as in many other passages, for frustrating a hope entertained, or for deceiving. The last thing mentioned, though many might at first sight think it trivial, is set down, not without good cause, as the crowning act of guilt, namely, that they had deposited the forbidden thing among their vessels. Persons who are otherwise not wholly wicked are sometimes tempted by a love of gain; but in the act of hiding the thing, and laying it up among other goods, a more obstinate perseverance in evil doing is implied, as the party shews himself to be untouched by any feelings of compunction. In the last part of the 12th verse, the term anathema is used in a different sense for execration; because it was on account of the stolen gold that the children of Israel were cursed, and almost devoted to destruction.

13. *Up, sanctify the people,* &c. Although the word קדש has a more extensive meaning, yet as the subject in question is the expiation of the people, I have no doubt that it prescribes a formal rite of sanctification. Those, therefore, who interpret it generally as equivalent to *prepare,* do not, in my judgment, give it its full force. Nay, as they were now to be in a manner brought into the divine presence, there was need of purification that they might not come while unclean. It is also to be observed in regard to the method of sanctifying, that Joshua intimates to the people a legal purgation. But though the ceremony might be in itself of little consequence, it had a powerful tendency to arouse a rude people. The external offering must have turned their thoughts to spiritual cleanness, while their abstinence from things otherwise lawful reminded them of the very high and unblemished purity which was required. And they are forewarned of what is to take place, in order that each may be more careful in examining himself. Nay, the Lord proceeds step by step, as if he meant to give intervals for repentance; for it is impossible to imagine any other reason for descending from tribe to family, and coming at length to the single individual.

In all this we see the monstrous stupor of Achan. Overcome perhaps by shame, he doubles his impudence, and putting on a bold front, hesitates not to insult his Maker. For why, when he sees himself discovered, does he not voluntarily come forward and confess the crime, instead of persisting in his effrontery till he is dragged forward against his will? But such is the just recompense of those who allow themselves to be blinded by the devil. Then when first by the taking of his tribe and next by that of his family, he plainly perceived that he was urged and held fast by the hand of God, why does he not then at least spring forward, and by a voluntary surrender deprecate punishment? It appears, then, that after he had hardened himself in his wickedness, his mind and all his senses were charmed by the devil.

Though God does not bring all guilty actions to light at the very moment, nor always employ the casting of lots for this purpose, he has taught us by this example that there is nothing so hidden as not to be revealed in its own time. The form of disclosure will, indeed, be different; but let every one reflect for himself, that things which escape the knowledge of the whole world are not concealed from God, and that to make them public depends only on his pleasure. For though a sin may seem as it were to have fallen asleep, it is however awake before the door, and will beset the miserable man till it overtake and crush him.

19. And Joshua said unto Achan, My son, give, I pray thee, glory to the Lord God of Israel, and make confession unto him; and tell me now what thou hast done; hide *it* not from me.

20. And Achan answered Joshua, and said, Indeed I have sinned against the Lord God of Israel, and thus and thus have I done:

21. When I saw among the spoils a goodly Babylonish garment, and two hundred shekels of silver, and a wedge of gold of fifty shekels weight, then I coveted them, and took them; and, behold, they *are* hid in the earth in the midst of my tent, and the silver under it.

22. So Joshua sent messengers, and they ran unto the tent; and, behold, *it was* hid in his tent, and the silver under it.

23. And they took them out of the midst of the tent, and brought them unto Joshua, and unto all the children of Israel, and laid them out before the Lord.

19. Tunc dixit Josue ad Achan, Fili mi, da nunc gloriam Jehovæ Deo Israel, et ede ei confessionem, atque indica mihi quid feceris, ne abscondas a me.

20. Respondit Achan ad Josuam, et ait, Vere ego peccavi Jehovæ Deo Israel, et sic et sic feci.

21. Vidi inter spolia pallium, Babylonicum bonum, et ducentos siclos argenteos, et ligulam auream unam, cujus pondus erat quinquaginta siclorum, quæ concupivi et abstuli; et ecce abscondita sunt in terra, in medio tabernaculi mei, et argentum subtus.

22. Misit itaque Josue nuncios qui currerunt ad tabernaculum; ecce absconditum erat in tabernaculo ejus et argentum sub eo.

23. Acceperuntque ea e medio tabernaculi, et attulerunt ea ad Josuam et ad omnes filios Israel, statueruntque coram Jehova

24. And Joshua, and all Israel with him, took Achan the son of Zerah, and the silver, and the garment, and the wedge of gold, and his sons, and his daughters, and his oxen, and his asses, and his sheep, and his tent, and all that he had; and they brought them unto the valley of Achor.

25. And Joshua said, Why hast thou troubled us? the Lord shall trouble thee this day. And all Israel stoned him with stones, and burned them with fire, after they had stoned them with stones.

26. And they raised over him a great heap of stones unto this day. So the Lord turned from the fierceness of his anger: wherefore the name of that place was called The valley of Achor, unto this day.

24. Tollensque igitur Josue Achan filium Zera, et argentum, et pallium, et ligulam auream, et filios ejus, et filias ejus, et boves ejus, et asinos ejus, et pecudes ejus, et tabernaculum ejus, et omnia quæ erant ejus, simulque universus Israel cum eo deduxerunt in vallem Achor.

25. Et dixit Josue, Cur turbasti nos? Turbet te Jehova hodie, et obruerunt eum universus Israel lapidibus, combusseruntque eos igni postquam lapidaverunt eos lapidibus.

26. Et statuerunt super eum acervum lapidum magnum usque ad hunc diem, et aversus est Jehova ab ira excandescentiæ suæ; ideo vocarunt nomen loci illius vallem Achor usque in hunc diem.

19. *And Joshua said unto Achan*, &c. Although only by lot, which seems to fall out fortuitously, Achan is completely caught; yet, as God has declared that he will point out the guilty party, as if with the finger, Joshua interrogates without having any doubt, and when the discovery is made, urges Achan to confess it. It is probable, indeed, that this was the usual form of adjuration, as we read in John's Gospel, (John ix. 24,) that the scribes and priests used the same words in adjuring the blind man whose sight our Saviour had restored, to answer concerning the miracle. But there was a special reason why Joshua exhorted Achan to give God the glory, because by denying or equivocating he might have impaired the credit of the decision. The matter had already been determined by lot. Joshua, therefore, simply orders him to subscribe to the divine sentence, and not aggravate the crime by vain denials.

He calls him son, neither ironically nor hypocritically, but truly and sincerely declares that he felt like a father toward him whom he had already doomed to death. By this example, judges are taught that, while they punish crimes, they ought so to temper their severity as not to lay aside the feelings of humanity, and, on the other hand, that they ought to be merciful without being reckless and remiss;

that, in short, they ought to be as parents to those they condemn, without substituting undue mildness for the sternness of justice. Many by fawning kindness throw wretched criminals off their guard, pretending that they mean to pardon them, and then, after a confession has been extracted, suddenly hand them over to the executioner, while they were flattering themselves with the hope of impunity. But Joshua, satisfied with having cited the criminal before the tribunal of God, does not at all flatter him with a vain hope of pardon, and is thus more at liberty to pronounce the sentence which God has dictated.

20. *And Achan answered Joshua*, &c. As he was now struck with astonishment, he neither employs subterfuge, nor palliates the crime, nor endeavours to give any colouring to it, but rather ingeniously details the whole matter. Thus the sacred name of God was more effectual in extorting a confession than any tortures could have been. Nor was the simplicity he thus displayed a sure indication of repentance; being, as it were, overcome with terror, he openly divulged what he would willingly have concealed. And it is no new thing for the wicked, after they have endeavoured for some time to escape, and have even grown hardened in vice, to become voluntary witnesses against themselves, not properly of their own accord, but because God drags them against their will, and, in a manner, drives them headlong. The open answer here given will condemn the hypocrisy of many who obscure the clear light by their subterfuges. The expression is emphatic—thus and thus did I; meaning that each part of the transaction was explained distinctly and in order. Nor does he only acknowledge the deed, but by renouncing all defence, and throwing aside all pretext, he condemns himself in regard to its atrocity. I have sinned, he says; this he would not have said had he not been conscious of sacrilege, and hence it appears that he did not pretend mistake or want of thought.

22. *So Joshua sent messengers*, &c. Although it is not singular for messengers to prove their obedience by running and making haste, yet the haste which is here mentioned, shews how intent all were to have the work of expiation

performed as speedily as possible, as they had been filled with the greatest anxiety in consequence of the stern denunciation—I will not be with you until you are purged of the anathema. They therefore ran swiftly, not merely to execute the commands of Joshua, but much more to appease the Lord. The things carried off by stealth, when placed before their eyes, were more than sufficient to explain the cause of the disgrace and overthrow which had befallen them.

It had been said that they had turned their backs on the enemy, because, being polluted with the accursed thing, they were deprived of the wonted assistance of God; it is now easy to infer from the sight of the stolen articles, that the Lord had deservedly become hostile to them. At the same time, they were reminded how much importance God attached to the delivery of the first-fruits of the whole land of Canaan in an untainted state, in order that his liberality might never perish from their memory. They also learned that while the knowledge of God penetrates to the most hidden recesses, it is in vain to employ concealments for the purpose of eluding his judgment.[1]

24. *And Joshua, and all Israel with him*, &c. Achan is led without the camp for two reasons; first, that it might not be tainted and polluted by the execution, (as God always required that some trace of humanity should remain, even in the infliction of legitimate punishments,) and secondly, that no defilement might remain among the people. It was customary to inflict punishment without the camp, that the people might have a greater abhorrence at the shedding of blood: but now, a rotten member is cut off from the body, and the camp is purified from pollution. We see that the example became memorable, as it gave its name to the spot.

If any one is disturbed and offended by the severity of the punishment, he must always be brought back to this point, that though our reason dissent from the judgments of God, we must check our presumption by the curb of a pious modesty

[1] French, "C'est folie de chercher couverture et deguisement pour eschapper son jugement et l'abuser;" "It is folly to seek cover and disguise in order to escape his judgment and deceive him."—*Ed.*

and soberness, and not disapprove whatever does not please us. It seems harsh, nay, barbarous and inhuman, that young children, without fault, should be hurried off to cruel execution, to be stoned and burned. That dumb animals should be treated in the same manner is not so strange, as they were created for the sake of men, and thus deservedly follow the fate of their owners. Everything, therefore, which Achan possessed perished with him as an accessary, but still it seems a cruel vengeance to stone and burn children for the crime of their father; and here God publicly inflicts punishment on children for the sake of their parents, contrary to what he declares by Ezekiel. But how it is that he destroys no one who is innocent, and visits the sins of fathers upon children, I briefly explained when speaking of the common destruction of the city of Jericho, and the promiscuous slaughter of all ages. The infants and children who then perished by the sword we bewail as unworthily slain, as they had no apparent fault; but if we consider how much more deeply divine knowledge penetrates than human intellect can possibly do, we will rather acquiesce in his decree, than hurry ourselves to a precipice by giving way to presumption and extravagant pride. It was certainly not owing to reckless hatred that the sons of Achan were pitilessly slain. Not only were they the creatures of God's hand, but circumcision, the infallible symbol of adoption, was engraven on their flesh; and yet he adjudges them to death. What here remains for us, but to acknowledge our weakness and submit to his incomprehensible counsel? It may be that death proved to them a medicine; but if they were reprobate, then condemnation could not be premature.[1]

[1] These admirable remarks are well fitted to satisfy every candid mind, not only as to the nature of this very remarkable execution, but also as to its expediency and strict justice, notwithstanding its admitted severity. Several expositors, however, continue to be dissatisfied, and to bring it more into accordance with their views, attempt to explain parts of it away by means of a minute and forced criticism. On finding this process not very successful, they endeavour to supply its deficiency by extraordinary conjectures. First, with regard to the criticism, it is said that in the directions which the Lord gives to Joshua, (ver. 10-15,) he receives no authority to put any person to death, except the one who should be found to have actually committed the crime. When the words of the 15th verse, " he and all that he hath," are quoted in opposition to this view, the answer is, that

It may be added, that the life which God has given he may take away as often as pleases him, not more by disease than by any other mode. A wild beast seizes an infant and tears it to pieces ; a serpent destroys another by its venomous bite ; one falls into the water, another into the fire, a third is overlain by a nurse, a fourth is crushed by a falling stone ; nay, some are not even permitted to open their eyes on the light. It is certain that none of all these deaths happens except by the will of God. But who will presume to call his procedure in this respect in question ? Were any man so insane as to do so, what would it avail ? We must hold, indeed, that none perish by his command but those whom he had doomed to death. From the enumeration of Achan's oxen, asses, and sheep, we gather that he was sufficiently rich, and that therefore it was not poverty that urged him to the crime. It must therefore be regarded as a proof of his insatiable cupidity, that he coveted stolen articles, not for use but for luxury.

25. *And Joshua said*, &c. The invective seems excessively harsh ; as if it had been his intention to drive the wretched man to frantic madness, when he ought rather to have exhorted him to patience. I have no doubt that he spake

the expression does not necessarily mean more than the man himself, his cattle, and other property, and therefore *may* not have included his family, properly so called, or the persons who formed his household. Another criticism, still more extraordinary, would scarcely be deserving of notice had it not received the countenance of so distinguished a name as that of Grotius, who insists that Achan was the only person who actually suffered death, though his children were taken out to the place of execution and compelled to witness it. This view he attempts to support by the 25th verse, in which it is said that " All Israel stoned *him* (Achan) with stones, and burned *them* with fire ;" *i.e.*, as he explains, stoned Achan only, and then burnt his dead body, and his cattle, and other effects designated by *them*. Such are specimens of the criticism which this transaction has called forth, and it would almost be an insult to the reader to give a serious refutation of them. The *conjectures* to which we have referred are equally extravagant. One of them is given in the Cyclopædia of Biblical Literature, under the article Achan, and as the writer appears both to have invented it, and to plume himself on the invention, it is but fair to give it in his own words :—" We prefer the supposition that they (Achan's family) were included in the doom by one of those sudden impulses of indiscriminate popular vengeance, to which the Jewish people were exceedingly prone, and which, in this case, it would not have been in the power of Joshua to control by any authority which he could, under such circumstances, exercise."—*Ed.*

thus for the sake of the people, in order to furnish a useful example to all, and my conclusion, therefore, is, that he did not wish to overwhelm Achan with despair, but only to shew in his person how grievous a crime it is to disturb the Church of God. It may be, however, that the haughty Achan complained that his satisfaction, by which he thought that he had sufficiently discharged himself, was not accepted,[1] and that Joshua inveighed thus bitterly against him with the view of correcting or breaking his contumacy. The question seems to imply that he was expostulating, and when he appeals to God as judge, he seems to be silencing an obstinate man. The throwing of stones by the whole people was a general sign of detestation, by which they declared that they had no share in the crime which they thus avenged, and that they held it in abhorrence. The heap of stones was intended partly as a memorial to posterity, and partly to prevent any one from imprudently gathering particles of gold or silver on the spot, if it had remained unoccupied. For although the Lord had previously ordered that the gold of Jericho should be offered to him, he would not allow his sanctuary to be polluted by the proceeds of theft.

CHAPTER VIII.

1. And the Lord said unto Joshua, Fear not, neither be thou dismayed: take all the people of war with thee, and arise, go up to Ai: see, I have given into thy hand the king of Ai, and his people, and his city, and his land.

2. And thou shalt do to Ai and her king as thou didst unto Jericho and her king: only the spoil thereof, and the cattle thereof, shall ye take for a prey unto yourselves: lay thee an ambush for the city behind it.

3. So Joshua arose, and all the people of war, to go up against Ai: and Joshua chose out thirty thousand

1. Dixitque Jehova ad Josuam, Ne timeas, nec formides, sume tecum omnem populum bellicosum, et surge, ascende in Hai. Vide, dedi in manu tua regem Hai, ac populum ejus, urbem ejus, et terram ejus.

2. Faciesque Hai, et regi ejus, quemadmodum fecisti Jericho, et regi ejus; tamen spolia ejus, et animalia ejus prædabimini vobis. Colloca autem insidias urbi a tergo ejus.

3. Surrexit itaque Josue, et omnis populus bellicosus, ut ascenderent in Hai, et elegit Josue triginta

[1] French, "Combien qu'il se peut faire, qu'Achan estant fier se soit plaint de ce qu'on ne se contentoit pas de la reparation, et payement qu'il avoit fait, par lequel il pensoit s'estre bien acquitté, et avoir grand devoir;" "Although it may be that Achan complained of their not being contented with the reparation and payment which he had made, and by which he thought that he had acquitted himself well, and performed a great duty."—*Ed.*

mighty men of valour, and sent them away by night.

4. And he commanded them, saying, Behold, ye shall lie in wait against the city, *even* behind the city; go not very far from the city, but be ye all ready:

5. And I, and all the people that *are* with me, will approach unto the city; and it shall come to pass, when they come out against us, as at the first, that we will flee before them,

6. (For they will come out after us,) till we have drawn them from the city; for they will say, They flee before us, as at the first: therefore we will flee before them.

7. Then ye shall rise up from the ambush, and seize upon the city: for the Lord your God will deliver it into your hand.

8. And it shall be, when ye have taken the city, *that* ye shall set the city on fire: according to the commandment of the Lord shall ye do. See, I have commanded you.

9. Joshua therefore sent them forth: and they went to lie in ambush, and abode between Beth-el and Ai, on the west side of Ai: but Joshua lodged that night among the people.

10. And Joshua rose up early in the morning, and numbered the people, and went up, he and the elders of Israel, before the people to Ai.

11. And all the people, *even the people* of war that *were* with him, went up, and drew nigh, and came before the city, and pitched on the north side of Ai: now *there was* a valley between them and Ai.

12. And he took about five thousand men, and sent them to lie in ambush between Beth-el and Ai, on the west side of the city.

13. And when they had set the people, *even* all the host that *was* on the north of the city, and their liers in wait on the west of the city, Joshua went that night into the midst of the valley.

14. And it came to pass, when the king of Ai saw *it*, that they hasted,

millia virorum fortium robore, misitque eos nocte.

4. Ac præcepit eis, dicendo, Attendite vos, Insidiabimini urbi a tergo ejus, nec removeatis vos ab ea procul, sed estote omnes vos parati.

5. Et ego et omnis populus, qui mecum est, accedemus ad urbem: quum autem egredientur in occursum nostrum, sicut prius, fugiemus ante eos:

6. Tunc egredientur post nos, donec avellamus eos ab urbe: dicent enim, Fugiunt ante nos, ut prius: et fugiemus ante eos.

7. Vos autem surgetis ex insidiis, et expelletis habitatores urbis, tradetque eam Jehova Deus vester in manu vestra.

8. Quum ceperitis urbem, succendetis eam igni, secundum sermonem Jehovæ facietis. Videte, præcepi vobis.

9. Misitque itaque eos Josue, et perrexerunt ad insidias, manseruntque inter Bethel et Hai, ab occidente Hai. Mansit autem Josue nocte illa in medio populi.

10. Postea surrexit Josue summo mane, recensuitque populum, atque ascendit ipse et seniores Israel ante populum versus Hai.

11. Omnisque populus bellicosus, qui erat cum eo ascenderunt et appropinquarunt, veneruntque e regione urbis, et castrametati sunt ab aquilone Hai. Vallis autem erat inter ipsum et Hai.

12. Tulitque præterea circiter quinque millia virorum, quos locavit in insidiis inter Bethel et Hai ab occidente urbi.

13. Et propius accessit populus tota castra quæ erant ab aquilone urbi, et insidiæ ejus ab occidente ipsi urbi, perrexitque Josue nocte illa in medium vallis.

14. Porro quum videret rex Hai, festinaverunt et mane surrexerunt,

and rose up early; and the men of the city went out against Israel to battle, he and all his people, at a time appointed, before the plain: but he wist not that *there were* liers in ambush against him behind the city.

15. And Joshua and all Israel made as if they were beaten before them, and fled by the way of the wilderness.

16. And all the people that *were* in Ai were called together to pursue after them: and they pursued after Joshua, and were drawn away from the city.

17. And there was not a man left in Ai or Beth-el that went not out after Israel: and they left the city open, and pursued after Israel.

18. And the Lord said unto Joshua, Stretch out the spear that *is* in thy hand toward Ai; for I will give it into thine hand. And Joshua stretched out the spear that *he had* in his hand toward the city.

19. And the ambush arose quickly out of their place, and they ran as soon as he had stretched out his hand: and they entered into the city, and took it, and hasted and set the city on fire.

20. And when the men of Ai looked behind them, they saw, and, behold, the smoke of the city ascended up to heaven; and they had no power to flee this way or that way: and the people that fled to the wilderness turned back upon the pursuers.

21. And when Joshua and all Israel saw that the ambush had taken the city, and that the smoke of the city ascended, then they turned again, and slew the men of Ai.

22. And the other issued out of the city against them; so they were in the midst of Israel, some on this side, and some on that side: and they smote them, so that they let none of them remain or escape.

23. And the king of Ai they took alive, and brought him to Joshua.

24. And it came to pass, when

atque egressi sunt homines urbis in occursum Israel ad prælium, ipse et universus populus ejus ad tempus constitutum ante campestria: nesciebat autem quod insidiæ sibi essent a tergo urbis.

15. Et profligati sunt Josue, et universus Israel ante eos, et fugerunt per viam deserti.

16. Et congregati sunt totus populus qui in urbe erat, ut persequeretur eos. Et persequuti sunt Josuam, abstractique sunt ab urbe.

17 Neque remansit quisquam ex Hai et Bethel, qui non egressus sit post Israel, et reliquerunt urbem apertam, et persequuti sunt Israelem.

18. Dixit autem Jehova ad Josuam, Eleva hastam quæ est in manu tua contra Hai, quia in manu tua dabo eam. Et elevavit Josue hastam quæ erat in manu sua contra urbem.

19. Tum insidiæ surrexerunt repente e loco suo, et cucurrerunt quum elevasset manum suam, veneruntque ad urbem, et ceperunt eam, et festinarunt urbem succendere igni.

20. Vertentes autem sese viri Hai viderunt, et ecce ascendebat fumus urbis in cœlum, neque erant eis spatia ad fugiendum huc et illuc. Populus autem qui fugerat in desertum versus est contra persequentes.

21. Josue itaque et universus Israel ubi viderunt quod insidiæ cepissent urbem, ascendissetque fumus urbis, reversi sunt, et percusserunt viros Hai.

22. Illi præterea egressi sunt ex urbe in occursum eorum, fueruntque Israeli in medio, isti hinc, et illi inde, et percusserunt eos, donec nemo remaneret eis superstes et evasor.

23. Regem quoque Hai ceperunt vivum, et stiterunt eum coram Josue.

24. Quum autem finem fecisset

Israel had made an end of slaying all the inhabitants of Ai in the field, in the wilderness wherein they chased them, and when they were all fallen on the edge of the sword, until they were consumed, that all the Israelites returned unto Ai, and smote it with the edge of the sword.

25. And *so* it was, *that* all that fell that day, both of men and women, *were* twelve thousand, *even* all the men of Ai.

26. For Joshua drew not his hand back, wherewith he stretched out the spear, until he had utterly destroyed all the inhabitants of Ai.

27. Only the cattle, and the spoil of that city, Israel took for a prey unto themselves, according unto the word of the Lord which he commanded Joshua.

28. And Joshua burnt Ai, and made it an heap for ever, *even* a desolation unto this day.

29. And the king of Ai he hanged on a tree until even-tide: and as soon as the sun was down, Joshua commanded that they should take his carcase down from the tree, and cast it at the entering of the gate of the city, and raise thereon a great heap of stones, *that remaineth* unto this day.

Israel cædendi omnes habitatores Hai in deserto quo persequuti fuerant eos, et cecidissent omnes ipsi acie gladii donec consumerentur, reversus est universus Israel ad Hai, et percusserunt eam acie gladii.

25. Fuitque numerus omnium qui ceciderunt die illa a viro usque ad mulierem circiter duodecim millia, omnes viri Hai.

26. Porro Josue non reduxit manum suam quam elevaverat ad lanceam, donec interficeret omnes habitatores Hai.

27. Tantum animalia et spolia urbis ejus sibi prædati sunt filii Israel secundum sermonem Jehovæ, quem præceperat ipsi Josue.

28. Succendit igitur Josue Hai et posuit eam acervum sempiternum vastitatum usque ad hunc diem.

29. Regem vero Hai suspendit in ligno usque ad tempus vespertinum: cumque occubuisset sol, præcepit Josue, et deposuerunt cadaver ejus e ligno, et projecerunt illud ad introitum portæ urbis, et statuerunt super illud acervum lapidum grandem usque ad hunc diem.

1. *And the Lord said unto Joshua,* &c. It was of great consequence to Joshua, as well as the people, to inspire new courage, that they might prepare with confidence to assault the city of Ai, from which they had lately been repulsed with loss and greater disgrace. God, therefore, to inspire them with intrepidity on this expedition, promises that he will give them the city. With the same view he enjoins them to fight by stratagem more than open war, to entice the enemy out, and to select a secret place for an ambuscade which might take them by surprise. A few thousands might without any difficulty have been overthrown by an immense host attacking the city suddenly and unexpectedly. But as we formerly saw that the hearts of all had melted away, God consulted for their weakness by laying no greater burden upon them than they were able to bear, until they had

recovered from their excessive panic, and could execute his commands with alacrity.

It is true, indeed, that he now used their own exertion, partly that they might not always keep looking for miracles, and so give themselves up to laziness, and partly that in different and unequal modes of acting they might nevertheless recognise that his power is the same. But care must be taken not to omit the special reason, namely, that not having yet recovered from their terror, they could scarcely have been induced to engage in an open conflict, had they not seen stratagem employed as a subsidiary aid. The first place, however, is due to the promise, Fear not, for I have delivered it into thy hands: for although it is verbally directed to Joshua, it belongs in common to the whole people, as it was most necessary that all to a man should be freed from anxiety and furnished with new confidence. The order to burn the city like Jericho, appears to be a concession to the popular feeling, the vengeance thus taken serving to wipe out the remembrance of their disgrace. At the same time that they may engage in the expedition more willingly, the spoils are left to them as the reward of victory.

13. *Joshua went that night,* &c. It is not probable that all were called out from the camp, but the army was composed of those who were more accustomed to war. That it was sufficiently numerous appears from the fact, that five thousand were withdrawn from it for ambuscade. At first thirty-five thousand appear to be enumerated, but it is clear from the context that the number was not so great. I am rather inclined to conjecture that thirty thousand were led out for open fight, and that five thousand were specially set apart for an ambuscade. Joshua hastens to execute the task assigned to him, commencing his march in the morning, and in this haste we see how effectual the promise had proved. Had not the mind of all been freed from fear he never could have found them so prompt to obey.

Apparently, indeed, little prudence is shewn in sending so large a body to proceed by hidden paths to a place suitable for ambuscade. For with whatever silence and composure they might proceed, the mere movement of their feet must have caused a considerable noise. Should any one say that there was nobody to meet them, as all the inhabitants of the district had deserted the fields and taken refuge in the city, we will find it mentioned shortly after, that before the Israelites came near to the city their arrival was known by the king of Ai; and this could scarcely have been without scouts. But granting that they met no one in the fields, it was certainly a difficult matter to pass by, to select a suitable place during night for an ambuscade, and to take possession of it without giving some indication of their presence. With regard to the procedure of Joshua, though he might see that the business could be accomplished by a smaller force, he seems to have been compelled by the recent trepidation of the people to be very careful not to engage them in any enterprise of danger. For had only a few of the army been despatched they would perhaps have declined a part by which they were to be particularly exposed.

The Lord meanwhile displays the greatest indulgence to his people in delivering up an enemy that was to be so easily conquered. His wonderful favour especially appears in blinding all of them, so that they have no suspicion of the ambuscade. I have no doubt that when it is said they knew not of it, the writer of the history means to draw attention to the rare and extraordinary kindness of God in so covering, as it were, with the shadow of his hand, first, the thirty thousand who accompanied Joshua, and then the five thousand, that they all escaped the notice of the enemy. When mention is now made of five thousand, I do not understand it to mean that Joshua furnished a new ambuscade, as if the number, already excessive, were not sufficient, but that the writer now merely shews how the thirty-five thousand whom Joshua had armed were distributed. For to what end would so small a reinforcement have been given to so great a multitude? Besides, the place where they are ordered to halt is the same as that which had been previously pointed out; this could not apply to two separate bodies of troops.

15. *And Joshua and all Israel made as if they were beaten,* &c. This is another stratagem. By pretending flight they

draw off the enemy to a distance, leaving them no retreat afterwards into the city, which was in flames before they suspected that any disaster was to be apprehended in their rear. Hence, while the king of Ai pursues the Israelites as vanquished, the part of the army which lay hid towards Bethel had sufficient time to take the city, and make it too late for the inhabitants to perceive that they were utterly undone. For after they had been already repulsed, and were everywhere slaughtered, they were overwhelmed with despair on beholding the flames of the city, and so completely surrounded that not an individual could escape.

The question here asked by some, as to whether it is lawful to overcome an enemy by wiles and stratagem, originates in gross ignorance. First, it is certain that wars are carried on not merely by striking blows; for those are considered the best commanders who accomplish more by art and counsel than by mere violence; and secondly, the longer any one has served so as to acquire experience, the better soldier he makes. If war, then, is lawful, it is beyond all controversy that the usual methods of conquering may be lawfully employed, provided always that there be no violation of faith once pledged either by truce or in any other way.

17. *And there was not a man left in Ai*, &c. It will be clear from the context that some were taken in the city and slain, and therefore we must hold that the sally was not by all universally, and that the old men and women and many others unfit for war, did not rush forth into the fields; the meaning simply is, that no garrison was left to defend the city. The same thing is said of Bethel, and hence we may easily conjecture that Bethel, as it was a small unimportant town, belonged to another power. The inhabitants, however, from being unable to defend their own city, abandoned it, and offered their whole force to the king of Ai, to whom they were perhaps tributaries. It is uncertain whether they went to the king of Ai before the arrival of the Israelites, to unite their forces with his in the contest, but the probability is, that as they were unable to resist they had come by agreement into a fortified and more populous city. They thought that they could not possibly be safe unless they were pre-

served under the shadow of a neighbouring city superior to their own.

18. *And the Lord said unto Joshua,* &c. This passage shews, that owing either to the strong fortifications of the city, or the valour of its inhabitants, or the trepidation of the Israelites, the victory was difficult, since God promises that he himself would take it by the lifting up of a spear. Had success been beyond doubt, the symbol would have been superfluous; their minds must therefore have been anxious and perplexed, since the Lord, to prevent them from fainting, raises up a banner of confidence in the hand of Joshua. It is true, indeed, that shortly after a different motive for raising the spear is mentioned, when it is said, that in this way a signal was given to the ambuscade, which accordingly rushed forth. But if it really was so used as a signal, it will scarcely do to regard the spear as a manifestation of the victorious power of God dispelling all doubt. Still, however, as it is not expressly said that the spear was the cause which brought forth the soldiers who had been placed in ambuscade, the truth may be that they came forth of their own accord, either because it was the suitable time, or because the shouting and noise made them aware that the battle had actually commenced. For it is scarcely possible to believe that the spear was seen by them, when we consider the long space which intervened, and more especially that Joshua was standing in a valley. Moreover, if we hold that the lifting up of the spear, though intended for a different purpose, had also the effect of inspiring them with additional courage, there will be no absurdity in it.

This much ought to be regarded as certain, *first,* that by this solemn badge they were rendered more certain of the happy issue of the battle; and *secondly,* that Joshua had no other intention than to incite his troops according to the command of God. For it is at last added, that Joshua did not draw back his hand until the city was taken, the enemy everywhere destroyed, and the war itself terminated. Hence it appears that he exhibited it in the middle of the conflict as an ensign of triumph, that the Israelites might have no doubt of success. For although he ordered them to engage and use their arms bravely, he at the same time distinctly declared that they had already conquered.

The course of the battle is rendered somewhat obscure by the same thing being told twice, but the substance is sufficiently plain. The children of Israel retreated feigning fear, and the battle had not actually commenced before the inhabitants of Ai were precluded from returning and defending their city. After the two armies had come to close quarters, the ambuscade arose and made such haste that the flames of the conflagration were rising from the city when the enemy turned their backs. From this we may infer that the city was in the possession of the Israelites, but that the chief slaughter took place when those who were in the city came forth to take part in the battle, because the inhabitants, hemmed in on all sides, found resistance and flight equally unavailing. They were thus seized with despair, and, huddled together in a narrow space, were everywhere cut down.

The statement, that the slaughter did not take place in the city before those who had feigned flight returned, I understand to mean, that the whole troops uniting their forces rushed in, seized the prey, and slew all who might have been left. If any one objects that the city was burnt while the battle was going on, I answer, that the fire was indeed applied so as to let both armies know that the city was in possession of the Israelites, but it was not actually destroyed by fire. It was not practicable in a moment of time to seize and carry off the booty, nay, to bring the vessels and a large part of the property without the walls; and it would have been absurd voluntarily to destroy spoils which God had granted. We see, then, that the first fire was not kindled for the purpose of destroying the whole city, but was merely a partial conflagration giving intimation of its capture, and that the Israelites entered at the open gates without bloodshed or a struggle. This is confirmed shortly after, when the burning is ascribed to Joshua himself, not only because it was burnt under his command, but because he was careful, after returning from the battle, to see that it was utterly destroyed; as it is immediately added that he made it a heap of stones in order that it might be a perpetual desolation.[1]

25. *And so it was that all that fell that day*, &c. The meaning is not that all the slain were inhabitants of Ai, but that all who dwelt in it were slain, that not one escaped. It has already been seen that the inhabitants of Bethel were mingled along with them; and as no mention of that city is afterwards made, it may be conjectured with some probability that they had abandoned their own town, which was little fortified, and betaken themselves for greater safety to one which they hoped could be easily defended. The words, therefore, simply mean, that all who had come out of the city and all who were found in it were slain to a man. If any are rather disposed to think that this number of those whose slaughter took place within the walls is confined to the aged, the sick, the women and the children, I will not dispute the matter. Still, if we consider that only a small town was conjoined with a city of no great extent or population, it is more probable that the number comprehends those also who fell in battle.

26. *For Joshua drew not his hand back*, &c. As by raising the spear he gave sign and pledge of hope as it were from heaven, he did not cease to keep the minds of his followers fixed upon it until they were masters of the city. By thus persevering he sufficiently proved how far removed he was from ambition; how free from doing anything in the way of vain ostentation. For it was just as if he had resigned

[1] Ai and its apparently tributary town Bethel, thus subjected to a fearful destruction, were situated about twelve miles north from Jerusalem, and seventeen miles west-north-west from Jericho, and had previously been brought under the notice of the Israelites in very different circumstances. For they had read in the interesting narrative of Moses how Abraham had pitched his tent on a mountain, "having Bethel on the west and Hai (Ai) on the east; and there he built an altar unto the Lord, and called upon the name of the Lord," (Gen. xii. 8; xiii. 3;) and how Bethel, formerly called Luz, had changed its name, because Jacob, on awaking out of his wonderful dream, had declared it to be "none other but the house of God," and "the gate of heaven." (Gen. xxviii. 11-19.) Notwithstanding of the doom pronounced and executed upon Ai, it appears to have been rebuilt, was occupied by the Benjamites after their return from the captivity, (Neh. vii. 32; xi. 32; Ezra ii. 28,) is mentioned by Josephus under the name of Aina, and still exhibits some indications of its site. —*Ed.*

the office of leader, and transferred the whole praise of the victory to God. How intrepid a warrior he was is plain from other passages. He might now, too, have willingly discharged his military functions, and thus done what was far better fitted to promote his reputation and glory. But as if his hand had been fastened to the spear, he exhorts the soldiers to look to God alone, to whom he resigns the success of the battle. By thus standing aloof he profited more than if he had in all directions, and by his own hand, struck down heaps of the enemy: at the same time his remaining at ease was more praiseworthy than any degree of agility could have been.

29. *And the king of Ai he hanged,* &c. Though he seems to have treated the king with great severity in order to satisfy the hatred of the people, I cannot doubt that he studied faithfully to execute the divine judgment. Conquerors, indeed, are wont to spare captive kings, because their rank seems to carry something venerable along with it, but the condition of kings was different among those nations in which God wished particularly to shew how greatly he detested the wickedness which he had so long tolerated. For while all were doomed to destruction, the divine vengeance justly displayed itself with greater sternness and severity on the leaders, with whom the cause of destruction originated.

We may add, that the ignominious punishment inflicted on the king rendered it still less necessary to deal leniently with the common people, and thus prevented the Israelites from indulging an unseasonable mercy, which might have made them more sluggish or careless in executing the work of universal extermination.

God purposely delivered the king alive into the hand of Joshua, that his punishment might be more marked and thus better adapted for an example Had he fallen in the conflict promiscuously with others, he would have been exempted from this special mark of infamy; but now even after his death, the divine vengeance pursues his corpse. Nay, after being hung, he is thrown forth at the gate of the city where he had sat on his throne in judgment, and a monument is erected for the purpose of perpetuating his ignominy to posterity. His burial, however, is mentioned to let us know that nothing was done through tumultuous impetuosity, as Joshua carefully observed what Moses had prescribed in the Law, (Deut. xxi. 23,) namely, that those hung on gibbets should be taken down before sunset, as a spectacle of the kind was held in abomination. And, certainly, while it is humane to bury the dead under ground, it is inhumanly cruel to cast them forth to be torn by wild beasts or birds. Therefore, that the people might not be accustomed to barbarity, God allowed criminals to be hung, provided they did not hang unburied for more than one day. And that the people might be more attentive to this duty, which otherwise might readily have been neglected, Moses declares that every one who hangs on a tree is accursed; as if he had said, that the earth is contaminated by that kind of death, if the offensive object be not immediately taken away.

30. Then Joshua built an altar unto the Lord God of Israel in mount Ebal;

31. As Moses, the servant of the Lord, commanded the children of Israel, as it is written in the book of the law of Moses, an altar of whole stones, over which no man hath lift up *any* iron; and they offered thereon burnt-offerings unto the Lord, and sacrificed peace-offerings.

32. And he wrote there, upon the stones, a copy of the law of Moses, which he wrote in the presence of the children of Israel.

33. And all Israel, and their elders, and officers, and their judges, stood on this side the ark, and on that side, before the priests the Levites, which bare the ark of the covenant of the Lord, as well the stranger, as he that was born among them; half of them over against mount Gerizim, and half of them over against mount Ebal; as Moses, the servant of the Lord, had commanded before, that they should bless the people of Israel.

30. Tunc ædificavit Josue altare Jehovæ Deo Israel in monte Ebal,

31. Quemadmodum præceperat Moses servus Jehovæ filiis Israel: sicut scriptum est in libro legis Mosis, altare ex lapidibus integris, super quos non levaverant ferrum: et immolaverunt super illud holocausta Jehovæ, et sacrificaverunt hostias prosperitatum.

32. Scripsit quoque ibi in lapidibus repetitam legem Mosis, quam scripsit coram filiis Israel.

33. Universus autem Israel, et seniores ejus, et præfecti, et Judices ejus stabant hinc et inde ad arcam coram sacerdotibus Levitis portantibus arcam fœderis Jehovæ, tam peregrinus quam indigena: dimidia pars ejus contra montem Garizin, et dimidia pars ejus contra montem Ebal: quemadmodum præceperat Moses servus Jehovæ, ut benediceret populo Israel primum.

34. And afterward he read all the words of the law, the blessings and cursings, according to all that is written in the book of the law.

35. There was not a word of all that Moses commanded, which Joshua read not before all the congregation of Israel, with the women, and the little ones, and the strangers that were conversant among them.

34. Et post hæc legit omnia verba legis, benedictionem et maledictionem, secundum id totum quod scriptum est in libro legis.

35. Non fuit quidquam ex omnibus quæ præceperat Moses quod non legerit Josue coram universo cœtu Israel, et mulieribus, et parvulis, et peregrinis versantibus in medio ipsorum.

30. *Then Joshua built an altar*, &c. God had been pleased that this should be the first extraordinary sacrifice offered to him in the land of Canaan, that thus the people might attest their gratitude, and the land begin to be consecrated in regular form. It was not possible for the people to do it before freely and on their own soil, till they had obtained possession of some vacant region.[1] Now, God had at the same time given them two commands—*first*, that they should erect an altar on Mount Ebal; and *secondly*, that they should set up two stones plastered over with lime, on which they should write the Law, in order that every passer by might be able to see it and read it. We now read that both were

[1] The 29th verse concludes the account of the destruction of Ai, and the 30th opens abruptly with the building of an altar on Mount Ebal. The distance between the two places is not less than twenty miles, Ai being only twelve and Ebal thirty miles north from Jerusalem. The journey of so many miles by the whole body of the Israelites, and through a country which, at least up to the victory of Ai, was in undisputed possession of the enemy, must have occupied a considerable time, and have been accomplished with no small labour and difficulty. How comes it that not one word is said in regard to it, and that we are led at once from Ai to Ebal just as if the two places, instead of being widely separated, had been actually contiguous to each other? Were the incidents of the journey so unimportant as not to require the slightest notice? or is the narrative contained in the Book of Joshua so very succinct that even transactions which might occupy a large place in a more copious work have been purposely excluded from it? If both these questions are answered in the negative, and it would seem that they must be so answered, the only other question is, Has the order of time been observed? in other words, have we not in the interesting account now about to be given of one of the most wonderful national conventions on record, another instance of anticipation of narrative similar to that which we have already seen in the first chapter? Assuming this to be the case, the continuation of the narrative is to be looked for in the ninth chapter, while the account of the transactions on Mounts Ebal and Gerizim is to be regarded in the light of an episode. It is very remarkable that the whole episode is omitted by the Septuagint at this place, and not introduced before giving the account of the league of the Amorites, contained in the beginning of the ninth chapter.—*Ed.*

faithfully performed. A third command related to the recitation of blessings and cursings: this, too, Joshua performed with no less care.

To begin with the altar,—it is said, that according to the divine command, it was formed of unhewn stones. For entire stones on which the masons' iron has not been employed, are called rough and unworked.[1] This is specially said in Deut. xxvii., of the altar, of which mention is now made. But the same thing had before been said in general of all others. Some expounders, in searching for the reason, needlessly have recourse to allegory, and allege that the hand and industry of men are forbidden, because the moment we introduce any devices of our own, the worship of God is vitiated. This is indeed truly and wisely said, but it is out of place, as the divine intention simply was to prohibit the perpetuity of altars. For we know, that in order to sacrifice duly, it was enjoined that all should have one common altar, in order both to cherish mutual agreement, and to obviate all sources of corruption from the introduction of an adventitious superstition; in short, in order that religion might remain one and simple, as a variety of altars would soon have led to discord, thereby distracting the people and putting sincere piety to flight.

Then it was not left to the choice of the people to select a place, but God uniformly in the books of Moses claims this for himself. He therefore confines the exercises of piety to that place where he may have put the remembrance of his name. Moreover, as the divine will was not immediately manifested, nor the place designated, that worship might not in the mean time cease, it was permitted to build an altar where the ark should happen to be stationed, but an altar formed only of a rude pile of stones, or of turf, that it might be only temporary.

Let the reader observe that an option was given to the

[1] French, "Car quand il est parlé de pierres entieres sur lesquelles le fer n'avoit point passé, cela signifie des pierres, telles qu'elles viennent de la carriere, qui ne sont point polies ni accoustrees par artifice;" "For when mention is made of entire stones on which no tool had passed, it means stones as they are when they come from the quarry, without having been polished or hewn artificially."—*Ed.*

people to make it of rough stones, that its form might not attract veneration, or of earth, which would crumble away of its own accord. In one word, this arrangement tended to give a pre-eminence to the perpetual altar, after God made choice of Mount Zion for its locality. Hence it is said in the Psalm, I was glad because our feet will stand in thy courts, O Jerusalem! (Ps. cxxii. 1, 2.) What other translators render *peace offerings*, I have, not without cause, rendered by *sacrifices of prosperity*, because they were offered up either to solicit successful results, or to render thanks; and the Hebrew term is not unsuitable, as the reader will find more fully explained in my commentaries on the books of Moses.

32. *And he wrote there upon the stones*, &c. A different rule is applicable to the stones here mentioned, on which God wished that a memorial of his Law should always appear, in order that a kind of barrier might be interposed to protect the pure religion against the superstitions of Egypt. They were therefore covered with lime, that they might be more conspicuous, and the writing upon them more distinct. I willingly subscribe to the opinion of those who understand by the repeated Law a written form, or what is commonly called a copy or duplicate. I cannot, however, believe that the whole volume was traced upon it; for no stones however large could suffice to contain all the details. I therefore think that by the term Law only its substance and sanctions[1] are denoted. This made it palpable even to strangers entering the land what God was worshipped in it, and all excuse for error was taken away, when the Law was not treasured up in a book, but made manifest to the eyes of all. In short, though the priests should have been dumb, the stones themselves spoke clearly.

33. *And all Israel, and their elders*, &c. The third instance of obedience was the placing all the tribes on Mount Gerizim and Mount Ebal to stand in six rows each over against each other. For they were so arranged that six stood on Mount Ebal, and an equal number on the opposite

[1] French, "Le sommaire, et les defenses et commandemens;" "The summary, and the prohibitions and commands."—*Ed.*

Mount Gerizim. The intervening space was occupied by the Levites with the ark of the covenant, that the Lord might be surrounded on all sides by his own people. It is said that Joshua stood that he might first bless the people, as it was the purpose of God to allure the people to himself by sweetness and winning condescension. For although Moses, to rebuke the obstinacy of the people, makes mention of curses only, it is certain that these were in a manner accidental, because the genuine method was to employ blessings as a means of gaining over to obedience those who might otherwise have proved refractory. But when humane invitation proved unavailing, curses were added as a new resource and remedy.

God had promised ample rewards to his servants who should obey the Law. On the other hand, curses were denounced in order to deter transgressors. Each is now forced to subscribe his own condemnation, while an amen is responded to every single sentence. For in this way they not only hear themselves condemned by the mouth of God, but as if they had been heralds sent by him, they denounce the punishment which may await themselves. A similar promulgation was made in the plain of Moab beyond the Jordan, but now they are bound more solemnly, and acknowledge on what condition they are to dwell in the land of Canaan. It added no little weight to the whole, that the children also were admitted as witnesses.

CHAPTER IX.

1. And it came to pass, when all the kings which *were* on this side Jordan, in the hills, and in the valleys, and in all the coasts of the great sea over against Lebanon, the Hittite, and the Amorite, the Canaanite, the Perizzite, the Hivite, and the Jebusite, heard *thereof*,

1. Quum autem audissent omnes reges qui erant trans Jordanem in monte, et in planitie, et in toto tractu maris magni e regione Libani, Hitthæus, Amorrhæus, Chananæus, Pherisæus, Hivæus, et Jebusæus,

2. That they gathered themselves together, to fight with Joshua and with Israel, with one accord.

2. Congregaverunt se pariter ad pugnandum cum Josue et Israel uno consensu.

3. And when the inhabitants of Gibeon heard what Joshua had done unto Jericho and to Ai,

4. They did work wilily, and went and made as if they had been ambassadors, and took old sacks upon their asses, and wine-bottles, old, and rent, and bound up;

5. And old shoes and clouted upon their feet, and old garments upon them; and all the bread of their provision was dry *and* mouldy.

6. And they went to Joshua unto the camp at Gilgal, and said unto him, and to the men of Israel, We be come from a far country; now therefore make ye a league with us.

7. And the men of Israel said unto the Hivites, Peradventure ye dwell among us; and how shall we make a league with you?

8. And they said unto Joshua, We *are* thy servants. And Joshua said unto them, Who *are* ye? and from whence come ye?

9. And they said unto him, From a very far country thy servants are come because of the name of the Lord thy God: for we have heard the fame of him, and all that he did in Egypt,

10. And all that he did to the two kings of the Amorites, that *were* beyond Jordan, to Sihon king of Heshbon, and to Og king of Bashan, which *was* at Ashtaroth.

11. Wherefore our elders, and all the inhabitants of our country, spake to us, saying, Take victuals with you for the journey, and go to meet them, and say unto them, We *are* your servants: therefore now make ye a league with us.

12. This our bread we took hot *for* our provision out of our houses on the day we came forth to go unto you; but now, behold, it is dry, and it is mouldy:

13. And these bottles of wine which we filled *were* new; and, behold, they be rent: and these our garments and our shoes are become old by reason of the very long journey.

14. And the men took of their

3. Habitatores vero Gibeon audientes quod fecerat Josue urbi Jericho et Hai,

4. Egerunt etiam ipsi callide. Nam abierunt et finxerunt se legatos esse, et tulerunt saccos vetustos, in suis asinis, et utres vini vestustos, et ruptos ac colligatos,

5. Et calceamenta vetusta, et resarta in pedibus suis, et vestes vetustas super se, et totus panis viatici eorum aridus ac mucidus.

6. Perrexerunt ergo ad Josuam in castra in Gilgal, dixeruntque ei et viris Israel, E terra longinqua venimus, itaque nunc percutite nobiscum fœdus.

7. Tunc responderunt viri Israel ad Hivæum, Forte in medio mei tu habitas, et quomodo percutiam tecum fœdus?

8. At illi dixerunt ad Josuam, Servi tui sumus. Quibus ait Josua, Quinam estis, et unde venistis?

9. Responderunt ei, E terra longinqua valde venerunt servi tui in nomine Jehovæ Dei tui. Audivimus enim famam ejus, et quæcunque fecit in Ægypto,

10. Quæcunque item fecit duobus regibus Amorrhæi, qui erant trans Jordanem, Sihon regi Hesebon, et Og regi Basan in Astaroth.

11. Dixeruntque nobis seniores nostri, et emnes habitatores terræ nostræ, Tollite in manu vestra escam pro itinere, et ite in occursum eorum, ac dicite illis, Servi vestri sumus, et nunc percutite nobiscum fœdus.

12. Iste est panis noster, calidum pro viatico paravimus e domibus nostris quo die egressi sumus ut veniremus ad vos, nunc autem aruit, et siccus est.

13. Et isti sunt utres vini, quos impleverimus novos, et ecce rupti sunt. Et ista vestimenta nostra, et calceamenta nostra vetustate attrita sunt ob longum iter.

14. Sumpserunt ergo viri de via-

victuals, and asked not *counsel* at the mouth of the Lord.

15. And Joshua made peace with them, and made a league with them, to let them live: and the princes of the congregation sware unto them.

tico eorum, et os Jehovæ non interrogaverunt.

15. Et fecit cum eis Josue pacem, et percussit cum eis fœdus quod sineret eos vivere, juraveruntque eis principes congregationis.

1. *And it came to pass when all the kings*, &c. As the arrival of the people was well known to these kings from the very first, it is certain that their minds were intoxicated from above with security or lethargy, so that they did not forthwith league together to oppose them. It implied excessive stupor not to provide for themselves till they were violently roused to exertion by the overthrow of two cities.[1] For as the war was common, it was a kind of voluntary surrender to send no aid to their neighbours, nay, to have no army ready, which might make a powerful impression for their defence. But in this way God spared the weakness of his people, to whom the combined forces of so many nations would have caused no small fear.

It is certain, then, that by the sloth and torpor of their enemies, the Israelites were rendered more expeditious. For an interval was, in the meanwhile, given them to compose themselves, and thus those whom the mere name of enemies might have alarmed, prepare leisurely to encounter them.[2] In the same way, although the reprobate are desirous, by every possible device, to destroy the Church, God, to take away their power of hurting her, scatters and confounds their counsels, nay, destroys their spirit.[3] On the other hand, these nations display their frantic audacity. Instead of being overcome by manifest miracle, they continue to rage like wild beasts against the unassailable

[1] French, "Car c'estoit une stupidité par trop grande de ne se point tenir sur ses gardes, jusqu'à tant qu'ils fussent resveillez comme par force de leur paresse oyans la ruine et le sac de deux villes;" "For it implied excessive stupidity not to stand upon their guard, until they were awakened, as if by force, from their indolence, on hearing of the ruin and sacking of two towns."—*Ed.*

[2] "To encounter them." Latin, "Ad eos excipiendos." French, "To give them a good reception, and repulse them bravely."—*Ed.*

[3] French, "Dissippe et renverse leur conseils, entreprises, et machinations: et mesme il leur oste le sens et l'entendement;" "Dissipates and overturns their counsels, enterprises, and machinations; and even deprives them of sense and understanding."—*Ed.*

power of God. A report of the taking of Jericho had reached them. Had it been overthrown by the counsel, or the acting, or the prowess, or the engines of men? Nay, the walls had fallen of their own accord. With what confidence then can they league to take up arms against heaven?

3. *And when the inhabitants of Gibeon heard,* &c. The inhabitants of Gibeon alone rejecting the proposal to make war have recourse to fraud, and endeavour to obtain peace by pretending to live at a great distance. To make such an attempt was very odious to their neighbours, because it was, in a manner, to make a schism among them, to open a door to the Israelites, and weaken the strength of their allies. And though blame is justly due to the foolish credulity of Joshua and the rulers, who were under no obligation to bargain rashly in regard to a matter not properly investigated, yet the Lord, who is wont to bring light out of darkness, turned it to the advantage of his people; for it procured them an interval of relaxation, while they halted in a tranquil district.

The Gibeonites, indeed, judged rightly and prudently, when they resolved to bear anything sooner than provoke God more against them, by a vain resistance. But the employment of fraud and illicit arts, to circumvent those whose favour and protection they desired to enjoy, was no less absurd and ridiculous than at variance with reason and equity. For what could be the stability of a league which was founded in nothing but gross fraud? They pretend that they are foreigners who had come from a far distant country. Joshua, therefore, is bargaining with mere masks, and contracts no obligation except in accordance with their words. Hence the craft by which they insinuated themselves ought not to have availed them. Still, as a great degree of integrity yet existed among men, they deemed it enough to obtain an oath even extorted by fraud, feeling fully persuaded, that the people of Israel would not violate it.

The expression, that they too acted cunningly, is erroneously supposed by some to contain an allusion to the stratagem which Joshua had employed in deceiving the citizens of Ai: no less inaccurately do others make it refer to the time of Jacob, whose sons, Simeon and Levi,[1] had treacherously destroyed the Sichemites. (Gen. xxxiv.) The antithesis is merely between the hostile preparations of the kings and the secret wiles with which the Gibeonites accosted Joshua. Accordingly, after it is stated, that some had leagued with the intention of trying the result of open war, the trick of the Gibeonites is subjoined, and hence the meaning is, that Joshua had to do not only with professed enemies, who had gathered themselves together to battle, but with the crafty dissimulation of one nation.

It is asked, however, why the Gibeonites laboured so anxiously in a matter which was not at all necessary? For we shall see elsewhere that the Israelites were ordered to offer peace to all, that they might thereafter have a just and legitimate cause for declaring war. But as it was everywhere rumoured, that they were seeking a permanent settlement in the land of Canaan, (which they could not obtain except by expelling the inhabitants,) the Gibeonites conclude that there is no means of binding them to mercy except by imposing upon them in some way or other; as they would never have spontaneously and knowingly allowed the land which they had invaded to be occupied by others. Nay, as it was known that they had been commanded to destroy all, they had no alternative left but to have recourse to fraud, as all hope of obtaining safety was otherwise taken away. And for this reason they shortly after ask pardon for a fraud wrung from them by necessity.

Here, however, a question arises; as the Israelites object that they are not at liberty to make any paction with the nations of Canaan, but are bound to exterminate them utterly. There is certainly a discrepancy between the two things—to exhort to submission, and at the same time refuse to admit suppliants and volunteers. But although God required that the laws of war should be observed according to use and wont, and that, therefore, peace should be offered on condition of submitting, he merely wished to try the minds of those nations, that they might bring

[1] French, "Duquel les trois enfans, assavoir, Ruben, Levi et Simeon;" "Whose three sons, Reuben, Levi, and Simeon."—*Ed.*

destruction upon themselves by their own obstinacy. At the same time, it was intimated to the Israelitish people, that they must destroy them; and hence the conclusion necessarily followed, that those who dwelt in the land of Canaan could not be tolerated, and that it was unlawful to make a covenant with them.

We shall afterwards find both things distinctly expressed, viz., that all persisted in carrying on war, because it had been the divine intention that their hearts should be hardened, and that they should perish. It was, therefore, a legitimate inference that those who were doomed to death could not be preserved. If any one object that the Gibeonites, who voluntarily applied for peace, were therefore exceptions, I answer, that the Israelites were not at present considering that formal custom which produced no result, but are merely attending to the promise and the command of God. Hence it is, that they allow no hope to remain, because they had been simply and precisely commanded to purge the land by putting every individual to death, and to succeed to the place of those they had slain.

6. *And they went to Joshua*, &c. I have said that in strict law, a covenant of this description was null and void. For when they obtain their prayer, what is stipulated but just that they should be kept safe, provided they come from a distant and remote region of the globe? And the oftener they reiterate the same falsehood, the more do they annul a compact elicited by fraud, since its true meaning only amounts to this, that the Israelites will offer no molestation to a foreign people, living at a remote distance. This is shewn to be more especially the meaning, from the fact, that the Israelites expressly exclude all the inhabitants of the land of Canaan. They could not, therefore, gain anything by the fraud. Nor are they more assisted by making a fallacious pretext of the name of God, and thus throwing a kind of mist over the mind of Joshua. They pretend that they had come in the name of God; as if they were professing to give glory to God, even the God of Israel; inasmuch as there is a tacit rejection of the superstitions to which they had been accustomed. For if it is true, that they had

come, moved by the faith of the miracles which had been performed in Egypt, they concede supreme power to the God of Israel, though to them a God unknown.

14. *And the men took of their victuals*, &c. Some commentators here have recourse to the insipid fictions that they ate the bread, to ascertain from the taste whether it were stale from age, or that they confirmed the covenant by a feast. The words rather, in my opinion, are an indirect censure of their excessive credulity in having, on slight grounds acquiesced in a fabulous narrative, and in having attended merely to the bread, without considering that the fiction was devoid of colour. And, certainly, had not their senses been blunted, many things would have instantly occurred to refute the Gibeonites.[1] But as it sometimes happens, that the most piercing eyes are dazzled by an empty spectacle, they are more severely condemned for not having ascertained the pleasure of God. The remedy was at hand, had they attempted nothing without consulting the oracle. It was a matter deserving of careful inquiry, and it was therefore a sign of gross carelessness, when a priest was ready to seek an answer from God, by means of Urim and Thummim, to decide rashly in an obscure case, as if they had no means of obtaining advice. Their rashness was the less excusable, from being combined with such supine neglect of the grace of God.

16. And it came to pass, at the end of three days after they had made a league with them, that they heard that they *were* their neighbours, and *that* they dwelt among them.

16. Post tres autem dies a fœdere cum illis inito audierunt, quod propinqui essent ipsis, et in medio ipsorum habitarent.

17. And the children of Israel

17. Profectique sunt filii Israel,

[1] Nothing could be more gross than the imposition thus practised. The capital of the Gibeonites was not above fourteen miles west from Jericho, and scarcely half that distance south-west from Ai, where the Israelites had recently gained so signal a victory, and it is therefore not improbable that the Israelites, while pursuing the fugitives, had actually been within the territory which their leaders now ignorantly believe to be so very distant, as to be altogether beyond the limits of the promised land. The compliments paid to their prowess so flattered their pride, and the alliance of a powerful though distant nation held out the hope of so many advantages in the further prosecution of their conquests, that they fell at once into the snare, as if they had almost been willing to be deceived. —*Ed.*

journeyed, and came unto their cities on the third day. Now their cities *were* Gibeon, and Chephirah, and Beeroth, and Kirjath-jearim.

et venerunt ad urbes ipsorum die tertio. Urbes autem eorum erant Gibeon, Chephirat, Beeroth, Ciriat-jearim.

18. And the children of Israel smote them not, because the princes of the congregation had sworn unto them by the Lord God of Israel. And all the congregation murmured against the princes.

18. Et non percusserunt eos filii Israel, eo quod jurassent eis principes congregationis per Jehovam Deum Israel: et murmuravit tota congregatio contra principes.

19. But all the princes said unto all the congregation, We have sworn unto them by the Lord God of Israel: now therefore we may not touch them.

19. Tunc dixerunt omnes principes ad totam congregationem, Nos juravimus eis per Jehovam Deum Israel, ideo nunc non possumus attingere eos.

20. This we will do to them; we will even let them live, lest wrath be upon us, because of the oath which we sware unto them.

20. Hoc faciemus eis, servabimus eos vivos, ne sit contra nos ira propter jusjurandum quod juravimus eis.

21. And the princes said unto them, Let them live; but let them be hewers of wood, and drawers of water, unto all the congregation; as the princes had promised them.

21. Dixerunt itaque illis principes, Vivant, et cædant ligna, et fodiant aquam toti congregationi, quemadmodum loquuti sunt eis cuncti principes.

22. And Joshua called for them, and he spake unto them, saying, Wherefore have ye beguiled us, saying, We *are* very far from you; when ye dwell among us?

22. Vocavit itaque eos Josue, et loquutus est ad eos, dicendo: Ut quid decepistis nos, dicendo, Remoti sumus a vobis valde, cum in medio nostri habitetis?

23. Now therefore ye *are* cursed; and there shall none of you be freed from being bond-men, and hewers of wood, and drawers of water, for the house of my God.

23. Nunc ergo maledicti estis, nec delebuntur ex vobis servi, et cædentes ligna, et fodientes aquam pro domo Dei mei.

24. And they answered Joshua, and said, Because it was certainly told thy servants, how that the Lord thy God commanded his servant Moses to give you all the land, and to destroy all the inhabitants of the land from before you, therefore we were sore afraid of our lives because of you, and have done this thing.

24. Qui responderunt ad Josuam, atque dixerunt, Cum renunciando renunciatum fuit servis tuis quomodo præceperat Jehova Deus tuus Mosi servo suo ut daret vobis terram, et disperderet omnes habitatores terræ a facie vestra, timuimus valde animabus nostris a facie vestra, et fecimus istud.

25. And now, behold, we *are* in thine hand: as it seemeth good and right unto thee to do unto us, do.

25. Et nunc ecce sumus in manu tua, sicut placet, et sicut rectum est in oculis tuis, ut facias nobis, facies.

26. And so did he unto them, and delivered them out of the hand of the children of Israel, that they slew them not.

26. Et fecit eis ita, liberavitque eos de manu filiorum Israel, nec interfecerunt eos.

27. And Joshua made them that day hewers of wood, and drawers of water, for the congregation, and for

27. Constituitque eos Josue eo die cæsores lignorum, et haustores aquæ congregationi, et altari Jehovæ

the altar of the Lord, even unto this day, in the place which he should choose.

usque in hunc diem in loco quem elegerit.

16. *And it came to pass*, &c. The chastisement of their levity by the discovery of the fraud, three days after, must, by the swiftness of the punishment, have made them more sensible of the shame and disgrace. For it was thus known, that through sloth and lethargy, they had very stupidly fallen into error from not having taken the trouble to inquire into a matter almost placed before their eyes. Their marching quietly through that region, entering cities without trouble, and finding free means of sustenance, was owing to the paternal indulgence of God, who not only pardons their fault, but causes that which might justly have been injurious to turn out to their good. Here it is related that the children of Israel did not act in a hostile manner in that region, because the Gibeonites had received a promise of safety confirmed by an oath.

Now two questions arise—*first*, Whether the children of Israel, who had no intention whatever to pledge their faith to impostors, had contracted any obligation? and, *secondly*, Whether it was not in the option of the people to rescind a promise which their leaders had foolishly and erroneously made? In regard to the general position, the obligation of an oath ought to be held in the greatest sacredness, so that we may not, under the pretext of error, resile from pactions, even from those in which we have been deceived, since the sacred name of God is more precious than the wealth of a whole world.[1] Hence though a man may have sworn with

[1] Calvin was well qualified, by his legal education, to discuss the important question here raised, and it is impossible to dispute the soundness of his general positions in regard to it, both here and in the previous sections of the Commentary on this chapter. There is, however, an appearance of inconsistency in some of the statements. In the section beginning with the third verse, he says in Latin, "Cum larvis ergo paciscitur Josue, nec quidquam obligationis contrahit, nisi secundum eorum verba;" or as it is in French, "Josue donques traitte alliance avec des masques ou phantosmes et n'est nullement obligé, sinon suivant leurs paroles;" "Joshua, then, makes an alliance with masks or phantoms, and is in no way bound, except according to their words." Again, in the section beginning with verse the sixth, he says, "Dixi summo jure evanidum et irritum fuisse ejusmodi fœdus," or as it is in French, "J'ay dit qu'a la rigueur de droit une telle alliance estoit nulle et cassée;" "I have said, that in strict law such an

little consideration, no loss or expense will free him from performance. I have no doubt, that in this sense David says, (Psalm xv. 4,) that the true worshippers of God, if they have sworn to their hurt, change not, because they will bear loss sooner than expose the name of God to contempt, by retracting their promises.

I conclude, therefore, that if a private interest only is to be affected, everything which we may have promised by oath must be performed. And it is apparent from the words, that the Israelites were afraid lest they should expose the name of their God to disgrace among the nations of Canaan. For I think there is an emphasis in the expression—because they had sworn by the God of Israel. But a special reason left the Israelites at liberty to recede from the deceitful compact; for they had not only given up their own right, but improperly departed from the command of God, with which it was not lawful to interfere in the smallest iota. It was not in their power either to spare the vanquished or enact laws of surrender, whereas they now transact as if the business had been committed to them. We see, accordingly, that they twice profaned the name of God, while,

alliance was null and void." And he gives the reason in the form of a question, when he asks, "What do they (the Gibeonites) gain when their request is granted, but just that they are to be kept safe, provided they have come from a distant country?" But if the Gibeonites did not gain, or, in other words, were not entitled to demand anything, it is perfectly obvious that the Israelites could not be bound to grant anything. They were the two parties to a mutual contract, in which the claims of the one party were exactly the counterpart or measure of the obligations of the other. It might have been expected, therefore, that after Calvin had decided that the Gibeonites had no claim, he would, of course, have decided that the Israelites had incurred no obligation. Here, however, when considering this latter point, he seems to change his ground, by distinctly asserting, that we may not resile even from pactions in which we have been deceived. The inconsistency, however, is only apparent. He does not say that we are bound by such pactions, as if they were valid in themselves, but he adverts to circumstances which may lay us under a formal obligation to act as if we were bound by them. In other words, he removes the case from a court of law into the court of conscience, and thus brings it under the class of cases to which St. Paul referred, when he drew a distinction between things lawful and things expedient. Joshua and the elders had sworn rashly, but having by so doing put the honour of the God of Israel, so to speak, in pledge, they were bound, at whatever cost, to redeem it.—*Ed.*

under pretence of the oath, they persevered in defending what they had foolishly promised.

In the deference which the common people pay to their leaders, by abstaining from all violence to the Gibeonites, we behold the integrity of the age. Elsewhere it would have readily occurred to elude the promise by asserting that a whole people were not bound by the agreement of a few individuals, as the Romans did, in repudiating the Caudine peace, to which only the consuls, legates, and tribunes had sworn without the orders of the senate and people. The more praise, therefore, is due to that rude simplicity in which the religious obligation prevailed more than the too subtle arguments which the greater part of men in the present day approve and applaud. The people are indeed indignant that their leaders had taken more upon them than they were entitled to do, but their moderation does not allow them to proceed beyond murmur and noise.[1]

20. *This we will do to them*, &c. Although, according to agreement, they give the Gibeonites their lives, they ratify the whole covenant only in part. For while the Gibeonites were entitled to be made perfectly secure, they are deprived of liberty, which is dearer than life. From this we infer that Joshua and the others had, as in a case of doubt and perplexity, devised a kind of middle course, so as not to make the oath altogether void. The principal object of this device was to appease the multitude: at the same time, while they were indignant at having been imposed upon by the Gibeonites, they punished the fraud, and did not allow impunity to increase their derision. It was a harsh condition, in this arrangement, that the Gibeonites were not only doomed to servile labours but withdrawn from their homes, to lead a vagrant and wandering life. The office of scullions imposed on them was no less mean than laborious, but the worst of all was to hew wood and draw water, wherever God should be pleased to station the ark.

22. *And Joshua called for them*, &c. As he was to de-

[1] French, " Quand il ne passe point outre le murmure, et qu'il se contente de cela ;" " When they do not proceed beyond murmuring, and rest contented with it."—*Ed.*

liver a sad and severe sentence, he premises that the resolution involves no injustice, because nothing would be more unbecoming than to allow tricks and wiles to be profitable to those who employ them. He therefore first expostulates with them for having warded off danger by falsehood, and then immediately pronounces them cursed. By this I understand that he throws the blame of their servitude upon themselves, because they bear nothing worse than they have deserved by their guile or perfidy; as if he had said that the ground of the condemnation which he pronounces is in themselves. It is hard, indeed, that no end is assigned to the labours to which they are doomed, for this is implied in the words, Slaves shall never cease from among you: but he declares that no injustice is done them, as they were cursed of their own accord, or by their own fault. They, indeed, extenuate the offence, by alleging the necessity which compelled them, and yet they decline not the punishment, which they acknowledge to be justly inflicted. It may indeed be, that overcome with fear, they refused nothing, nay, calmly and flatteringly[1] acquiesced in the terms imposed on them. For what could they gain by disputing? I have no doubt, however, that as they were conscious of having done wrong, and had no means of completely exculpating themselves, they considered themselves very humanely dealt with, so long as their lives were saved.[2]

CHAPTER X.

1. Now it came to pass, when Adoni-zedek king of Jerusalem had heard how Joshua had taken Ai, and had utterly destroyed it; as he had done to Jericho and her king, so he had done to Ai and her king; and how the inhabitants of Gibeon had made peace with Israel, and were among them;

1. Quum audisset Adoni-zedec rex Jerusalem quod cepisset Josue Hai, et eam perdidisset (quemadmodum fecerat Jericho, et regi ejus, quod sic fecisset Hai et regi ejus) et quod pacem fecissent habitatores Gibeon cum Israel, et essent inter ipsos:

[1] Latin, "Nec sine assentatione;" "Nor without flattery." French, "Et sans flatterie;" "And without flattery."—*Ed.*

[2] Among the many pernicious consequences resulting from this arrangement, was the formation of a degraded caste in the heart of the Israelitish commonwealth, and the consequent introduction of domestic slavery, in one of its worst forms.—*Ed.*

2. That they feared greatly, because Gibeon *was* a great city, as one of the royal cities, and because it *was* greater than Ai, and all the men thereof *were* mighty.

3. Wherefore Adoni-zedek king of Jerusalem sent unto Hoham king of Hebron, and unto Piram king of Jarmuth, and unto Japhia king of Lachish, and unto Debir king of Eglon, saying,

4. Come up unto me, and help me, that we may smite Gibeon: for it hath made peace with Joshua, and with the children of Israel.

5. Therefore the five kings of the Amorites, the king of Jerusalem, the king of Hebron, the king of Jarmuth, the king of Lachish, the king of Eglon, gathered themselves together, and went up, they and all their hosts, and encamped before Gibeon, and made war against it.

6. And the men of Gibeon sent unto Joshua to the camp to Gilgal, saying, Slack not thy hand from thy servants; come up to us quickly, and save us, and help us: for all the kings of the Amorites, that dwell in the mountains, are gathered together against us.

7. So Joshua ascended from Gilgal, he, and all the people of war with him, and all the mighty men of valour.

8. And the Lord said unto Joshua, Fear them not: for I have delivered them into thine hand; there shall not a man of them stand before thee.

9. Joshua therefore came unto them suddenly, *and* went up from Gilgal all night.

10. And the Lord discomfited them before Israel, and slew them with a great slaughter at Gibeon, and chased them along the way that goeth up to Beth-horon, and smote them to Azekah, and unto Makkedah.

11. And it came to pass, as they fled from before Israel, *and* were in the going down to Beth-horon, that the Lord cast down great stones from heaven upon them unto Aze-

2. Tunc timuerunt valde, quod civitas magna esset Gibeon tanquam una e civitatibus regiis, quia major erat quam Hai, omnesque viri ejus fortes.

3. Propterea misit Adoni-zedec rex Jerusalem ad Hoham regem Hebron et ad Piram regem Jarmuth, et ad Japhiam regem Lachis, et ad Debir regem Eglon, dicendo,

4. Ascendite ad me et suppetias ferte mihi, ut percutiamus Gibeon qui pacem fecit cum Josue et filiis Israel.

5. Congregati sunt itaque, et ascenderunt quinque reges Amorrhæi, rex Jerusalem, rex Hebron, rex Jarmuth, rex Lachis, rex Eglon, ipsi et omnes exercitus eorum, et castrametati sunt juxta Gibeon, pugnaveruntque adversus eam.

6. Miserunt ergo viri Gibeon ad Josuam ad castra in Gilgal, dicendo, Ne contrahas manus tuas a servis tuis: ascende ad nos cito, et serva nos, atque auxiliare nobis: congregati enim sunt contra nos omnes reges Amorrhæi habitantes in monte.

7. Ascendit itaque Josue de Gilgal, ipse, et universus populus bellator cum eo, omnes potentes viribus.

8. Dixit autem Jehova ad Josue, Ne timeas ab eis: in manum enim tuam tradidi eos, nec consistet quisquam ex eis in conspectu tuo.

9. Et venit ad eos Josue repente: tota enim nocte ascendit de Gilgal.

10. Et contrivit eos Jehova coram Israel, percussitque eos plaga magna in Gibeon, et persequutus est eos per viam ascensus Beth-horon, et percussit eos usque Azecah et usque Makedah.

11. Dum autem fugerent a facie Israel, et essent in descensu Beth-horon, Jehova demisit super eos lapides magnos e cœlo usque ad Azecah, et mortui sunt, plures mor-

kah, and they died: *they were* more which died with hail-stones than *they* whom the children of Israel slew with the sword.

tui sunt lapidibus grandinis, quam quos interfecerunt filii Israel gladio.

12. Then spake Joshua to the Lord, in the day when the Lord delivered up the Amorites before the children of Israel, and he said in the sight of Israel, Sun, stand thou still upon Gibeon; and thou, Moon, in the valley of Ajalon.

12. Tunc loquutus est Josue ad Jehovam die qua tradidit Jehova Amorrhæum coram filiis Israel.[1] Dixitque in oculis Israel, Sol in Gibeon expecta, et Luna in valle Ajalon.

13. And the sun stood still, and the moon stayed, until the people had avenged themselves upon their enemies. *Is* not this written in the book of Jasher? So the sun stood still in the midst of heaven, and hasted not to go down about a whole day.

13. Et expectavit Sol, et luna constitit donec ulcisceretur se gens de inimicis suis. Annon hoc scriptum est in libro Jasar? (*vel*, recti) Stetit ergo sol in medio cœli, nec festinavit occumbere circiter die una integra.

14. And there was no day like that before it, or after it, that the Lord hearkened unto the voice of a man: for the Lord fought for Israel.

14. Et non fuit sicut dies illa ante eam nec post eam, qua exaudivit Jehova vocem viri: Jehova enim pugnabat pro Israel.

1. *Now it came to pass*, &c. He had formerly briefly glanced at, but now more fully details the conspiracy of the kings, who dwelt both in the mountains and in the plain. For after mentioning that they were struck with fear, and leagued together to make common war, he had broken off abruptly, and proceeded to speak of the Gibeonites. But what he had previously said of the kings in general, he now applies only to one individual; not because Adoni-zedek alone was afraid, but because he stirred up all the others, and was the principal originator and leader in carrying on the war against the Israelites. This is sufficiently expressed by the plural number of the verb; for it is said, When Adoni-zedek had heard—they feared greatly. From this it appears that they were all of the same mind, but that while some of them held back from fear, he who possessed greater authority, and was nearer the danger, invited the four others to arms.[2]

[1] An additional clause not found in the original, and excluded by the common versions, is here inserted in the Septuagint in the following terms, "ἡνίκα συνέτριψεν αὐτοὺς ἐν Γαβαὼν, καὶ συνετρίβησαν ἀπὸ προσώπου υἱῶν Ισραήλ;" "When he crushed them in Gibeon, and they were crushed before the face of the children of Israel."—*Ed.*

[2] French, "Appela et suscita les autres à prendre les armes;" "Called

In the beginning of the chapter it is again told, how the five kings formed an alliance to meet the Israelites, and ward off the overthrow with which they were all threatened. But as the Gibeonites had meanwhile surrendered, they first turned their arms against them, both that by inflicting punishment upon them, as the betrayers of their country, they might make them an example to all their neighbours, and that by striking terror into those vanquished enemies, they might also inspire their own soldiers with confidence. They resolve, therefore, to attack the Gibeonites who, by their embassy, had made a disruption and opened a passage to the Israelites. They had, indeed, a fair pretext for war, in resolving to punish the effeminacy of those who had chosen to give their sanction to strangers, about to lay the whole country waste, rather than faithfully defend their neighbours. And the Gibeonites experienced how useless their crafty counsel must have been, had they not been saved in pity by the Israelites. Meanwhile the Lord allowed them to be involved in danger, in order that, being twice freed, they might more willingly and meekly submit to the yoke.

6. *And the men of Gibeon sent unto Joshua, &c.* The course of the narrative is inverted; for the Gibeonites certainly did not wait till they were besieged, but on seeing an army levied and prepared, and having no doubt that they would have to sustain the first onset, as they had incurred general hatred, they anticipate the attack, and hasten to have recourse to the protection of Joshua.[1] To desert those to whom life had been given, would have been at once unlawful, unjust, and inhumane. Nay, as their surrender had been consequent on the agreement, they were entitled to be defended against violence and injury. With justice, there-

upon, and stirred up the others to take up arms." Jerusalem was only about five miles S.S.E. from Gibeon, while the other towns, situated S.S.W., were at distances varying from twenty to thirty miles.—*Ed.*

[1] The conjecture that the narrative is here inverted, seems somewhat gratuitous. Lachish, the most remote of the towns, was not more than thirty miles distant, and Jerusalem, as has been mentioned, was only five; and, therefore, in so far as distance merely is concerned, there is nothing to prevent us from holding in accordance with the literal purport of the narrative, that the kings had suddenly advanced against Gibeon, and were actually besieging it when the Gibeonites dispatched their embassy to Joshua.

fore, they implore the Israelites, under whose protection they were; and there is no hesitation on the part of Joshua, who judges it to be his duty to defend those whose submission he had agreed to accept. They had deceived him, it is true, but after the fraud had been detected, and they had confessed it, interposing some palliating circumstances, they had obtained pardon.

Equity and a sense of duty thus did not allow the Israelites to abandon the Gibeonites to their fate. Still, Joshua is entitled to praise for his promptitude in complying with the request, and sending assistance without delay. He is said to have marched during the whole night, and thus could not have proceeded with greater haste had the safety of the whole people been at stake. Had the same sincerity always been evinced by profane nations, they would rather have assisted their allies in due time than avenged their disasters after they had suffered them. The term *suddenly* ought not, however, to be confined to a single day, as if Joshua had accomplished three days' journey in a single night, and made his appearance among the Gibeonites next morning. All that is meant to be expressed is his great speed, and his not delaying his departure till next day.[1]

Though the Israelites moved their camp from Ai or that neighbourhood, it was the third day before they entered the confines of the Gibeonites. Granting that they then proceeded slowly in order of battle, Joshua was still at some distance when application is made to him to assist the Gibeonites. We have seen that Gilgal was the first station

[1] Here, again, apparently from exaggerating the distance, Calvin thinks it necessary to resort to an ingenious explanation, and give a kind of colouring to the narrative. The distance from Gilgal to Gibeon was not more than eighteen miles, and this might certainly be accomplished by a forced march in the course of a single night. Calvin says we are not to suppose that "Joshua accomplished three days' journey in a single night." But it is nowhere said that Gibeon was *three days' journey* from Gilgal. The words are, "The Israelites journeyed and came into the cities on the third day." (Chap. ix. 17.) In other words, the Israelites, on this particular occasion, employed three days, or rather, if we adopt the common Hebrew mode of computation, part of a first, the whole of a second, and part of a third day. Such a statement scarcely justifies the inference that the average time of making the journey between the two places was three days.—*Ed.*

after crossing the Jordan, and therefore more remote than Jericho. If any one deems it absurd, that after receiving the submission of several cities, he should have turned backwards, and left an empty district, the recovery of which from the enemy might again cost new labour, I answer, there was no ground to fear that the enemy would come forward to occupy it, and engage in an expedition attended with great danger and difficulty. It is probable that when a body of troops was selected to attack Jericho, the women, children, and all others unfit for war remained in that quiet corner, where they might have the protection of those of the Reubenites, Gadites, and half tribe of Manasseh, who had been left on the opposite bank of the Jordan. For to what end would they have carried with them into their battles children and women heavy with child, or nursing babes at their breasts? How, during the incursions of the enemy, could food be found for such a multitude, or water sufficient to supply all their flocks and herds? I conclude, therefore, that Joshua and his soldiers returned to their tents that they might refresh themselves for a little with their wives and children, and there deposit the spoils with which they had been enriched.

8. *And the Lord discomfited them*, &c. It is uncertain whether the Lord anticipated the movement, and armed Joshua by his oracle, drawing him forth from Gilgal before he had taken any step, or whether he only confirmed him after he had made his preparations for setting out. It seems to me more likely that Joshua did not rush forth as soon as he was asked without consulting God, but at length, after being informed of his will, took up arms boldly and speedily. As he had lately been chastised for excessive facility, it is at least a probable conjecture that in this case of difficulty, he attempted nothing except in so far as he had a divine command. The Lord, therefore, had respect to the wretched Gibeonites when he did not allow them to remain destitute without the assistance of his people.

Joshua is made confident of victory in order that he may succour them; for God stimulates us more powerfully to the performance of duty by promising than by ordering. That which is here promised to one belongs to all, but for the sake of honouring Joshua, it is specially deposited with him that he may afterwards be the bearer of it to his army. For God does not speak from heaven indiscriminately to all sorts of persons, but confers the honour only on excellent servants and chosen prophets.

It is moreover worthy of notice that Joshua did not abuse the divine promise by making it an excuse for sluggishness, but felt the more vehemently inflamed after he was assured of a happy issue. Many, while they ostentatiously express their faith, become lazy and slothful from perverse security. Joshua hears that victory is in his hand, and that he may gain it, runs swiftly to battle. For he knew that the happy issue was revealed, not for the purpose of slackening his pace or making him more remiss, but of making him exert himself with greater zeal. Hence it was that he took the enemy by surprise.

10. *And the Lord discomfited them,* &c. In the first slaughter the Lord exerted his own might, but used the swords of the people. Hence we infer that whenever he works by men, nothing is detracted from his glory, but whatever is done redounds to him alone. For when he employs the co-operation of men, he does not call in allies as a subsidiary force, or borrow anything from them; but as he is able to accomplish whatever he pleases by a mere nod, he uses men also as instruments to shew that they are ruled by his hand and will. Meanwhile it is said with truth in either way, that the enemy were routed and crushed by God, or by the Israelites, inasmuch as God crushed them by the instrumentality of the Israelites.

In the second slaughter the hand of God appeared more clearly, when the enemy were destroyed by hail. And it is distinctly stated that more were destroyed by hail than were slain by the sword, that there might be no doubt of the victory having been obtained from heaven. Hence again it is gathered that this was not common hail, such as is wont to fall during storms. For, in the first place, more would have been wounded or scattered and dispersed than suddenly destroyed; and secondly, had not God darted it directly, part would have fallen on the heads of the Israelites. Now, when the one army is attacked separately, and the other, kept free from injury, comes forward as it were to join auxiliary troops, it becomes perfectly clear that God is fighting from heaven. To the same effect it is said that God threw down great stones of hail from heaven: for the meaning is that they fell with extraordinary force, and were far above the ordinary size. If at any time, in common battles, a storm has suddenly arisen, and has proved useful to one of the parties, God has seemed to give that party a token of his favour, and hence the line, Dearly beloved of heaven is he on whose side the elements are enlisted.[1] Here we have the account of a more distinguished miracle, in which the omnipotence of God was openly displayed.

12. *Then spake Joshua to the Lord,* &c. Such is the literal reading, but some expound it as meaning *before* Jehovah: for to speak to God, who, as piety dictates, is to be suppliantly petitioned, seems to be little in accordance with the modesty of faith, and it is immediately subjoined that Joshua addressed his words to the sun. I have no doubt that by the former clause prayer or vow is denoted, and that the latter is an expression of confidence after he was heard: for to command the sun to stand if he had not previously obtained permission, would have been presumptuous and arrogant. He first, then, consults God and asks: having forthwith obtained an answer, he boldly commands the sun to do what he knows is pleasing to God.

And such is the power and privilege of the faith which Christ inspires, (Matt. xvii. 20; Luke xvii. 6,) that mountains and seas are removed at its command. The more the godly feel their own emptiness, the more liberally does God transfer his power to them, and when faith is annexed to the word, he in it demonstrates his own power. In short, faith borrows the confidence of command from the word on which it is founded. Thus Elias, by the command of God, shut

[1] The passage here inserted is a quotation from the Latin poet Claudian, who, in his panegyric on Theodosius, referring to a victory of that emperor, in which the elements seem to war in his favour, exclaims—

O nimium dilecte Deo, tibi militat æther,
Et conjurati veniunt ad classica venti!—*Ed.*

and opened the heaven, and brought down fire from it; thus Christ furnished his disciples with heavenly power to make the elements subject to them.

Caution, however, must be used, lest any one may at his own hand presume to give forth rash commands. Joshua did not attempt to delay and check the course of the sun before he was well instructed as to the purpose of God. And although, when he is said to have spoken with God, the words do not sufficiently express the modesty and submission which become the servant of God in giving utterance to his prayers, let it suffice us briefly to understand as implied, that Joshua besought God to grant what he desired, and on obtaining his request, became the free and magnanimous herald of an incredible miracle unlike any that had previously taken place. He never would have ventured in the presence of all to command the sun so confidently, if he had not been thoroughly conscious of his vocation. Had it been otherwise, he would have exposed himself to a base and shameful affront. When, without hesitation, he opens his mouth and tells the sun and the moon to deviate from the perpetual law of nature, it is just as if he had adjured them by the boundless power of God with which he was invested. Here, too, the Lord gives a bright display of his singular favour toward his Church. As in kindness to the human race he divides the day from the night by the daily course of the sun, and constantly whirls the immense orb with indefatigable swiftness, so he was pleased that it should halt for a short time till the enemies of Israel were destroyed.[1]

13. *And the sun stood still*, &c. The question how the sun stood in Gibeon, is no less unseasonably raised by some than unskilfully explained by others.[2] For Joshua did not

[1] One might almost suspect from this concluding sentence, that Calvin was a stranger to the Copernican system, and still continued to believe that it was not the earth but the sun that revolved. As we know, however, that he was before his age in many points, so we cannot believe that he was behind it in this.—*Ed.*

[2] The rebuke here administered to those who attempt to explain the miracle applies with double force to those who attempt to explain it away. It is rather strange that among this number are some of the most distinguished Jewish rabbis as Levi-ben-Gerson and Maimonides, both of whom maintain that there was no miracle, but only something very like

subtilely place the sun in any particular point, making it necessary to feign that the battle was fought at the summer solstice, but as it was turning towards the district of Ajalon as far as the eye could discern, Joshua bids it stay and rest there, in other words, remain above what is called the horizon. In short, the sun, which was already declining to the west, is kept from setting.[1]

I do not give myself any great anxiety as to the number of the hours; because it is enough for me that the day was continued through the whole night. Were histories of that period extant, they would doubtless celebrate this great miracle; lest its credibility, however, should be questioned, the writer of this book mentions that an account of it was given elsewhere, though the work which he quotes has been lost, and expounders are not well agreed as to the term Jazar. Those who think Moses is meant, insist on referring the example which is here given to general predictions. As Moses applies this name to the chosen people, it is more congruous to hold that commentaries on the events in their history are meant. I, for my part, understand by it either God or Israel, rather than the author of a history.[2]

one. Their chief inducement to adopt this very extraordinary view, is zeal for the honour of Moses, which they think would be seriously impugned by admitting that a miracle which he never performed was performed by the instrumentality of his successor Joshua.—*Ed.*

[1] French, "En somme, le soleil remonte estant ja commencé a se coucher;" "In a word, the sun remounts after he had begun to set." —*Ed.*

[2] French, "Quant a moy, pour dire la verité, je le prends comme s'il estoit parlé de Dieu ou du peuple d'Israel, plutost que de celuy qui a escrit l'histoire;" "For my part, to tell the truth, I understand it as if it were spoken of God, or of the people of Israel, rather than of him who wrote the history." The view here adopted as to the meaning of Jasher has the sanction of many expositors of eminence, both ancient and modern, who consider it to have been some record in which an account of the leading events in the history of the chosen people was regularly inserted, and which might thus come to be commonly spoken of as the Book of the Just, very much in the same way as we are accustomed to speak of the Book of Worthies, the Book of Martyrs, &c. The only other allusion to the Book of Jasher is in 2 Sam. i. 18, where it is referred to as containing, or at least in connection with David's lament over Saul and Jonathan. Founding on this reference, De Wette and other rationalists argue that the Book of Joshua is not of the early date usually ascribed to it, and must have been written after the time of David. This argument assumes that Jasher is the name of an author living in the time, or subsequently to the

14. *And there was no day like that,* &c. We read in Isaiah and in the Sacred History, that the course of the sun was afterwards changed as a favour to King Hezekiah. (Is. xxxviii. 5-8.) For to assure him that his life was still to be prolonged fifteen years, the shadow of the sun was carried back over ten degrees on which it had gone down. It is not, therefore, absolutely denied that anything similar had ever been conceded to any other person, but the miracle is extolled as singular. The rendering of the word שמע, by *obeyed,* as adopted by some, I reject as too harsh. For although it is said in the Psalm, that the Lord does according to the desire of his servants, which may be held to be equivalent to obeying, it is better to avoid anything which seems to give a subordinate office to God.[1] Simply, therefore, the excellence of the miracle is praised, as nothing like it had been seen before or had happened after. The second clause of the verse celebrates the kindness and condescension of God in hearing Joshua, as well as his paternal favour towards the people, for whom he is said to have fought.

15. And Joshua returned, and all Israel with him, unto the camp to Gilgal.

16. But these five kings fled, and hid themselves in a cave at Makkedah.

17. And it was told Joshua, saying, The five kings are found hid in a cave at Makkedah.

18. And Joshua said, Roll great stones upon the mouth of the cave, and set men by it for to keep them;

19. And stay ye not, *but* pursue after your enemies, and smite the hindmost of them; suffer them not

15. Reversus autem est Josue et universus Israel cum eo ad castra in Gilgal.

16. Fugerant vero ipsi reges, et absconderant se in spelunca in Makeda.

17. Et nuntiatum est Josue his verbis, Inventi sunt quinque reges absconditi in spelunca in Makeda.

18. Tunc dixit Josue, Devolvite saxa magna ad os speluncæ, et constituite juxta eam viros ut custodiant eos.

19. Vos autem persequimini[2] inimicos vestros, et caudam eorum cædite, nec sinatis eos ingredi urbes

time, of David, and, but for this assumption, for which no good grounds are shewn, is utterly destitute of plausibility.—*Ed.*

[1] French, "Neantmoins si est-ce meilleur d'eviter toujours toutes façons de parler derogantes à la majesté de Dieu, comme s'il estoit question de la ranger;" "Nevertheless it is better to avoid all modes of speaking derogatory to the majesty of God, as if it were intended to make him subordinate."—*Ed.*

[2] The words "stay ye not," contained in the original, and in the Septuagint, the English, and other versions, are omitted in Calvin's Latin.—*Ed.*

to enter into their cities: for the Lord your God hath delivered them into your hand.

suas: tradidit enim eos Jehova Deus vester in manum vestram.

20. And it came to pass, when Joshua and the children of Israel had made an end of slaying them with a very great slaughter, till they were consumed, that the rest *which* remained of them entered into fenced cities.

20. Quum autem finem fecisset Josue, et filii Israel percutiendi plaga magna valde, donec consumerentur, et superstites qui evaserant ex ipsis ingressi essent urbes munitas.

21. And all the people returned to the camp to Joshua at Makkedah in peace: none moved his tongue against any of the children of Israel.

21. Reversi sunt universus populus ad castra ad Josue in Makeda in pace: non movit contra filios Israel quisquam linguam suam.

22. Then said Joshua, Open the mouth of the cave, and bring out those five kings unto me out of the cave.

22. Tunc dixit Josue, Aperite os speluncæ, et adducite ad me quinque illos reges de spelunca.

23. And they did so, and brought forth those five kings unto him out of the cave, the king of Jerusalem, the king of Hebron, the king of Jarmuth, the king of Lachish, *and* the king of Eglon.

23. Atque ita fecerunt, nempe adduxerunt ad eum quinque illos reges de spelunca, regem Jerusalem, regem Hebron, regem Jarmuth, regem Lachis, regem Eglon.

24. And it came to pass, when they brought out those kings unto Joshua, that Joshua called for all the men of Israel, and said unto the captains of the men of war which went with him, Come near, put your feet upon the necks of these kings. And they came near, and put their feet upon the necks of them.

24. Quumque eduxissent quinque reges illos ad Josue, vocavit Josue omnes viros Israel, dixitque ducibus virorum bellatorum, qui profecti erant secum, Accedite, ponite pedes vestros super colla regum istorum. Et accesserunt, posueruntque pedes suos super colla ipsorum.

25. And Joshua said unto them, Fear not, nor be dismayed; be strong, and of good courage: for thus shall the Lord do to all your enemies against whom ye fight.

25. Tunc dixit ad eos Josue, Ne timeatis, et ne paveatis, fortes estote, et roborate vos: sic enim faciet Jehova omnibus inimicis vestris contra quos pugnatis.

26. And afterward Joshua smote them, and slew them, and hanged them on five trees: and they were hanging upon the trees until the evening.

26. Posthæc percussit eos Josue, et interfecit eos, et suspendit in quinque lignis, fueruntque suspensi in lignis usque ad vesperum.

27. And it came to pass at the time of the going down of the sun, *that* Joshua commanded, and they took them down off the trees, and cast them into the cave wherein they had been hid, and laid great stones in the cave's mouth, *which remain* until this very day.

27. Fuit præterea tempore quo occumbit sol præcepit Josue, et deposuerunt eos e lignis, projeceruntque eos in speluncam in qua se absconderant, et posuerunt lapides magnos ad os speluncæ usque in hunc diem.

28. And that day Joshua took Makkedah, and smote it with the edge of the sword, and the king

28. Makedam vero cepit Josue eo die, et percussit eam acie gladii, et regem ejus occidit una cum illis,

thereof he utterly destroyed, them, and all the souls that *were* therein; he let none remain: and he did to the king of Makkedah as he did unto the king of Jericho.	et nullam animam quæ esset in ea reliquit superstitem, fecitque regi Makeda quemadmodum fecerat regi Jericho.

15. *And Joshua returned*, &c. This verse is not inserted in its proper place,[1] for shortly after the end of the battle is added, and the punishment inflicted on the kings, which was subsequent to the battle. We are then told of the encampment in Makkedah, and at last, in the end of the chapter, the return to Gilgal, which was introduced at the beginning without regard to the order of time, is repeated. Hence the narrative of the flight and concealment of the kings is connected with the former transactions. For having been informed during the heat of the battle that they were hiding in a cave, Joshua, fearing that if he were to set about capturing them, the others might escape, prudently contented himself with ordering the mouth of the cave to be blocked up with large stones, and setting sentinels over them, that being thus shut up, as it were in prison, they might at a fit time be brought forth and put to death. Hence, too, it appears that the army of the enemy was very large, because although the Israelites pressed closely upon them in their flight, and the sun himself gave an additional period for slaying them, it was impossible, notwithstanding, to prevent numbers of them from escaping into fortified cities. The divine assistance afforded to the Israelites was, however, sufficiently attested by the fact that they continued till they were wearied slaying at will all whom they met, and then returned safe. For the expression, that no one dared to move the tongue, implies that the Israelites gained a bloodless victory,[2] as if they had gone forth not to fight, but merely to slay.

18. *And Joshua said, Roll*, &c. The enemy having been completely routed, Joshua is now free, and, as it were, at leisure, to inflict punishment on the kings. In considering

[1] It is altogether omitted in the Septuagint.—*Ed.*

[2] "A bloodless victory." Latin, "Incruenta victoria." French, "De la part des Israelites ils ont acquis la victoire sans qu'il leur ait cousté la vie d'un seul homme;" "On the part of the Israelites they gained the victory without its having cost them the life of a single man."—*Ed.*

this, the divine command must always be kept in view. But for this it would argue boundless arrogance and barbarous atrocity to trample on the necks of kings, and hang up their dead bodies on gibbets. It is certain that they had lately been raised by divine agency to a sacred dignity, and placed on a royal throne. It would therefore have been contrary to the feelings of humanity to exult in their ignominy, had not God so ordered it. But as such was his pleasure, it behoves us to acquiesce in his decision, without presuming to inquire why he was so severe.

At the same time, we must recollect, as I formerly hinted, first, that all from the least even to the greatest were deserving of death, because their iniquity had reached the highest pitch, and the kings, as more criminal than the others, deserved severer punishment; and secondly, that it was expedient to give an example of inexorable rigour in the person of the kings, whom the people, from a perverse affectation of clemency, might have been too much disposed to pardon. It was the will of God that all should be destroyed, and he had imposed the execution of this sentence on his people. Had he not stimulated them strongly to the performance of it, they might have found specious pretexts for giving pardon. But a mercy which impairs the authority of God at the will of man, is detestable.[1] Now, however, when regal honour is not spared, all handle for humanity to the plebeians and common vulgar is cut off.

By this instance, the Lord shews us the great interest he takes in his elect people; for it was an instance of rare condescension to place kings under their feet, and allow them to insult over their dignity, as if they had been petty robbers; as it is said in the Psalm, A two-edged sword is in their hand to execute vengeance on the nations, to bind their kings with fetters, and their nobles with chains of iron; to execute the judgment written: this honour have all the saints. (Ps. cxlix. 6-9.) That fearful sight had at

[1] French, " Or c'este une misericorde qui merite d'estre detestee, quand elle derogue à l'authorité de Dieu, et qu'elle la deminue selon qu'il semble bon aux hommes;" "Now it is a mercy which deserves to be detested, when it derogates from the authority of God, and lessens it according as it seems good to men."—*Ed.*

the same time the effect of striking terror, so as to prevent the Israelites from imitating the manners of nations whose crimes they had seen so severely punished. Accordingly, we repeatedly meet in the books of Moses with this warning, You have seen how God took vengeance on the nations who were in the land of Canaan before you. Beware, therefore, of provoking the wrath of your God by their perverse doings. In one word, that God might be worshipped with greater sanctity, he ordered the land to be purged of all pollutions, and as the inhabitants had been excessively wicked, he willed that his curse should rest upon them in a new and unwonted manner.

25. *And Joshua said unto them, Fear not,* &c. Joshua now triumphs in the persons of the five kings over all the others who remained. For he exhorts his own people to confidence, just as if those who still stood unsubdued were actually prostrate under their feet. Hence we gather, that by the trampling down of a few, the whole people were so elated, that they looked down with contempt on all the others, as if they were already overthrown. And, certainly, we have here a brighter display of the divine power, which could thus inspire confidence for the future.

It is to be observed, however, that the kings were hung up, not for the purpose of exercising greater severity upon them, but merely by way of ignominy, as they were already slain. It was expedient that this memorable act of divine vengeance should be openly displayed in the view of all. Perhaps, also, it was the divine purpose to infuriate the other nations by despair, and drive them to madness, that they might bring down swifter destruction on themselves, whetting the wrath of the Israelites by their obstinacy. The same ignominy is inflicted on the king of Makkedah, though he had not led out his forces, and a similar destruction is executed on the whole people, who had kept quiet within their walls.[1] It is probable, indeed, that they had made some hostile attempt, but the special reason was, that

[1] French, "Tout le peuple qui n'estoit point sorti de la ville n'en a pas eut meilleur conte;" "All the people who had not come out from the town did not get easier off."—*Ed.*

God had passed the same sentence upon all. Why the dead bodies were thrown into the cave at evening, I have elsewhere explained. Moreover, this whole history holds up to us as in a mirror, how, when the Lord is seated on his tribunal, all worldly splendour vanishes before him, and the glory of those who seemed to excel is turned by his judgment into the greatest disgrace.

29. Then Joshua passed from Makkedah, and all Israel with him, unto Libnah, and fought against Libnah:

30. And the Lord delivered it also, and the king thereof, into the hand of Israel; and he smote it with the edge of the sword, and all the souls that *were* therein: he let none remain in it; but did unto the king thereof as he did unto the king of Jericho.

31. And Joshua passed from Libnah, and all Israel with him, unto Lachish, and encamped against it, and fought against it:

32. And the Lord delivered Lachish into the hand of Israel, which took it on the second day, and smote it with the edge of the sword, and all the souls that *were* therein, according to all that he had done to Libnah.

33. Then Horam king of Gezer came up to help Lachish; and Joshua smote him and his people, until he had left him none remaining.

34. And from Lachish Joshua passed unto Eglon, and all Israel with him; and they encamped against it, and fought against it:

35. And they took it on that day, and smote it with the edge of the sword; and all the souls that *were* therein he utterly destroyed that day, according to all that he had done to Lachish.

36. And Joshua went up from Eglon, and all Israel with him, unto Hebron; and they fought against it:

37. And they took it, and smote it with the edge of the sword, and the king thereof, and all the cities thereof, and all the souls that *were*

29. Transivit deinde Josue et universus Israel cum eo de Makeda in Libna, et oppugnavit Libna.

30. Traditque Jehova illam etiam in manum Israel, et regem ejus, et percussit eam acie gladii, omnemque animam quæ erat in ea: non reliquit in ea superstitem, fecitque regi ejus quemadmodum fecerat regi Jericho.

31. Postea transivit Josue, et universus Israel cum eo de Libna in Lachis, et castrametatus est juxta eam, et oppugnavit eam.

32. Deditque Jehova Lachis in manum Israel, et cepit eam die secunda, et percussit eam acie gladii, omnemque animam quæ erat in ea prorsus ut fecerat Libna.

33. Ascendit autem Horam rex Geser ad opem ferendam Lachis, et percussit eum Josue ac populum ejus, ut non reliquerit ei superstitem.

34. Transivit insuper Josue et universus Israel cum eo de Lachis in Eglon, et castrametati sunt contra eam, et oppugnaverunt eam.

35. Ceperuntque eam die illo, et percusserunt acie gladii, et omnem animam quæ illic erat, die illa interfecit prorsus ut fecerat Lachis.

36. Ascendit postea Josue et universus Israel cum eo ab Eglon in Hebron, et oppugnaverunt eam.

37. Et ceperunt eam, et percusserunt acie gladii, et regem ejus, et omnia oppida ejus, atque omnem animam quæ illic erat: non reliquit

therein; he left none remaining, according to all that he had done to Eglon, but destroyed it utterly, and all the souls that *were* therein.

superstitem prorsus ut fecerat Eglon. Perdidit ergo eam atque omnem animam quæ illic erat.

38. And Joshua returned, and all Israel with him, to Debir, and fought against it:

38. Postea reversus est Josue, et universus Israel cum eo in Debir, et oppugnavit eam.

39. And he took it, and the king thereof, and all the cities thereof, and they smote them with the edge of the sword, and utterly destroyed all the souls that *were* therein; he left none remaining: as he had done to Hebron, so he did to Debir, and to the king thereof; as he had done also to Libnah, and to her king.

39. Et ceperunt eam, et percusserunt acie gladii, et regem ejus, et omnia oppida ejus, percusseruntque eos acie gladii, atque interfecerunt omnem animam quæ illic erat. Non reliquit superstitem, quemadmodum fecerat Hebron, sic fecit Debir, et regi ejus: et quemadmodum fecerat Libna, et regi ejus.

40. So Joshua smote all the country of the hills, and of the south, and of the vale, and of the springs, and all their kings: he left none remaining, but utterly destroyed all that breathed, as the Lord God of Israel commanded.

40. Percussit itaque Josue omnem terram montanam, et meridianam, et campestrem, descensus acclives, et omnes reges earum: non reliquit superstitem: et omnem animam interfecit, quemadmodum præceperat Jehova Deus Israel.

41. And Joshua smote them from Kadesh-barnea even unto Gaza, and all the country of Goshen, even unto Gibeon.

41. Percussit itaque Josue a Cades Barne usque ad Asa, et universam terram Gosen usque ad Gibeon.

42. And all these kings, and their land, did Joshua take at one time, because the Lord God of Israel fought for Israel.

42. Cunctos vero reges istos, et terram eorum cepit Josue simul: quia Jehova Deus Israelis pugnabat pro Israele.

43. And Joshua returned, and all Israel with him, unto the camp to Gilgal.

43. Inde reversus est Josue et universus Israel cum eo in castra in Gilgal.

29. *Then Joshua passed*, &c. We have now a description of the taking of the cities, out of which the army of the enemy had been raised; and herein God displayed his power no less wonderfully than in the open field, especially when the rapidity is considered. For although those who had fled hither in trepidation might have produced some degree of panic, still, when the fear was allayed, they might be useful for defence.[1] The garrison had been increased by their numbers. When, therefore, in a short period of time, Joshua takes all the cities, and gains possession of the smaller towns, the presence of God was conspicuously manifested in a success no less incredible than unexpected. For

[1] French, "Ils pourroyent servir de defense pour garder les villes;" "They might serve for defence to guard the towns."—*Ed.*

had they, when attacked, only shut their gates, as Joshua had not brought either ladders by which he might scale the walls, or engines by which he might throw them down, each siege might have been attended with considerable fatigue and delay. Therefore, when he takes one the following day, and another the very day after attacking it, these continued, easy, and rapid victories, are evidently beyond human agency

Not without cause, then, in the end of the chapter, is the goodness of God expressly celebrated, as it had been made manifest that he was fighting for Israel, when Joshua at once took and vanquished so many kings, with their territories. Indeed, he could never, even in a course of inspection, have passed so quickly from city to city, had not a passage been divinely opened by the removal of obstacles. The miracle was increased when the king of Geser, who had come to the help of others, doubtless with full confidence in the result, was suddenly put to rout, almost without an effort, and did not even delay the advance of the Israelites. Those who were slain in the cities represent, as in a mirror, those whose punishment the Almighty holds suspended, while he actually takes vengeance on others. For though they plume themselves on the reprieve thus afforded them, their condition is worse than if they were immediately dragged to death.[1] It looks as if it would have been a dire calamity to fall in the field of battle; and making their escape, they seek safety within their walls. But what awaited them there was much more dreadful. Their wives and their children are butchered in their sight, and their own death is more ignominious than if they had perished sword in hand. Hence there is no reason to envy the reprobate the short time which the Lord sometimes grants them, because when they have begun to promise themselves safety, sudden destruction will come upon them. (2 Thess. v. 3.) Meanwhile, let us learn not to abuse the patience of God when he defers to execute his judgment, and, instead of indulging in self-complacency when we seem to have been

[1] Latin, "Quam si mox ad mortem traherentur." French, "Que s'ils estoyent depeschez soudainement sur le champ;" "Than if they were despatched suddenly on the spot."—*Ed.*

delivered from any danger, or when means of escape from it present themselves, let us reflect on the words of Jeremiah, (Jer. xxiv. 2,) that while the basket of early figs[1] had at least some savour, the other was so sour that they could not be eaten.

40. *So Joshua smote all the country,* &c. Here the divine authority is again interposed in order completely to acquit Joshua of any charge of cruelty. Had he proceeded of his own accord to commit an indiscriminate massacre of women and children, no excuse could have exculpated him from the guilt of detestable cruelty, cruelty surpassing anything of which we read as having been perpetrated by savage tribes scarcely raised above the level of the brutes. But that at which all would otherwise be justly horrified, it becomes them to embrace with reverence, as proceeding from God. Clemency is justly praised as one of the principal virtues; but it is the clemency of those who moderate their wrath when they have been injured, and when they would have been justified, as individuals, in shedding blood. But as God had destined the swords of his people for the slaughter of the Amorites, Joshua could do nothing else than obey his command.

By this fact, then, not only are all mouths stopped, but all minds also are restrained from presuming to pass censure. When any one hears it said that Joshua slew all who came in his way without distinction, although they threw down their arms and suppliantly begged for mercy, the calmest minds are aroused by the bare and simple statement, but when it is added, that so God had commanded, there is no more ground for obloquy against him, than there is against those who pronounce sentence on criminals. Though, in our judgment at least, the children and many of the women also were without blame, let us remember that the judgment-seat of heaven is not subject to our laws. Nay, rather when we see how the green plants are thus burned, let us, who are dry wood, fear a heavier judgment for ourselves. And certainly, any man who will thoroughly examine himself, will

[1] Latin, "Ficus præcoces." French, "Les figues hastives;" "Precocious figs, or figs too hastily ripened."—*Ed.*

find that he is deserving of a hundred deaths. Why, then, should not the Lord perceive just ground for one death in any infant which has only passed from its mother's womb? In vain shall we murmur or make noisy complaint, that he has doomed the whole offspring of an accursed race to the same destruction; the potter will nevertheless have absolute power over his own vessels, or rather over his own clay.[1]

The last verse[2] confirms the observation already made, that the fixed station of the whole people was in Gilgal; and that the soldiers who had gone out to war, returned thither, both that they might rest from their fatigues, and place their booty in safety. It would not have been proper to allow them to be more widely scattered till the casting of the lot had shewn where each was to have his permanent abode.

CHAPTER XI.

1. And it came to pass, when Jabin king of Hazor had heard *those things*, that he sent to Jobab king of Madon, and to the king of Shimron, and to the king of Achshaph,

2. And to the kings that *were* on the north of the mountains, and of the plains south of Chinneroth, and in the valley, and in the borders of Dor on the west;

3. *And to* the Canaanite on the east and on the west, and *to* the Amorite, and the Hittite, and the Perizzite, and the Jebusite in the mountains, and *to* the Hivite under Hermon in the land of Mizpeh.

4. And they went out, they and all their hosts with them, much people, even as the sand that *is* upon the sea-shore in multitude, with horses and chariots very many.

5. And when all these kings were met together, they came and pitched together at the waters of Merom, to fight against Israel.

1. Quum autem Jabim rex Hasor, misit ad Jobab regem Madam, et ad regem Simeron, et ad regem Achsaph,

2. Ad reges quoque qui habitabant ab aquilone in montanis, et in planitie ad meridiem Cineroth, et in planitie in Naphoth-Dor ab occidente.

3. Ad Chananæum ab oriente et occidente, et Amorrhæum, et Hitthæum, et Pherisæum, et Jebusæum in montanis, et Hivæum sub Hermon in terra Mispath.

4. Et egressi sunt ipsi, et omnes exercitus eorum cum ipsis, populus multus tanquam arena quæ est juxta littus maris, præ multitudine, et equi, et currus multi valde.

5. Congregati sunt omnes reges isti, et venientes castrametati sunt pariter ad aquas Merom, ut pugnarent cum Israele.

[1] French, "Car cela n'empeschera point que le potier n'ait puissance de faire de ses pots tout ce qu'il luy plaira;" "For that will not hinder the potter from having power to make of his pots whatever he pleases."—*Ed.*

[2] This verse is also omitted by the Septuagint.—*Ed.*

6. And the Lord said unto Joshua, Be not afraid because of them; for to-morrow, about this time, will I deliver them up all slain before Israel: thou shalt hough their horses, and burn their chariots with fire.

6. Dixit autem Jehova ad Josuam, Ne timeas a facie eorum: cras enim hoc tempore tradam omnes istos occisos coram Israele, equos eorum subnervabis, et currus eorum combures igni.

7. So Joshua came, and all the people of war with him, against them by the waters of Merom suddenly, and they fell upon them.

7. Venit itaque Josue, et cunctus populus bellator cum eo adversus ipsos ad aquam Merom repente, et irruerunt in eos.

8. And the Lord delivered them into the hand of Israel, who smote them, and chased them unto great Zidon, and unto Misrephoth-maim, and unto the valley of Mizpeh eastward; and they smote them, until they left them none remaining.

8. Et tradidit eos Jehova in manum Israelis, percusseruntque eos, et persequuti sunt usque ad Sidonem magnam, et usque ad fervores aquarum, et usque ad campum Mispe ad orientem: ac percusserunt eos donec non reliquerit eis superstitem.

9. And Joshua did unto them as the Lord bade him: he houghed their horses, and burnt their chariots with fire.

9. Fecitque eis Josue quemadmodum dixerat eis Jehova, equos eorum subnervavit, et currus eorum combussit igni.

10. And Joshua at that time turned back, and took Hazor, and smote the king thereof with the sword: for Hazor beforetime was the head of all those kingdoms.

10. Et reversus Josue eodem tempore cepit Hasor, et regem ejus percussit gladio, Hasor enim antea fuerat caput omnium istorum regnorum.

11. And they smote all the souls that *were* therein with the edge of the sword, utterly destroying *them*; there was not any left to breathe: and he burnt Hazor with fire.

11. Percusserunt quoque omnem animam quæ illic erat, acie gladii perdendo: non remansit ulla anima: et Hasor combussit igni.

12. And all the cities of those kings, and all the kings of them, did Joshua take, and smote them with the edge of the sword; *and* he utterly destroyed them, as Moses, the servant of the Lord, commanded.

12. Omnes urbes regum istorum, et universos reges earum cepit Josue, percussitque eos acie gladii, perdendo eos sicuti præceperat Moses servus Jehovæ.

13. But *as for* the cities that stood still in their strength, Israel burned none of them, save Hazor only; *that* did Joshua burn.

13. Tantummodo omnes urbes quæ manebant in statu suo non combussit Israel, præter Hasor solam quam combussit Josue.

14. And all the spoil of these cities, and the cattle, the children of Israel took for a prey unto themselves; but every man they smote with the edge of the sword, until they had destroyed them, neither left they any to breathe.

14. Et omnia spolia urbium istarum, et jumenta prædati sunt sibi filii Israel: veruntamen omnes homines percusserunt acie gladii quousque perderent eos: non reliquerunt ullam animam.

15. As the Lord commanded Moses his servant, so did Moses command Joshua, and so did Joshua: he left nothing undone of all that the Lord commanded Moses.

15. Quemadmodum præceperat Jehova Mosi servo suo: sic præcepit Moses Josue, et Josue sic fecit, ut non omitteret quidquam ex omnibus quæ præceperat Jehova Mosi.

1. *And it came to pass when Jabin,* &c. In this new league also we have a bright manifestation of the more than paternal care of God, in warding off dangers from his people, and also in assisting their weakness by kindness and indulgence. Had Jabin, with the confederates of whom mention is now made, openly declared himself the ally of the neighbouring kings, a much more formidable war would have broken out against the Israelites, and greater solicitude and anxiety must have seized their minds. It would, indeed, have been easy for the Lord, as well to put all their forces at once to the rout, as to dissipate all fear and dread of them. He was unwilling, however, to press beyond measure his own people, who were otherwise feeble, lest the excessive numbers of the enemy should strike them with terror, and drive them to despair. He therefore kept the many nations, whose interest it was to have rushed hastily to arms, in a state of lethargy and amazement, until the chosen people had been animated by signal victories, to carry on the wars which still remained. They pillage and devastate a large territory, and leave it destitute of inhabitants and stript of resources. None of the neighbouring powers, who were afterwards to act on the offensive, makes the least movement. The Israelites revisit their wives and children in safety. When they had gathered courage, and were ready for a new war, suddenly a very large army appears, composed of different nations, who had hitherto, by remaining quiet, furnished opportunity for victory. Their coming thus forward at a later period, was the same as if they had entered into a truce. Thus God not only fought for his chosen people, but by dividing the enemy, increased their strength manifold.

How formidable must the onset have been, had not the Israelites been gradually trained to confidence in battle, and at the same time experienced the manifest assistance of God? First, their numbers are compared to the sand of the sea, and then they have horses and chariots. As the Israelites were altogether destitute of cavalry, it is strange that they were not terrified at this array. Therefore they were gradually brought forward till they were able to bear it. For, in their former battles, he had only exercised them by a kind of pleasing preludes.[1] It may be added, that the Lord had, by several victories, ever and anon borne testimony to his power, that they might not think more lightly of it than was meet. Had all their enemies been routed at once, they might, indeed, have magnificently celebrated the praises of God, but they might also have easily lost the remembrance of them. It was necessary, therefore, that repeated proofs distinct and apart from each other, should be held forth to their view, lest they might attribute one victory to a stroke of fortune.

6. *And the Lord said unto Joshua, &c.* The greater the labour and difficulty of destroying an army, so numerous and so well equipped, the more necessary was it to inspire them with new confidence. The Lord, therefore, appears to his servant Joshua, and promises the same success as he had previously given him on several occasions. It is to be carefully observed, that as often as he reiterates his promises men are reminded of their forgetfulness, or their sloth, or their fickleness. For unless new nourishment is every now and then given to faith, they forthwith faint and fall away.[2] And yet such is our perverse fastidiousness, that to hear the same thing twice is usually felt to be irksome. Wherefore let us learn, as often as we are called to engage in new contests, to recall the remembrance of the divine promises, which may correct our languor, or rouse us from our sloth. And especially let us make an application of that which is here said in general, to our daily practice; as the Lord now intimates, that that which he had declared concerning all nations would be specially sure and stable on the present occasion.

We infer from the account of the time employed, that these kings had marched a considerable distance, in order to attack Joshua and the people in Gilgal. For immediately after the divine intimation, mention is made of the expedition used by Joshua.[3] He is promised the victory on the following

[1] Latin, "Jucundis præludiis." French, "Escarmouches plaisantes;" "Pleasing skirmishes."—*Ed.*

[2] French, "Elle secoule et evanouist; "It" (faith) "melts and vanishes." —*Ed.*

[3] Latin, "Oraculo enim subnectitur expeditio Josue." French, "Car l'expedition de Josué est conjointe avec l'avertissement que Dieu luy

day. Hence they were not far distant. And the lake of Merom, where they had pitched their camp, is contiguous to the Jordan, and much nearer to Gilgal than Gennesaret, from which district some of the enemy had come.[1] It is said that this lake diminishes or increases according to the freezing of the snow on the mountains, or to its melting. Moreover, the

donne;" "For the expedition of Joshua is conjoined with the intimation which God gives him."—*Ed.*

[1] Latin, "Et lacus Merom, ubi castra locaverant, qui Jordani contiguus est, longe propius accedit ad Gilgal quam Gennesara ex cujus tractu pars hostium profecta erat." French, "Et le lac de Merom ou ils s'estoyent campez, qui est contigu au Jourdain, approche beaucoup plus pres de Gilgal que ne fait Genesara, du rivage duquel une partie des ennemis s'estoit levée;" "And the lake of Merom, where they had encamped, which is contiguous to the Jordan, approaches much nearer to Gilgal than Gennesaret does, on the shores of which a part of the enemy had been raised." The geographical details here given, and more especially those relating to the lake of Merom, are both defective and inaccurate. The impression left by the Commentary is, that after the kings, composing this formidable league, had united their forces, they began to march southwards, and had arrived within a moderate distance of Gilgal, where they probably expected to come suddenly on Joshua, and take him by surprise. Meanwhile they encamped by the lake of Merom, and Joshua having, in consequence of a divine intimation, set out hastily with his army, gives them the surprise which they expected to have given him. According to this view, the lake of Merom was comparatively near to Gilgal, and hence this is distinctly asserted in the Latin and French quotation which commences this note. The French says plainly, that there was a shorter distance to Gilgal from the lake of Merom than from that of Gennesaret. And the Latin, though not free from ambiguity, says, either the same thing or something still more inacurate, namely, that the lake of Merom was nearer to Gilgal than to the lake of Gennesaret. On the contrary, it is now well known, that the lake of Merom, the modern El Hule, is situated ten miles to the north of the lake of Gennesaret, and consequently is exactly that number of miles farther from Gilgal than the lake of Gennesaret is, the distances of the lakes from Gilgal being respectively, for Merom, about seventy-five, and for Gennesaret sixty-five miles. Such being the fact, it is obvious that Joshua could not have been at Gilgal when he was honoured with a divine communication, promising him the victory on the following day. The true state of the case seems to be, that after Joshua had conquered the central and southern parts of the country, a number of kings or chiefs, whose territories extended over the whole of the north of the promised land, entered into a common league, and appointed the lake of Merom as their place of rendezvous. Joshua, well informed of the league, and alive to its formidable nature, did not wait to give the enemy time to mature their schemes, or remain inert till they were actually within a day's march of his camp, but set out with a determination to act on the offensive, and with this view had advanced far to the north, into the very heart of the enemy's country, when any fears which their formidable array might have produced, either in himself or his army, were completely removed by the assurance of speedy and signal success.—*Ed.*

command given to Joshua and the people, to cut the legs or thighs of the horses, and to burn the chariots, was undoubtedly intended to prevent them from adopting those more studied modes of warfare which were in use among profane nations. It was indeed necessary that they should serve as soldiers, and fight strenuously with the enemy, but still they were to depend only on the Lord, to consider themselves strong only in his might, and to recline on him alone.

This could scarcely have been the case, if they had been provided with cavalry, and an array of chariots. For we know how such showy equipment dazzles the eye, and intoxicates the mind with overweening confidence. Moreover, a law had been enacted, (Deut. xvii. 16,) that their kings were not to provide themselves with horses and chariots, obviously because they would have been extremely apt to ascribe to their own military discipline that which God claimed for himself. Hence the common saying, (Psalm xx. 7,) "Some trust in chariots and some in horses, but we will remember the name of the Lord our God." God wished to deprive them of all stimulants to audacity, in order that they might live quietly contented with their own limits, and not unjustly attack their neighbours. And experience shewed, that when a bad ambition had impelled their kings to buy horses, they engaged in wars not less rashly than unsuccessfully. It was necessary, therefore, to render the horses useless for war, by cutting their sinews, and to destroy the chariots, in order that the Israelites might not become accustomed to the practices of the heathen.

8. *And the Lord delivered them*, &c. The greatness of the overthrow may be inferred from this, that the slaughter continued as far as Sidon, which was far distant from the lake of Merom. Sidon is called great, from its celebrity as a commercial emporium and the great number of its inhabitants. There is no comparison instituted between it and a minor town of same name. The Hebrew noun Mozerephoth, which some retain without change as a proper name, we have preferred to translate "the boiling of the waters," because it is probable that there were thermal springs there, which boiled. Moreover, as the panic which hurried them away

into such a scattered flight, plainly shews that they were driven headlong by the secret terror of the Lord. So it is certain that the Israelites who dared to follow the fugitives through so many dangers were carried to a higher pitch of valour than human by celestial agency.

Praise is bestowed on Joshua as well for his abstinence as for his prompt obedience. Nor would he have submitted so willingly to the loss of so many horses and chariots, had not the fear of God overawed him. For such is our ingenuity in devising pretexts, it would have been plausible to allege, that though he could not fit them for military use, still their value was by no means to be despised. But he thought that he had no right to take anything into consideration but the pleasure of God. Then, as he had succeeded by his own good conduct, in making the people willing and obedient, he, as an individual, justly received the praise of what had been performed generally by all.

12. *And all the cities of those kings*, &c. Having routed the army, they began to plunder and lay waste the country, and to take and demolish the towns. From its being said that the cities which remained entire were not burned, it may be inferred with some probability, that some were taken by force and assault, and so razed. Hazor, alone, after the siege was over, and the heat of the struggle had cooled, was destroyed by fire, because it had held forth the torch which enkindled the war. But in accordance with the explanation already given, it is repeatedly and more clearly stated in this passage, that Joshua did not give loose reins to his passion, when he slew all from the least to the greatest. For there is now a distinct statement of what had not yet been expressed, namely, that Joshua faithfully performed his part, by fulfilling everything which the Lord had enjoined by Moses. It is just as if he had placed his hands at the disposal of God, when he destroyed those nations according to his command. And so ought we to hold that, though the whole world should condemn us, it is sufficient to free us from all blame, that we have the authority of God.[1] Meanwhile, it becomes us pru-

[1] Latin, "Deum habere authorem." French, "Que nous ayons Dieu pour garant et autheur de ce que nous faisons;" "That we have God as guarantee and author for what we do."—*Ed.*

dently to consider, what each man's vocation requires, lest any one, by giving license to his zeal, as wishing to imitate Joshua, may be judged cruel and sanguinary, rather than a strict servant of God.

16. So Joshua took all that land, the hills, and all the south country, and all the land of Goshen, and the valley, and the plain, and the mountain of Israel, and the valley of the same;

17. *Even* from the mount Halak, that goeth up to Seir, even unto Baalgad in the valley of Lebanon, under mount Hermon: and all their kings he took, and smote them, and slew them.

18. Joshua made war a long time with all those kings.

19. There was not a city that made peace with the children of Israel, save the Hivites, the inhabitants of Gibeon: all *other* they took in battle.

20. For it was of the Lord to harden their hearts, that they should come against Israel in battle, that he might destroy them utterly, *and* that they might have no favour, but that he might destroy them, as the Lord commanded Moses.

21. And at that time came Joshua, and cut off the Anakims from the mountains, from Hebron, from Debir, from Anab, and from all the mountains of Judah, and from all the mountains of Israel: Joshua destroyed them uttely with their cities.

22. There was none of the Anakims left in the land of the children of Israel: only in Gaza, in Gath, and in Ashdod, there remained.

23. So Joshua took the whole land, according to all that the Lord said unto Moses, and Joshua gave it for an inheritance unto Israel, according to their divisions by their tribes. And the land rested from war.

16. Et cepit Josue omnem terram istam montanam, et omnem australem, omnemque Gosen et planitiem atque campestria, montem quoqueIsrael et planitiem ejus.

17. A monte Lævi qui assurgit versus Seir usque ad Baalgad in campo Libani sub monte Hermon: omnes quoque reges eorum cepit, et percussit eos et interfecit.

18. Diebus multis gessit Josue cum omnibus regibus istis bellum.

19. Non fuit urbs quæ pacem fecerit cum filiis Israel præter Hivæos habitatores Gibeon: omnes cœperunt prælio.

20. Quia a Jehova fuit, ut induraret cor eorum in occursum belli cum Israel: ut deleret eos, nec restaret illis misericordia: sed ut disperderet eos, sicut præceperat Jehova Mosi.

21. Venit autem Josue tempore illo, et excidit Anakim e montanis: ex Hebron, ex Debir, ex Anab, et ex omni monte Jehuda, et ex omni monte Israel: una cum urbibus eorum delevit eos Josue.

22. Non remansit ex Anakim in terra filiorum Israel: tantum in Gad et in Asdod residui fuerunt.

23. Accepit itaque Josue totam terram prorsus ut dixerat Jehova Mosi, et tradidit eam in hæreditatem Israeli secundum divisiones eorum per tribus suas: et terra quievit a bello.

16. *So Joshua took all that land,* &c. In the uninterrupted series of victories, when the land, of its own accord, spued out its old inhabitants, to give free possession to the Israelites, it was visibly manifest, as is said in the Psalm, (Ps. xliv. 3,) " They got not the land in possession by their own

sword, neither did their own arm save them; but thy right hand, and thine arm, and the light of thy countenance, because thou hadst a favour unto them." The design of enumerating the places and districts is to let us know that the work which God had begun he continued to carry on without interruption. But it is a mistake to suppose, as some do, that by the name Israel a certain mountain is meant. For it will be plain, from the end of the chapter, (ver. 21,) that the term is applied indiscriminately to the mountainous part of Israel and Judah. There is therefore an enallage in the enumeration, because the mountains of the ten tribes are tacitly compared with the mountains of Judah. Accordingly, an antithesis is to be understood. In the other mountain (ver. 17) the surname is ambiguous. Some understand it to mean *division*, as if it had been cut in two;[1] others to mean *smooth*, as it was destitute of trees, just as a head is rendered smooth by baldness. As the point is uncertain, and of little importance, the reader is at liberty to make his choice.

18. *Joshua made war a long time*, &c. Before, he had in a short time, and, as it were, with the swiftness of running, seized possession of five kingdoms; in the others the case was different, not from hesitation, or weariness, or sloth, but because the Lord exercised his people variously, that he might give a brighter display of his manifold grace, which usually loses its value in our eyes, if it is exhibited only in one and the same way. Therefore, as the divine power had formerly been signally manifested by incredible facility of accomplishment, when the enemy were routed in an instant, so a lingering warfare now furnished numerous proofs of heavenly aid.[2] Nor did this happen suddenly and unex-

[1] Latin, "Dissectus." French, "Couppée ou fendue;" "Cut, or cleft." —*Ed.*

[2] According to Josephus, (Antiquit., v. 2,) the time which Joshua spent in his wars was five years; others make it seven, and justify their estimate by the following calculation:—In Joshua xiv. 7-10, Caleb says that he was forty years old when he was sent from Kadesh-Barnea to spy out the land, and that since then to the present time (apparently that when the wars had just terminated) forty-five years had elapsed. Of these forty-five years, thirty-eight were spent in the desert, and consequently the remaining seven constitute the whole period which had elapsed from the passage of the Jordan up to the time when Caleb made his statement.—*Ed.*

pectedly; for God had foretold by Moses that so it would be, lest, if the land were at once converted into a desert, the wild beasts might gain the ascendency. (Deut. vii. 22.) In short, we here perceive, as in a mirror, that whatever the Lord had promised by Moses was accomplished in reality, and by no dubious event. But while we recognise the certainty of the promises of God, we ought also to meditate on the favour confirmed towards his chosen people, in that he acted as the provident head of a family, not neglecting or omitting anything which tended to their advantage.

19. *There was not a city that made peace*, &c. This sentence appears, at first sight, contradictory to what is everywhere said in the books of Moses, that the Israelites were not to enter into any league with those nations, or make any terms of peace with them, but, on the contrary, to destroy them utterly, and wipe out their race and name. (Exod. xxiii. 32; Deut. vii. 2.)[1] Seeing the nations were thus excluded from the means of making any paction, and would in vain have made any proposals for peace, it seems absurd to ascribe the destruction, which they had not even the means of deprecating, to their obstinacy.

For, let us suppose that they had sent ambassadors before them with olive branches in their hands, and had been intent on pacific measures, Joshua would at once have answered that he could not lawfully enter into any negotiation, as the Lord had forbidden it. Wherefore, had they made a hundred attempts to avoid war, they must, nevertheless, have perished. Why, then, are they blamed for not having sought peace, as if they had not been driven by necessity to fight, after they saw they had to do with an implacable people? But if it was not free to them to act otherwise, it is unjust to lay any blame upon them when they acted under compulsion in opposing the fury of their enemy.

[1] The Septuagint, as if influenced by considerations similar to those here mentioned, has evaded the apparent inconsistency, by rendering the 19th verse as follows, "And there was not a city which Israel did not take: they took all in war." There is a various reading, however, which corresponds almost verbatim with the common rendering.—*Ed.*

To this objection, I answer, that the Israelites, though they were forbidden to shew them any mercy, were met in a hostile manner, in order that the war might be just. And it was wonderfully arranged by the secret providence of God, that, being doomed to destruction, they should voluntarily offer themselves to it, and by provoking the Israelites be the cause of their own ruin. The Lord, therefore, besides ordering that pardon should be denied them, also incited them to blind fury, that no room might be left for mercy. And it behoved the people not to be too wise or prying in this matter. For while the Lord, on the one hand, interdicted them from entering into any covenant, and, on the other, was unwilling that they should take hostile measures without being provoked, a too anxious discussion of the procedure might have greatly unsettled their minds. Hence the only way of freeing themselves from perplexity was to lay their care on the bosom of God. And he in his incomprehensible wisdom provided that when the time for action arrived, his people should not be impeded in their course by any obstacle. Thus the kings beyond the Jordan, as they had been the first to take up arms, justly suffered the punishment of their temerity. For the Israelites did not assail them with hostile arms until they had been provoked. In the same way, also, the citizens of Jericho, by having shut their gates, were the first to declare war. The case is the same with the others, who, by their obstinacy, furnished the Israelites with a ground for prosecuting the war.

It now appears how perfectly consistent the two things are. The Lord commanded Moses to destroy the nations whom he had doomed to destruction; and he accordingly opened a way for his own decree when he hardened the reprobate. In the first place, then, stands the will of God, which must be regarded as the principal cause. For seeing their iniquity had reached its height, he determined to destroy them. This was the origin of the command given to Moses, a command, however, which would have failed of its effect had not the chosen people been armed to execute the divine judgment, by the perverseness and obstinacy of those who were to be destroyed. God hardens them for this very end, that they may shut themselves out from mercy.[1] Hence that hardness is called his work, because it secures the accomplishment of his design. Should any attempt be made to darken so clear a matter by those who imagine that God only looks down from heaven to see what men will be pleased to do, and who cannot bear to think that the hearts of men are curbed by his secret agency, what else do they display than their own presumption? They only allow God a permissive power, and in this way make his counsel dependent on the pleasure of men. But what saith the Spirit? That the hardening is from God, who thus precipitates those whom he means to destroy.

21. *And at that time came Joshua,* &c. Of the sons of Anak we have spoken elsewhere. They were a race of giants, with the account of whose mighty stature the spies so terrified the people, that they refused to proceed into the land of Canaan. Therefore, seeing they were objects of so much dread, it was of importance that they should be put out of the way, and the people made more alert by their good hopes of success. It would have been exceedingly injurious[2] to keep objects which filled them with alarm and anxiety always present before their minds, inasmuch as fear obscured the glory ascribed to God for former victories, and overthrew their faith, while they reflected that the most difficult of all their contests still awaited them. Therefore, not without cause is it mentioned among the other instances of divine aid, that by purging the land of such monsters, it was rendered a fit habitation for the people. The less credible it seemed that they could be warred against with success, the more illustriously was the divine power displayed.

23. *So Joshua took the whole land,*[3] &c. Although it was

[1] French, "Dieu les endurcit, afin qu'ils se monstrent indigne de toute pitié et compassion qu'on eust peu avoir d'eux;" "God hardens them in order that they may show themselves unworthy of all pity and compassion which might have been felt for them."—*Ed.*

[2] Latin, "Perquam noxium." French, "Fort dangereuse;" "Very dangerous."—*Ed.*

[3] The Latin text of the 23d verse, beginning thus, "Accepit itaque Josue totam terram prorsus ut dixerat Jehova Mosi;" "Joshua, therefore, received the whole land entirely, as the Lord had said to Moses," removes the apparent inaccuracy, but it is only by a sacrifice of the literal meaning,

far from being true that Joshua had actually acquired the whole land, yet he is truly said to have obtained it as God had declared to Moses, the latter clause restricting the meaning of the general sentence. For it had been expressly added that the conquest which God had promised would be made gradually, lest it should afterwards become necessary to war with the ferocious wild beasts of the woods, if they pressed forward into a desert waste. Therefore, we are at liberty to say, that though the Lord had not yet placed his people in possession of the promised land, yet he had virtually performed what he had agreed to do, inasmuch as he gave a commodious habitation, and one which was sufficient for the present time. And the words used imply that other districts, which had not yet come into their full and actual possession, are included; for it is said that that which they had acquired was distributed according to families. And, in short, we afterwards see in the division that the lands were divided into lots which were not actually subdued by the people till Joshua was dead, nay, till many ages after.[1] The meaning of the words, which is now plain, is simply this, that while Joshua was still alive, a certain specimen of the promise was exhibited, making him feel perfectly secure in dividing the land by lot.[2]

which is perfectly rendered by the English version. "So (And) Joshua took the whole land, *according to all* that the Lord said unto Moses." This is certainly superior to the Latin, which endeavours to obtain by a gloss that which the English equally well obtains by a literal rendering. In the commentary, the words of the 23d verse, as quoted, are, *Et cepit Josue.* This makes it not improbable that the *Accepit* of the text is only a misprint for *Et cepit.—Ed.*

[1] French, "Or en la division nous verrons puis apres, que les regions qui furent assujetties à l'empire du peuple apres la mort de Josué, voire plusieurs siecles depuis, furent mises en sort pour voir à qui elles escherroyent;" "Now, in the division, we shall afterwards see that the countries which were subjected to the dominion of the people after the death of Joshua, nay, several ages after, were put into the lot, in order to see to whom they should fall."

[2] Latin, "Exhibitum fuisse certum specimen promissionis ut secure licuerit terram sorte dividere." French, "La promesse fut tellement ratifiee, et si bien eprouvee par effect, qu'il leur fut loisible de diviser la terre par sort;" "The promise was so far ratified and proved by fact, that they were able at leisure to divide the land by lot."—*Ed.*

CHAPTER XII.

1. Now these *are* the kings of the land, which the children of Israel smote, and possessed their land on the other side Jordan, toward the rising of the sun, from the river Arnon unto mount Hermon, and all the plain on the east:

2. Sihon king of the Amorites, who dwelt in Heshbon, *and* ruled from Aroer, which *is* upon the bank of the river Arnon, and from the middle of the river, and from half Gilead, even unto the river Jabbok, *which is* the border of the children of Ammon:

3. And from the plain to the sea of Chinneroth on the east, and unto the sea of the plain, *even* the salt sea on the east, the way to Beth-jeshimoth; and from the south, under Ashdoth-pisgah:

4. And the coast of Og king of Bashan, *which was* of the remnant of the giants, that dwelt at Ashtaroth and at Edrei,

5. And reigned in mount Hermon, and in Salcah, and in all Bashan, unto the border of the Geshurites, and the Maachathites, and half Gilead, the border of Sihon king of Heshbon:

6. Them did Moses, the servant of the Lord, and the children of Israel, smite: and Moses, the servant of the Lord, gave it *for* a possession unto the Reubenites, and the Gadites, and the half-tribe of Manasseh.

7. And these *are* the kings of the country which Joshua and the children of Israel smote on this side Jordan on the west, from Baal-gad in the valley of Lebanon, even unto the mount Halak, that goeth up to Seir; which Joshua gave unto the tribes of Israel *for* a possession, according to their divisions:

8. In the mountains, and in the valleys, and in the plains, and in the springs, and in the wilderness, and in the south country; the Hittites, the Amorites, and the Canaanites, the Perizzites, the Hivites, and the Jebusites:

1. Hi sunt reges terræ quos percusserunt filii Israel, et quorum possederunt terram trans Jordanem, ad ortum solis a torrente Arnon usque ad montem Hermon, et omnem planitiem orientalem.

2. Sihon rex Æmorrhæus qui habitabat in Hesbon, qui dominabatur ab Aroer ad ripam torrentis Arnon, et ad medium torrentis, et ad mediam partem Gilead, usque ad Jabbok torrentem, qui est terminus filiorum Ammon.

3. Et a planitie usque ad mare Cineroth ad orientem, et usque ad mare deserti, mare salis ad orientem per viam Beth-hagesimoth, et ab austro sub effusionibus Pisga.

4. Terminus præterea Og regis Basan ex residuo Raphaim qui habitabat in Astaroth, et in Hedrei.

5. Qui dominabatur in monte Hermon, et in Salchah, et in toto Basan, usque ad terminum Gessuri, et Maachati: et mediam partem Gilead, terminus Sihon regis Hesbon.

6. Moses servus Jehovæ, et filii Israel percusserunt eos, et dedit eam Moses servus Jehovæ in possessionem Rubenitis, et Gaditis, et dimidiæ tribui Manasse.

7. Isti autem sunt reges terræ quos percussit Josue, et filii Israel trans Jordanem ad occidentem, a Baal-gad in campo Libani, usque ad montem Lævem qui assurgit in Seir, et tradidit eam Josue tribubus Israel in possessionem secundum partes eorum.

8. In montanis, et in planitie, et in campestribus, et in Asdoth, et in deserto, et in austro: Hithæus, Æmorrhæus, Chananæus, Pherisæus, Hivæus, et Jebusæus.

9. The king of Jericho, one; the king of Ai, which *is* beside Beth-el, one;

10. The king of Jerusalem, one; the king of Hebron, one;

11. The king of Jarmuth, one; the king of Lachish, one;

12. The king of Eglon, one; the king of Gezer, one;

13. The king of Debir, one; the king of Geder, one;

14. The king of Hormah, one; the king of Arad, one;

15. The king of Libnah, one; the king of Adullam, one;

16. The king of Makkedah, one; the king of Beth-el, one;

17. The king of Tappuah, one; the king of Hepher, one;

18. The king of Aphek, one; the king of Lasharon, one;

19. The king of Madon, one; the king of Hazor, one;

20. The king of Shimron-meron, one; the king of Achshaph, one;

21. The king of Taanach, one; the king of Megiddo, one;

22. The king of Kedesh, one; the king of Jokneam of Carmel, one;

23. The king of Dor, in the coast of Dor, one; the king of the nations of Gilgal, one;

24. The king of Tirzah, one: all the kings thirty and one.

9. Rex Jericho unus, rex Ai, qui erat e latere Bethel unus.

10. Rex Jerusalem unus, rex Hebron unus.

11. Rex Jarmuth unus, rex Lachis unus.

12. Rex Eglon unus, rex Jeser unus.

13. Rex Debir unus, rex Jeder unus.

14. Rex Hormah unus, rex Arad unus.

15. Rex Libna unus, rex Adullam unus.

16. Rex Makeda unus, rex Beth-el unus.

17. Rex Tapua unus, rex Epher unus.

18. Rex Aphek unus, rex Lasaron unus.

19. Rex Madon unus, rex Asor unus.

20. Rex Simron-Meron unus, rex Achsaph unus.

21. Rex Taanach unus, rex Megiddo unus.

22. Rex Kedesch unus, rex Jocnam ad Carmelum unus.

23. Rex Dor ad Naphath-dor unus, rex Goim in Gilgal unus.

24. Rex Thirsa unus: omnes reges triginta et unus.

1. *Now these are the kings,* &c. This chapter does not need a lengthened exposition, as it only enumerates the kings of whose territories the Israelites gained possession. Two of them are beyond the Jordan, Og and Sihon, whose rule was extensive; in the land of Canaan there are thirty-one. But though each of those now summarily mentioned was previously given more in detail, there is very good reason for here placing before our eyes as it were a living picture of the goodness of God, proving that there had been a complete ratification and performance of the covenant made with Abraham as given in the words, "Unto thy seed will I give this land." (Gen. xii. 7; xiii. 15; xv. 18.) This living image of the grace of God is here set before us as if

the reality were actually present.[1] Joshua was eighty years of age when he entered the land. In this aged man how could there be so much vigour[2] as to fit him for carrying on so many wars and enduring the fatigues of warfare, had not celestial virtue furnished him with more than mortal strength? And were not his uninterrupted career of victory, his success under all circumstances, the ease, free from doubt and uncertainty, with which he stormed cities, the rapidity of his movements, and his inflexible firmness—were not all these clear evidences of the hand of God, just as if it had appeared from heaven?

The object of defining the countries by their boundaries was to give a better display of the divine power by setting forth their extent; but this of course was only for those to whom their site was known. Hence, for any one not acquainted with the geography to dwell upon the names, would be vain and foolish curiosity. I admit, indeed, that it is useful to pay attention to the places with which, from their being often mentioned in Scripture, our knowledge ought to be somewhat more familiar, as when the boundaries are fixed by the brook Jabok, in the district of Lebanon and the lake of Gennesaret, here called the Sea of Cineroth, and elsewhere Cinereth. For a slight attention will help us to understand the narrative. If we cannot go farther, let us leave those who are better skilled to give a more searching discussion of what is beyond our reach.[3] But although the dominions of these petty kings were narrow and not very populous, we shall however see that many towns were annexed to their principal cities; their number may be

[1] Latin, " Quam si nos Deus in rem præsentem adduceret." French, " Comme si Dieu nous mettoit presentement sur le faict, pour nous faire voire la chose de nos yeux;" " As if God were putting us actually upon the spot to make us see the thing with our own eyes."—*Ed.*

[2] French, " Comment un povre vieillard pouvoit-il estre si vigoureux;" " How could a poor old man be so vigorous."—*Ed.*

[3] It is evident from these remarks, that though in some other passages Calvin seems to speak rather disparagingly of the elucidation which the Scripture narrative may receive from geography, he did not so much underrate its importance as lament its imperfection at the period when he wrote. All complaint on this head has now been happily removed; and it may safely be affirmed, that nothing has done more to clear up obscurities in the Sacred Volume and triumphantly establish its strict and literal accuracy, than the labours and discoveries of recent travellers.

ascertained especially from what is said of the lot of the Levites. On the other hand, if we reflect how one small territory could receive and maintain old men, women, and children, nay, a great part of the people with their domestic animals, we cannot fail to admire the inestimable goodness of God which prevented all things from being thrown into complete and irremediable confusion.[1]

CHAPTER XIII.

1. Now Joshua was old *and* stricken in years; and the Lord said unto him, Thou art old *and* stricken in years, and there remaineth yet very much land to be possessed.

2. This *is* the land that yet remaineth: all the borders of the Philistines, and all Geshuri,

3. From Sihor, which *is* before Egypt, even unto the borders of Ekron northward, *which* is counted to the Canaanite: five lords of the Philistines; the Gazathites, and the Ashdothites, the Eshkalonites, the Gittites, and the Ekronites; also the Avites.

4. From the south, all the land of the Canaanites, and Mearah that *is* beside the Sidonians, unto Aphek, to the borders of the Amorites;

5. And the land of the Giblites, and all Lebanon toward the sun-rising, from Baal-gad under mount Hermon, unto the entering into Hamath:

6. All the inhabitants of the hill-country, from Lebanon unto Misrephoth-maim, *and* all the Sidonians, them will I drive out from before the children of Israel; only divide thou it by lot unto the Israelites for an inheritance, as I have commanded thee.

7. Now therefore divide this land for an inheritance unto the nine tribes, and the half-tribe of Manasseh;

1. Quum autem senuisset Josue, et venisset in dies, dixit ei Jehova, Tu senuisti, venisti in dies, et multa terra admodum superest ad possidendum.

2. Hæc est terra quæ residua est, omnes limites Philisthinorum, et omnis Gessuri.

3. A Nilo qui est e regione Ægypti usque ad terminum Ecron, qui est ab aquilone, quæ Chananeæ reputatur, quinque principatus Philisthinorum, Azathæus, Asdodæus, Ascalonæus, Gitthæus et Ekronæus et Auæi.

4. Ab austro universa terra Chananæi et Meara, quæ est Sidoniorum usque ad Pæra, usque ad terminum Æmorrhæi.

5. Et terra Gibli, et totus Libanus ad ortum solis a Baal-gad sub monte Hermon, donec pervenias Hemath.

6. Omnes habitatores montis a Libano usque ad fervores aquarum: omnes Sidonios ego expellam a facie filiorum Israel: tantum jacias sortem, ut sit in hæreditatem Israeli, sicut præcepi tibi.

7. Nunc ergo divide terram istam in hæreditatem novem tribubus, et dimidiæ tribui Manasse.

[1] Latin, "Ne horribili confusione, omnia miscerentur." French, "Que tout ne vint à estre brouillé pesle mesle d'une confusion horrible;" "That every thing was not hurled pell-mell into horrible confusion."—*Ed.*

8. With whom the Reubenites and the Gadites have received their inheritance, which Moses gave them, beyond Jordan eastward, *even* as Moses, the servant of the Lord, gave them;

9. From Aroer, that *is* upon the bank of the river Arnon, and the city that *is* in the midst of the river, and all the plain of Medeba unto Dibon;

10. And all the cities of Sihon king of the Amorites, which reigned in Heshbon, unto the border of the children of Ammon;

11. And Gilead, and the border of the Geshurites and Maachathites, and all mount Hermon, and all Bashan unto Salcah;

12. All the kingdom of Og in Bashan, which reigned in Ashtaroth and in Edrei, who remained of the remnant of the giants: for these did Moses smite, and cast them out.

13. Nevertheless the children of Israel expelled not the Geshurites, nor the Maachathites; but the Geshurites and the Maachathites dwell among the Israelites until this day.

14. Only unto the tribe of Levi he gave none inheritance; the sacrifices of the Lord God of Israel made by fire *are* their inheritance, as he said unto them.

8. Præter eam Rubenitæ, et Gaditæ acceperunt partes suas, quas dedit iis Moses trans Jordanem ad orientem, sicut dedit eis Moses servus Jehovæ.

9. Ab Aroer quæ est juxta ripam fluminis Arnon, et urbem ipsam quæ est in medio vallis, et totam planitiem Medeba usque ad Dibon.

10. Et omnes urbes Sihon regis Æmorrhæi, qui regnabat in Hesbon, usque ad terminum filiorum Ammon.

11. Et Gilead et terminum Gessuri, et Maachati, et totum montem Hermon, et universum Basan usque ad Salchah.

12. Universum regnum Og in Basan, qui regnabat in Astaroth, et in Edrei: hic supererat ex residuo Rephaim, quos percussit Moses et expulit.

13. Non expulerunt autem filii Israel Gessuri et Maachati: propterea habitavit Gessur et Maachat in medio Israel usque ad hunc diem.

14. Tantum tribui Levi non dedit hæreditatem, sacrificia Jehovæ Dei Israel sunt hereditas ejus, quemadmodum loquutus est de ea.

1. *Now Joshua was old,* &c.[1] Since we have seen above that the land was pacified by the subjugation of thirty-one kings, it is probable that some cessation now took place for the purpose of resting from their fatigues, lest the people should be worn out by continual service. Nor could that

[1] The words, "old and stricken in years," do not contain a tautology, but accurately express the period of life according to a division which was long familiar to the Jews, and may have been not unknown to them even at this early period. According to this division, old age consisted of three stages,—the *first* extending from the sixtieth to the seventieth year, constituting the commencement of old age properly so called; the *second* extending from the seventieth to the eightieth year, and constituting what was called *hoary*, or *hoary-headed* age; and the *third* extending from the eightieth year to the end of life, and constituting what was called *advanced* age, and caused the person who had reached it to be described as one stricken in years. At this closing stage Joshua had now arrived.—*Ed.*

justly be blamed, provided they rested only for a time and continued always intent on the goal set before them. But lest that intermission which was given for the purpose of recruiting new vigour might prove an occasion of sloth, the Lord employs a new stimulus to urge them to proceed. For he orders the whole inheritance to be divided into tribes, and the whole line of the Mediterranean coast which was possessed by the enemy to be put into the lot. A division of this kind might indeed seem absurd and ludicrous, nay, a complete mockery, seeing they were dealing among themselves with the property of others just as if it had been their own. But the Lord so appointed for the best of reasons. *First*, they might have cast away the hope of the promise and been contented with their present state. Nay, although after the lot was cast they had security in full for all that God had promised, they by their own cowardice, as far as in them lay, destroyed the credit of his words. Nor was it owing to any merit of theirs that his veracity did not lie curtailed and mutilated. The allocation by lot must therefore have been to them an earnest of certain possession so as to keep them always in readiness for it. *Secondly*, Those who happened to have their portion assigned in an enemy's country, inasmuch as they were living in the meanwhile as strangers on precarious hospitality beyond their own inheritance, must have acted like a kind of task-masters spurring on the others. And it surely implied excessive stupor to neglect and abandon what had been divinely assigned to them.

We now see to what intent the whole land behoved to be divided by lot, and the seat of each tribe allocated. It was also necessary that this should be done while Joshua was alive, because after his death the Israelites would have been less inclined to obedience, for none of his successors possessed authority sufficient for the execution of so difficult a task. Moreover, as God had already by the mouth of Moses commanded it to be done, had he not performed the business thus committed to him, the whole work might have gone to wreck when the lawful minister was removed. Although the exact time is not stated, still it is probable that as there was no hope that while Joshua continued alive the people would again take up arms with the view of giving a wider extent to their boundaries, he then only attempted to divide the land, as if he were proclaiming and promising, by a solemn attestation, that the distribution would certainly be carried into effect, because the truth of God could not fail in consequence of the death of any man.

2. *This is the land,* &c. The ancient boundaries long ago fixed by God, are recalled to remembrance, in order that Joshua and the people may feel fully persuaded that the covenant made with Abraham would be fulfilled in every part. Wherefore they are enjoined to make it their study to acquire the parts still remaining to be possessed. The inference will be appropriate if we make a practical application of this perseverance to that which is required of us, viz., to forget the things which are behind, and reach forth unto those that are before, and press toward the mark for the prize of our high calling. (Phil. ii. 14.) For it would be of no use to run in the race without endeavouring to reach the goal.

The boundary commenced with a river separating Egypt toward the sea from the Holy Land, and most probably the river Nile, as we interpret it according to the received opinion, or a small stream which flowed past the town of Rhinocornea, believed by many to be Raphia or Raphane.[1]

[1] The opinion generally entertained in Calvin's time, that the river here meant was the Nile, or at least one of its branches, was founded partly on the meaning of the word *sihor*, which is literally *black*, and was explained by expositors as equivalent to *turbid*, a term strictly applicable to the Nile; and partly from a passage in Jeremiah, (ii. 18,) in which the Prophet asks, "What hast thou to do in the way of Egypt to drink the waters of Sihor?"—Sihor being here undoubtedly used as a proper name for the Nile. The second opinion mentioned by Calvin is now almost universally admitted to be the only one tenable. Even the description here given of Sihor, (ver. 3,) as "before Egypt," is totally inapplicable to the Nile, which, instead of being before Egypt, or on its frontiers, flows nearly through its centre. The river meant and expressly referred to both by Moses (Num. xxxiv. 5) and by Joshua (Josh. xv. 4) under the name of the river of Egypt, is now called the Wady El-Arisch, from the town of that name situated near its mouth, and not far from the site of the ancient Rhinocolura, or perhaps more properly Rhinocorura. Calvin spells Rhinocornea, which if it had not been repeated by the French, might seem to be a misprint.—*Ed.*

It is indeed beyond dispute that the inheritance of the people commencing in that quarter was contiguous to Egypt. But although I have followed the opinion of the majority of expositors, that the boundaries were not extended further than to the less cultivated and in a manner desert land, lest greater proximity might have been injurious by leading to too close familiarity with the Egyptians, I by no means repudiate a different opinion.

The third verse raises a question. After it is said that the territories towards the sea-coast were five, a sixth is added, namely, that of the Avites. Some think that it is not counted among the five because it was an insignificant province. But I would have my readers to consider whether there may not be an indirect antithesis between a free people, their own masters, and five territories ruled by sovereigns. Hence the Avites being in different circumstances are mentioned separately, the plural number being used for the sake of distinction. In the enumeration of the sovereignties they are not arranged in the order of their dignity or opulence, but the first place is given to Aza because of its nearness to Egypt, and the same remark applies to Ashdod and the others.

The Septuagint translators, according to their usual custom, employ the Greek γ (*gamma*) to express the Hebrew ע (*ain*), and thus give the name of Gaza to that which in Hebrew is Aza, in the same way as they convert Amorrha into Gomorrha.[1] This sufficiently exposes the mistake of those who suppose that its name is Persian, and derived from its resources[2] in consequence of Cambyses, when about to carry on war in Greece, having made it the depot of his treasures. But as in the Acts, (viii. 26,) Luke speaks of a

[1] It is here assumed that the only genuine sound represented by the Hebrew letter *Ain* is that of *a*. Is this the fact? Gesenius, on the contrary, while repudiating the modern Jewish pronunciation of it by the nasal *gn* or *ng* as decidedly false, says that its hardest sound is that of a *g* rattled in the throat, and, very remarkably, illustrates his statement by referring to Gaza and Gomorrha, the two words referred to by Calvin in illustration of the contrary. See Gesenius's Hebrew Grammar. (Bagster, 1852, p. 16.)

[2] The French adds, "Et qu'il signifie Richesses;" "And that it means Riches."—*Ed.*

"Gaza which is desert," it appears that a city of the same name was erected near it, but on a different site. Ashdod is the same as that which the Greeks called Azotus. The whole of this tract, which is either on the sea-coast or verging towards it, extends as far as Sidon. And there are some who think that the Phœnicians were once masters both of Gaza and Azotus. How far Lebanon extends is sufficiently known.[1] For it sometimes comprehends Mount Hermon; and on account of its length part of it is surnamed Antilibanus.[2] The reader will find the subject of Mount Hermon considered in the fourth chapter of Deuteronomy. Towards the east is Hamath, which is also Antioch of Syria.

6. *All the inhabitants of the hill country*, &c. Joshua is again admonished, though the Israelites do not yet possess those regions, not to defer the partition, but trust to the promise of God, because it would detract injuriously from his honour if there were any doubt as to the event. It is accordingly said: Only do what is thy duty in the distribution of the land; nor let that which the enemy still hold securely be exempted from the lot; for it will be my care to fulfil what I have promised. Hence let us learn in undertaking any business, so to depend on the lips of God as that no doubt can delay us. It is not ours, indeed, to fabricate vain hopes for ourselves; but when our confidence is founded on the Lord, let us only obey his commands, and there is no reason to fear that the event will disappoint us.

He afterwards assigns the land of Canaan to nine tribes and a half tribe, because the portion of the Reubenites, Gadites, and half tribe of Manasseh had already been assigned beyond the Jordan. Though there is a seeming tautology in the words, Which Moses gave them, as Moses gave them, there is nothing superfluous, because in the second clause the donation is confirmed; as if God were

[1] French, "Quant au Liban, c'est une chose assez notoire quelle longeur d'étendue il a;" "As to Lebanon it is sufficiently well known what length of extent it has."

[2] This is certainly incorrect. Antilibanus received its name, not from its length, but from its being a mountain chain opposite and parallel to Libanus or Lebanon proper, from which it is separated by the beautiful valley known to the Greeks and Romans by the name of Coele-Syria, or rather Koilé (Hollow) Syria, and watered by the Leontes.—*Ed.*

ordering that which was done to be ratified, or saying, in other words, As Moses gave them that land, so let them remain tranquil in the possession of it.[1] For this reason also he is distinguished by the title of servant of God, as if it were said, Let no one interfere with that decree which a faithful minister has pronounced on the authority of God. It was certainly necessary to provide by anticipation against the disputes which otherwise must have daily arisen.

14. *Only unto the tribe of Levi,* &c. This exception was also necessary, lest the Levites might allege that they were unjustly disinherited, and thus excite great commotions in regard to their right. He therefore reminds them that Moses was the author of this distinction, and, at the same time, shews that they have no reason to complain of having been in any way defrauded, because an excellent compensation was given them. For although the sacrifices were not equally divided among the Levites, their subsistence was sufficiently provided for by all the first-fruits and the tithes. Moreover, as God allures them by hire to undertake the charge of sacred things, so he exhorts the people in their turn to be faithful in paying the sacred oblations by declaring that their sacrifices are the maintenance of the Levites.[2]

15. And Moses gave unto the tribe of the children of Reuben *inheritance* according to their families.	15. Dedit ergo Moses tribui filiorum Ruben per familias suas :
16. And their coast was from Aroer, that *is* on the bank of the river Arnon, and the city that *is* in the midst of the river, and all the plain by Medeba ;	16. Fuitque illis terminus ab Aroer, quæ est juxta ripam torrentis Arnon, et urbs quæ est in medio vallis, et universa planities quæ est juxta Medeba.
17. Heshbon, and all her cities	17. Hesbon et omnes urbes ejus,

[1] The Septuagint avoids the appearance of tautology, both by abridging the verse and adopting a different punctuation, rendering it thus: "To Reuben and Gad the Lord gave (*an inheritance*) on the other side of the Jordan ; towards the sun-rising did Moses the servant of the Lord give it to them." This, however, is not the only alteration made by the Septuagint version. For immediately before the verse now quoted, it interpolates another in the following terms, "From the Jordan unto the Great Sea on the west shalt thou give it : the Great Sea will be the boundary of the two tribes and of the half tribe of Manasse."—*Ed.*

[2] To the end of this verse the Septuagint adds the following clause : "καὶ οὗτος ὁ καταμερισμὸς, ὃν κατεμέρισε Μωυσῆς τοῖς υἱοῖς Ἰσραὴλ ἐν Ἀραβὼθ Μωὰβ ἐν τῷ πέραν τοῦ Ἰορδάνου κατὰ Ἰεριχὼ ;" "And this is the division which Moses divided to the children of Israel in Araboth-Moab beyond Jordan opposite to Jericho."—*Ed.*

that *are* in the plain; Dibon, and Bamoth-baal, and Beth-baal-meon,

18. And Jahaza, and Kedemoth, and Mephaath,

19. And Kirjathaim, and Sibmah, and Zareth-shahar in the mount of the valley,

20. And Beth-peor, and Ashdoth-pisgah, and Beth-jeshimoth,

21. And all the cities of the plain, and all the kingdom of Sihon king of the Amorites, which reigned in Heshbon, whom Moses smote with the princes of Midian, Evi, and Rekem, and Zur, and Hur, and Reba, *which were* dukes of Sihon dwelling in the country.

22. Balaam also the son of Beor, the soothsayer, did the children of Israel slay with the sword among them that were slain by them.

23. And the border of the children of Reuben was Jordan, and the border *thereof*. This *was* the inheritance of the children of Reuben after their families, the cities and the villages thereof.

24. And Moses gave *inheritance* unto the tribe of Gad, *even* unto the children of Gad, according to their families:

25. And their coast was Jazer, and all the cities of Gilead, and half the land of the children of Ammon, unto Aroer that *is* before Rabbah;

26. And from Heshbon unto Ramath-mizpeh, and Betonim; and from Mahanaim unto the border of Debir;

27. And in the valley, Beth-aram, and Beth-nimrah, and Succoth, and Zaphon, the rest of the kingdom of Sihon king of Heshbon, Jordan and *his* border, *even* unto the edge of the sea of Chinnereth, on the other side Jordan eastward.

28. This *is* the inheritance of the children of Gad after their families, the cities, and their villages.

29. And Moses gave *inheritance* unto the half-tribe of Manasseh: and *this* was *the possession* of the half-tribe of the children of Manasseh by their families.

30. And their coast was from

quæ erant in planitie: Dibon et Bamoth-baal, et Beth-baalmeon.

18. Et Jahasah, et Cedemoth, et Mephaath.

19. Et Ciriathaim, et Sibmah, et Sereth-sahar in monte vallis.

20. Et Beth-peor, et Asdoth-Pisgah, et Beth-jesimoth.

21. Et omnes urbes planitiei, et universum regnum Sihon regis Æmorrhæi, qui regnabat in Hesbon, quem percussit Moses: et principes Midian, Evi, et Rekem, et Sur, et Hur, et Reba duces Sihon habitatores terræ.

22. Et Bileam filium Beor divinatorem occiderunt filii Israel gladio cum interfectis eorum.

23. Fuit autem terminus filiorum Ruben, Jordanes et terminus. Hæc est hæreditas filiorum Ruben per familias suas, urbes et villæ earum.

24. Deditque Moses tribui Gad, filiis Gad per familias suas.

25. Et fuit eis terminus Jazer, et omnes urbes Gilead, et dimidium terræ filiorum Ammon usque ad Aroer, quæ est coram Rabbah.

26. Et ab Hesbon usque ad Ramath ipsius Mispe, et Bethonim: et a Mahanaim usque ad terminum ipsius Debir.

27. Et in valle Beth-haram, et Beth-nimrah, et Succoth, et Saphon: residuum regni Sihon, regis Hesbon, Jordanem, et confinium, usque ad extremum maris Chinnereth, trans Jordanem ad orientem.

28. Hæc est hæreditas filiorum Gad per familias suas, urbes et villæ earum.

29. Dedit præterea Moses dimidiæ tribui Manasse: fuitque dimidiæ tribui filiorum Manasse per familias suas:

30. Fuit, inquam, terminus eo-

Mahanaim, all Bashan, all the kingdom of Og king of Bashan, and all the towns of Jair, which *are* in Bashan, threescore cities;

31. And half Gilead, and Ashtaroth, and Edrei, cities of the kingdom of Og in Bashan, *were pertaining* unto the children of Machir, the son of Manasseh, *even* to the one half of the children of Machir by their families.

32. These *are the countries* which Moses did distribute for inheritance in the plains of Moab, on the other side Jordan, by Jericho, eastward.

33. But unto the tribe of Levi Moses gave not *any* inheritance: the Lord God of Israel *was* their inheritance, as he said unto them.

rum a Mahanaim omnis Basan totius regni Og regis Basan, et omnes Havoth-Jair, quæ sunt in Basan, sexaginta urbes.

31. Et dimidium Gilead, et Astaroth, et Edrei, urbes regni Og in Basan, filiorum Machir, filii Manasse, dimidiæ parti filiorum Machir, per familias suas.

32. Istæ sunt hereditates quas tradidit Moses in campestribus Moab a transitu Jordanis ipsi Jericho ad orientem.

33. Tribui autem Levi non dedit Moses hæreditatem: Jehova Deus Israel ipse est hæreditas eorum, quemadmodum dixit illis.

15. *And Moses gave unto the tribe*, &c. What he seemed to have said with sufficient clearness he now follows more fully in detail, not only that the reading might incite the people to gratitude, seeing the divine goodness recorded in public documents, and, as it were, constantly before their eyes, but also that each might enjoy his inheritance without molestation and quarrel. For we know how ingenious human cupidity is in devising pretexts for litigation, so that no one can possess his right in safety unless a plain and perspicuous definition of his right make it impossible to call it in question. That country had been given without casting lots. It was therefore open to others to object that the just proportion had not been kept, and that the inequality behoved to be corrected. Therefore, that no unseasonable dispute might ever disturb the public peace, the boundaries are everywhere fixed by the authority of God, and disputes of every kind are removed by setting up landmarks. God does not by one single expression merely adjudge the whole kingdom of Sihon to the tribe of Reuben, but he traces their extreme limit from Aroer to the banks of the Arnon, and thus, making an entire circuit, contracts or widens their territory so as not to leave the possession of a single acre ambiguous. Moreover, how useful this exact delineation was may be learned from profane history, where

we everywhere meet, not only with invidious but pernicious disputes among neighbours as to their boundaries.

We may add that the care which the Lord condescended to take in providing for his people, and in cherishing mutual peace among them, demonstrates his truly paternal love, since he omitted nothing that might conduce to their tranquillity. And, indeed, had not provision been thus early made, they might have been consumed by intestine quarrels.[1]

I again beg my readers to excuse me if I do not labour anxiously in describing the situation of towns, and am not even curious in regard to names. Nay, I will readily allow those names which it was thought proper to leave as proper nouns in Hebrew to be used appellatively, and so far altered as to give them a Latin form.[2]

It is worthy of notice, that when the land of the Midianites is referred to, the princes who ruled over it are called Satraps of Sihon, to let us know that they shared in the same overthrow, because they had involved themselves in an unjust war, and belonged to the government of Sihon, an avowed enemy. And to make it still more clear that they perished justly, it is told that among the slain was Balaam, by whose tongue they had attempted to wound the Israelites more grievously than by a thousand swords;[3] just as if it had been said that in that slaughter they found the hostile banner, by which they had declared themselves at open war with the Israelites. When it is said that the Jordan was a boundary, and a boundary, it will be proper, in order to prevent

[1] French, "Et de faict, s'il n'euste pourveu a cela de bonne heure, ils se fussent mangez et consumez les uns les autres en debatant entre eux;" "And in fact, had not this been provided for in good time, they would have eaten and consumed one another while debating among themselves."—*Ed.*

[2] French, "Qui plus est, je suis content qu'on traduise en d'autres langues certains noms, qu'il m'a semblé bon de laisser ici en la langue Hebraique comme noms propres;" "Moreover, I am content that certain words which I have thought good to leave here in the Hebrew tongue as proper names be translated into other languages."—*Ed.*

[3] The curious contradictions in the behaviour of this remarkable man whose fate is here recorded, and analogous exemplifications of them in ordinary life, are admirably delineated by Bishop Butler in a sermon on the subject.—*Ed.*

useless repetition, to interpret that Jordan was a boundary to them according to its limits.[1]

24. *And Moses gave inheritance unto the tribe of Gad*, &c. The observation made above applies also to the tribe of Gad, namely, that their legitimate boundaries were carefully defined in order to prevent disputes as to their possession. Meanwhile God is extolled for his liberality in having expelled nations of great celebrity, and substituted them in their stead. This is expressed more clearly in regard to the half tribe of Manasseh, when sixty cities are enumerated as included in their inheritance. Hence, too, it is manifest that Moses was not munificent through mistake, because it was well known to God how many cities he was giving them out of his boundless liberality. In a short clause the tribe of Levi is again excluded, that the Levites might not be able at some future period to pretend that the grant which the Reubenites, Gadites, and half tribe of Manasseh had obtained without the casting of lots, belonged in common to them also; for they are expressly forbidden to share with their brethren. This made it easy for them to interpret shrewdly for their advantage, that they were entitled to share with others. Here, however, it is not the sacrifices, as a little before, but God himself that is said to be their inheritance; if they are not satisfied with it, they only convict themselves of excessive pride and insufferable fastidiousness.[2]

CHAPTER XIV.

1. And these *are the countries* which the children of Israel inherited in the land of Canaan, which Eleazar the priest, and Joshua the son of Nun, and the heads of the fathers of the tribes of the children of Israel, distributed for inheritance to them.

2. By lot *was* their inheritance, as the Lord commanded by the hand

1. Hæc sunt quæ in hæreditatem acceperunt filii Israel in terra Chanaan, quæ illis tradiderunt in hæreditatem Eleazar sacerdos, et Josue filius Nun, et capita tribuum filiorum Israel.

2. Per sortem hæreditatis eorum, sicut præceperat Jehova per manum

[1] Latin, "Terminum illis fuisse Jordanem secundum suos fines." French, "Que le Jordain estoit leur borne selon ses limites;" "That the Jordan was their boundary according to its limits." The repetition is omitted by the Septuagint.—*Ed.*

[2] The thirty-third verse is entirely omitted by the Septuagint.—*Ed.*

of Moses, for the nine tribes, and *for* the half-tribe.

3. For Moses had given the inheritance of two tribes and an half-tribe on the other side Jordan; but unto the Levites he gave none inheritance among them.

4. For the children of Joseph were two tribes, Manasseh and Ephraim; therefore they gave no part unto the Levites in the land, save cities to dwell *in*, with their suburbs for their cattle and for their substance.

5. As the Lord commanded Moses, so the children of Israel did, and they divided the land.

6. Then the children of Judah came unto Joshua in Gilgal: and Caleb the son of Jephunneh the Kenezite said unto him, Thou knowest the thing that the Lord said unto Moses, the man of God, concerning me and thee, in Kadesh-barnea.

7. Forty years old *was* I when Moses, the servant of the Lord, sent me from Kadesh-barnea to espy out the land; and I brought him word again as *it was* in mine heart.

8. Nevertheless my brethren that went up with me made the heart of the people melt: but I wholly followed the Lord my God.

9. And Moses sware on that day, saying, Surely the land whereon thy feet have trodden shall be thine inheritance, and thy children's for ever, because thou hast wholly followed the Lord my God.

10. And now, behold, the Lord hath kept me alive, as he said, these forty and five years, even since the Lord spake this word unto Moses, while *the children of* Israel wandered in the wilderness; and now, lo, I *am* this day fourscore and five years old.

11. As yet I *am as* strong this day as *I was* in the day that Moses sent me: as my strength *was* then, even so *is* my strength now, for war, both to go out, and to come in.

12. Now therefore give me this mountain, whereof the Lord spake in that day: (for thou heardest in

Mosis, ut daret novem tribubus, et dimidiæ tribui.

3. Dederat enim Moses duabus tribubus, et dimidiæ tribui citra Jordanem: Levitis autem non dederat hæreditatem in medio eorum.

4. Fuerunt enim filii Joseph duæ tribus Manasse et Ephraim: ideo non dederunt partem Levitis in terra præter urbes ad habitandum, et suburbana earum pro armentis et gregibus ipsorum.

5. Quemadmodum præceperat Moses sic fecerunt filii Israel, et diviserunt terram.

6. Accesserunt autem filii Juda ad Josuam in Gilgal, dixitque ad eum Caleb filius Jephune Kenisæus, Tu nosti verbum quod loquutus est Jehova ad Mosen virum Dei de me, et de te, in Cades-barnea:

7. Quadragenarius eram quando misit me Moses servus Jehovæ de Cades-barnea ad explorandam terram, et retuli ei rem sicuti erat in corde meo.

8. Et quum fratres mei qui descenderant mecum dissolverent cor populi, ego perseveranter sequutus sum Jehovam Deum meum.

9. Et juravit Moses illo die, dicendo, Si non terra quam calcavit pes tuus, tua erit in hæreditatem et filiis tuis in æternum, quia perseveranter sequutus es Jehovam Deum meum.

10. Nunc autem Jehova concessit mihi vitam sicuti dixerat. Jam quadraginta quinque anni sunt, ex quo tempore pronunciavit Jehova hanc rem Mosi, ex quo ambulavit Israel per desertum: et nunc quidem hodie sum quinque et octoginta annorum.

11. Et adhuc sum hodie vegetus ut eo die, quo misit me Moses: quantus erat tunc vigor meus, tantus hodie est vigor meus ad prælium, et ad exeundum, et ad ingrediendum:

12. Nunc ergo da mihi montem istum, ut loquutus est Jehova eo die. Tu enim audivisti eo die quod Ana-

that day how the Anakims *were* there, and *that* the cities *were* great *and* fenced;) if so be the Lord *will be* with me, then I shall be able to drive them out, as the Lord said.	kim sint ibi, et urbes magnæ et munitæ: forte Jehova erit mecum, et expellam eos quemadmodum dixit Jehova.
13. And Joshua blessed him, and gave unto Caleb the son of Jephunneh Hebron for an inheritance.	13. Et benedixit ei Josue, deditque Hebron ipsi Caleb filio Jephune in hæreditatem.
14. Hebron therefore became the inheritance of Caleb the son of Jephunneh the Kenezite unto this day, because that he wholly followed the Lord God of Israel.	14. Idcirco fuit Hebron ipsius Caleb filii Jephune Kenisæi in hæreditatem, usque ad diem hunc, eo quod perseveranter sequutus est Jehovam Deum Israel.
15. And the name of Hebron before *was* Kirjath-arba; *which Arba was* a great man among the Anakims. And the land had rest from war.	15. Nomen autem Hebron antea fuit Ciriath-arba, qui Arba homo magnus inter Anakim fuit: et terra quievit a bello.

1. *And these are the countries*, &c. He now proceeds to the land of Canaan, from which nine tribes and a half were to obtain their lots. And he will immediately break off the thread of the narrative, as we shall see. Yet the transition is seasonably made from that region whose situation was different, to let the reader know that the discourse was to be concerning the land of Canaan, which was to be divided by lot. We have said that Joshua and Eleazar not only divided what the Israelites had already acquired, but trusting in the promise of God, confidently included whatever he had promised to his people, just as if they had been in actual possession of it. We shall see, indeed, that the division was not all at once made complete, but when the first lot turned up in favour of Judah, the turns of the others were left in hope.

Here a difficult question arises. How can it be said that the distribution of the land was made by Joshua, Eleazar, and the princes, if lots were cast? For the lot is not regulated by the opinion or the will or the authority of man. Should any one answer, that they took charge and prevented any fraud from being committed, the difficulty is not removed, nay, this evasion will be refuted from the context. It is to be known, therefore, that they were not selected simply to divide the land by lot, but also afterwards to enlarge or restrict the boundaries of the tribes by giving to each its due proportion. That this business could not be accomplished by a naked lot is very apparent. For while, according to human ideas, nothing is more fortuitous than the result of a lot, it was not known whether God might choose to place the half tribe of Manasseh where the tribe of Judah obtained its settlement, or whether Zebulun might not occupy the place of Ephraim. Therefore they were not at liberty at the outset to proceed farther than to divide the land into ten districts or provinces. In this way, however, the space belonging to each would remain indefinite. For had an option been given to each, some would have chosen to fix themselves in the centre, others would have preferred a quiet locality, while others would have been guided in their choice by the fertility of the soil, or the climate and beauty of the scenery. But the lot placed the tribe of Judah, as it were, at the head, while it sent that of Zebulun away to the sea-shore, placed the tribe of Benjamin adjacent to that of Judah, and removed that of Ephraim to a greater distance. In short, the effect of the lot was that ten divisions fell out from Egypt towards Syria, and from the north quarter to the Mediterranean Sea, making some neighbours to the Egyptians, and giving to others maritime positions, to others hilly districts, to others intervening valleys.

This being understood, the office remaining for the rulers of the people was to trace out the boundaries on all sides in accordance with the rules of equity. It remained, therefore, for them to calculate how many thousand souls there were in every tribe, and to assign more or less space to each, according to the greatness or the smallness of their numbers. For in conformity to the divine command, a due proportion was to be observed, and a larger or narrower district was to be assigned, according as the census which was taken had ascertained the numbers to be. (Num. xxvi.) To the judgment of the princes was it in like manner left to shape the territories, regulating the length and breadth as circumstances might require. It is necessary also to bear in mind what is said in Numbers xxiv., that the ten who are here called heads of families were appointed to execute this office, not by the suffrages of men, but by the voice of God. Thus each tribe had its own overseers to prevent either fraud or violence from being committed. Then it would have been impious to have any suspicion of those who had been nominated by God. Such is the manner in which Joshua may be said to have distributed the land, though it was portioned out by lot.

4. *They gave no part unto the Levites,* &c. It is here repeated for the third time with regard to the Levites, that they were not included in the number, so as to have the portion of a tribe assigned to them ; but it is mentioned for a different purpose, for it is immediately after added, that the sons of Joseph were divided into two tribes, and were thus privileged to obtain a double portion. Thus had Jacob prophesied, (Gen. xlix.,) or rather, like an arbiter appointed by God, he had in this matter preferred the sons of Joseph to the others. God therefore assumed the Levites to himself as a peculiar inheritance, and in their stead substituted one of the two families of Joseph.

6. *Then the children of Judah came,* &c. Here the account which had been begun as to the partition of the land is broken off to make way for the insertion of a narrative, namely, that Caleb requested Mount Hebron to be given to him as he had been promised by Moses. This happened a long time before the people had ceased from making war, and it became necessary to cast lots. It is stated to be the fifth year since their entrance into the land, and he does not ask for a locality to be given up to him which was already subdued and cleared of the enemy, but in the midst of the noise and heat of warfare, he asks to be permitted to acquire it by routing and slaying its giants. He only seeks to provide, that when his valour has subdued the giants, he is not to be defrauded of the reward of his labour. The method of so providing, is to prevent its being included in the common lot of a tribe. Accordingly, he does not put forth the claim by himself alone, but the members of his tribe, the sons of Judah also concur with him, because the effect of conferring this extraordinary benefit on one family was so far to make an addition to all. Hence though Caleb alone speaks, all the tribe whose interest it was that his request should be granted were present.

I am not clear why the surname of Kenite was given to Caleb. He is so called also in Numbers xxxii. I am not unaware of the conjecture of some expositors, that he was so surnamed from Kenas, because either he himself or some one of his ancestors dwelt among the Kenites. But I see no solid foundation for this. What if he gained this title by some illustrious deed, just as victors sometimes assume a surname from the nations they have subdued? As the promise had not been inserted into any public record, and Joshua was the only witness now surviving, he makes his application to him. And it is probable that when the ten spies made mention of the names of the Anakim, with the view of terrifying the people, Caleb, to refute their dishonesty, answered with truth, that when he beheld them on Mount Hebron, they were so far from being terrible, that he would attack them at his own hand, provided that on their expulsion he should succeed to their lands; and that on these conditions Moses ceded to him a habitation in that locality which he should have acquired by his own prowess.

7. *Forty years old was I*, &c. He seems to talk of his own virtue in rather loftier terms than becomes a pious and modest man. But let us remember that, seeing the thing was in itself invidious and liable to many objections, it stood in need of special commendation as a means of suppressing envy. He therefore mentions that he had acted in good faith in bringing back an account of what he had learned concerning the land. For the expression, " As it was in my heart," evidently denotes sincerity, the heart being thus opposed to deceitful words. It is a ridiculous fiction to imagine that he had said it in his heart, because from fear of being killed by his companions he had not ventured to mention anything of the kind by the way. Nothing more is meant than simply this, that he acted honestly according to the command given him, without gloss or dissimulation. He enlarges on the merit of his integrity, because though he was opposed by all his colleagues, with the exception of Joshua, he did not yield to their malice, nor was dispirited by their iniquitous conspiracy, but steadfastly pursued his purpose. The words taken in their most literal sense are, I

filled or fulfilled to go after thy God; but the obvious meaning is, that he was not seduced from a faithful discharge of his duty by the wicked machination of ten men, however difficult it was to resist them, because he followed God with inflexible perseverance, feeling perfectly assured that God was the author of the expedition, from which those perfidious men were endeavouring to draw off the people.

Let us learn from this passage, first, that unless the last part corresponds to the first, good beginnings vanish away; secondly, that constancy is deserving of praise only when we follow God.

9. *And Moses sware on that day*, &c. Here, then, is one fruit of the embassy honestly and faithfully performed—to gain possession of an inheritance of which the whole people is deprived. For although long life is justly accounted one of the mercies of God, the end proposed by it is here added, viz., that Caleb may obtain the inheritance which is denied to others. This was no ordinary privilege. He next extols the faithfulness of God in having prolonged his life, and not only so, but supplied vigour and strength, so that though he was now above eighty years of age, he was not a whit feebler than when in the flower of his youth. Others, too, had a green old age, but they were few in number, and then in their case there was not added to the even tenor of their days a manly vigour, remaining wholly unimpaired up to their eighty-fifth year. For he lays claim not only to the skill and valour of a leader, but also to the physical strength of a soldier.

He next adds the other offices and actions of his life. For to go out and in is equivalent in Hebrew to the observance and execution of all parts of our duty. And this Caleb confirms by fact, when he demands it as his task to assail and expel the giants. He is not, however, elated by stolid pride to a confident assurance of victory, but hopes for a prosperous event from the assistance of God. There seems, indeed, to be an incongruous expression of doubt in the word Perhaps, as if he were begirting himself fortuitously for the fight.[1] Those expositors who think that he is

[1] French, "Il est vrai que ce mot *Peut estre*, qui est une marque ordi-

distrusting himself from a feeling of modesty and considering his own weakness, say something to the point, but do not say the whole. They certainly omit what is of principal import, viz., that this Perhaps refers to the common feelings which men would entertain on taking a view of the actual state of matters.

The first thing necessary is duly to consider what his design is. Had he asked the gift of a mountain, which he could have seized without any great exertion, it would have been more difficult to obtain it. But now when the difficulty of the task is plainly set forth, he gains the favour of Joshua and the princes, because in assenting to his prayer, they grant him nothing but the certainty of an arduous, doubtful, and perilous contest. Knowing, then, that the children of Israel trembled and were in terror at the very name of the giants, he speaks according to their opinion as of a matter attended with doubt and uncertainty. As regards himself, the words clearly demonstrate how far he was from viewing that which had been said to him with a dubious or vacillating mind. I shall drive them out, he says, as the Lord hath declared. Shall we say that when he utters the declaration of God, he is in doubt whether or not God will do what he promised? It is quite plain that he only reminded them how dangerous the business was, in order that he might the more easily obtain their assent. Although it is not uncommon in Hebrew to employ this term to denote difficulty merely, without meaning to imply that the mind is agitated by distrust or disquietude. How very difficult it was to drive out the giants from that fastness,[1] may be inferred from the fact that the death of Joshua took place before Caleb ventured to attack them.

13. *And Joshua blessed him*, &c. He prayed thus earnestly to shew the delight he felt. For it was expedient by way of example to extol his valour, by which others might be in-

naire de doute, semble estre estrange et ne convenir point, comme s'il se preparoit au combat a l'adventure;" "It is true, indeed, that this word *Perhaps*, which is an ordinary mark of doubt, seems strange and unsuitable, as if he were preparing himself for the combat at hap-hazard."—*Ed.*

[1] Latin, "Ea munitione." French, "Cette forteresse si bien munie;" "That stronghold so well fortified."—*Ed.*

cited to surmount all their fears. For it was just as if he had gained an eminence from which he could look down upon the giants. The blessing of Caleb, therefore, includes in it praise which may have the effect of an exhortation to the people. In the end of the chapter it is said, that the name of Hebron was Ciriath-Arba, (Kirjath-Arba.) Here it is to be observed, that it is not the mountain itself that is meant, but the principal city, of which there is frequent mention in Scripture. It is said to have received the surname from a giant famous for his stature. And this refutes the imagination of those expositors who insist that it was so called from having been the burial-place of four patriarchs —Adam, Abraham, Isaac, and Jacob.

It is plain that Caleb, in making the request, had not been looking to present ease or private advantage, since he does not aspire to the place that had been given him till many years after. Wherefore it was no less the interest of the whole people than of one private family, that that which as yet depended on the incomprehensible grace of God, and was treasured up merely in hope, should be bestowed as a special favour. A grant which could not take effect without a wonderful manifestation of divine agency could scarcely be invidious.

A question, however, arises. Since Hebron not only became the portion of the Levites, but was one of the cities of refuge, how could the grant stand good? If we say that Caleb was contented with other towns, and resigned his right to the Levites, it is obvious that the difficulty is not solved, because Caleb is distinctly appointed owner of that city. But if we reflect that the right of dwelling in the cities was all that was granted to the Levites, there will be no inconsistency. Meanwhile, no small praise is due to the moderation of Caleb, who, in a locality made his own by extraordinary privilege, did not refuse an hospitable reception to the Levites.[1]

[1] According to the explanation here given, the Levites held Hebron only by a kind of precarious tenure, dependent on the good will of Caleb, who gave them an hospitable reception, but might have declined it. It would seem, however, from other passages, and more particularly from chaps. xx. 7, and xxi. 9-13, that their right to Hebron was as complete and ab-

CHAPTER XV.

1. *This* then was the lot of the tribe of the children of Judah by their families; *even* to the border of Edom, the wilderness of Zin, southward, *was* the uttermost part of the south coast.

2. And their south border was from the shore of the salt sea, from the bay that looketh southward:

3. And it went out to the south side to Maaleh-acrabbim, and passed along to Zin, and ascended up on the south side unto Kadesh-barnea, and passed along to Hezron, and went up to Adar, and fetched a compass to Karkaa:

4. *From thence* it passed toward Azmon, and went out unto the river of Egypt; and the goings out of that coast were at the sea. This shall be your south coast.

5. And the east border *was* the salt sea, *even* unto the end of Jordan: and *their* border in the north quarter *was* from the bay of the sea, at the uttermost part of Jordan.

6. And the border went up to Beth-hogla, and passed along by the north of Beth-arabah; and the border went up to the stone of Bohan the son of Reuben.

7. And the border went up toward Debir, from the valley of Achor, and so northward, looking toward Gilgal, that *is* before the going up to Adummim, which *is* on the south side of the river: and the border passed toward the waters of En-shemesh, and the goings out thereof were at En-rogel.

8. And the border went up by the valley of the son of Hinnom unto the south side of the Jebusite; the same *is* Jerusalem: and the border went up to the top of the mountain

1. Fuitque sors tribui filiorum Jehuda per familias eorum juxta terminum Edom, et desertum Sin ad austrum ab extremo austri.

2. Fuitque ejus terminus meridiei ab extremo maris salis, hoc est a petra quæ respicit ad meridiem.

3. Et egreditur versus meridiem Maale-acrabim, et illinc transit in Sin: progrediens autem a meridie in Cades-barnea transit illinc in Esron, et rursum ascendit in Adar, unde circuit in Carcaa.

4. Inde transit in Asmon, et egreditur ad torrentem Ægypti: suntque egressus hujus termini ad occidentem: iste erit vobis terminus ad meridiem.

5. Terminus vero ad orientem, est mare salis usque ad extremitatem Jordanis, terminus autem anguli aquilonaris a petra maris ab extremo Jordanis.

6. Ascenditque terminus iste in Beth-hoglah, et transit ab aquilone ad Betharaba, atque illinc ascendit terminus iste ad lapidem Bohan filii Ruben.

7. Ascendit præterea terminus iste in Debir a valle Achor, et versus aquilonem respicit ad Gilgal, quæ est e regione ascensus Adummim, quæ quidem est ab austro torrenti: et transit terminus iste ad aquas En-semes, suntque exitus ejus ad En-rogel.

8. Et ascendit terminus iste ad vallem filii Hinnom, ad latus Jebusæi a meridie, ipsa est Jerusalem: ascendit insuper terminus iste ad verticem montis qui est e regione

solute as that which they possessed to any of their other cities. Moreover, as these cities were allocated by lot, or in other words, by divine arrangement, no injustice was done to Caleb, and it would have been strangely inconsistent with all that we have previously learned of his conduct and character, had he on this occasion offered any remonstrance.—*Ed.*

that *lieth* before the valley of Hinnom westward, which *is* at the end of the valley of the giants northward.

9. And the border was drawn from the top of the hill unto the fountain of the water of Nephtoah, and went out to the cities of mount Ephron; and the border was drawn to Baalah, which *is* Kirjath-jearim.

10. And the border compassed from Baalah westward unto mount Seir, and passed along unto the side of mount Jearim, (which *is* Chesalon,) on the north side, and went down to Beth-shemesh, and passed on to Timnah.

11. And the border went out unto the side of Ekron northward: and the border was drawn to Shicron, and passed along to mount Baalah, and went out unto Jabneel; and the goings out of the border were at the sea.

12. And the west border *was* to the great sea, and the coast *thereof*. This *is* the coast of the children of Judah round about, according to their families.

13. And unto Caleb the son of Jephunneh he gave a part among the children of Judah, according to the commandment of the Lord to Joshua, *even* the city of Arba, the father of Anak, which *city is* Hebron.

vallis Hinnom ad occidentem, quæ quidem est in extremitate vallis Rephaim ad aquilonem.

9. Circuit autem terminus a vertice ipsius montis, ad fontem aquæ Nephthoah, et egreditur ad urbes montis Ephron, circuitque terminus iste in Baala, ipsa est Cirjath-jearim.

10. Et illinc gyrat terminus iste a Baala ad occidentem ad montem Seir, et illinc pertransit ad latus montis Jearim ab aquilone, ipsa est Chesalon, descenditque in Bethsemes, et pertransit in Timna.

11. Egrediturque terminus ad latus Ecron ad Aquilonem, et circuit terminus iste ad Sichron, pertransitque ad montem Baala, et illinc egreditur in Jabneel, suntque exitus hujus termini ad mare.

12. Porro terminus occidentalis ad mare magnum, et terminum, iste est terminus filiorum Jehuda per circuitum, per familias suas.

13. Caleb autem filio Jephune dedit partem in medio filiorum Jehuda, secundum sermonem Jehovæ ad Josue, Cirjath-arba patris Anac, ipsa est Hebron.

1. I have already premised, that I would not be very exact in delineating the site of places, and in discussing names, partly because I admit that I am not well acquainted with topographical or chorographic science, and partly because great labour would produce little fruit to the reader;[1] nay, per-

[1] French, "Jai desia par ci devant adverti que je ne seroye point curieux a descrire ou peindre la situation des lieux, et a espulcher tous les noms, en partie parce que je confesse franchement que je ne suis pas bien exercé a faire descriptions de lieux ou de regions; en partie d'autant que d'un grand travail qu'il faudroit prendre, il n'en reviendroit que bien peu de fruict aux lecteurs;" "I have already before this intimated that I would not be curious in describing or painting the situation of places, and in expiscating all the names, partly because, I frankly confess, that I am not much experienced in making descriptions of places or countries, partly because from the great labour which it would be necessary to take, very little benefit would redound to the reader." It may be added that these de-

haps the greater part of readers would toil and perplex themselves without receiving any benefit. With regard to the subject in hand, it is to be observed, that the lot of the tribe of Judah not only falls on elevated ground, the very elevation of the territory, indicating the dignity of the future kingdom, but a similar presage is given by its being the first lot that turns up. What had already been obtained by arms, they begin to divide. The names of the ten tribes are cast into the urn. Judah is preferred to all the others. Who does not see that it is raised to the highest rank, in order that the prophecy of Jacob may be fulfilled? Then within the limits here laid down, it is well known that there were rich pastures, and vineyards celebrated for their productiveness and the excellence of their wines. In this way, while the lot corresponds with the prophecy of Jacob, it is perfectly clear that it did not so happen by chance; the holy patriarch had only uttered what was dictated by the Spirit.

If any are better skilled in places, a more minute investigation will be pleasant and useful to them. But lest those who are less informed feel it irksome to read unknown names, let them consider that they have obtained knowledge of no small value, provided they bear in mind the facts to which I have briefly and summarily adverted—that the tribe of Judah was placed on elevated ground, that it might be more conspicuous than the others, until the sceptre should arise from it—and that a region of fruitful vineyards and rich pastures was assigned to his posterity—and, finally, all this was done, in order that the whole people might recognise that there was nothing of the nature of chance in the turning up of a lot, which had been foretold three centuries

scriptions of boundaries, how minutely soever they may be detailed, must, from their very nature, leave a very vague impression on the mind of the most careful reader, and are much less adapted for the ear than for the eye, which, by a single glance at a map, furnishes information much more vivid, distinct, and accurate than can be obtained from pages of description. At the same time it ought to be remembered, that accurate and detailed descriptions of the boundaries of the different tribes were absolutely indispensable to the Israelites themselves, to whom they formed a kind of title-deeds, vindicating their right of possession, and securing them against encroachment.—*Ed.*

before. Besides, it is easy for the unlearned to infer from the long circuit described, that the territory thus allocated to one tribe was of great extent.[1] For although some diminution afterwards took place, its dominions always continued to be the largest.

It is necessary, however, to bear in mind what I formerly observed, that nothing else was determined by the lot than that the boundary of the children of Judah was to be contiguous to the land of Edom and the children of Sin, and that their boundary, in another direction, was to be the river of Egypt and the Mediterranean Sea—that those who had been selected to divide the country proceeded according to the best of their judgment, in proportioning the quantity of territory allotted to the number of their people, without extending their boundaries any farther—and that they followed the same method in other cases, as vicinity or other circumstances demanded.

Any error into which they fell, did not at all affect the general validity of their decision. For as they were not ashamed partly to recall any partition that might have been made without sufficient consideration, so the people in their turn, while they acknowledged that they had acted in the matter with the strictest good faith and honesty, submitted the more willingly to whatever they determined. Thus, notwithstanding any particular error, their general arrangements received full effect.

It will be worth while to make one remark on the city Jebus, whose name was afterwards Jerusalem. Although it had been already chosen, by the secret counsel of God, for his sanctuary, and the seat of the future kingdom, it however continued in the possession of the enemy down to the time of David. In this long exclusion from the place on which the sanctity, excellence, and glory of the rest of the land were founded, there was a clear manifestation of the divine curse inflicted to punish the people for their sluggishness: since it was virtually the same as if the land had been deprived of its principal dignity and ornament. But on the other hand, the

[1] As originally laid out, it contained nearly a third of the whole Israelitish territory west of the Jordan.—*Ed.*

wonderful goodness of God was conspicuous in this, that the Jebusites who, from the long respite which had been given them, seemed to have struck their roots most deeply, were at length torn up, and driven forth from their secure position.

13. *And unto Caleb the son of Jephunneh*, &c. Were we to judge from the actual state of matters, it would seem ridiculous repeatedly to celebrate an imaginary grant from which Caleb received no benefit while Joshua was alive. But herein due praise is given both to the truth of God, and to the faith of his saint in resting on his promise. Therefore, although sneering men, and the inhabitants of the place itself, if the rumour had reached them, might have derided the vain solicitude of Caleb, and the empty liberality of Joshua, the contempt thus expressed would only have proved them to be presumptuous scoffers. God at length evinced the firmness of his decree by the result, and Caleb, though he saw himself unable to obtain access to the mountain, testified that he was contented with the mere promise of God, the true exercise of faith, consisting in a willingness to remain without the fruition of things which have been promised till the period actually arrive. Moreover, this passage, and others similar to it, teach us that the giants who are usually called Enakim, were so named after their original progenitor, Enac, and that the word is hence of Gentile origin. The time when Caleb routed the sons of Enac we shall see in a short time. This passage also shews us that Caleb, when he brought forward the name of Moses, did not make a mere pretence, or utter anything that was not strictly true; for it is now plainly declared, that Moses had so appointed, in conformity with the command of God.

14. And Caleb drove thence the three sons of Anak, Sheshai, and Ahiman, and Talmai, the children of Anak.

15. And he went up thence to the inhabitants of Debir: and the name of Debir before *was* Kirjath-sepher.

16. And Caleb said, He that smiteth Kirjath-sepher, and taketh

14. Expulit inde Caleb tres filios Enac, Sezadi, et Ahiman, et Thalmai qui fuerunt filii Enac.

15. Ascenditque inde ad habitatores Debir, cujus nomen antea fuit Ciriath-sepher.

16. Dixitque Caleb, qui percusserit Ciriath-sepher, et ceperit eam,

it, to him will I give Achsah my daughter to wife.

17. And Othniel the son of Kenaz, the brother of Caleb, took it: and he gave him Achsah his daughter to wife.

18. And it came to pass, as she came *unto him*, that she moved him to ask of her father a field: and she lighted off *her* ass; and Caleb said unto her, What wouldest thou?

19. Who answered, Give me a blessing: for thou hast given me a south land; give me also springs of water. And he gave her the upper springs, and the nether springs.

20. This *is* the inheritance of the tribe of the children of Judah, according to their families.

21. And the uttermost cities of the tribe of the children of Judah, toward the coast of Edom, southward, were Kabzeel, and Eder, and Jagur,

22. And Kinah, and Dimonah, and Adadah,

23. And Kedesh, and Hazor, and Ithnan,

24. Ziph, and Telem, and Bealoth,

25. And Hazor, Hadattah, and Kerioth, *and* Hezron, which *is* Hazor,

26. Amam, and Shema, and Moladah,

27. And Hazar-gaddah, and Heshmon, and Beth-palet,

28. And Hazar-shual, and Beersheba, and Bizjothjah,

29. Baalah, and Iim, and Azem,

30. And Eltolad, and Chesil, and Hormah,

31. And Ziklag, and Madmannah, and Sansannah,

32. And Lebaoth, and Shilhim, and Ain, and Rimmon: all the cities *are* twenty and nine, with their villages.

33. *And* in the valley, Eshtaol, and Zoreah, and Ashnah,

34. And Zanoah, and En-gannim, Tappuah, and Enam,

35. Jarmuth, and Adullam, Socoh, and Azekah,

36. And Sharaim, and Adithaim,

dabo ei Achsa filiam meam in uxorem.

17. Cepit autem eam Othniel filius Cenas fratris Caleb: deditque ei Achsa filiam suam in uxorem.

18. Fuitque quum veniret ipsa suasit illi, ut peteret a patre suo agrum, et descendit de asino, dixitque ei Caleb, Quid tibi est?

19. Illa respondit, Da mihi benedictionem: quandoquidem terram aridam dedisti mihi, da mihi fontes aquarum. Et dedit ei fontes superiores, et fontes inferiores.

20. Ista est hæreditas tribus filiorum Jehuda per familias suas.

21. Fuerunt autem urbes in extremitate tribus filiorum Jehudæ juxta terminum Edom ad meridiem, Cabseel, et Eder, et Jagur.

22. Et Cina, et Dimona, et Adada,

23. Et Cedes, et Hasor, et Ithnan,

24. Ziph, et Telem, et Bealoth,

25. Et Hasor in Hadatha, et Cerioth, Hesron, ipsa est Hasor,

26. Amam, et Sema, et Molada,

27. Et Hasar-gadda, et Hesmon, Beth-phelet,

28. Et Hasar-sual, et Beerseba, et Bizjotheja,

29. Baala, et Iim, et Asem,

30. Et Eltholad, et Chesil, et Horma,

31. Et Siclag, et Madmannah, et Sensannah,

32. Et Lebaoth, et Silhim, et Ain, et Rimon: omnes urbes viginti et novem, et villæ earum.

33. In planitie Esthaol, et Sora, et Asnah,

34. Et Zanoah, et Engannim, et Taphuah, et Enam,

35. Jarmuth, et Adulam, Socoh, et Azecah,

36. Et Saaraim, et Adithaim, et

and Gederah, and Gederothaim: fourteen cities with their villages.

37. Zenan, and Hadashah, and Migdal-gad,

38. And Dilean, and Mizpeh, and Joktheel,

39. Lachish, and Bozkath, and Eglon,

40. And Cabbon, and Lahmam, and Kithlish,

41. And Gederoth, Beth-dagon, and Naamah, and Makkedah: sixteen cities with their villages.

42. Libnah, and Ether, and Ashan,

43. And Jiphtah, and Ashnah, and Nezib,

44. And Keilah, and Achzib, and Mareshah: nine cities with their villages.

45. Ekron, with her towns and her villages.

46. From Ekron even unto the sea, all that *lay* near Ashdod, with their villages.

47. Ashdod with her towns and her villages, Gaza with her towns and her villages, unto the river of Egypt, and the great sea, and the border *thereof.*

48. And in the mountains, Shamir, and Jattir, and Socoh,

49. And Dannah, and Kirjath-sannah, which *is* Debir,

50. And Anab, and Eshtemoh, and Anim,

51. And Goshen, and Holon, and Giloh: eleven cities with their villages.

52. Arab, and Dumah, and Eshean,

53. And Janum, and Beth-tappuah, and Aphekah,

54. And Humtah, and Kirjath-arba, (which *is* Hebron,) and Zior: nine cities with their villages.

55. Maon, Carmel, and Ziph, and Juttah,

56. And Jezreel, and Jokdeam, and Zanoah,

57. Cain, Gibeah, and Timnah: ten cities with their villages.

58. Halhul, Beth-zur, and Gedor,

59. And Maarath, and Beth-anoth, and Eltekon: six cities with their villages.

Gederah, et Gederothaim: urbes quatuordecim, et villæ earum.

37. Senam, et Hadasa, et Migdalgad,

38. Et Dilan, et Mispeh, et Jocteel,

39. Lachis, et Boscath, et Eglon,

40. Et Chabbon, et Lahmam, et Chithlis,

41. Et Gederoth, Beth-dagon, et Naamah, et Makeda: urbes sexdecim, et villæ earum.

42. Libna, et Ether, et Asan,

43. Et Jeptha, et Asna, et Nesib,

44. Et Cheila, et Achzib, et Maresah: urbes novem et villæ earum.

45. Ecron, et oppida ejus et villæ ejus.

46. Ab Ecron, et ad mare, omnes quæ sunt ad latus Asdod, et villæ earum.

47. Asdod, oppida ejus, et villæ ejus: Azza, oppida ejus et villæ ejus usque ad torrentem Ægypti, et mare magnum, et terminus,

48. Et in monte, Samir, et Jathir, et Sochoh,

49. Et Dannah, et Ciriath-sannah, ipsa est Debir,

50. Et Anab, et Eshtemoh, et Anim,

51. Et Gosan, et Holon, et Giloh: urbes undecim, et villæ earum.

52. Arab, et Dumah, et Esan,

53. Et Janum, et Beth-thappuah, et Aphecah,

54. Et Huntha, et Ciriath-arba, ipsa est Hebron, et Sior: urbes novem, et villæ earum.

55. Mahon, Carmel, et Ziph, et Juttah,

56. Et Jezrael, et Jocdean, et Zaura,

57. Cain, Giba, et Thimna: urbes decem, et villæ earum.

58. Hal-hul, et Beth-sur, et Gedor,

59. Et Maarath, et Bethanoth, et Elthecon: urbes sex, et villæ earum.

60. Kirjath-baal, (which *is* Kirjath-jearim,) and Rabbah: two cities with their villages.	60. Ciriath-baal, ipsa est Ciriath-jearim, et Rabba: urbes duæ, et villæ earum.
61. In the wilderness, Beth-arabah, Middin, and Secacah,	61. In deserto, Beth-arabah, Middin, et Sech-acha,
62. And Nibshan, and the city of Salt, and En-gedi: six cities with their villages.	62. Et Nibsan, et urbs salis, et Engedi: urbes sex, et villæ earum.
63. As for the Jebusites, the inhabitants of Jerusalem, the children of Judah could not drive them out: but the Jebusites dwell with the children of Judah at Jerusalem unto this day.	63. Porro Jebusæos habitatores Jerusalem non potuerunt filii Jehuda expellere: itaque habitavit Jebusæus cum filiis Jehuda in Jerusalem usque ad diem hanc.

Here we have a narrative of what plainly appears from the book of Joshua to have taken place subsequent to the death of Joshua; but lest a question might have been raised by the novelty of the procedure, in giving a fertile and well watered field as the patrimony of a woman, the writer of the book thought proper to insert a history of that which afterwards happened, in order that no ambiguity might remain in regard to the lot of the tribe of Judah. First, Caleb is said, after he had taken the city of Hebron, to have attacked Debir or Ciriath-sepher, and to have declared, that the person who should be the first to enter it, would be his son-in-law. And it appears, that when he held out this rare prize to his fellow-soldiers for taking the city, no small achievement was required. This confirms what formerly seemed to be the case, that it was a dangerous and difficult task which had been assigned him, when he obtained his conditional grant. Accordingly, with the view of urging the bravest to exert themselves, he promises his daughter in marriage as a reward to the valour of the man who should first scale the wall.

It is afterwards added that Othniel who was his nephew by a brother, gained the prize by his valour. I know not how it has crept into the common translation that he was a younger brother of Caleb; for nothing in the least degree plausible can be said in defence of the blunder. Hence some expositors perplex themselves very unnecessarily in endeavouring to explain how Othniel could have married his niece, since such marriage was forbidden by the law. It is easy to see that he was not the uncle, but the cousin of his wife.

But here another question arises, How did Caleb presume to bargain concerning his daughter until he was made acquainted with her inclinations?[1] Although it is the office of parents to settle their daughters in life, they are not permitted to exercise tyrannical power and assign them to whatever husbands they think fit without consulting them. For while all contracts ought to be voluntary, freedom ought to prevail especially in marriage that no one may pledge his faith against his will. But Caleb was probably influenced by the belief that his daughter would willingly give her consent, as she could not modestly reject such honourable terms;[2] for the husband to be given her was no common man, but one who should excel all others in warlike prowess. It is quite possible, however, that Caleb in the heat of battle inconsiderately promised what it was not in his power to perform. It seems to me, however, that according to common law, the agreement implied the daughter's consent, and was only to take effect if it was obtained.[3] God certainly

[1] If we are to indulge in conjectures on the subject, this question might be answered by another, How do we know that Caleb had not consulted her inclinations, and instead of resting satisfied with the vague imaginings here ascribed to him, actually obtained her consent to the proposal which he was about to make? It may not have been, as Calvin supposes, a sudden thought which struck him in the heat of battle, but a calm resolve formed before he set out on his expedition against Debir, and intended to reward the most valiant of those who had assisted him in his war against the giants. And it is even not impossible that both he and his daughter, to whom Othniel, from his near relationship, must have been well known, had no doubt from the prowess he had previously exhibited, that he would outstrip all his competitors and carry off the prize. These, of course, are mere conjectures, but they are at least as plausible as those indulged in by other expositors, who, after raising the question, appear to have given themselves much unnecessary trouble in attempting to solve it.—*Ed.*

[2] French, "Pource qu'un tel partie et condition si honorable ne pouvoit estre refusée honnestement et sans impudence;" "Because such a party and so honourable a condition could not be refused honestly (honourably) and without impudence."—*Ed.*

[3] In other words, Caleb promises his daughter not absolutely to the man who should take the city, but to the man who, in addition to the prowess exerted in taking it, should also have the address to gain the daughter's consent. It is difficult to believe that the promise made was either so meant by Caleb, or so interpreted by his followers. He very probably and, as the event shewed, justly judged that his influence as a parent would either win or command his daughter's consent.—*Ed.*

heard the prayer of Caleb, when he gave him a son-in-law exactly to his mind. For had the free choice been given him, there was none whom he would have preferred.

18. *And it came to pass as she came unto him,* &c. Although we may conjecture that the damsel Acsa was of excellent morals and well brought up, as marriage with her had been held forth as the special reward[1] of victory, yet perverse cupidity on her part is here disclosed. She knew that by the divine law women were specially excluded from hereditary lands, but she nevertheless covets the possession of them, and stimulates her husband by unjust expostulation. In this way ambitious and covetous wives cease not to molest their husbands until they force them to forget shame, modesty, and equity. For although the avarice of men also is insatiable, yet women are apt to be much more precipitate. The more carefully ought husbands to be on their guard against being set as it were on flame by the blast of such importunate counsels.[2]

But a greater degree of intemperance is displayed when she acquires additional boldness from the facility of her husband and the indulgence of her father. Not contented with the field given to her, she demands for herself a well-watered district. And thus it is when a person has once overleaped the bounds of rectitude and honesty, the fault is forthwith followed up by impudence. Moreover, her father in refusing her nothing gives proof of his singular affection for her. But it does not therefore follow that the wicked thirst of gain which blinds the mind and perverts right judgment is the less hateful. In regard to Acsa's dismounting from the ass, some interpreters ascribe it to dissimulation and craft, as if she were pretending inability to retain

[1] French, "Pour un salaire exquis et precieux;" "As an exquisite and precious recompense."—*Ed.*

[2] Latin, "Fœminæ tamen magis præcipites feruntur." French, "Les femmes sont beaucoup plus bouillantes, et se laissent transporter plus aisément. Et d'autant plus sogneusement les maris se doyvent donner garde, de peur que par leurs conseils importuns, qui sont comme des soufflets, ils ne soyent embrasez;" "Women are much more fervid, and allow themselves to be more easily carried away. And so much the more carefully should husbands be on their guard, lest by their importunate counsels, which are like bellows, they be blown into flame."—*Ed.*

her seat from grief. In this way her dismounting or falling off is made an indication of criminality and defective character. It is more simple, however, to suppose that she placed herself at her father's feet with the view of accosting him as a suppliant. Be this as it may, by her craft and flattery she gained his consent, and in so far diminished the portion of her brothers.[1]

20. *This is the inheritance*, &c. He had formerly, indeed, traced out the boundaries of the children of Judah ; but it is now shewn for a different reason how large and fertile the territory was which the Lord in his great liberality had bestowed upon them. One hundred and thirteen cities with their towns and villages are enumerated. The number attests not only the populousness, but also the fertility of the country. And there cannot be a doubt that by the divine blessing a new degree of fertility was imparted to it. The goodness of God was, however, manifested in the very nature of the land selected for his people, a land abounding in all kinds of advantages. If we attend to the number of souls in the tribe, we shall find that one half of the country would have been amply sufficient for their habitation. For when eight hundred were allocated in each of the cities, the remainder had the towns and the villages. It is no doubt true that a portion was afterwards withdrawn and given to the tribe of Simeon. For in this was accomplished the dispersion of which Jacob had prophesied, "I will divide them in Jacob, and scatter them in Israel." (Gen. xlix. 7.) They were accordingly admitted by the children of Judah as a kind of guests.

63. *As for the Jebusites*, &c. This furnishes no excuse for the people, nor is it set down with that view ; for had they exerted themselves to the full measure of their strength, and failed of success, the dishonour would have

[1] French, " Quoy qu'il en soit, cette femme attira a soy par astuce et flatteries le droit d'autruy, et par ce moyen, la part et portion de ses freres en fut d'autant amoindrie ;" " Be this as it may, this woman attracted to herself by craft and flattery the right of another, and by this means the part and portion of her brothers was so far lessened." The censure here passed upon Achsah is rather more severe than the circumstances seem to warrant. It ought to be remembered, that in cases of succession the preference given to males is only conventional, and that by natural law her brothers' title was not a whit better than her own.—*Ed.*

fallen on God himself, who had promised that he would continue with them as their leader until he should give them full and free possession of the land, and that he would send hornets to drive out the inhabitants. Therefore, it was owing entirely to their own sluggishness that they did not make themselves masters of the city of Jerusalem. This they were not able to do; but their own torpor, their neglect of the divine command from a love of ease, were the real obstacles.

This passage is deserving of notice: we ought to learn from it to make vigorous trial of our strength in attempting to accomplish the commands of God, and not to omit any opportunity, lest while we are idly resting the door may be shut. A moderate delay might have been free from blame; but a long period of effeminate ease in a manner rejected the blessing which God was ready to bestow.[1]

CHAPTER XVI.

1. And the lot of the children of Joseph fell from Jordan by Jericho, unto the water of Jericho on the east, to the wilderness that goeth up from Jericho, throughout mount Beth-el,	1. Egressa est autem sors filiis Joseph a Jordane Jericho, ad aquas Jericho ad orientem, ad desertum quod ascendit a Jericho in montem Beth-el.
2. And goeth out from Beth-el to Luz, and passeth along unto the borders of Archi to Ataroth,	2. Egrediturque a Beth-el in Luz, et hinc pertransit ad terminum Archi-Ataroth.
3. And goeth down westward to the coast of Japhleti, unto the coast of Beth-horon the nether, and to Gezer: and the goings out thereof are at the sea.	3. Postea ascendit ad mare, ad terminum Japhleti usque ad terminum Beth-horon inferiorem et usque ad Gazer, suntque exitus ejus ad mare.
4. So the children of Joseph, Manasseh and Ephraim, took their inheritance.	4. Itaque hæreditatem acceperunt filii Joseph, Manasses et Ephraim.
5. And the border of the children of Ephraim, according to their	5. Fuit autem terminus filiorum Ephraim per familias suas: fuit,

[1] Some of the Jewish expositors, unwilling to admit the cowardice and sluggishness of their countrymen, fable that the Jebusites were permitted to remain in possession because they were descendants of Abimelech, and in consequence of the covenant made between him and Abraham, (Gen. xxi. 22, 32,) could not be lawfully expelled.—*Ed.*

families, was *thus:* even the border of their inheritance on the east side was Ataroth-adar, unto Beth-horon the upper;

6. And the border went out toward the sea to Michmethah on the north side; and the border went about eastward unto Taanath-shiloh, and passed by it on the east to Janohah;

7. And it went down from Janohah to Ataroth, and to Naarath, and came to Jericho, and went out at Jordan.

8. The border went out from Tappuah westward unto the river Kanah; and the goings out thereof were at the sea. This *is* the inheritance of the tribe of the children of Ephraim by their families.

9. And the separate cities for the children of Ephraim *were* among the inheritance of the children of Manasseh, all the cities with their villages.

10. And they drave not out the Canaanites that dwelt in Gezer; but the Canaanites dwell among the Ephraimites unto this day, and serve under tribute.

inquam, terminus hæreditatis eorum ad orientem ab Atroh-Addar, usque ad Beth-horon superiorem.

6. Et exit terminus ille ad mare, ad Michmethah ab aquilone: et circumit terminus ad orientem, ad Thaanath-siloh, et transit illam ab oriente ad Janoah.

7. Et descendit a Janoah in Ataroth, et Naarath, et pervenit in Jericho, egrediturque ad Jordanem.

8. A Thappuah pergit terminus ad mare ad torrentem arundinis, suntque exitus ejus ad mare, hæc est hereditas tribus filiorum Ephraim per familias suas.

9. Et urbes separatæ filiis Ephraim in medio hæreditatis filiorum Manasse, omnes urbes, et villæ earum.

10. Neque expulerunt Chananæum habitantem in Gazer. Itaque habitavit Chananæus in medio Ephraim usque ad diem hanc, et fuit tributo serviens.

1. *And the lot of the children of Joseph fell,* &c. The sacred writer first states what the lot was which fell to the two children of Joseph, and then describes the lot of Ephraim. It is strange, however, that when the half of the tribe of Manasseh had already been settled beyond the Jordan, more words are employed in describing the remaining half than in describing the whole of the inheritance of the tribe of Ephraim, though the latter was the more populous, and justly claimed for itself a larger territory. But the longer detail given concerning the posterity of Manasseh is owing to particular circumstances. First, the writer repeats how a settlement had been given them without lot in the country of Basan. Secondly, he mentions the ratification by Joshua of the command which Moses had given by divine authority in regard to the daughters of Selophead. Seeing, then, there was no doubt in regard to the boundaries of

Ephraim, and there was no danger of dispute, their allocation is only briefly glanced at.

But here a new question arises. When the right of primogeniture had passed from Manasseh to Ephraim, how did the posterity of that tribe which had precedence in rank obtain their cities among the children of Manasseh? For theirs seems in this way to have been the inferior condition. My explanation is this, When the portion of Manasseh was too extensive in proportion to the amount of population, a calculation was made, and certain cities were deducted to complete the just share of the tribe of Ephraim; not that they were mixed up with the children of Manasseh, to hold their dwellings among them by a precarious tenure,[1] but their boundaries were merely extended in the direction of the Manassites whom a narrower possession might suffice.

In the end of the chapter, Ephraim is severely censured for his effeminacy in not having expelled the Canaanites from Gezer. For had they proceeded in a manly and hearty manner to make good their right to the land which had fallen to them by lot, the victory was in their hands. There would have been no temerity in the attempt, since the decision of the lot was as valid as if the Lord himself had stretched forth his hand from heaven. But their disgraceful sloth is more clearly expressed and their culpability greatly heightened by the fact, that they made tributaries of those with whom it was not lawful to enter into any kind of arrangement. Seeing, then, God had distinctly forbidden his people to transact business of any kind with those nations, and least of all to enter into pactions with them, stipulating for their pardon and safety, the Ephraimites sinned much more grievously in exacting tribute than if they had tolerated them without paction.[2]

[1] Latin, "Quasi precario." French, "Comme par emprunt ou par prieres;" "As by loan or by entreaty."—*Ed.*

[2] A long clause is here added by the Septuagint, to the effect that the Canaanite continued to dwell in Ephraim till Pharaoh, king of Egypt, came up and took it, drove out the Canaanites, Perizzites, and dwellers in Gezer, and gave it as a dowry to his daughter, (who had married Solomon.)—*Ed.*

CHAPTER XVII.

1. There was also a lot for the tribe of Manasseh, (for he *was* the first-born of Joseph,) *to wit*, for Machir, the first-born of Manasseh, the father of Gilead: because he was a man of war, therefore he had Gilead and Bashan.

2. There was also *a lot* for the rest of the children of Manasseh by their families; for the children of Abiezer, and for the children of Helek, and for the children of Asriel, and for the children of Shechem, and for the children of Hepher, and for the children of Shemida: these *were* the male-children of Manasseh the son of Joseph by their families.

3. But Zelophehad, the son of Hepher, the son of Gilead, the son of Machir, the son of Manasseh, had no sons, but daughters: and these *are* the names of his daughters, Mahlah, and Noah, Hoglah, Milcah, and Tirzah.

4. And they came near before Eleazar the priest, and before Joshua the son of Nun, and before the princes, saying, The Lord commanded Moses to give us an inheritance among our brethren: therefore, according to the commandment of the Lord, he gave them an inheritance among the brethren of their father.

5. And there fell ten portions to Manasseh, besides the land of Gilead and Bashan, which *were* on the other side Jordan;

6. Because the daughters of Manasseh had an inheritance among his sons: and the rest of Manasseh's sons had the land of Gilead.

7. And the coast of Manasseh was from Asher to Michmethah, that *lieth* before Shechem; and the border went along on the right hand unto the inhabitants of En-tappuah.

8. *Now* Manasseh had the land of Tappuah: but Tappuah, on the

1. Fuit quoque sors tribui Manasse (ipse enim fuit primogenitus Joseph) ipsi Machir primogenito Manasse patri Gilead (ipse enim fuit vir bellicosus), fuit inquam, ei Gilead et Basan.

2. Fuit item filiis Manasse reliquis per familias suas, filiis Abiezer, et filiis Helec, et filiis Asriel, et filiis Sechem, et filiis Hepher, et filiis Semida. Isti sunt filii Manasse, filii Joseph mares per familias suas.

3. Porro Selophead filio Hepher, filii Gilead, filii Machir, filii Manasse non fuerunt filii sed filiæ: quarum ista sunt nomina, Mahala, et Noa, Hogla, Melcha, et Thirza.

4. Hæ accesserunt in conspectum Eleazar sacerdotis, et in conspectum Josue filii Nun, atque in conspectum principum, dicendo, Jehova præcepit Mosi ut daret nobis hæreditatem in medio fratrum nostrorum. Itaque dedit eis juxta sermonem Jehovæ, hæreditatem in medio fratrum patris earum.

5. Et ceciderunt hæreditates Manasse decem, præter terram Gilead et Basan, quæ erant trans Jordanem.

6. Filiæ enim Manasse sortitæ sunt hereditatem in medio filiorum ejus: terra autem Gilead fuit filiis Manasse reliquis.

7. Fuit autem terminus Manasse ab Aser ad Michmethah, quæ est coram Sechem, et pergit terminus ad dextram ad habitatores En-thappua.

8. Ipsius Manasse fuit terra Thappua: ab Thappua quæ erat ad

border of Manasseh, *belonged* to the children of Ephraim;

9. And the coast descended unto the river Kanah, southward of the river: these cities of Ephraim *are* among the cities of Manasseh: the coast of Manasseh also *was* on the north side of the river, and the outgoings of it were at the sea.

10. Southward *it was* Ephraim's, and northward *it was* Manasseh's, and the sea is his border; and they met together in Asher on the north, and in Issachar on the east.

terminum Manasse, est filiorum Ephraim.

9. Descenditque terminus ad torrentem arundinis ad meridiem ipsius torrentis: civitates istæ tribus Ephraim sunt in medio civitatum Manasse: at terminus Manasse est ab aquilone ipsius torrentis, suntque exitus ejus ad mare.

10. Ad meridiem est ipsius Ephraim, et ad aquilonem ipsius Manasse, estque terminus ejus, et in Aser occurrunt inter se ab aquilone, et in Issachar ab oriente.

The historian returns to the tribe of Manasseh with the view of confirming what we formerly saw with regard to the daughters of Selophead. For though it was a novelty for females to succeed indiscriminately with males, yet as five of them had survived their father, they proved it to be equitable that they should be admitted to a portion, lest while he was innocent he should lie under the reproach of having died childless. God had replied to Moses by his oracle, that in regard to succession they should be counted as one head. They now demand that the decision thus given by the mouth of the Lord shall be carried into effect. As to the name of first-born, still given to Manasseh, it must be understood so as not to be at variance with the prophecy of Jacob; or rather his primogeniture is here in a manner buried, and his dignity restricted to the past. Here, however, it is to be observed, that men are so tenacious and so much devoted to their own interests, that it seldom occurs to them to give others their due. The daughters of Selophead had obtained a portion by a heavenly decree; nor had any one dared to utter a word against it; and yet if they had remained silent no regard would have been paid to them. Therefore, lest the delay should prove injurious to them, they apply to Joshua and Eleazar, and insist that they shall not be deprived of their legitimate succession. No delay is interposed by Joshua to prevent their immediately obtaining what is just, nor is there any murmuring on the part of the people. Hence we infer, that all were disposed to act equitably; but every one is occupied with his own interest, and too apt carelessly to overlook that of others.

5. *And there fell ten portions to Manasseh, &c.* The children of Manasseh are in this passage classed under seven stems. Machir, the first-born, is placed apart; the other six follow. Here the question arises, How was the inheritance divided into ten parts? Some expositors cunningly disguise the difficulty;[1] others, because they are unable to solve it, indulge in the merest trifling. It is certainly very absurd that four portions should be given to five daughters; and it is not a whit more congruous that their share should be doubled because their father was the first-born. It is beyond all controversy, that Gilead, son of Machir, and great-grandfather of the females of whom we are now speaking, chose his settlement in mount Gilead and Bashan. Therefore, seeing he had already obtained an inheritance by privilege without lot, he ought not to have obtained one by lot in the land of Canaan, unless perhaps he settled only a part of his family beyond the Jordan. For Hepher was one of his sons, but not the only one; and likewise the offspring of five other brothers might be distinguished into several heads according to the number of which the allocation by lot might be made. For it is not known in what degree families whose portion fell in the land of Canaan were taken. And all we read here is, that ten lots were cast among the sons of Manasseh in addition to the country which they had formerly acquired for themselves beyond the Jordan. It is thus vain to dispute concerning the number, which cannot be ascertained with certainty from the present narrative, because the first thing necessary to be known is the exact number of families to whom the divison was common. Nay, it is not impossible that the daughters of Selophead obtained their patrimony there. They are said, indeed, to have dwelt among the brethren of their father; but the place is not given. Be this as it may, I have no

[1] Latin, "Quidam astute hunc scrupulum dissimulant." French, "Aucuns y vont à la finesse ne faisans nulle mention de ceste difficulté;" "Some have recourse to finesse, making no mention of this difficulty."—*Ed.*

doubt that mutual equity was observed, and that after provision was made for others, the land which had been submitted to lot was distributed among ten families whose names are here omitted.

11. And Manasseh had in Issachar, and in Ashur, Beth-shean and her towns, and Ibleam and her towns, and the inhabitants of Dor and her towns, and the inhabitants of En-dor and her towns, and the inhabitants of Taanach and her towns, and the inhabitants of Megiddo and her towns, *even* three countries.

12. Yet the children of Manasseh could not drive out *the inhabitants of* those cities; but the Canaanites would dwell in that land.

13. Yet it came to pass, when the children of Israel were waxen strong, that they put the Canaanites to tribute; but did not utterly drive them out.

14. And the children of Joseph spake unto Joshua, saying, Why hast thou given me *but* one lot and one portion to inherit, seeing I *am* a great people, forasmuch as the Lord hath blessed me hitherto?

15. And Joshua answered them, If thou *be* a great people, *then* get thee up to the wood-*country*, and cut down for thyself there in the land of the Perizzites, and of the giants, if mount Ephraim be too narrow for thee.

16. And the children of Joseph said, The hill is not enough for us: and all the Canaanites that dwell in the land of the valley have chariots of iron, *both they* who *are* of Beth-shean and her towns, and *they* who *are* of the valley of Jezreel.

17. And Joshua spake unto the house of Joseph, *even* to Ephraim and to Manasseh, saying, Thou *art* a great people, and hast great power; thou shalt not have one lot *only:*

18. But the mountain shall be thine; for it *is* a wood, and thou shalt cut it down; and the outgoings

11. Fuitque ipsi Manasse in Issachar, et in Aser, Beth-sean, et oppida ejus: et Ibleam, et oppida ejus: et habitatores Dor, et oppida ejus: et habitatores Endor, et oppida ejus: et habitatores Thaanach, et oppida ejus: et habitatores Magiddo, et oppida ejus, tres regiones.

12. Et non potuerunt filii Manasse expellere habitatores urbium istarum, sed cœpit Chananæus habitare in terra ipsa.

13. Quum autem roborati essent filii Israel, posuerunt Chananæum tributarium, nec expellendo expulerunt eum.

14. Loquuti sunt autem filii Joseph ad Josue, dicendo, Cur dedisti mihi in hæreditatem sortem unam, et hæreditatem unam, quum ego sim populus multus, ita quod hucusque benedixerit mihi Jehova?

15. Dixitque ad eos Josue, Si populus multus es, ascende in sylvam, et succide tibi illic in terra Perizæi, et Rephaim, si angustus est tibi mons Ephraim.

16. Cui responderunt filii Joseph, Non sufficiet nobis mons ille: et currus ferrei sunt in omni Chananæo qui habitat in terra vallis, et ei qui habitat in Beth-sean et oppidis ejus, et ei qui habitat in valle Jezrael.

17. Dixitque Josue ad domum Joseph, nempe ad Ephraim et Manasse, dicendo, Populus multus es, et fortitudo magna est tibi: non erit tibi sors unica:

18. Mons enim erit tibi, quia sylva est: succides ergo eam, et erunt tibi exitus ejus: quia expelles Chana-

of it shall be thine: for thou shalt drive out the Canaanites, though they have iron chariots, *and* though they *be* strong.

næum, quanquam currus ferrei sint ei, quanquam fortis sit.

11. *And Manasseh had in Issachar,* &c. How they were so mingled as to possess some cities in the lot of Asher and Issachar, while the tribe of Ephraim dwelt between their limits, it is not easy to divine, unless, perhaps, it was perceived that a more commodious habitation would not be liable to many complaints,[1] or, perhaps, after the whole country had become more certainly known, some change was made on principles of equity in the former partition. This, therefore, seems to have been a new acquisition after it was discovered that the children of Manasseh might occupy a wider extent without loss to others. Nor was the habitation given to them a subjugated one, which they might immediately enjoy, but it was an inheritance treasured up in hope, and founded more upon heavenly promise than on actual possession. And yet their not gaining possession of those cities is attributed to their fault, because the lot assigning it to them was an indubitable pledge of victory. The reason, therefore, why they could not expel the inhabitants was, because they were not fully persuaded in their minds that God is true, and stifled his agency by their own sluggishness. But another crime still less pardonable was committed when, having it in their power easily to destroy all, they not only were slothful in executing the command of God, but, induced by filthy lucre,[2] they preserved those alive whom God had doomed to destruction. For persons, on whom we impose tribute, we in a manner take under our faith and protection. God had appointed them the ministers of his vengeance, and he supplies them with strength to execute it:

[1] Latin, "Nisi quia forte perspectum est; nec habitatio commodior obnoxia esset multis querimoniis." French, "Sinon possible qu'on voulust avoir esgard que s'ils eussent esté plus à leur aise, cela eust engendré des complaintes;" "Unless it be possible that they were pleased to take it into consideration that if they had been more at their ease, that might have engendered complaints."—*Ed.*

[2] Latin, "Turpi lucro adducti." French, "Sous couleur de quelque gain vilain et infame;" "Under colour of some vile and infamous gain."—*Ed.*

they not only delay, but deprive themselves of the liberty of acting rightly. It is not strange, therefore, that God severely punished this perverse heartlessness, by making those nations whom they had pardoned in the face of a clear prohibition, to become like thorns to pierce their eyes and pricks to gall their sides.

Here, again, a question arises, How were cities granted to them in the tribe of Asher and Issachar, when the portions of both were as yet unknown? Here, therefore, that which had not yet taken place is related by way of anticipation. Be this as it may, we gather that from ignorance of the localities, single portions were not divided so exactly as not to make it necessary afterwards to correct what had been more or less decided.[1] And we must hold in general, with regard both to the tribe of Ephraim and the others, that many of the cities which they gained were of no account because of the devastation. I doubt not that many ruins here lie buried. On the other hand, we must conclude that in fertile spots, or spots possessed of other advantages, where petty villages only existed, their famous cities were founded. It is certain that Sichem was of sufficient importance to hold both a name and rank, and yet there is no mention of it here. The same is the case with Samaria, which, as is well known, belonged to the same tribe of Ephraim when it was the metropolis of the kingdom of Israel. It is plain, therefore, that each tribe possessed several cities, which are here passed over in silence.

14. *And the children of Joseph spake unto Joshua,* &c. Although they clothe their complaint with some colour of excuse, yet they dishonestly disguise the fact, that more was comprehended in one lot than was proper for one tribe. I know not, however, whether or not the lot was cast indefinitely for the sons of Joseph: it certainly does not seem congruous that it should be so. Joshua and the other dividers were not unaware that Ephraim and Manasseh

[1] In the French this section of the commentary stops here, and all that follows in the Latin is omitted. It only amounts, however, to a transposition, as the omitted paragraph is inserted under the section of verse 14, at the place indicated by a note.—*Ed.*

formed two heads, or two stems: and it has repeatedly been said before that the land was divided into ten tribes, which number was not accurate, unless the tribe of Manasseh was considered distinct from that of Ephraim. It is certain, therefore, that they had not fallen into such a gross blunder as to throw the two names into one lot. Now, to conceal two tribes under the name of Joseph, in order to defraud them of half their right, would have been intolerable injustice. We may add, that the domain of each was distinctly explained and described by its proper boundaries.[1]

We are therefore led to conclude, that when the lots were cast for the two tribes, the admirable counsel of God arranged that the brothers, who had a common father, should be contiguous and neighbours to each other. It is unworthy in them, therefore, to complain and plead that only one inheritance had been given to them, because Joshua had neither such heartlessness nor so much malice as to defraud them of a clear right either through thoughtlessness or envy.[2] But

[1] The omitted paragraph of the section of verse 11 is inserted here.—*Ed.*

[2] It is impossible, of course, to make any suppositions at variance with the honour and integrity of Joshua, and it must therefore be held that in whatever manner the lot was taken for the children of Joseph, the strictest equity was observed. Is it necessary, however, to adopt one of the two alternatives,—either that separate lots were taken for Ephraim and Manasseh, or that Joshua deceived them? Though they counted as two tribes, they had only one patriarch for their ancestor, and it may therefore have been most expedient that, as they were brethren, their settlements should be adjacent to each other. This might, perhaps, have been obtained by taking separate lots, for we have already seen, on several occasions, how the lot, though apparently fortuitous, was providentially controlled, so as to give results at once confirmatory of ancient predictions, and conducive to the public good; and we may therefore presume that even if separate lots had been taken, the result might still have been to place the two kindred tribes in juxtaposition. But this was only problematical, and the only way of placing the matter beyond doubt was to make one lot serve for both. And there was no necessary injustice in this, since, as has been repeatedly observed, the lot only fixed the locality, without determining its precise limits, and thus left it open to enlarge or curtail them according to the extent of the population. If injustice had been done to the children of Joseph, it would not have been merely because they had been placed in one lot, but because this lot, though really intended for two tribes, had been left as small as if it had been intended only for one. The unreasonableness and dishonesty of the complaint, therefore, lay, according to this view, in their insisting on the fact that only one lot had been taken, and at the same time keeping out of view the other equally important fact,

herein lay the falsehood of their complaint concerning narrow boundaries, that they counted all that was yet to be acquired by warlike prowess as nothing; as if the lot had assigned portions to the other tribes only in subjugated territory. Joshua, accordingly, in a single sentence, refutes and disposes of their plea, and retorts upon them a charge by which they were trying to throw obloquy upon him. If your resources and your numbers are so great, why, he asks, do you not make an inroad on the enemy, whose country has been given to you? Nor will the event disappoint you, if, trusting to the promise of God, you boldly proceed to the inheritance which he has bestowed upon you. We see how, although proper provision had been made for them, they were so blinded by sloth as to complain that they were straitened for room, because they were unwilling to move their finger to seek the full possession of their inheritance. Wherefore, this passage teaches us, that if at any time we think less is performed for us than is due, we ought carefully to shake off all delays, and not rashly throw upon others the blame which is inherent in ourselves.

16. *And the children of Joseph said,* &c. It is too apparent that they were thinking only of themselves, because they quibble as much as they can, in order to avoid following the suggestion of Joshua, than which, however, nothing was more reasonable. They object, that the mountain is rugged and little better than a desert, and therefore, though it were added to them, they would derive very little benefit from it. In regard to the plain, which was cultivated and fertile, they

that in fixing its boundaries due allowance had been made for their numbers, and distinct settlements of sufficient magnitude given to each. That only one lot had been taken is strongly confirmed by the whole tenor of the narrative: *First,* When the children distinctly put the question to Joshua, "Why hast thou given me but one lot and one portion to inherit?" he does not silence them at once by answering that the assertion which they thus broadly made in the form of a question was not true. On the contrary, the indirectness of his answer seems to imply that the truth of the assertion could not be denied. *Secondly,* The narrative in chapter xvi., in describing the allocations of Ephraim and Manasseh, speak of them as forming only one lot. Thus, it is said, (ver. 1,) "The lot of the children of Joseph fell from Jordan by Jericho, unto the water of Jericho on the east;" and, (ver. 4,) "So the children of Joseph, Manasseh and Ephraim, took their inheritance."—*Ed.*

object that they are shut out and debarred from it because of the formidable array of the enemy. Accordingly, they make mention of their iron chariots, as if they had not already learned by experience that the Lord was able, without any difficulty, to trample down both horses and chariots. Joshua, however, by a simple and right-hearted answer, administers due castigation, as well to their avarice as their effeminacy and torpor. If the forest, as it now stands, is not sufficiently productive, cut down the trees and convert it into good fields; provided you are not sparing of your labour, you will have no reason to be dissatisfied with your habitation. Iron chariots, moreover, cannot prevent the Lord from performing what he has promised to you. The inheritance is yours; do only your part by entering with due confidence on the possession of it.

CHAPTER XVIII.

1. And the whole congregation of the children of Israel assembled together at Shiloh, and set up the tabernacle of the congregation there: and the land was subdued before them.

2. And there remained among the children of Israel seven tribes, which had not yet received their inheritance.

3. And Joshua said unto the children of Israel, How long *are* ye slack to go to possess the land, which the Lord God of your fathers hath given you?

4. Give out from among you three men for *each* tribe: and I will send them, and they shall rise and go through the land, and describe it, according to the inheritance of them; and they shall come *again* to me.

5. And they shall divide it into seven parts: Judah shall abide in their coast on the south, and the house of Joseph shall abide in their coasts on the north.

6. Ye shall therefore describe the land *into* seven parts, and bring *the*

1. Congregata est autem universa multitudo filiorum Israel in Silo, et collocaverunt ibi tabernaculum conventionis, postquam terra subjecta erat coram eis.

2. Remanserunt autem e filiis Israel quibus non diviserant hæreditatem suam, septem tribus.

3. Dixitque Josue ad filios Israel, Usquequo cessatis ingredi, ut possideatis terram quam dedit vobis Jehova Deus patrum vestrorum?

4. Tradite ex vobis tres viros per tribum, quos mittam: surgentque et ambulabunt per terram, describentque eam juxta hæreditatem suam, postea revertentur ad me.

5. Et partientur eam in septem portiones: Judas stabit in finibus suis a meridie: et familia Joseph stabunt in finibus suis ab aquilone.

6. Vosque describatis terram in septem partes, et afferatis ad me

description hither to me, that I may cast lots for you here before the Lord our God.

7. But the Levites have no part among you; for the priesthood of the Lord *is* their inheritance: and Gad, and Reuben, and half the tribe of Manasseh, have received their inheritance beyond Jordan on the east, which Moses, the servant of the Lord, gave them.

8. And the men arose, and went away: and Joshua charged them that went to describe the land, saying, Go and walk through the land, and describe it, and come again to me, that I may here cast lots for you before the Lord in Shiloh.

9. And the men went and passed through the land, and described it by cities into seven parts in a book, and came *again* to Joshua to the host at Shiloh.

10. And Joshua cast lots for them in Shiloh before the Lord: and there Joshua divided the land unto the children of Israel, according to their divisions.

huc: tum projiciam vobis sortem hic coram Jehova Deo nostro.

7. Non est enim pars Levitis in medio vestri, quia sacerdotium Jehovæ est hæreditas ejus: Gad autem et Ruben, et dimidia tribus Manasse acceperunt hæreditatem suam citra Jordanem ad orientem, quam dedit ei Moses servus Jehovæ.

8. Surrexeruntque viri illi, atque abierunt, præcepitque Josue istis qui ibant, ut describerent terram, dicendo: Ite, et ambulate per terram, ac describite eam: postea revertemini ad me, et hic projiciam vobis sortem coram Jehova in Silo.

9. Abierunt itaque viri, et transierunt per terram, atque descripserunt eam per urbes in septem partes, in libro: reversique sunt ad Josuam ad castra in Silo.

10. Misit autem eis Josua sortem in Silo coram Jehova: partitusque est ibi Josua terram filiis Israel secundum partes eorum.

1. *And the whole congregation of the children of Israel*, &c. Here we have a narrative of the celebrated convention held in Shiloh, where it was deliberated, as to the casting of the remaining lots. For although with pious zeal they had attempted the casting of lots, yet the proceeding had been interrupted, as if victory behoved to precede the distribution which depended solely on the mouth of God. They assemble, therefore, in Shiloh to determine what was necessary to be done in future. And there is no doubt that Joshua summoned this meeting in order to raise them from their lethargy. For they do not come forward spontaneously with any proposal, but he begins with upbraiding them with having been sluggish and remiss in entering on the inheritance which God had bestowed upon them. It is easy to infer from his speech that they had shewn great alacrity at the outset, but that there had been no perseverance.

And yet that obedience, which shortly after grew languid, was honoured with the approbation of the Holy Spirit. It is to be observed that the people are blamed, not for neglecting to proceed to the lot, but for not occupying the inheritance divinely offered to them. And, certainly, as the distribution by lot was a sign of confidence, so each district which fell out to each was a sure and faithful pledge of future possession ; for the Lord was by no means deluding them in assigning to each his portion.

The word רפה, which I have translated "to cease," signifies also to be remiss or feeble. He charges them, therefore, with base heartlessness, in that while the full time for routing the enemy had arrived, they by their delays retard and suspend the effect of the divine goodness. For had they been contented with the bare lot, and faithfully embraced the results which it gave, they would doubtless have been prompt and expeditious in carrying on the war, nay, would have hastened like conquerors to a triumph.

The ark is said to have been stationed at Shiloh,[1] not only that the consultation might be graver and more sacred, as held in the presence of God, but because it was a completely subjugated place, and safe from all external violence and injury. For it behoved to be their special care to prevent its exposure to sudden assault. No doubt the hand of God would have been stretched to ward off attacks of the enemy from any quarter ; still, however, though God dwelt among them, they were to be regarded as its guardians and attendants.

But although a station for the ark was then chosen, it was not a perpetual abode, but only a temporary lodging. For it was not left to the will or suffrages of the people to fix the seat where God should dwell, but they behoved to wait

[1] This place, which afterwards became so celebrated as the fixed station of the ark and tabernacle during the remainder of Joshua's life and the rule of the Judges, down to the tragical death of Eli, is described in Judges xxi. 19, as "On the north side of Bethel, on the east side of the highway that goeth up from Bethel to Shechem, and on the south of Lebonah." This minute description corresponds with a place now called Seilun, which is situated about twenty miles N.N.E. from Jerusalem, and has several ruins indicative of an ancient site. If this was the place, it stood nearly in the centre of the country, and was thus the most convenient which could have been selected. While its locality made it easily accessible from all quarters, its site, in the heart of a basin completely enclosed by hills except on the south, where a narrow valley opens into a plain, admirably adapted it for the still and solemn performance of religious services.—*Ed.*

for the period so often referred to in the Law, when he was to establish the memorial of his name elsewhere. This was at length accomplished when Mount Zion was set apart for the Temple. For this reason it is said in the Psalm, " Our feet shall stand within thy gates, O Jerusalem." (Ps. cxxii. 2.) These words intimate that up to that time the ark was pilgrimating. At last the ruin and devastation of Shiloh shewed that no rank or dignity can screen those who corrupt the blessings of God from his vengeance. Up to the death of Eli, God allowed his sacred name to be worshipped there; but when all religion was polluted by the impiety of the priests, and almost abolished by the ingratitude of the people, that spot became to posterity a signal monument of punishment. Accordingly, Jeremiah tells the inhabitants of Jerusalem, who were proudly boasting of their Temple, to turn their eyes to that example. Speaking in the name of the Lord, he says, " Go ye now unto my place which was in Shiloh, where I set my name at the first, and see what I did to it for the wickedness of my people Israel." (Jer. vii. 12.)

4. *Give out from among you three men*, &c. Caleb and Joshua had already surveyed those regions, and the people had learned much by inquiry: Joshua, however, wishes the land to be divided as if according to actual survey,[1] and orders three surveyors to be appointed for each of the seven tribes, in order that by the mouth of two or three persons every dispute may be settled. But nothing seems more incongruous than to send twenty-one men, who were not only to pass directly through a hostile country, but to trace it through all its various windings and turnings, so as not to leave a single corner unexamined, to calculate its length and breadth, and even make due allowance for its inequalities. Every person whom they happened to meet must readily have suspected who they were, and for what reason they had been employed on this expedition. In short, no free return lay open for them except through a thousand deaths. Assuredly they would not have encountered

[1] Latin, " Quasi ex præsenti aspectu." French, " Comme s'ils eussent esté presens sur le lieu;" " As if they had been present on the spot."—*Ed.*

so much danger from blind and irrational impulse, nor would Joshua have exposed them to such manifest danger had they not been aware that all those nations, struck with terror from heaven, desired nothing so much as peace. For although they hated the children of Israel, still, having been subdued by so many overthrows, they did not dare to move a finger against them, and thus the surveyors proceeded in safety as through a peaceful territory, under the pretext either of trading, or at least of making a harmless visit.[1] It is also possible that they arranged themselves in different parties, and thus made the journey more secretly. It is certain, indeed, that there was only one source from which they could have derived all this courage and confidence, from trusting under the shadow of the wings of the Almighty, and thus having no fear of blind and stupid men. Hence the praise here bestowed on their ready will. For had they not been persuaded that the hands of those nations were tied up by supernal power, they would have had a just and honest cause for refusing.[2]

9. *And the men went and passed*, &c. Here not only is praise bestowed on the ready obedience by which their virtue shone forth conspicuous, but the Lord gives a signal manifestation of his favour by deigning to bestow remarkable success on pious Joshua and the zeal of the people. Had they crept along by subterranean burrows, they could scarcely

[1] Latin, "Innoxii hospites." French, "Estrangers innocens qui passent leur chemin;" "Innocent strangers passing on their way."—*Ed.*

[2] These observations are made on the understanding that the survey made on this occasion was very minute, embracing, as Calvin here expresses it, all the "various windings and turnings," so as not to leave a single corner unexamined, and extending with the same minuteness, not only to the lands actually conquered, but to those still in the undisputed possession of the original inhabitants. Assuming this to be the fact, the dangers to be encountered by the surveyors are certainly not exaggerated in the very graphical description of them here given, and nothing but a series of miraculous interpositions could have saved them. It may be suggested, however, that the object of the surveyors was only to obtain such a general measurement as might suffice, in the manner already explained, for the taking of the lot, and that such a measurement might possibly have been made without much danger of awakening the suspicion, or rousing the hostility of the actual inhabitants. That the survey was more cursory than minute seems to be indicated by the description given of it in verse 9, "And the men went and passed through the land, and described it by cities."—*Ed.*

have escaped innumerable dangers, but now, when they are taking notes of the cities and their sites, of the fields, the varying features of the districts, and all the coasts, and without meeting with any adverse occurrence, return in safety to their countrymen, who can doubt that their life had been kept safe among a thousand deaths by a wonderful exertion of divine power? It is accordingly said emphatically, that they returned to celebrate the grace of God, which is just equivalent to saying that they were brought back by the hand of God. This made the people proceed more willingly to the casting of lots. For their minds would not yet have been well purged of fastidiousness had they not perceived in that journey a signal display of divine favour, promising them that the final issue would be according to their wish. Joshua is hence said to have divided according to the inheritance of each, as if he were sending them to enter on a quiet possession, though the effect depended on the divine presence, because it ought to have been enough for them that the whole business was carried on by the authority of God, who never deceives his people, even when he seems to sport with them. In what sense the ark of the covenant is called God, or the face of God, I have already explained in many passages.

11. And the lot of the tribe of the children of Benjamin came up according to their families: and the coast of their lot came forth between the children of Judah and the children of Joseph.

11. Ascendit autem sors tribus filiorum Benjamin per familias suas, et exivit terminus sortis eorum inter filios Jehuda, et filios Joseph:

12. And their border on the north side was from Jordan; and the border went up to the side of Jericho on the north side, and went up through the mountains westward; and the goings out thereof were at the wilderness of Bethaven.

12. Fuitque eis terminus ad latus Aquilonis a Jordane: et ascendit terminus ad latus Jericho ab Aquilone, ascenditque in montem ad mare, ac exitus ejus sunt ad desertum Bethaven.

13. And the border went over from thence toward Luz, to the side of Luz, (which *is* Beth-el,) southward; and the border descended to Ataroth-adar, near the hill that *lieth* on the south side of the nether Beth-horon.

13. Illinc autem pertransit terminus in Luz ad latus Luz Australe, (ipsa est Beth-el,) et descendit terminus in Ateroth-Adar, juxta montem, qui est a meridie ipsi Beth-horon inferiori.

14. And the border was drawn *thence*, and compassed the corner of

14. Et designatur terminus, circuitque ad latus maris ad meridiem,

the sea southward, from the hill that *lieth* before Beth-horon southward; and the goings out thereof were at Kirjath-baal, (which *is* Kirjath-jearim,) a city of the children of Judah. This *was* the west quarter.

a monte qui est e regione Beth-horon ad meridiem: suntque exitus ejus ad Cirjath-Baal, (ipsa est Cirjath-Jearim,) urbem filiorum Jehuda, hoc est latus maris.

15. And the south quarter *was* from the end of Kirjath-jearim, and the border went out on the west, and went out to the well of waters of Nephtoah;

15. Latus autem ad meridiem, ab extremo Cirjath-Jearim: itaque exit terminus ad mare, exit, inquam, ad fontem aquarum Nephthoah.

16. And the border came down to the end of the mountain that *lieth* before the valley of the son of Hinnom, *and* which *is* in the valley of the giants on the north, and descended to the valley of Hinnom, to the side of Jebusi on the south, and descended to En-rogel,

16. Et descendit terminus ad extremum montis, qui est e regione vallis Benhinnom, quique est in valle Rephaim ad aquilonem, descenditque ad vallem Hinnom ad latus Jebusi, ad meridiem, et illinc descendit ad Enrogel.

17. And was drawn from the north, and went forth to En-shemesh, and went forth toward Geliloth, which *is* over against the going up of Adummim, and descended to the stone of Bohan the son of Reuben,

17. Et circuit ab aquilone, et exit ad En-semes, atque egreditur ad Geliloth, quæ est e regione contra ascensum Adummim: et descendit Eben Bohan filii Ruben.

18. And passed along toward the side over against Arabah northward, and went down unto Arabah;

18. Illinc pertransit ad latus quod est e regione planitiei ad aquilonem, et descendit in Arabah.

19. And the border passed along to the side of Beth-hoglah northward: and the outgoings of the border were at the north bay of the salt sea, at the south end of Jordan. This *was* the south coast.

19. Inde pertransit terminus ad latus Beth-hogla ad aquilonem: suntque exitus termini ad limitem maris salis ad aquilonem, ad extremum Jordanis ad meridiem: iste est terminus austri.

20. And Jordan was the border of it on the east side. This *was* the inheritance of the children of Benjamin, by the coasts thereof round about, according to their families.

20. Et Jordanes terminat eum ad latus orientis. Ista est hæreditas filiorum Benjamin per terminos suos in circuitu per familias suas.

21. Now the cities of the tribe of the children of Benjamin, according to their families, were Jericho, and Beth-hoglah, and the valley of Keziz;

21. Fueruntque urbes istæ tribus filiorum Benjamin per familias suas, Jericho, et Beth-hoglah, et vallis Cesis,

22. And Beth-arabah, and Zemaraim, and Beth-el,

22. Et Beth-araba, et Semaraim, et Beth-el,

23. And Avim, and Parah, and Ophrah,

23. Et Avim, et Parah, et Ophrah,

24. And Chephar-haammonai, and Ophni, and Gaba: twelve cities with their villages.

24. Et villa Haamonai, et Ophni, et Gaba: civitates duodecim, et villæ earum.

25. Gibeon, and Ramah, and Beeroth,

25. Gibon, et Ramah, et Beeroth,

26. And Mizpeh, and Chephirah, and Mozah,

27. And Rekem, and Irpeel, and Taralah,

28. And Zelah, Eleph, and Jebusi, (which *is* Jerusalem,) Gibeath, *and* Kirjath: fourteen cities with their villages. This *is* the inheritance of the children of Benjamin, according to their families.

26. Et Mispeh, et Chephirah, et Mosah,

27. Et Recem, et Irpeel, et Tharalah.

28. Et Sela, Eleph, et Jebusi, (ipsa est Jerusalem,) Gibath, Cirjath: civitates quatuordecim, et villæ earum. Ista est hæreditas filiorum Benjamin per familias suas.

In the lot of Benjamin nothing occurs particularly deserving of notice, unless that a small tribe takes precedence of the others. I admit, indeed, that its limits were narrowed in proportion to the fewness of its numbers, because it obtained only twenty-six cities; but still an honour was bestowed upon it in the mere circumstance of its receiving its inheritance before more distinguished tribes. We may add, that in this way they were conjoined and made neighbours to the other[1] children of Joseph, with whom their relationship was more immediate. For they were placed in the middle between the children of Ephraim and Manasseh on the one side, and those of Judah on the other. They had also the distinguished honour of including Jerusalem in their inheritance, though they afterwards granted it by a kind of precarious tenure to the children of Judah for a royal residence.[2]

It is strange, however, that having obtained such a quiet locality, they did not live on peaceful and friendly terms with their neighbours. But we possess the prophecy of Jacob, "Benjamin shall raven as a wolf; in the morning he shall devour the prey, and at night he shall divide the spoil." (Gen. xlix. 27.) They must, therefore, have been by nature

[1] Latin, "Reliquis filiis." French, "Des autres enfans;" "The other children,"—an apparent oversight, as if Benjamin had been a son and not a brother of Joseph.—*Ed.*

[2] Latin, "Postea filiis Juda quasi precario sedem regiam concederent." French, "Depuis ils la baillerent aux enfans de Juda comme par emprunt, pour en faire le siege royal;" "Afterwards they let it to the children of Judah as by loan, to make it the royal residence." These words seem to imply that at some time or other a regular agreement to this effect had been made, but we nowhere find any mention of such an agreement. It would rather seem from Josh. xv. 63, and Judges i. 8, 21, that the inhabitants of Judah possessed Jerusalem in consequence of their having wrested it from the Jebusites.—*Ed.*

of a covetous and turbulent disposition, or from some necessity not now known to us, they must have been impelled to live upon plunder. In regard to the city of Luz, the other name is added, ("the same is Bethel,") because then only did the name given by Jacob come into common use. (Gen. xxviii. 19.) It was at no great distance from Beth-Aven, whose name, as it was opprobrious and infamous, was transferred to Bethel itself, after it was corrupted and polluted by impious superstitions.[1] It is probable that Ciriath-Baal was called Ciriath-Jeharim, to take away the name of the idol, which would have been a stain on its true piety. For it certainly would have been base and shameful that the lips of the people should have been polluted by the name of a protector who was an enemy to the true God.

CHAPTER XIX.

1. And the second lot came forth to Simeon, *even* for the tribe of the children of Simeon, according to their families: and their inheritance was within the inheritance of the children of Judah.	1. Egressa est autem sors secunda ipsi Simeon, tribui filiorum Simeon per familias suas: et fuit hæreditas eorum in medio hæreditatis filiorum Jehuda.
2. And they had in their inheritance Beer-sheba, and Sheba, and Moladah,	2. Fuitque eis in hæreditate eorum Beer-seba, et Seba, et Moladah,
3. And Hazar-shual, and Balah, and Azem,	3. Et Hasar-sual, et Balah, et Asen,
4. And Eltolad, and Bethul, and Hormah,	4. Et Eltholad, et Bethul, et Hormah,
5. And Ziklag, and Beth-marcaboth, and Hazar-susah,	5. Et Siclag, et Beth-Marcaboth, et Hasarsusa,
6. And Beth-lebaoth, and Sharuhen: thirteen cities and their villages.	6. Et Beth-Lebaoth, et Saruhen: urbes tredecim, et villæ earum.
7. Ain, Remmon, and Ether, and	7. Aim, Rimmon, et Ether, et

[1] This refers to the setting up of the golden calves by Jeroboam, and the idolatrous worship which thus impiously originated by him was long practised by his successors. See 1 Kings xii. 28-33; xiii.; 2 Kings x. 29-31; xxiii. 15; Amos iv. 4; v. 5; Hosea iv. 15; x. 5, 8. Bethel or "the house of God," so called by Jacob the morning after he had risen from his wonderful vision, having forfeited its name in consequence of the abominations practised at it, became afterwards known by that of Beth-aven, "the house of idols," or of vanity and iniquity.—*Ed.*

Ashan: four cities and their villages.	Asan: urbes quatuor, et villæ earum.
8. And all the villages that *were* round about these cities to Baalath-beer, Ramath of the south. This *is* the inheritance of the tribe of the children of Simeon, according to their families.	8. Et omnes villæ quæ erant per circuitus urbium istarum usque ad Baalath-beer, Ramath Australem. Ista est hæreditas tribus filiorum Simeon per familias suas.
9. Out of the portion of the children of Judah *was* the inheritance of the children of Simeon: for the part of the children of Judah was too much for them; therefore the children of Simeon had their inheritance within the inheritance of them.	9. De portione filiorum Jehuda facta fuit hæreditas filiorum Simeon: erat enim portio filiorum Jehuda major ipsis; itaque hæreditatem acceperunt filii Simeon in medio hæreditatis eorum.

Next followed the lot of the tribe of Simeon, not as a mark of honour, but rather as a mark of disgrace. Jacob had declared with regard to Simeon and Levi, "I will divide them in Jacob, and scatter them in Israel." (Gen. xlix. 7.) The punishment of Levi, indeed, was not only mitigated, but converted into an excellent dignity, inasmuch as his posterity were placed on a kind of watch-towers to keep the people in the paths of piety. In regard to Simeon, the dispersion of which Jacob prophesied, manifestly took place when certain cities within the territory of Judah were assigned to his posterity for their inheritance. For although they were not sent off to great distances, yet they dwelt dispersed, and as strangers in a land properly belonging to another. Therefore, on account of the slaughter which they had perpetrated with no less perfidy than cruelty, they were placed separately in different abodes. In this way the guilt of the father was visited upon his children, and the Lord ratified in fact that sentence which he had dictated to his servant. The truth of the lot also was clearly proved.

In the circumstance of a certain portion being withdrawn from the family of Judah, we again perceive that though the dividers had carefully endeavoured to observe equity, they had fallen into error, which they were not ashamed to correct as soon as it was discovered. And though they were guided by the Spirit, there is nothing strange in their having been partially mistaken, because God sometimes leaves his servants destitute of the spirit of judgment, and suffers them to act like men on different occasions, that they may not plume themselves too much on their clear-sightedness. We may add that the people were punished for their carelessness and confident haste, because they ought at the outset to have ascertained more accurately how much land could be properly assigned to each. This they neglected to do. Through their unskilful procedure, the children of Judah had received a disproportioned accumulation of territory, and equity required that they should relinquish a part. It would also have been better for themselves to have their limits fixed with certainty at once than to be subjected to a galling spoliation afterwards. Add that each tribe had indulged the vain hope that its members would dwell far and wide, as if the land had been of unlimited extent.

9. *Out of the portion of the children of Judah*, &c. The praise of moderation is due to the tribe of Judah for not contending that the abstraction of any part of the inheritance already assigned to them was unjust. They might easily have obtruded the name of God, and asserted that it was only by his authority they had obtained that settlement. But as it is decided by the common consent of all the tribes that more has been given to them than they can possess without loss and injury to the others, they immediately desist from all pretext for disputing the matter. And it is certain that if they had alleged the authority of God, it would have been falsely and wickedly, inasmuch as though their lot had been determined by him in regard to its situation, an error had taken place with regard to its extent, their limits having been fixed by human judgment wider than they ought. Therefore, acknowledging that it would have been wrong to give them what would occasion loss to others, they willingly resign it, and give a welcome reception to their brethren, who must otherwise have remained without inheritance, nay, submit to go shares with them in that which they supposed they had acquired beyond controversy.

10. And the third lot came up for the children of Zebulun, according to their families; and the border of their inheritance was unto Sarid.

11. And their border went up to-

10. Ascendit autem sors tertia filiis Zabulon per familias suas: et fuit terminus hæreditatis eorum usque ad Sarid.

11. Ascenditque terminus eorum

ward the sea, and Maralah, and reached to Dabbasheth, and reached to the river that *is* before Jokneam;

12. And turned from Sarid eastward, toward the sun-rising, unto the border of Chisloth-tabor, and then goeth out to Dabereth, and goeth up to Japhia,

13. And from thence passeth on along on the east to Gittah-hepher, to Ittah-kazin, and goeth out to Remmon-methoar, to Neah;

14. And the border compasseth it on the north side to Hannathon; and the outgoings thereof are in the valley of Jiphthah-el;

15. And Kattath, and Nahallal, and Shimron, and Idalah, and Beth-lehem: twelve cities with their villages.

16. This *is* the inheritance of the children of Zebulun, according to their families, these cities with their villages.

17. *And* the fourth lot came out to Issachar, for the children of Issachar, according to their families.

18. And their border was toward Jezreel, and Chesulloth, and Shunem,

19. And Haphraim, and Shihon, and Anaharath,

20. And Rabbith, and Kishion, and Abez,

21. And Remeth, and En-gannim, and En-haddah, and Beth-pazzez;

22. And the coast reacheth to Tabor, and Shahazimah, and Beth-shemesh; and the outgoings of their border were at Jordan: sixteen cities with their villages.

23. This *is* the inheritance of the tribe of the children of Issachar, according to their families, the cities and their villages.

24. And the fifth lot came out for the tribe of the children of Asher, according to their families.

25. And their border was Helkath, and Hali, and Beten, and Achshaph,

26. And Alammelech, and Amad, and Misheal; and reacheth to Carmel westward, and to Shihor-libnath;

ad mare: et Maralah, et pertingit ad Dabbaseth: pervenitque ad flumen quod est e regione Jocneam.

12. Revertiturque a Sarid ad orientem, id est, ad ortum solis, ad terminum Chisloth-Thabor, et illinc egreditur ad Dobrath, et ascendit in Japhia.

13. Inde præterea transit ad orientem, ad ortum, ad Githah-Hepher, et ad Ihtah-casin: et illinc exit in Rimmon, et gyrat ad Neah:

14. Gyrat item idem terminus ab aquilone ad Hannathon: suntque egressus ejus ad vallem Iphthael.

15. Et Catthath, et Nahalal, et Simron, et Idalah, et Bethlehem: urbes duodecim, et villæ earum.

16. Hæc est hæreditas filiorum Zabulon per familias suas: urbes istæ, et villæ earum.

17. Ipsi Issachar egressa est sors quarta, filiis inquam, Issachar per familias suas.

18. Et fuit terminus eorum Jezrael, et Chesuloth, et Sunem,

19. Et Hapharaim, et Sion, et Anaharath,

20. Et Rabbith, et Cicion, et Abeth,

21. Et Remeth, et Engannin, et Enhaddah, et Beth-passeth.

22. Et pervenit terminus in Thabor, et Sahasima, et Beth-semes: eruntque exitus termini eorum ad Jordanem: urbes sedecim, et villæ earum.

23. Hæc est hæreditas tribus filiorum Issachar per familias suas: urbes et villæ earum.

24. Egressa est autem sors quinta tribui filiorum Aser per familias suas.

25. Fuitque terminus eorum Helcath, et Hali, et Bethen, et Achsaph,

26. Et Alamelech, et Amad, et Misal, et pervenit in Carmel ad mare, et in Sihor Libnath.

27. And turneth toward the sun-rising to Beth-dagon, and reacheth to Zebulun, and to the valley of Jiphthah-el, toward the north side of Beth-emek, and Neiel, and goeth out to Cabul on the left hand;

28. And Hebron, and Rehob, and Hammon, and Kanah, *even* unto great Zidon;

29. And *then* the coast turneth to Ramah, and to the strong city Tyre; and the coast turneth to Hosah; and the outgoings thereof are at the sea, from the coast to Achzib:

30. Ummah also, and Aphek, and Rehob: twenty and two cities with their villages.

31. This *is* the inheritance of the tribe of the children of Asher, according to their families, these cities with their villages.

27. Et revertitur ad ortum solis in Beth-dagon, et pervenit in Zabulon, et in vallem Iphtahel ad aquilonem, et in Beth-emec, et Neel: et exit ad Chabul a sinistra.

28. Et Ebron, et Rehob, et Hammon, et Canah, usque ad Sidon magnam:

29. Revertiturque terminus in Rama, usque ad urbem munitam petræ: inde revertitur terminus in Hosah: suntque exitus ejus ad mare a funiculo Achzib,

30. Et Ummah, et Aphec, et Rehob: urbes viginti duæ, et villæ earum.

31. Hæc est hæreditas tribus filiorum Aser per familias suas: urbes istæ, et villæ earum.

10. *And the third lot came up*, &c. In the lot of Zebulun there is a clear fulfilment of the prophecy of Jacob, which had foretold that they would dwell on the sea-coast. An old man, an exile who could not set a foot on his own land,[1] assigned a maritime district to the posterity of his son Zebulun. What could be more extravagant? But now, when the lot assigns them a maritime region, no clearer confirmation of his decision could be desired. It was just as if God were twice thundering from heaven. The tribe of Zebulun, therefore, do not occupy the shore of their own accord or by human suffrage, but a divine arrangement fixes their habitation contiguous to the sea. Thus, although men erred, still the light was always seen shining brightly in the darkness. Jacob goes farther, and makes a clear distinction between Zebulun and Issachar. The former tribe will travel far and wide, carrying on trade and commerce; the latter remaining in his tents, will cultivate ease and a sedentary life. (Gen. xlix. 13-15.) Hence it is probable that the sea-coast where Zebulun settled, was provided with harbours and well adapted for the various forms of commercial inter-

[1] French, "Estant un vieillard, povre banni, qui n'avoit pas un pied de terre à luy ou il peust marcher;" "Being an old man, a poor exile, who had not a foot of land of his own on which he could walk."—*Ed.*

course,[1] whereas the children of Issachar were contented with their own produce, and consumed the fruits which they had raised by their own labour and culture at home.

Those who are thought to be well acquainted with these countries, affirm that the land of the tribe of Asher was fertile in corn.[2] This is in complete accordance both with the letter and the spirit of Jacob's prophecy. (Gen. xlix. 20.) From the fact that only a small number of cities are designated by name, we may infer that there were then many ruined cities which were not taken into account, and from the other fact that the people dwelt commodiously, we may also infer that they built many cities, with which it is plain from other passages that the land was adorned. And it is certainly apparent that only a summary of the division is briefly glanced at, and that thus many things were omitted which no religious feeling forbids us to investigate, provided we do not indulge in an excessive curiosity leading to no beneficial result. There cannot be a doubt that those to whom twenty or even only seventeen cities are attributed, had more extensive territories. Therefore, all we have here is a compendious description of the division as it was taken from the general and confused notes of the surveyors.

32. The sixth lot came out to the children of Naphtali, *even* for the children of Naphtali, according to their families.

33. And their coast was from Heleph, from Allon to Zaanannim, and Adami, Nekeb, and Jabneel, unto Lakum; and the outgoings thereof were at Jordan:

34. And *then* the coast turneth westward to Aznoth-tabor, and go-

32. Filiis Nephtali exivit sors sexta, filiis inquam, Nephtali, per familias suas.

33. Fuitque terminus eorum ab Heleph, et ab Elon in Saanannim, et Adami, Neceb, et Jabneel, usque ad Lacum: suntque exitus ejus ad Jordanem.

34. Postea revertitur terminus ad mare ad Aznoth-thabor: et progre-

[1] The extent of coast possessed by Zebulun was of very limited extent, but included the large and beautiful bay of Acre, which commences in the north at the promontory on which the town of Acre stands, and is terminated magnificently in the south by the lofty heights of Mount Carmel.—*Ed.*

[2] The greater part of it consisted of a rich and undulating plain, diversified by gentle hills, well watered by the Leontes and other streams which derived their supplies from the snowy heights of Lebanon, and sloping gradually to that part of the sea-coast, on which were built the famous cities of Tyre and Sidon. According to Clarke, the plain of Asher and Zebulun bore a considerable resemblance to the southern districts of England.—*Ed.*

eth out from thence to Hukkok, and reacheth to Zebulun on the south side, and reacheth to Asher on the west side, and to Judah upon Jordan toward the sun-rising.

35. And the fenced cities *are* Ziddim, Zer, and Hammath, Rakkath, and Chinnereth,

36. And Adamah, and Ramah, and Hazor,

37. And Kedesh, and Edrei, and En-hazor,

38. And Iron, and Migdal-el, Horem, and Beth-anath, and Beth-shemesh: nineteen cities with their villages.

39. This *is* the inheritance of the tribe of the children of Naphtali, according to their families, the cities and their villages.

40. *And* the seventh lot came out for the tribe of the children of Dan, according to their families.

41. And the coast of their inheritance was Zorah, and Eshtaol, and Ir-shemesh,

42. And Shaalabbin, and Ajalon, and Jethlah,

43. And Elon, and Thimnathah, and Ekron,

44. And Eltekeh, and Gibbethon, and Baalath,

45. And Jehud, and Bene-berak, and Gath-rimmon,

46. And Me-jarkon, and Rakkon, with the border before Japho.

47. And the coast of the children of Dan went out *too little* for them; therefore the children of Dan went up to fight against Leshem, and took it, and smote it with the edge of the sword, and possessed it, and dwelt therein, and called Leshem, Dan, after the name of Dan their father.

48. This *is* the inheritance of the tribe of the children of Dan, according to their families, these cities with their villages.

49. When they had made an end of dividing the land for inheritance by their coasts, the children of Israel gave an inheritance to Joshua the son of Nun among them:

50. According to the word of the Lord, they gave him the city which

ditur illinc in Huccoc, et pervenit ad Zabulon a meridie, et ad Aser pervenit ab occidente, et ad Jehuda in Jordanem, ad ortum solis.

35. Et urbes munitæ, Siddim, Ser, et Hammath, Raccath, et Chinnereth.

36. Et Adamah, et Ramah, et Hasor,

37. Et Cedes, et Hedrei, et En-Hasor,

38. Et Iron, et Migdal-el, Horem, et Beth-anath, et Beth-semes: urbes novemdecim, et villæ earum.

39. Hæc est hæreditas tribus filiorum Nephtali per familias suas, urbes istæ et villæ earum.

40. Tribui filiorum Dan per familias suas exivit sors septima.

41. Fuitque terminus hæreditatis eorum, Sorah, et Esthaol, et Itsemes,

42. Et Saalabbin, et Ajalon, et Ithlah,

43. Et Elon, et Thimnathah, et Ecron,

44. Et Elthece, et Gibbethon, et Baalath,

45. Et Jehud, et Bene-berak, et Gath-rimon,

46. Et Mehajarcon, et Raccon, cum termino contra Japho.

47. Et exivit terminus filiorum Dan ab eis, ascenderuntque filii Dan, et pugnaverunt cum Lesem, ceperuntque eam, ac percusserunt eam acie gladii, et hæreditate acceperunt eam, habitaveruntque in ea: et vocaverunt Lesem Dan, secundum nomen Dan patris sui.

48. Hæc est hæreditas tribus filiorum Dan per familias suas, civitates istæ, et villæ earum.

49. Quum autem finem fecissent partiendi terram ut possiderent singuli terminos suos, dederunt filii Israel hæreditatem ipsi Josue filio Nun in medio sui.

50. Secundum sermonem Jehovæ dederunt ei urbem quam petivit,

he asked, *even* Timnath-serah in mount Ephraim: and he built the city, and dwelt therein.	Thimnath-serah in monte Ephraim, et edificavit urbem, habitavitque in ea.
51. These *are* the inheritances, which Eleazar the priest, and Joshua the son of Nun, and the heads of the fathers of the tribes of the children of Israel, divided for an inheritance by lot in Shiloh before the Lord, at the door of the tabernacle of the congregation. So they made an end of dividing the country.	51. Istæ sunt hæreditates quas tradiderunt possidendas Eleazar sacerdos, et Josue filius Nun, et principes patrum tribuum filiorum Israel per sortem in Silo coram Jehova ad ostiam tabernaculi conventionis, et finem fecerunt dividendi terram.

The next lot mentioned is that of Naphtali, and it seems to correspond with the disposition and manners of that tribe. For Jacob had testified, Naphtali is a hind let loose; he giveth goodly words. For this reason they seem to have been contiguous on one side to the children of Judah, and to have been surrounded on other sides by the enclosures of their brethren.[1] Indeed, in its being said that the tribe of Dan took Lesen, there seems to be a tacit comparison, because the children of Naphtali did not employ arms to force their way into their inheritance, but kept themselves quietly in a subdued territory, and thus enjoyed safety and tranquillity under the faith, and, as it were, protection of Judah and the other tribes. The capture of Lesen by the children of Dan, in accordance with the divine grant which they had

[1] The tribe of Naphtali, as marked out by Joshua, Eleazar, and the heads of the tribes, harmonizes well with the figurative description of it given by Jacob, for both in scenery and fertility it is one of the fairest in the Promised Land, but the locality assigned to it in the Commentary is singularly inaccurate. In the Latin, it is said that the children of Naphtali "Videntur contigui ab una parte fuisse filiis Juda: alibi autem cincti fuisse fratrum suorum præsidiis;" and in the French, "Il semble que d'un costé ils estoyent contigus aux enfans de Juda; et d'autrepart qu'ils estoyent environnez du secours de leurs freres;" "It seems that on one side they were contiguous to the children of Judah, and on the other sides that they were surrounded by the help of their brethren." The fact, however, is, that Judah and Naphtali are at the opposite extremities of the country, and so far from being contiguous to each other, are widely separated by the intervention of no fewer than five tribes, which commencing on the frontiers of Judah, and proceeding northwards, are, in succession, Benjamin, Ephraim, Manasseh, Issachar, and Zebulun. Then, as it stretched from the shores of the lake of Gennesaret, north to the roots of Lebanon, it cannot well be said to have been surrounded on all sides by the enclosures of other tribes. It certainly had Zebulun on the south-west, and Asher on the west, but on the north and east, it formed the extreme frontiers of the Promised Land, and, of course, bounded with foreign and hostile settlements.—*Ed.*

received of it, did not take place till after the death of Joshua. But the fact which is more fully detailed in the book of Judges is here mentioned in passing, because praise was due to them for their boldness and activity in thus embracing the right which God had bestowed upon them, and so trusting in him as to go down bravely and defeat the enemy.

49. *When they had made an end of dividing*, &c. We have here, at length, an account of the gratitude of the people towards Joshua. For although the partition of the land of Canaan, among the posterity of Abraham, behoved to be equitable, yet Joshua, by his excellent virtues, deserved some honorary reward. Nor could any complain that a single individual was enriched at their expense. For, first, in the delay there was a striking proof of the moderation of this holy servant of God. He does not give any heed to his own interest till the commonweal has been secured. How seldom do we find any who, after they have given one or two specimens of valour, do not forthwith make haste to the prey? Not so Joshua, who thinks not of himself till the land has been divided. In the reward itself also the same temperance and frugality are conspicuous. The city he asks to be given to himself and his family was a mere heap of stones, either because it had been demolished and converted into a heap of ruins, or because no city had yet been built upon it.

It is conjectured with probability, that with the view of making the grant as little invidious as possible, the city he requested was of no great value. If any one thinks it strange that he did not give his labour gratuitously, let him reflect that Joshua liberally obeyed the divine call, and had no mercenary feelings in undergoing so many labours, dangers, and troubles; but having spontaneously performed his duty, he behoved not to repudiate a memorial of the favour of God, unless he wished by perverse contempt to suppress his glory. For the grant voted to him was nothing else than a simple testimonial of the divine power, which had been manifested through his hand. Truly no ambition can be detected here, inasmuch as he desires nothing for himself, and does not rashly act from a feeling of covetousness, but seeks in the popular consent a confirmation of the honour which God had already bestowed upon him. To have been silent in such a case, would have been more indicative of heartlessness than of modesty. The statement in the concluding verse of the chapter, that Joshua and Eleazar made an end of dividing the land, points to the perpetuity of the boundaries, which had been fixed, and warns the children of Israel against moving in any way to unsettle an inviolable decree.

CHAPTER XX.

1. The Lord also spake unto Joshua, saying,

2. Speak to the children of Israel, saying, Appoint out for you cities of refuge, whereof I spake unto you by the hand of Moses;

3. That the slayer that killeth *any* person unawares, *and* unwittingly, may flee thither: and they shall be your refuge from the avenger of blood.

4. And when he that doth flee unto one of those cities shall stand at the entering of the gate of the city, and shall declare his cause in the ears of the elders of that city, they shall take him into the city unto them, and give him a place, that he may dwell among them.

5. And if the avenger of blood pursue after him, then they shall not deliver the slayer up into his hand; because he smote his neighbour unwittingly, and hated him not beforetime.

6. And he shall dwell in that city, until he stand before the congregation for judgment, *and* until the death of the high priest that shall be in those days: then shall the slayer return, and come unto his own city, and unto his own house, unto the city from whence he fled.

7. And they appointed Kedesh in Galilee in mount Naphtali, and

1. Loquutus est autem Jehova ad Josue, dicendo,

2. Alloquere filios Israel, his verbis, Date urbes refugii, de quibus loquutus sum ad vos per manum Mosis:

3. Ut fugiat illuc homicida qui percusserit animam per errorem, absque scientia: eruntque vobis in refugium a propinquo sanguinis.

4. Et fugiet ad unam ex civitatibus istis, stabitque ad ostium portæ urbis, ac loquetur in auribus seniorum urbis ipsius verba sua, et recolligent eum in urbem ad se, dabuntque ei locum, ac habitabit apud eos.

5. Quum autem persequutus fuerit eum propinquus sanguinis, non tradent homicidam in manum ejus: quia absque scientia percussit proximum suum, neque odio habuerat eum ab heri et nudiustertius.

6. Et habitabit in ea civitate donec stet ante cœtum ad judicium, aut donec moriatur sacerdos magnus qui erit in diebus illis: tunc enim revertetur homicida venietque ad urbem suam, et ad domum suam, ad urbem unde fugerat.

7. Et addixerunt Cedes in Galil in monte Nephtali, et Sechem in

Shechem in mount Ephraim, and Kirjath-arba (which *is* Hebron) in the mountain of Judah.

8. And on the other side Jordan, by Jericho eastward, they assigned Bezer in the wilderness upon the plain out of the tribe of Reuben, and Ramoth in Gilead out of the tribe of Gad, and Golan in Bashan out of the tribe of Manasseh.

9. These were the cities appointed for all the children of Israel, and for the stranger that sojourneth among them, that whosoever killeth *any* person at unawares might flee thither, and not die by the hand of the avenger of blood, until he stood before the congregation.

monte Ephraim, et Cirjath-arba (ipsa est Hebron) in monte Jehudæ.

8. De trans Jordane autem Jericho, ad orientem dederunt Beser in deserto in planitie, de tribu Ruben: et Ramoth in Gilead, de tribu Gadi: et Golan in Basan, de tribu Manasse.

9. Istæ fuerunt urbes conventionis omnibus filiis Israel, et peregrino qui peregrinatur in medio eorum: ut fugeret illuc quicunque interfecisset aliquem per errorem, et non moreretur manu propinqui sanguinis, donec stetisset coram cœtu.

1. *The Lord also spake unto Joshua, &c.* In the fact of its not having occurred to their own minds, to designate the cities of refuge, till they were again reminded of it, their sluggishness appears to be indirectly censured. The divine command to that effect had been given beyond the Jordan. When the reason for it remained always equally valid, why do they wait? Why do they not give full effect to that which they had rightly begun? We may add, how important it was that there should be places of refuge for the innocent, in order that the land might not be polluted with blood. For if that remedy had not been provided, the kindred of those who had been killed would have doubled the evil, by proceeding without discrimination to avenge their death. It certainly did not become the people to be idle in guarding the land from stain and taint.[1] Hence we perceive how tardy men are, not only to perform their duty, but to provide for their own safety, unless the Lord frequently urge them, and prick them forward by the stimulus of exhortation. But that they sinned only from thoughtlessness, is apparent from this, that they are forthwith ready

[1] Calvin is somewhat singular in holding that the message communicated to Joshua was an indirect censure of the Israelites, for not having previously of their own accord appointed cities of refuge. Other expositors think that till now the proper time of appointing them had not arrived, as it could not well precede, but rather behoved to be subsequent to the allocation of cities to the Levites, inasmuch as the nature of the case required that every city of refuge should be Levitical.—*Ed.*

to obey, neither procrastinating nor creating obstacles or delays to a necessary matter, by disputing the propriety of it.

The nature of the asylum afforded by the cities of refuge has been already explained. It gave no impunity to voluntary murder, but if any one, by mistake, had slain a man, with whom he was not at enmity, he found a safe refuge by fleeing to one of these cities destined for that purpose. Thus God assisted the unfortunate, and prevented their suffering the punishment of an atrocious deed, when they had not been guilty of it. Meanwhile respect was so far paid to the feelings of the brethren and kindred of the deceased, that their sorrow was not increased by the constant presence of the persons who had caused their bereavement. Lastly, the people were accustomed to detest murder, since homicide, even when not culpable, was followed by exile from country and home, till the death of the high priest. For that temporary exile clearly shewed how precious human blood is in the sight of God. Thus the law was just, equitable, and useful, as well in a public as in a private point of view.[1] But it is to be briefly observed, that everything is not here mentioned in order. For one who had accidentally killed a man might have remained in safety, by sisting himself before the court to plead his cause, and obtaining an acquittal, after due and thorough investigation, as we explained more fully in the books of Moses, when treating of this matter.

7. *And they appointed Kedesh*, &c. The Hebrew word Kedesh here used, signifies also to fit and consecrate. Accordingly, I interpret, that cities were selected according as common use required.[2] Hence it is inferred that matters were well arranged so as to make private yield to public interest. Moreover, we shall see in the next chapter, that

[1] It may be observed in passing, how strikingly the humanity and wisdom conspicuous in the appointment of the Mosaic cities of refuge contrast with the manifold abuses and abominations to which the numerous asylums and sanctuaries of Popish countries have led.—*Ed.*

[2] Latin, "Prout communis usus ferebat." French, "Selon que le profit et l'utilité commune le requeroit;" "According as the common profit and utility required."—*Ed.*

Ciriath-Arbah, which was afterwards called Hebron, was transferred to the Levites, though it had formerly been the property of Caleb. Hence appeared the rare, nay, the incomparable moderation of this aged saint, who readily gave up to others both the city and suburbs, which he had justly claimed as his right, the moment the lot shewed that this was pleasing to God. It was necessary to advert briefly to this change, because the Lord was pleased that asylums should be found only in the Levitical cities, that their innocence might be defended with greater fidelity and authority.

CHAPTER XXI.

1. Then came near the heads of the fathers of the Levites unto Eleazar the priest, and unto Joshua the son of Nun, and unto the heads of the fathers of the tribes of the children of Israel;

2. And they spake unto them at Shiloh, in the land of Canaan, saying, The Lord commanded, by the hand of Moses, to give us cities to dwell in, with the suburbs thereof for our cattle.

3. And the children of Israel gave unto the Levites, out of their inheritance, at the commandment of the Lord, these cities and their suburbs.

4. And the lot came out for the families of the Kohathites: and the children of Aaron the priest, *which were* of the Levites, had by lot, out of the tribe of Judah, and out of the tribe of Simeon, and out of the tribe of Benjamin, thirteen cities.

5. And the rest of the children of Kohath *had* by lot, out of the families of the tribe of Ephraim, and out of the tribe of Dan, and out of the half-tribe of Manasseh, ten cities.

6. And the children of Gershon *had* by lot, out of the families of the tribe of Issachar, and out of the tribe of Asher, and out of the tribe of Naphtali, and out of the half-tribe of Manasseh in Bashan, thirteen cities.

1. Accesserunt autem principes patrum Levitarum ad Eleazar sacerdotem, et ad Josue filium Nun, et ad principes patrum tribuum filiorum Israel.

2. Loquutique sunt ad eos in Silo in terra Chanaan, dicendo, Jehova præcepit per manum Mosis ut daretis nobis urbes ad habitandum, et suburbana earum pro animalibus nostris.

3. Dederunt ergo filii Israel Levitis de hæreditate sua, secundum sermonem Jehovæ, urbes istas et suburbana earum.

4. Egressa est autem sors per familias Ceathitarum: fueruntque filiis Aaron sacerdotis de Levitis, de tribu Juda, et de tribu Simeon, et de tribu Benjamin per sortem, urbes tredecim.

5. Filiis autem Ceath reliquis, de familiis tribus Ephraim, et de tribu Dan, et de dimidia tribu Manasse, per sortem, urbes decem.

6. Filiis vero Gerson de familiis tribus Issachar, et de tribu Aser, et de tribu Nephthali, et de dimidia tribu Manasse in Basan per sortem, urbes tredecim.

7. The children of Merari, by their families, *had* out of the tribe of Reuben, and out of the tribe of Gad, and out of the tribe of Zebulun, twelve cities.

8. And the children of Israel gave by lot unto the Levites these cities with their suburbs, as the Lord commanded by the hand of Moses.

9. And they gave, out of the tribe of the children of Judah, and out of the tribe of the children of Simeon, these cities which are *here* mentioned by name,

10. Which the children of Aaron, *being* of the families of the Kohathites, *who were* of the children of Levi, had: for theirs was the first lot.

11. And they gave them the city of Arba, the father of Anak, (which *city is* Hebron,) in the hill *country* of Judah, with the suburbs thereof round about it.

12. But the fields of the city, and the villages thereof, gave they to Caleb the son of Jephunneh for his possession.

13. Thus they gave to the children of Aaron the priest, Hebron with her suburbs, *to be* a city of refuge for the slayer, and Libnah with her suburbs,

14. And Jattir, with her suburbs, and Eshtemoa with her suburbs,

15. And Holon with her suburbs, and Debir with her suburbs,

16. And Ain with her suburbs, and Juttah with her suburbs, *and* Bethshemesh with her suburbs: nine cities out of those two tribes.

17. And out of the tribe of Benjamin, Gibeon with her suburbs, Geba with her suburbs,

18. Anathoth with her suburbs, and Almon with her suburbs: four cities.

19. All the cities of the children of Aaron, the priests, *were* thirteen cities with their suburbs.

7. Filiis Merari per familias suas, de tribu Ruben, et de tribu Gad, et de tribu Zabulon, urbes duodecim.

8. Dederunt, inquam, filii Israel Levitis urbes has, et suburbana earum, sicut præceperat Jehova per manum Mosis, per sortem.

9. Dederunt ergo de tribu filiorum Juda, et de tribu filiorum Simeon, urbes istas quas vocavit nomine.

10. Fueruntque filiis Aaron de familiis Ceath, de filiis Levi: illis enim fuit sors prima.

11. Dederuntque eis Ciriath-arba patris Anac (ipsa est Hebron) in monte Juda, et suburbana ejus per circuitum ejus.

12. Agrum vero ejus urbis et villas ejus dederunt Caleb filio Jephune in possessionem ejus.

13. Filiis, inquam, Aaron sacerdotis dederunt urbem refugii homicidæ, Hebron, et suburbana ejus, et Libna et suburbana ejus.

14. Et Jathir et suburbana ejus, et Esthemoa et suburbana ejus.

15. Holon et suburbana ejus, et Debir et suburbana ejus.

16. Et Ain et suburbana ejus, et Jutta et suburbana ejus: et Bethsemes et suburbana ejus: urbes novem de duabus tribubus istis.

17. De tribu vero Benjamin, Gibeon et suburbana ejus, et Geba et suburbana ejus.

18. Anathoth et suburbana ejus, Almon et suburbana ejus: urbes quatuor.

19. Omnes urbes filiorum Aaron sacerdotum, tredecim urbes et suburbana earum.

1. *Then came near the heads*, &c. Here we have at a later period a narrative of what ought to have preceded. For no cities of refuge were appointed before they had been assigned

to the Levites. To this may be added what was formerly said, that Joshua and Eleazar had made an end of dividing the land. Now, the land was not truly divided till the habitation of the Levites was fixed. We must understand, therefore, that when the lot was cast in the name of the ten tribes, a reservation was made of cities in the land of Canaan for the habitation of the Levites. Beyond the Jordan their portion had already been assigned to them. But as the Levites come forward and request a ratification of the divine grant, it is probable that they were neglected till they pleaded their own cause. For so it is apt to happen, every one being so attentive in looking after his own affairs that even brethren are forgotten. It was certainly disgraceful to the people that they required to be pulled by the ear, and put in mind of what the Lord had clearly ordered respecting the Levites. But had they not demanded a domicile for themselves, there was a risk of their being left to lie in the open air; although, at the same time, we are permitted to infer that the people erred more from carelessness and forgetfulness than from any intention to deceive, as they make no delay as soon as they are admonished; nay, they are praised for their obedience in that they did what was just and right according to the word of the Lord.

4. *And the lot came out for the families*, &c. Here is first described the number of cities of which we shall have to speak by and bye. Secondly, it is distinctly said that the lot fell out to the children of Aaron in the tribe of Judah. This did not happen fortuitously, because God in his admirable counsel placed them in that locality where he had determined to choose a temple for himself. Thirdly, the narrative proceeds to give the exact names of the cities, of which the first mentioned is Hebron, of which Caleb, with great equanimity, allowed himself to be deprived. Should any one object that the first city of all that ought to have been given them was Jerusalem, where they were to have their future station, it is easy to answer, that moderate sized cities were delivered to them as their condition required. Moreover, Jerusalem was not then subjugated, as

it continued under the power of the Jebusites. In short, it would have been absurd to assign a royal seat to priests. And their religion and faith was the better proved by this, that they migrated of their own accord from their native soil to devote their attention to sacred things. For no priest performed the office without becoming a stranger. Their weakness, however, was so far indulged by giving them a grant of neighbouring cities, that they might not have the fatigue of a long journey in going to perform their function. Moreover, the giving of thirteen cities for a habitation to one family, and that not very numerous, confirms what I have elsewhere said, that the other tribes possessed very many cities,[1] of which no mention is made; in a short time this will be more certainly confirmed.

20. And the families of the children of Kohath, the Levites which remained of the children of Kohath, even they had the cities of their lot out of the tribe of Ephraim.

21. For they gave them Shechem with her suburbs, in mount Ephraim, *to be* a city of refuge for the slayer; and Gezer with her suburbs,

22. And Kibzaim with her suburbs, and Beth-horon with her suburbs: four cities.

23. And out of the tribe of Dan, Eltekeh with her suburbs, Gibbethon with her suburbs,

24. Aijalon with her suburbs, Gath-rimmon with her suburbs: four cities.

25. And out of the half-tribe of Manasseh, Taanach with her suburbs, and Gath-rimmon with her suburbs: two cities.

26. All the cities *were* ten, with their suburbs, for the families of the children of Kohath that remained.

27. And unto the children of Gershon, of the families of the Levites, out of the *other* half-tribe of Manasseh, *they gave* Golan in

20. Familiis vero filiarum Cahath Levitarum, qui residui erant de filiis Cahath (fuerunt autem urbes sortis eorum de tribu Ephraim.)

21. Dederunt, inquam, illis urbem refugii homicidæ Sechem, et suburbana ejus in monte Ephraim: et Geser et suburbana ejus.

22. Et Cibsaim et suburbana ejus: et Beth-horon et suburbana ejus: urbes quatuor.

23. De tribu vero Dan, Elthece et suburbana ejus: et Gibbethon et suburbana ejus.

24. Et Ajalon et suburbana ejus, et Gath-rimmon et suburbana ejus: urbes quatuor.

25. De dimidia vero tribu Manasse Thaanach, et suburbana ejus: Gathrimmon et suburbana ejus: urbes duæ.

26. Omnes urbes decem, et suburbana earum, familiis filiorum Cahath residuis.

27. Porro filiis Gerson de familiis Levitarum, de dimidia tribu Manasse urbem refugii homicidæ, Golan in Basan, et suburbana ejus,

[1] Latin, "Plurimis urbibus." French, "Plusieurs villes:" "Several cities."—*Ed.*

Bashan with her suburbs, *to be* a city of refuge for the slayer; and Beeshterah with her suburbs: two cities.

28. And out of the tribe of Issachar, Kishon with her suburbs, Dabareh with her suburbs,

29. Jarmuth with her suburbs, En-gannim with her suburbs: four cities.

30. And out of the tribe of Asher, Mishal with her suburbs, Abdon with her suburbs,

31. Helkath with her suburbs, and Rehob with her suburbs: four cities.

32. And out of the tribe of Naphtali, Kedesh in Galilee with her suburbs, *to be* a city of refuge for the slayer; and Hamoth-dor with her suburbs, and Kartan with her suburbs: three cities.

33. All the cities of the Gershonites, according to their families, *were* thirteen cities with their suburbs.

34. And unto the families of the children of Merari, the rest of the Levites, out of the tribe of Zebulun, Jokneam with her suburbs, and Kartah with her suburbs,

35. Dimnah with her suburbs, Nahalal with her suburbs: four cities.

36. And out of the tribe of Reuben, Bezer with her suburbs, and Jahazah with her suburbs,

37. Kedemoth with her suburbs, and Mephaath with her suburbs: four cities.

38. And out of the tribe of Gad, Ramoth in Gilead with her suburbs, *to be* a city of refuge for the slayer; and Mahanaim with her suburbs,

39. Heshbon with her suburbs, Jazer with her suburbs: four cities in all.

40. So all the cities for the children of Merari, by their families, which were remaining of the families of the Levites, were, *by* their lot, twelve cities.

41. All the cities of the Levites, within the possession of the children of Israel, *were* forty and eight cities with their suburbs.

Beesthera et suburbana ejus: urbes duæ.

28. De tribu Issachar, Cision et suburbana ejus: Dabrath et suburbana ejus.

29. Iarmuth et suburbana ejus: Engannim et suburbana ejus: urbes quatuor.

30. De tribu autem Aser, Misal et suburbana ejus: Abdon et suburbana ejus.

31. Helcath et suburbana ejus, et Rehob et suburbana ejus: urbes quatuor.

32. De tribu vero Nephthali urbem refugii homicidæ, Cedes in Galil et suburbana ejus: et Hamoth-dor et suburbana ejus: et Carthan et suburbana ejus: urbes tres.

33. Omnes urbes Gersonitarum per familias suas, tredecim urbes, et suburbana earum.

34. Familiis autem filiorum Merari Levitarum residuorum, de tribu Zabulon: Jocneam et suburbana ejus: Cartha et suburbana ejus.

35. Dimnah et suburbana ejus, Nahalal et suburbana ejus: urbes quatuor.

36. De tribu vero Ruben, Beser et suburbana ejus: et Jehasa et suburbana ejus.

37. Cedemoth et suburbana ejus: Mephaath et suburbana ejus: urbes quatuor.

38. Et de tribu Gad, urbem refugii homicidæ, Ramoth in Gileath et suburbana ejus: et Mahanaim et suburbana ejus.

39. Hesbon et suburbana ejus: Jaazer et suburbana ejus: urbes quatuor.

40. Omnes urbes filiorum Merari per familias suas qui residui erant de familiis Levitarum, ut fuit sors eorum, urbes duodecim.

41. Omnes urbes Levitarum, in medio possessionis filiorum Israel, urbes quadraginta octo et suburbana earum.

42. These cities were every one with their suburbs round about them: thus *were* all these cities.	42. Fuerunt urbes istæ singulæ, et suburbana earum per circuitum ipsarum: sic omnibus urbibus istis.
43. And the Lord gave unto Israel all the land which he sware to give unto their fathers; and they possessed it, and dwelt therein.	43. Dedit itaque Jehova Israeli universam terram de qua juraverat se daturum eam patribus eorum: et possederunt eam, habitaveruntque in ea.
44. And the Lord gave them rest round about, according to all that he sware unto their fathers: and there stood not a man of all their enemies before them; the Lord delivered all their enemies into their hand.	44. Requiem quoque dedit eis Jehova in circuitu prorsus ut juraverat Jehova patribus eorum: neque fuit quisquam qui resisteret illis ex omnibus inimicis eorum: omnes inimicos eorum tradidit Jehova in manum eorum.
45. There failed not ought of any good thing which the Lord had spoken unto the house of Israel; all came to pass.	45. Non cecidit ullum verbum ex omni bono quod loquutus fuerat Jehova ad domum Israel, omnia evenerunt.

20. *And the families of the children of Kohath*, &c. Why it was necessary that the Levites should be dispersed among the different tribes, the reader may see in my Commentaries on the Books of Moses. This dispersion had, indeed, been imposed on their progenitor as a punishment for the cruelty and perfidy of which he had been guilty toward the children of Shechem, but the disgrace of it had been converted into the highest honour by their appointment as a kind of guardians in every district to retain the people in the pure worship of God. It is true, they were everywhere strangers; but still it was with the very high dignity of acting as stewards for God, and preventing their countrymen from revolting from piety. This is the reason for stating so carefully how many cities they obtained from each tribe; they were everywhere to keep watch, and preserve the purity of sacred rites unimpaired.

41. *All the cities of the Levites*, &c. This passage more especially shews what I have already more than once adverted to, that the boundaries of the other tribes were not so confined as not to comprehend a far larger number of cities than is actually mentioned. It is perfectly well known that Levi was the least numerous of all the tribes. With what equity, then, could it have been allowed to expand itself over four times the space allowed to the tribe of Zebulun,

which, though more populous, is mentioned as only possessing twelve cities. Only sixteen are enumerated as belonging to the tribe of Issachar, nineteen to the tribe of Naphtali, and twenty-two to the tribe of Asher. It would surely have been an unequal division to give the greater number of cities for habitation to the smaller population. Hence we infer, that not only the villages which are here set down as accessories of the cities were fit for habitation, but that other cities also, of which no mention is made, were included. In short, the extent of the lot of Levi makes it perfectly obvious how large and ample the territories of the other tribes must have been.

43. *And the Lord gave unto Israel, &c.* Should any one raise a question as to this rest, the answer is easy. The nations of Canaan were so completely overcome with fear, that they thought they could not better consult their interest than by servilely flattering the Israelites, and purchasing peace from them on any terms.[1] Plainly, therefore, the country was subdued and rendered peaceful for habitation, since no one gave any annoyance, or dared to entertain any hostile intentions, since there were no threats, no snares, no violence, no conspiracies.

A second point, however, raises some doubt,[2] namely, how the children of Israel can be said to have been settled in the possession of the land promised to them, and to have become masters of it, in such a sense that in regard to the enjoyment of it, not one syllable of the promises of God had failed. For we have already seen that many of the enemy were intermingled with them. The divine intention was, that not one of the enemy should be permitted to remain; on the other hand, the Israelites do not drive out many, but

[1] French, "Ils penserent qu'il n'y avoit rien meilleur pour eux ni plus expedient, que de racheter la paix avec les enfans d'Israel, en faisans les chiens couchans (comme l'on dit) devant eux, et leur gratifiant en toutes choses;" "They thought there was nothing better for them, nor more expedient, than to purchase peace with the children of Israel by acting (so to speak) like fawning dogs before them, and gratifying them in all things."—*Ed.*

[2] Latin, "Verum de secundo ambigitur." French, "Mais il y a plus grande difficulté sur le second poinct;" "But there is greater difficulty as to the second point."—*Ed.*

admit them as neighbours, as if the inheritance had been common to them ; they even make pactions with them. How then can these two things be reconciled, that God, as he had promised, gave possession of the land to the people, and yet they were excluded from some portion by the power or obstinate resistance of the enemy ?

In order to remove this appearance of contradiction, it is necessary to distinguish between the certain, clear, and steadfast faithfulness of God in keeping his promises, and between the effeminacy and sluggishness of the people, in consequence of which the benefit of the divine goodness in a manner slipped through their hands. Whatever war the people undertook, in whatever direction they moved their standards, victory was prepared ; nor was there any other delay or obstacle to their exterminating all their enemies than their own voluntary torpor. Wherefore, although they did not rout them all so as to make their possession clear, yet the truth of God came visibly forth, and was realized, inasmuch as they might have obtained what was remaining without any difficulty, had they been pleased to avail themselves of the victories offered to them. The whole comes to this, that it was owing entirely to their own cowardice that they did not enjoy the divine goodness in all its fulness and integrity. This will be still clearer from the following chapter.

CHAPTER XXII.

1. Then Joshua called the Reubenites, and the Gadites, and the half-tribe of Manasseh,

2. And said unto them, Ye have kept all that Moses, the servant of the Lord, commanded you, and have obeyed my voice in all that I commanded you:

3. Ye have not left your brethren these many days unto this day, but have kept the charge of the commandment of the Lord your God.

4. And now the Lord your God hath given rest unto your brethren, as he promised them: therefore now

1. Tunc accersivit Josue Rubenitas et Gaditas ac dimidiam tribum Manasse,

2. Dixitque ad eos, Vos custodistis omnia quæ præcepit vobis Moses servus Jehovæ, et obedistis voci meæ in cunctis quæ præcepi vobis.

3. Non deseruistis fratres vestros jam diebus multis usque ad diem hanc, sed custodistis custodiam præcepti Jehovæ Dei vestri.

4. Nunc autem requiem dedit Jehova Deus vester fratribus vestris, quemadmodum dixerat eis:

return ye, and get you unto your tents, *and* unto the land of your possession, which Moses, the servant of the Lord, gave you on the other side Jordan.

5. But take diligent heed to do the commandment, and the law, which Moses, the servant of the Lord, charged you, to love the Lord your God, and to walk in all his ways, and to keep his commandments, and to cleave unto him, and to serve him with all your heart, and with all your soul.

6. So Joshua blessed them, and sent them away: and they went unto their tents.

7. Now to the *one* half of the tribe of Manasseh Moses had given *possession* in Bashan; but unto the *other* half thereof gave Joshua among their brethren on this side Jordan westward. And when Joshua sent them away also unto their tents, then he blessed them;

8. And he spake unto them, saying, Return with much riches unto your tents, and with very much cattle, with silver, and with gold, and with brass, and with iron, and with very much raiment: divide the spoil of your enemies with your brethren.

9. And the children of Reuben, and the children of Gad, and the half-tribe of Manasseh, returned, and departed from the children of Israel out of Shiloh, which *is* in the land of Canaan, to go unto the country of Gilead, to the land of their possession, whereof they were possessed, according to the word of the Lord by the hand of Moses.

nunc igitur revertimini, et proficiscimini ad tabernacula vestra, ad terram possessionis vestræ, quam dedit vobis Moses servus Jehovæ trans Jordanem.

5. Tantum observate diligenter ut faciatis præceptum et legem quam præcepit vobis Moses servus Jehovæ, ut diligatis Jehovam Deum vestrum, et ambuletis in omnibus viis ejus, servetisque præcepta ejus, et adhæreatis ei, atque serviatis ei toto corde vestro, et tota anima vestra.

6. Benedixitque eis Josue, ac dimisit eos, abieruntque in tabernacula sua.

7. Dimidiæ autem tribui Manasse dederat Moses in Basan: alteri autem ejus parti dedit Josue cum fratribus suis trans Jordanem ad occidentem. Et etiam quum dimitteret eos Josue in tabernacula sua, et benedixisset eis,

8. Tunc dixit ad eos, dicendo, Cum divitiis multis revertimini ad tabernacula vestra, et cum acquisitione multa valde, cum argento, et auro, et ære, et ferro, et vestibus multis valde: dividite spolia inimicorum vestrorum cum fratribus vestris.

9. Reversi sunt itaque, et abierunt filii Ruben, et filii Gad, et dimidia tribus Manasse a filiis Israel de Silo quæ est in terra Chanaan, ut irent ad terram Gilead, ad terram possessionis suæ, in qua possessionem acceperunt secundum sermonem Jehovæ per manum Mosis.

1. *Then Joshua called the Reubenites*, &c. Here is related the discharge of the two tribes and half-tribe, who had followed the rest of the people, not that they might acquire anything for themselves, but that, as they had already obtained dwellings and lands without lot, they might carry on war in common with their brethren, until they also should have a quiet inheritance. Now, as they had been faithful companions and helpers to their brethren, Joshua declares

that they were entitled to their discharge, and thus sends them back to their homes released and free. It is asked, however, how he can consider them to have performed their due measure of military service, while the enemy were still in possession of part of the land, of which the sole possession was to be the proper termination of the war?[1] But if we bear in mind what I lately said, the knot will be loosed. Had the Israelites followed the invitation of God, and seconded his agency, nay, when he was stretching out his hand to them, had they not basely drawn back,[2] the remaining part of the war would have been finished with no danger and little trouble. From their own sloth, therefore, they refused what God was ready to bestow. And thus it happened that the agreement by which the two tribes and half-tribe had bound themselves, ceased to be binding. For the only obligation they had undertaken was to accompany the ten tribes, and contend for their inheritance as strenuously as if their condition had been exactly the same. Now, when they have perseveringly performed their part as faithful allies, and the ten tribes contented with their present fortune, not only do not demand, but rather tacitly repudiate their assistance, a free return to their homes is justly allowed them. They, indeed, deserve praise for their patient endurance, in not allowing weariness of the service to make them request their discharge, but in waiting quietly till Joshua of his own accord sends for them.[3]

5. *But take diligent heed*, &c. He thus releases and frees them from temporary service, that he may bind them for ever to the authority of the one true God. He therefore permits them to return home, but on the condition that

[1] Latin, "Cujus sola possessio justum debuit bello imponere finem." French, "De laquelle il faloit qu'ils fussent paisibles possesseurs avant qu'ils peussent avoir licence de se desparter, et avant que finir la guerre;" "Of which it was necessary that they should be peaceful possessors before they could have license to depart, and before finishing the war."—*Ed.*

[2] French, "Ou pour mieux dire, s'ils n'eussent vilainement tourné le dos arriere, quand il leur tendoit la main;" "Or, to speak more properly, if they had not villanously turned their back when he stretched out his hand to them."—*Ed.*

[3] Jewish writers, founding on plausible *data*, calculate that the auxiliary tribes who crossed the Jordan to assist their brethren, had been absent from their homes for a period of fourteen years.—*Ed.*

wherever they may be they are to be the soldiers of God; and he at the same time prescribes the mode, namely, the observance of his Law. But since such is the vanity and inconstancy of the human mind, that religion easily fades away from the heart, while carelessness and contempt creep in, he requires of them zeal and diligence in executing the Law. He calls it the Law of Moses, that they may not be carried to and fro by airy speculations, but remain fixed in the doctrine which they had learned from the faithful servant of God. He touches also on the end and sum of the Law, love to God, and adherence to him, because outward worship would otherwise be of little value. He confirms the same thing by other words, by which sincerity is denoted, namely, serving the Lord with their whole heart and soul.

8. *Return with much riches*, &c. As it was formerly seen that the greater part of the two tribes were left in their territories beyond the Jordan, when the others passed over to carry on the war, it was fair that, as they had lived in ease with their families, or been only occupied with domestic concerns, they should be contented with their own livelihood and the produce of their own labour. And they certainly could not, without dishonesty, have demanded that any part of the booty and spoil should be distributed among them, when they had taken no share in all the toil and the danger. Joshua, however, does not insist on the strictly legal view, but exhorts the soldiers to deal liberally with their countrymen, by sharing the prey with them. Here some one may unseasonably raise the question, Whether or not the booty was common? For Joshua does not decide absolutely that it is their duty to do as he enjoins; he admonishes them that, after they have been enriched by the divine blessing, it would betray a want of proper feeling not to be liberal and kind towards their brethren, especially as it was not their fault that they did not take part in the same expedition. Moreover, when he bids them divide, he does not demand an equal partition, such as that which is usual among partners and equals, but only to bestow something that may suffice to remove all cause of envy and hatred.[1]

[1] The Septuagint alters the tenor of the whole passage by substituting

10. And when they came unto the borders of Jordan, that *are* in the land of Canaan, the children of Reuben, and the children of Gad, and the half-tribe of Manasseh, built there an altar by Jordan, a great altar to see to.

11. And the children of Israel heard say, Behold, the children of Reuben, and the children of Gad, and the half-tribe of Manasseh, have built an altar over against the land of Canaan, in the borders of Jordan, at the passage of the children of Israel.

12. And when the children of Israel heard *of it*, the whole congregation of the children of Israel gathered themselves together at Shiloh, to go up to war against them.

13. And the children of Israel sent unto the children of Reuben, and to the children of Gad, and to the half-tribe of Manasseh, into the land of Gilead, Phinehas the son of Eleazar the priest,

14. And with him ten princes, of each chief house a prince, throughout all the tribes of Israel; and each one *was* an head of the house of their fathers among the thousands of Israel.

15. And they came unto the children of Reuben, and to the children of Gad, and to the half-tribe of Manasseh, unto the land of Gilead, and they spake with them, saying,

16. Thus saith the whole congregation of the Lord, What trespass *is* this that ye have committed against the God of Israel, to turn away this day from following the Lord, in that ye have builded you an altar, that ye might rebel this day against the Lord?

17. *Is* the iniquity of Peor too little for us, from which we are not

10. Devenerunt autem ad limites Jordanis qui erant in terra Chanaan, et ædificaverunt filii Ruben, et filii Gad, et dimidia tribus Manasse, ibi altare juxta Jordanem, altare magnum visu.

11. Audierunt autem filii Israel dici, Ecce ædificaverunt filii Ruben, et filii Gad, et dimidia tribus Manasse, altare e regione terræ Chanaan, in confinibus Jordanis in transitu filiorum Israel.

12. Audierunt, inquam, filii Israel, et convenerunt universus cœtus filiorum Israel in Silo, ut ascenderent contra eos ad pugnam.

13. Miserunt autem filii Israel ad filios Ruben, et ad filios Gad, et ad dimidiam tribum Manasse, ad terram Gilead, Phinees filium Eleazar sacerdotis.

14. Et decem principes cum eo, singulos principes per singulas domos avitas ex omnibus tribubus Israel: singuli namque principes familiarum patrum suorum erant in millibus Israel.

15. Venerunt ergo ad filios Ruben, et ad filios Gad, et ad dimidiam tribum Manasse, ad terram Gilead, loquutique sunt cum eis, dicendo,

16. Sic dicunt universus cœtus Jehovæ, Quæ est prævaricatio ista, qua prævaricati estis contra Deum Israel, ut avertamini hodie ne eatis post Jehovam ædificando vobis altare, ut rebelletis hodie contra Jehovam?

17. An parum nobis est cum iniquitate Peor, a qua nec dum sumus

the past tense for the imperative, and making it read not as a part of Joshua's address, but as the statement of a fact, "They departed with much riches," &c., and "they divided the spoil of their enemies with their brethren."—*Ed.*

cleansed until this day, although there was a plague in the congregation of the Lord,

18. But that ye must turn away this day from following the Lord? and it will be, *seeing* ye rebel to-day against the Lord, that to-morrow he will be wroth with the whole congregation of Israel.

19. Notwithstanding, if the land of your possession *be* unclean, *then* pass ye over unto the land of the possession of the Lord, wherein the Lord's tabernacle dwelleth, and take possession among us; but rebel not against the Lord, nor rebel against us, in building you an altar, besides the altar of the Lord our God.

20. Did not Achan the son of Zerah commit a trespass in the accursed thing, and wrath fell on all the congregation of Israel? and that man perished not alone in his iniquity.

mundati etiam hodie, et tamen fuit plaga in cœtu Jehovæ?

18. Vos autem avertimini hodie ne eatis post Jehovam, et erit, vos rebellabitis hodie contra Jehovam, et cras in totum cœtum Israel irascetur.

19. Et quidem si immunda est terra possessionis vestræ, transite ad terram possessionis Jehovæ, in qua habitat tabernaculum Jehovæ, et possessiones accipite in medio nostrum, et contra Jehovam ne rebelletis: neque a nobis deficiatis, ædificando vobis altare præter altare Jehovæ Dei nostri.

20. Nonne Achan filius Zerah prævaricatus est prævaricatione in anathemate, et contra omnem cœtum Israel fuit ira? et ille vir unus non obiit propter iniquitatem suam.

10. *And when they came unto the borders,* &c. The history here is particularly deserving of notice, when the two tribes and half-tribe, intending to erect a memorial of common faith and fraternal concord, allowed themselves from inconsiderate zeal to adopt a method which was justly suspected by their brethren. The ten tribes, thinking that the worship of God was violated with impious audacity and temerity, were inflamed with holy wrath, and took up arms to use them against their own blood; nor were they appeased till they had received full satisfaction. The motive for erecting the altar was right in itself. For the object of the children of Reuben, Gad, and Manasseh, was to testify that though they were separated from their brethren by the intervening stream, they were, however, united with them in religion, and cherished a mutual agreement in the doctrine of the Law. Nothing was farther from their intention than to innovate in any respect in the worship of God. But they sinned not lightly in attempting a novelty, without paying any regard to the high priest, or consulting their brethren, and in a form which was very liable to be misconstrued.

We know how strictly the Law prohibited two altars,

(Exod. xx. 24;) for the Lord wished to be worshipped in one place only. Therefore, when on the very first blush of the case, all were at once led to think that they were building a second altar, who would not have judged them guilty of sacrilege in framing a ritual of a degenerate description, at variance with the Law of God? Seeing, then, that the work might be deemed vicious, they ought, at least, in so great and so serious a matter, to have made their brethren sharers in their counsel; more especially were they in the wrong in neglecting to consult the high priest, from whose lips the divine will was to be ascertained. They were, therefore, deserving of blame, because, as if they had been alone in the world, they considered not what offence might arise from the novelty of the example. Wherefore, let us learn to attempt nothing rashly, even should it be free from blame, and let us always give due heed to the admonition of St. Paul, (1 Cor. vi. 12; x. 23,) that it is necessary to attend not only to what is lawful, but to what is expedient; more especially let us sedulously beware of disturbing pious minds[1] by the introduction of any kind of novelty.

11. *And the children of Israel heard say*, &c. There is no doubt that they were inflamed with holy zeal, nor ought their vehemence to seem excessive in taking up arms to destroy their countrymen on account of a pile of stones. For they truly and wisely judged that the lawful sanctuary of God was polluted and his worship profaned, that sacred things were violated, pious concord destroyed, and a door opened for the license of superstitious practices, if in two places victims were offered to God, who had for these reasons so solemnly bound the whole people to a single altar. Not rashly, therefore, do the ten tribes, on hearing of a profane altar, detest its sacrilegious audacity.

Here, then, we have an illustrious display of piety, teaching us that if we see the pure worship of God corrupted, we must be strenuous, to the utmost of our ability, in vindicating it. The sword, indeed, has not been committed to the hands of all; but every one must, according to his call and office,

[1] Latin, "Pios animos." French, "Les bonnes consciences;" "Good consciences."—*Ed.*

study manfully and firmly to maintain the purity of religion against all corruptions. More especially deserving of the highest praise was the zeal of the half-tribe of Manasseh, who, setting aside all regard to the flesh, did not spare their own family. I admit, however, that this zeal, though pious, was not free from turbulent impetuosity, inasmuch as they hasten to declare war before they inquired concerning the mind of their brethren, and properly ascertained the state of the case. War, I admit, was declared only under conditions; for they send ambassadors to bring back word after they had carefully investigated the matter, and they move not a finger in the way of inflicting punishment till they are certified of the existence of the crime. Excuse, therefore, may be made for the fervour of their passion, while they prepare for battle in the event of any defection being discovered.[1]

16. *Thus saith the whole congregation*, &c. Just as if it had been known that this second altar was opposed to the one only altar of God, they begin with upbraiding them, and that in a very harsh and severe manner. They thus assume it as confessed, that the two tribes had built the altar with a view of offering sacrifices upon it. In this they are mistaken, as it was destined for a different use and purpose. Moreover, had the idea which they had conceived been correct, all the expostulation which they employ would have been just; for it was a clear case of criminal revolt to make any change in the Law of God, who values obedience more than all sacrifices, (1 Sam. xv. 22;) and there would have been perfect ground for condemning them as apostates, in withdrawing from the one only altar.

17. *Is the iniquity of Peor too little for us?* &c. They represent the crime as more heinous, from their perverse obstinacy in not ceasing ever and anon to provoke the Lord by their abominations. They bring forward one signal example of recent occurrence. While they were encircling the sanctuary of God from the four cardinal points, like good watchmen of God, and when they had received the form of due worship, and were habituated to it by constant exercise, they had

[1] French, "S'il se trouve que les autres se soyent revoltez de la religion;" "If it be found that the others have revolted from religion."—*Ed.*

allowed themselves, through the seductive allurements of harlots, to be polluted by foul superstitions, and had worshipped Baal-Peor. As the whole people were implicated in this crime, the ten ambassadors do not hesitate to admit, that they were partners in the guilt. They therefore ask, Is not the iniquity which we contracted in the matter of Baal-Peor sufficient? They add, that they were not yet purified from it, just as if they had said, that the remembrance of it was not yet entirely buried, or that the vengeance of God was not yet extinguished; and hence they infer, that the two tribes and the half tribe, while with impious contumacy they turn aside from God, and shake off his yoke, not only consult ill for themselves, but are calling down similar destruction on the whole people, because God will avenge the insult offered him to a wider extent. This they confirm by the example of Achan, who, though he was alone when he secretly stole of the accursed thing, did not alone undergo the punishment of his sacrilege, but also dragged others along with him, as it was seen that some fell in the line of battle, while all were shamefuly put to flight, because pollution attached to the people.

They reason from the less to the greater. If the anger of God burnt against many for the clandestine misdeed of one man, much less would he allow the people to escape if they connived at manifest idolatry. A middle view, however, is inserted, that if the two tribes and half tribe built up an altar, and if their condition was worse from not dwelling in the land of Canaan, let them rather come and obtain a settlement also in the land of Canaan, but let them not provoke God by a wicked rivalship.[1] Hence we infer, that they were not urged by some turgid impetus, since, even at their own loss and expense, they are willing kindly to offer partnership to those who had demanded a settlement and domicile for themselves elsewhere.

21. Then the children of Reuben, and the children of Gad, and the	21. Responderunt autem filii Ruben, et filii Gad, et dimidia

[1] Latin, "Prava æmulatione." French, "Abusant en mal de ce qu'ils ont veu faire aux autres;" "Making a wicked abuse of what they have seen others do."—*Ed.*

half-tribe of Manasseh, answered and said unto the heads of the thousands of Israel,

22. The Lord God of gods, the Lord God of gods, he knoweth, and Israel he shall know, if *it be* in rebellion, or if in transgression against the Lord, (save us not this day,)

23. That we have built us an altar to turn from following the Lord, or if to offer thereon burnt-offering or meat-offering, or if to offer peace-offerings thereon, let the Lord himself require *it;*

24. And if we have not *rather* done it for fear of *this* thing, saying, In time to come your children might speak unto our children, saying, What have ye to do with the Lord God of Israel?

25. For the Lord hath made Jordan a border between us and you, ye children of Reuben, and children of Gad; ye have no part in the Lord: so shall your children make our children cease from fearing the Lord.

26. Therefore we said, Let us now prepare to build us an altar, not for burnt-offering, nor for sacrifice:

27. But *that* it *may be* a witness between us and you, and our generations after us, that we might do the service of the Lord before him with our burnt-offerings, and with our sacrifices, and with our peace-offerings; that your children may not say to our children in time to come, Ye have no part in the Lord.

28. Therefore said we, that it shall be, when they should *so* say to us, or to our generations in time to come, that we may say *again*, Behold the pattern of the altar of the Lord, which our fathers made, not for burnt-offerings, nor for sacrifices; but it *is* a witness between us and you.

29. God forbid that we should rebel against the Lord, and turn this day from following the Lord, to build an altar for burnt-offerings,

tribus Manasse, loquutique sunt cum principibus millium Israel.

22. Deus deorum Jehova, Deus deorum Jehova ipse novit, et Israel cognoscet, si per rebellionem, et si per prevaricationem in Jehovam, ne serves nos die hac.

23. Si cogitavimus ædificare nobis altare, ut averteremur ne iremus post Jehovam, et si ad immolandum super illud holocausta et sacrificium, et si ad faciendum super illud sacrificia prosperitatum, Jehova ipse inquirat.

24. Et si non potius timore hujusce rei fecimus hoc dicendo: Cras dicent filii vestri filiis nostris dicendo: Quid vobis et Jehovæ Deo Israel?

25. Nam terminum posuit Jehova inter nos et vos filii Ruben et filii Gad, Jordanem: non est vobis portio in Jehova: et cessare facient filii vestri filios nostros, ut non timeant Jehovam.

26. Et diximus, Demus nunc operam ut ædificemus altare, non pro holocausto, nec pro sacrificio:

27. Sed ut testis sit inter nos et vos, et inter generationes nostras post nos, ut serviamus servitutem Jehovæ coram eo in holocaustis nostris, et in sacrificiis nostris, et prosperitatibus nostris: et ne dicant filii vestri cras filiis nostris, Non est vobis pars in Jehova.

28. Diximus itaque, Et erit, si dixerint nobis aut generationibus nostris cras, tum dicemus, Videte similitudinem altaris Jehovæ quod fecerunt patres nostri, non pro holocausto, neque pro sacrificio, sed ut testis sit inter nos et vos.

29. Absit a nobis ut rebellemus contra Jehovam, et avertamur hodie ne eamus post Jehovam, ædificando altare pro holocausto, pro oblatione,

for meat-offerings, or for sacrifices, besides the altar of the Lord our God that *is* before his tabernacle.

et pro sacrificio, ultra altare Jehovæ Dei nostri quod est ante tabernaculum ejus.

30. And when Phinehas the priest, and the princes of the congregation, and heads of the thousands of Israel which *were* with him, heard the words that the children of Reuben, and the children Gad, and the children of Manasseh spake, it pleased them.

30. Porro quum audisset Phinees sacerdos, et principes cœtus, capitaque millium Israel qui cum eo erant, verba quæ loquuti fuerant filii Ruben, et filii Gad, et filii Manasse, placuit in oculis eorum.

31. And Phinehas the son of Eleazar the priest said unto the children of Reuben, and to the children of Gad, and to the children of Manasseh, This day we perceive that the Lord *is* among us, because ye have not committed this trespass against the Lord: now ye have delivered the children of Israel out of the hand of the Lord.

31. Dixitque Phinees filius Eleazar sacerdotis filiis Ruben, et filiis Gad, et filiis Manasse, Hodie novimus quod in medio nostri sit Jehova, quod non prævaricati sitis contra Jehovam prævaricationem istam : tunc liberastis filios Israel de manu Jehovæ.

32. And Phinehas the son of Eleazar the priest, and the princes, returned from the children of Reuben, and from the children of Gad, out of the land of Gilead, unto the land of Canaan, to the children of Israel, and brought them word again.

32. Reversus est igitur Phinees filius Eleazar sacerdotis, et principes illi a filiis Ruben, et a filiis Gad, de terra Gilead ad terram Chanaan ad reliquos filios Israel, et retulerunt eis rem.

33. And the thing pleased the children of Israel; and the children of Israel blessed God, and did not intend to go up against them in battle, to destroy the land wherein the children of Reuben and Gad dwelt.

33. Placuitque res in oculis filiorum Israel, atque benedixerunt Deo filii Israel : neque decreverunt ascendere contra eos ad pugnam, ut disperderent terram in qua filii Ruben et filii Gad habitabant.

34. And the children of Reuben, and the children of Gad, called the altar *Ed:* for it *shall be* a witness between us that the Lord *is* God.

34. Vocaverunt autem filii Ruben et filii Gad altare Hed, dicendo : Quia testis erit inter nos quod Jehova est Deus.

21. *Then the children of Reuben,* &c. The state of the case turns on the definition. For the children of Reuben, Gad, and Manasseh, explain that they had a different intention, and thus exculpate themselves from the charge, inasmuch as the nature of the proceeding was quite different from what the others supposed. In not making a disturbance,[1] nor picking a quarrel for the injustice done to

[1] Latin, " Quod autem non tumultuantur." French, " Et en ce qu'ils n'escarmouchent point ;" " And in not skirmishing."—*Ed.*

them they give an example of rare modesty, which is held forth for our imitation ; so that if at any time anything we have rightly done happen to be unjustly and falsely blamed by those not acquainted with its nature, we may deem it sufficient to refute the censure only so far as may be necessary for clearing ourselves. Moreover, that the more credit may be given to them, and that they may the better attest their integrity, they, by a solemn protest, put far from them the wickedness of which they were suspected. For there is force and meaning in the reduplication, The Lord God of gods, the Lord God of gods, by which they with vehemence affirm, how faithfully they desire to persevere in the doctrine of the Law, and how greatly they abhor all contrary superstitions. But as their intention was not patent to men, and every one explained it variously, according to his own sense, they appeal to the judgment of God, and offer to submit to punishment if he decide that they had attempted anything wickedly. And to prove that they are not like hypocrites who, with abandoned wickedness, appeal to God a hundred times as judge even when they are convicted in their own minds, they not only bring forward conscience, but at the same time declare, that the whole people will be witness ; as if they had said, that it will be made palpable by the fact itself, that they never had any intention of devising any new form of worship ; and they rightly explain, how the altar would have been unlawful, namely, if they had built it for the purpose of offering sacrifice. For the Law did not condemn the mere raising of heaps of stones, but only enjoined that sacrifices should be offered in one place, for the purpose of retaining the people in one faith, lest religion should be rent asunder, lest license should be given to human presumption, and thus every man might turn aside to follow his own fictions. We thus see how an explanation of the nature of the deed removes the detestation which the ten tribes had conceived of it.[1]

[1] Several Romish writers endeavour to make the most of this transaction, and think they find in the apparent sanction which it gives to the erection of an altar similar to the one on which sacrifices were offered, though intended for a different purpose, an authority for their endless forms of image worship. It is scarcely possible to treat such an argu-

It is not strictly correct, though appropriate enough, for the rudeness of sense, to place our God above all gods. For it is impossible to compare him with others, seeing that no others actually exist. Hence, in order to avoid the apparent absurdity, some interpreters substitute *angels* for *gods;* this meaning holds in some cases, though not in all. It ought not, however, to seem harsh when he who is the one sole supreme being is called the God of gods, inasmuch as he has no equal, standing forth conspicuous above all other height, and so, by his glory, obscuring and annihilating all names of deity which are celebrated in the world. Hence this mode of speaking ought to be viewed with reference to the common sense of the vulgar.

26. *Therefore we said,* &c. The gross impiety of which they had been accused was now well refuted; and yet they seem not to have been in every respect free from blame, because the Law forbids the erection of any kind of statues. It is easy, however, to excuse this by saying, that no kind of statues are condemned except those which are intended to represent God. To erect a heap of stones as a trophy, or in testimony of a miracle, or a memorial of some signal favour of God, the Law has nowhere prohibited. (Exod. xx. 4; Levit. xxvi. 1; Deut. v. 8.) Otherwise, Joshua and many holy judges and kings after him, would have defiled themselves by profane innovation. But the only thing displeasing to God was to see the minds of men drawn hither and thither, so as to worship him in a gross and earthly manner. The children of Reuben, Gad, and Manasseh do all that is required for their exculpation, when they declare that they would use the altar only as a bond of brotherly union; and add a sufficient reason, namely, the danger there was, lest, after a long course of time, the ten tribes might exclude the others as strangers, because they did not inhabit

ment seriously, but it is surely sufficient to answer, that while the Reubenites and their associates justified the erection of their altar, by declaring in the most solemn manner, that they never intended, and were firmly determined never to employ it for religious service, the Romanists, on the other hand, erect their images for the express purpose of so employing them, and are continually extolling the imaginary benefits which this sacrilegious employment of them confers.—*Ed.*

the same land. For as the country beyond the Jordan was not at first comprehended in the covenant, a difference of habitation might ultimately prove a cause of dissension. They therefore consult timeously for their posterity, that they may be able by means of the altar as a kind of public document to defend their right, that they may mutually recognise each other, and unite in common in serving one God.

30. *And when Phinehas the priest,* &c. Phinehas and the ambassadors rightly temper their zeal, when, instead of harshly insisting and urging the prejudice which they had conceived, they blandly and willingly admit the excuse. Many persons, if once offended and exasperated by any matter, cannot be appeased by any defence, and always find something maliciously and unjustly to carp at, rather than seem to yield to reason. The example here is worthy of observation. It teaches us that if at any time we conceive offence in regard to a matter not sufficiently known, we must beware of obstinacy, and be ready instantly to take an equitable view. Moreover, when the children of Reuben, Gad, and Manasseh are found free from crime, Phinehas and the ambassadors ascribe it to the grace of God. For by the words, We know that Jehovah is in the midst of us, they intimate that God was propitious to them, and had taken care of their safety.

This is to be carefully observed; for we are able to infer from it that we never revolt from God, or fall off to impiety unless he abandon us, and give us up when thus abandoned to a reprobate mind. All idolatry, therefore, shews that God has previously been alienated, and is about to punish us by inflicting judicial blindness. Meanwhile, we must hold that we persevere in piety only in so far as God is present to sustain us by his hand, and confirm us in perseverance by the agency of his Spirit. Phinehas and the ambassadors speak as if they had been delivered by the children of Reuben, Gad, and Manasseh, because there was no longer any ground to fear the divine vengeance, when all suspicion of criminality had been removed. At last similar equity and humanity are displayed by the whole people, when accepting the defence of their brethren they gave thanks to God for having kept his people free from criminality.

Though they had been suddenly inflamed, they depart with calm minds. In like manner the two tribes and the half tribe carefully exert themselves to perform their duty by giving a name to the altar, which, by explaining its proper use, might draw off the people from all superstition.

CHAPTER XXIII.

1. And it came to pass, a long time after that the Lord had given rest unto Israel from all their enemies round about, that Joshua waxed old *and* stricken in age.

2. And Joshua called for all Israel, *and* for their elders, and for their heads, and for their judges, and for their officers, and said unto them, I am old *and* stricken in age:

3. And ye have seen all that the Lord your God hath done unto all these nations because of you: for the Lord your God *is* he that hath fought for you.

4. Behold, I have divided unto you by lot these nations that remain, to be an inheritance for your tribes, from Jordan, with all the nations that I have cut off, even unto the great sea westward.

5. And the Lord your God, he shall expel them from before you, and drive them from out of your sight; and ye shall possess their land, as the Lord your God hath promised unto you.

6. Be ye therefore very courage-

1. Fuit autem post dies multos postquam requiem dedit Jehova Israeli ab omnibus inimicis eorum in circuitu, Josue senuit, et venit in dies:

2. Tunc vocavit Josue omnem Israel, seniores ejus, et capita ejus, et judices ejus, et præfectos ejus, dixitque ad eos, Ego senui, et veni in dies:

3. Vosque vidistis omnia quæ fecerit Jehova Deus vester omnibus gentibus istis in conspectu[1] vestro, quod Jehova Deus vester pugnaverit pro vobis.

4. Videte, sorte distribui vobis gentes istas residuas in hæreditatem per tribus vestras, a Jordane, atque omnes gentes quas disperdidi usque ad mare magnum ab occasu solis.

5. Jehova autem Deus vester ipse propulsabit eas a facie vestra, et expellet eas a conspectu vestro, et jure hæreditario possidebitis[2] terram earum, quemadmodum loquutus est Jehova Deus vester vobis.

6. Roborate igitur vos valde, ut

[1] The original literally is "from before you," and is more exactly rendered by Calvin's Latin "In conspectu vestro," than by the English version "because of you." This English rendering is the more remarkable, as in the 5th verse the very same Hebrew word is literally rendered "From before you."

[2] Simply "Ye shall inherit," seems better than the English version, "Ye shall possess," which is too weak, or than Calvin's Latin, "Jure hæreditario possidebitis," which is too strong.—*Ed.*

ous to keep and to do all that is written in the book of the law of Moses, that ye turn not aside therefrom *to* the right hand or *to* the left;

7. That ye come not among these nations, these that remain among you; neither make mention of the name of their gods, nor cause to swear *by them*, neither serve them, nor bow yourselves unto them:

8. But cleave unto the Lord your God, as ye have done unto this day.

9. For the Lord hath driven out from before you great nations and strong: but *as for* you, no man hath been able to stand before you unto this day.

10. One man of you shall chase a thousand: for the Lord your God, he *it is* that fighteth for you, as he hath promised you.

11. Take good heed therefore unto yourselves, that ye love the Lord your God.

custodiatis, et faciatis quicquid scriptum est in libro Legis Mosis, ut non recedatis ab eo neque ad dextram, neque ad sinistram.

7. Neque commisceamini gentibus istis quæ remanent vobiscum et nomen deorum earum ne commemoretis, nec adjuretis, neque serviatis eis, neque incurvetis vos eis.

8. Sed Jehovæ Deo vestro adhæreatis, sicut fecistis usque ad diem hanc.

9. Propterea expulit a facie vestra gentes magnas et fortes, nec stetit quisquam in conspectu vestro usque ad diem hanc.

10. Vir unus ex vobis persequutus est mille, quia Jehova Deus vester est qui pugnat pro vobis sicut loquutus fuerat vobis.

11. Custodite valde super animabus vestris ut diligatis Jehovam Deum vestrum.

Here we have a narrative of the solemn protestation which Joshua used towards the time of his death, that he might leave the pure worship of God surviving him. But although the peace and quiet which the Israelites obtained among the nations of Canaan is described as an excellent blessing from God, it is necessary to keep in mind what I formerly taught, that it was owing to their cowardice that they dwelt among their enemies, whom it would not have been difficult to rout and destroy. But thanks are justly rendered to God for his goodness in pardoning their ingratitude.

The pious solicitude of Joshua is here also set forth, for the imitation of all who are in authority. For as the father of a family will not be considered sufficiently provident if he thinks of his children only till the end of his own life, and does not extend his care farther, studying as much as in him lies to do them good even when he is dead; so good magistrates and rulers ought carefully to provide that the well arranged condition of affairs as they leave them, be confirmed and prolonged to a distant period. For this reason Peter writes, (2 Pet. i. 25,) that he will endeavour after he has departed out of the world to keep the Church in remembrance of his admonitions, and able to derive benefit from them.

From its being said that he invited all Israel, and its being immediately after added that he invited their elders, and heads, and judges, and prefects, I understand the meaning to be that all were indeed permitted to come, but that the summons was addressed specially to the heads and prefects. And thus the last clause appears to me to be explanatory of the former. And, indeed, it is not at all credible that the whole people were invited; for no such meeting could possibly take place. The sense, therefore, in which the people were invited was simply this, that the elders, judges, and others were commanded to come, and might bring as many persons as were disposed to come along with them.

The speech of Joshua, as quoted, is double; but it appears to me that the historian first, as is often done, gives a brief summary of the whole speech, and then follows it out more in detail, introducing the particulars which he had omitted.[1] In the one which is first given, Joshua briefly animates the people, and exhorts them to sure confidence

[1] According to this view, the details given in chapters xxiii. and xxiv. refer only to one meeting. It may be so, but certainly the impression produced by a simple perusal of the chapters is, that they refer to two distinct meetings, between which some interval of time must have elapsed. It is only by means of laboured criticism, accompanied with a degree of straining, that some expositors have arrived at a different conclusion. But why should it be deemed necessary to employ criticism for such a purpose? There is surely no antecedent improbability that Joshua, after all the turmoils of war were over, should have more than once come forth from his retirement, and called the heads of the people, or even the whole body of them together to receive his counsels, when he felt that the time of his departure was at hand. Observe, moreover, that each meeting is ushered in by its own appropriate preamble, and has its own special business. In the one, Joshua speaks in his own name, and delivers his own message; in the other, all the tribes are regularly assembled, and are said to have "presented themselves before God," because, although Joshua was still to be the speaker, he was no longer to speak in his own name, but with the authority of a divine messenger, and in the very terms which had been put into his mouth. Accordingly, the very first words he utters are, "Thus saith the Lord God of Israel." The message thus formally and solemnly announced in chap. xxiv. 2, is continued verbatim and without interruption to the end of verse 13.—*Ed.*

in the continued and unwearying grace of God. For, seeing they had experienced that God is true in all things, they could have no doubt for the future, that they might safely hope for the same success in vanquishing and destroying the enemy. The partition also by which he had distributed the remainder of the land, he set before them as an earnest or pledge of their undoubted fruition, because it was not at random but by the order of God he had marked out the seat, and fixed the boundaries of each tribe.

6. *Be ye therefore very courageous*, &c. He now shews them the mode of conquering,—not to indulge gross security, as too often happens, as a substitute for genuine confidence. He affirms that God will be propitious to them, and promises that whatever they attempt will turn out prosperously, provided they are stedfast in obeying the Law. However confidently hypocrites may contemn and deride God, they would wish, however, to have him astricted to them; nay, they often, with no small pomposity, boast of his promises. But true faith, while it reclines upon God, keeps those who possess it in his fear. In short, those who would find God must seek him sincerely, and if we desire to be regarded by him, we must beware of turning our backs upon him. The expression, Be ye very courageous, as has elsewhere been said, denotes serious study, because in the great weakness of our nature no man will set about the thorough observance of the Law, if he does not exert himself above his strength. Attention ought also to be paid to the definition of true obedience which is here repeated from Moses, (Deut. v. 32,) and said to consist in not turning either to the right hand or the left.

7. *That ye come not among these nations*, &c. He distinctly admonishes them that it will be impossible rightly to discharge their duty if they be not carefully on their guard against all sources of corruption. This it was very necessary to enforce upon them. For they were surrounded on all sides by the snares of Satan, and we know how great their proneness to superstition was, or rather how headlong their eagerness for it. First, then, he warns them that intimate intercourse with the nations may involve them in fellowship in crime; for the term *mingling* used in this pas-

sage is equivalent to what is termed by St. Paul, *being yoked.* (2 Cor. vi. 14.) In short, he first removes the incitements or allurements to idolatry, and then declares his detestation of idolatry itself. It is to be observed, however, that he does not expressly mention either bending of the knee, or sacrifices, or other rites, but designates all perverse modes of worship by the terms *naming* them and *swearing* by them. Whence we infer that God is defrauded of his honour whenever any particle, however small, of all the things which he claims for himself is transferred to idols. He accordingly concludes that they are to adhere to God alone; in other words, they are to be bound to him out and out.

9. *For the Lord hath driven out from before you,* &c. He intimates that so long as they do not themselves change, there will certainly be no change on the part of God. Therefore he asserts that, provided they conciliate the favour of God, they shall have an uninterrupted course of victory. At length he again exhorts them, as they value their life and safety, to be careful in maintaining love to God. From this source all true obedience springs; for if we do not cling to him with free and ardent affection, we shall study in vain to frame our lives in accordance with the external form of the Law.

12. Else, if ye do in any wise go back, and cleave unto the remnant of these nations, *even* these that remain among you, and shall make marriages with them, and go in unto them, and they to you:

13. Know for a certainty, that the Lord your God will no more drive out *any of* these nations from before you; but they shall be snares and traps unto you, and scourges in your sides, and thorns in your eyes, until ye perish from off this good land which the Lord your God hath given you.

14. And, behold, this day I *am* going the way of all the earth: and ye know in all your hearts, and in all your souls, that not one thing hath failed of all the good things which the Lord your God spake concerning you; all are come to pass

12. Quia si avertendo aversi fueritis, et adhæseritis residuis gentibus istis, residuis, inquam, istis quæ sunt vobiscum: et affinitatem contraxeritis cum eis, et misceatis vos cum eis, et ipsæ vobiscum:

13. Jam nunc scitote quod posthac Jehova Deus vester non expellet omnes gentes istas a facie vestra: sed potius erunt vobis in laqueum, et offendiculum, et flagellum in lateribus vestris, et in spinas in oculis vestris, donec pereatis e terra optima ista quam dedit vobis Jehova Deus vester.

14. En autem ego ingredior hodie viam universæ terræ: cognoscite ergo toto corde vestro, et tota anima vestra quod non cecidit verbum unum ex omnibus verbis optimis quæ loquutus est Jehova Deus vester super vos: omnia evenerunt

unto you, *and* not one thing hath failed thereof.

15. Therefore it shall come to pass, *that* as all good things are come upon you, which the Lord your God promised you; so shall the Lord bring upon you all evil things, until he have destroyed you from off this good land which the Lord your God hath given you.

16. When ye have transgressed the covenant of the Lord your God, which he commanded you, and have gone and served other gods, and bowed yourselves to them; then shall the anger of the Lord be kindled against you, and ye shall perish quickly from off the good land which he hath given unto you.

vobis, non cecidit ex eis verbum unum.

15. Sicut ergo evenit vobis omne verbum bonum quod loquutus est Jehova Deus vester ad vos, sic adducet Jehova super vos omne verbum malum, donec disperdat vos e terra optima ista, quam dedit vobis Jehova Deus vester.

16. Quum transgressi fueritis pactum Jehovæ Dei vestri quod præcepit vobis, et abieritis, et servieritis diis alienis, incurvaveritisque vos eis, irascetur furor Jehovæ contra vos, et peribitis cito e terra optima quam dedit vobis.

12. *Else if ye do in any wise go back*, &c. According to the usual method observed in the Law, he adds threatenings, in order that if they are not sufficiently allured by the divine goodness, they may be aroused by fear to the performance of their duty. It is, indeed, disgraceful for men, when God graciously condescends to invite them, not at once to run forward and meet the invitation by prompt and alert obedience; but such is the lethargy of the flesh, that it always requires to be stimulated by threats. Joshua, therefore, adopts the usual method of the Law, while he reminds the Israelites of the terrors of the Lord, provided they do not of their own accord embrace his offered favour. Moreover, it is not once only that he sets before them the denunciation that the nations of Canaan will be scourges to their sides and thorns in their eyes if they become familiar with them. *First*, inasmuch as God had consecrated the land to himself, he wished it to be purged of all impurities; and *secondly*, inasmuch as he saw how prone the people were to be corrupted by bad example, he wished also to provide a remedy for this evil. Then, while on the one hand the people counted it as nothing that the land should be contaminated by impious superstitions, and that idols should be worshipped in it instead of the true God, and on the other hand, eagerly contracted contagion from their vices, it was only a just punishment of this gross contempt that they should expe-

rience molestation and hostility from those whom they had improperly[1] spared.

That the threatenings which both Moses and Joshua thus denounced were openly accomplished, is but too plain from the Book of Judges. And yet this promulgation of the divine vengeance was not altogether useless; for after Joshua was dead, they became courageous enough to engage in war. Their ardour, however, proved evanescent,[2] and they shortly after were initiated in nefarious Gentile rites. Hence, we perceive in the human mind an intemperate longing for perverse worship, a longing which no curbs are able to restrain.

It is now proper to consider how far this doctrine is applicable to us. It is true a special command was given to the ancient people to destroy the nations of Canaan, and keep aloof from all profane defilements. To us, in the present day, no certain region marks out our precise boundaries; nor are we armed with the sword to slay all the ungodly; we have only to beware of allowing ourselves to become involved in fellowship with wickedness, by not keeping at a sufficient distance from it. For it is almost impossible, if we mingle with it, spontaneously to avoid receiving some spot or blemish. But this point having been elsewhere expounded, I now merely advert to it in passing.

14. *And, behold, this day I am going,* &c. As it has been appointed unto all men once to die, (Heb. ix. 27,) Joshua says that in regard to himself the common end of all is at hand, inasmuch as he, too, was born mortal. These expressions are evidently adapted to console the people, and prevent them from feeling immoderate grief at the bereavement when he should be taken from them. For there cannot be a doubt that his loss filled the people with the deepest regret, when they saw themselves reduced, as it were, to a mutilated trunk, by being deprived of their head. He there-

[1] Latin, "Male." French, "A tort et contre leur devoir;" "Wrongfully and contrary to their duty."—*Ed.*

[2] Latin, "Verum evanidus fuit fervor ille." French, "Mais ç'a esté un feu de paille comme on dit: car leur ardeur n'a gueres duré;" "But it was a fire of straw, as it is called; for their ardour was not durable."—*Ed.*

fore admonishes them, that since the race of life is ended by having reached the goal, they were not to ask that his condition should be different from that of the whole human race. Meanwhile he does not intimate that the form of dying is the same in all, because the believers of heavenly doctrine are distinguished from unbelievers by an incorruptible seed, not allowing them in like manner to perish, but only adverts to that which is common, namely, departure from the world after the course of life is ended. The substance of his whole address amounts to this, that as God had proved himself true by his favours and the fulfilment of his promises, so his threatenings would not be empty or vain, and he would certainly avenge the profanation of his worship by their final destruction.[1]

CHAPTER XXIV.

1. And Joshua gathered all the tribes of Israel to Shechem, and called for the elders of Israel, and for their heads, and for their judges, and for their officers; and they presented themselves before God.

1. Congregavit itaque[2] Josue omnes tribus Israel in Sichem, vocavitque seniores Israel, et capita ejus, judicesque ejus, ac præfectos ejus: steteruntque coram Deo.

2. And Joshua said unto all the people, Thus saith the Lord God of Israel, Your fathers dwelt on the other side of the flood in old time, *even* Terah, the father of Abraham, and the father of Nahor: and they served other gods.

2. Dixitque Josue ad universum populum, Sic dicit Jehova Deus Israel, Trans flumen habitaverunt patres vestri a seculo, ut Thare pater Abraham, et pater Nachor, servieruntque diis alienis.

3. And I took your father Abraham from the other side of the flood, and led him throughout all the land of Canaan, and multiplied his seed, and gave him Isaac.

3. Et tuli patrem vestrum Abraham e loco qui erat trans flumen, et deduxi per universam terram Chanaan: multiplicavique semen ejus, et dedi ei Isaac.

[1] Latin, "Ultimo eorum interitu." French, "En les destruisant à toute rigeur;" "By destroying them in all rigour," (without mercy.)—*Ed.*

[2] The "itaque" is here inserted without authority, but Calvin, as he explains in the commentary on the verse, thinks it necessary, in order to keep up the connection with the previous chapter, and shew, according to his hypothesis, that both chapters contain the account of only one meeting. On the contrary, as has been observed in note, p. 264, the whole tenor of the narrative here given seems to indicate that it refers not to a continuation of the former meeting, but to one held on a subsequent occasion, and for a still more solemn purpose.—*Ed.*

4. And I gave unto Isaac Jacob and Esau: and I gave unto Esau mount Seir, to possess it; but Jacob and his children went down into Egypt.

5. I sent Moses also and Aaron, and I plagued Egypt, according to that which I did among them; and afterward I brought you out.

6. And I brought your fathers out of Egypt: and ye came unto the sea; and the Egyptians pursued after your fathers with chariots and horsemen unto the Red sea.

7. And when they cried unto the Lord, he put darkness between you and the Egyptians, and brought the sea upon them, and covered them; and your eyes have seen what I have done in Egypt: and ye dwelt in the wilderness a long season.

8. And I brought you into the land of the Amorites, which dwelt on the other side Jordan; and they fought with you: and I gave them into your hand, that ye might possess their land; and I destroyed them from before you.

9. Then Balak the son of Zippor, king of Moab, arose, and warred against Israel, and sent and called Balaam the son of Beor to curse you:

10. But I would not hearken unto Balaam; therefore he blessed you still: so I delivered you out of his hand.

11. And ye went over Jordan, and came unto Jericho: and the men of Jericho fought against you, the Amorites, and the Perizzites, and the Canaanites, and the Hittites, and the Girgashites, the Hivites, and the Jebusites; and I delivered them into your hand.

4. Et dedi ipsi Isaac Jacob et Esau: tradidique ipsi Esau montem Seir, ut possideret eum: Jacob autem et filii ejus descenderunt in Ægyptum.

5. Misique Mosen et Aharon, et percussi Ægyptum, quemadmodum feci in medio ejus, et postea eduxi vos.

6. Et eduxi patres vestros ex Ægypto, devenistisque ad mare, et persequuti sunt Ægyptii patres vestros cum curribus, et equitibus usque ad mare rubrum.

7. Tum clamaverunt[1] ad Jehovam, et posuit caliginem inter vos et Ægyptios: induxitque super eum mare, ac operuit eum: et viderunt oculi vestri quæ feci in Ægypto, et habitastis in solitudine in diebus multis.

8. Postea adduxi vos ad terram Æmorrhæi habitantis trans Jordanem: præliatique sunt vobiscum, et tradidi eos in manum vestram: possedistisque terram eorum, ac delevi eos a facie vestra.

9. Surrexit autem Balac filius Sippor rex Moab, et præliatus est cum Israel: misitque et vocavit Bileam filium Beor, ut malediceret vobis:

10. Et nolui audire Bileam, sed benedixi benedicendo vobis, et liberavi vos e manu ejus.

11. Transistisque Jordanem, et venistis ad Jericho: pugnaveruntque contra vos viri Jericho, Æmorrhæus, et Perizæus, et Chananæus, et Hittæus, et Girgasæus, et Hivæus, et Jebusæus: tradidique eos in manum vestram.

[1] There is here a very abrupt transition from the first to the third person in the verbs "they cried"—"he put"—"he brought"—"he covered," as if Joshua had ceased to deliver an actual message, and became merely a narrator. The message, however, is immediately resumed, "Your eyes have seen what *I* have done." The Septuagint, at the commencement of the verse, renders "ἀνεβοήσαμεν," "we cried," and thereafter uses the narrative form to the end of the 13th verse, saying, in the 8th verse, "he brought," and in the 10th, "the Lord your God would not."—*Ed.*

12. And I sent the hornet before you, which drave them out from before you, *even* the two kings of the Amorites; *but* not with thy sword, nor with thy bow.

12. Et misit ante vos crabrones, qui expulerunt eos a facie vestra, duos reges Æmorrhæi, non gladio tuo, nec arcu tuo.

13. And I have given you a land for which ye did not labour, and cities which ye built not, and ye dwell in them; of the vineyards and oliveyards which ye planted not do ye eat.

13. Dedique vobis terram in qua non laborastis, et urbes quas non ædificastis, et habitastis in eis: vineas et oliveta quæ non plantastis, comedetis.

14. Now therefore fear the Lord, and serve him in sincerity and in truth: and put away the gods which your fathers served on the other side of the flood, and in Egypt; and serve ye the Lord.

14. Nunc ergo timete Jehovam, et servite ei in perfectione, et veritate, et auferte deos quibus servierunt patres vestri trans flumen, et in Ægypto, et servite Jehovæ.

1. *And Joshua gathered all the tribes*, &c. He now, in my opinion, explains more fully what he before related more briefly. For it would not have been suitable to bring out the people twice to a strange place for the same cause. Therefore by the repetition the course of the narrative is continued. And he now states what he had not formerly observed, that they were all standing before the Lord, an expression which designates the more sacred dignity and solemnity of the meeting. I have accordingly introduced the expletive particle *Therefore*, to indicate that the narrative which had been begun now proceeds. For there cannot be a doubt that Joshua, in a regular and solemn manner, invoked the name of Jehovah, and, as in his presence, addressed the people, so that each might consider for himself that God was presiding over all the things which were done, and that they were not there engaged in a private business, but confirming a sacred and inviolable compact with God himself. We may add, as is shortly afterwards observed, that there was his sanctuary. Hence it is probable that the ark of the covenant was conveyed thither, not with the view of changing its place, but that in so serious an action they might sist themselves before the earthly tribunal of God.[1] For there was no religious obligation forbidding the ark to be moved, and the situation of Sichem was not far distant.

[1] Latin, "Terrestre Dei tribunal." French, "Le siege judicial que Dieu avoit en terre;" "The judicial seat which God had on earth."—*Ed.*

2. *Your fathers dwelt on the other side*, &c. He begins his address by referring to their gratuitous adoption by which God had anticipated any application on their part, so that they could not boast of any peculiar excellence or merit. For God had bound them to himself by a closer tie, having, while they were no better than others, gathered them together to be his peculiar people, from no respect to anything but his mere good pleasure. Moreover, to make it clearly appear that there was nothing in which they could glory, he leads them back to their origin, and reminds them how their fathers had dwelt in Chaldea, worshipping idols in common with others, and differing in nothing from the great body of their countrymen. Hence it is inferred that Abraham, when he was plunged in idolatry, was raised up, as it were, from the lowest deep.

The Jews, indeed, to give a false dignity to their race, fabulously relate that Abraham became an exile from his country because he refused to acknowledge the Chaldean fire as God.[1] But if we attend to the words of the inspired writer, we shall see that he is no more exempted from the guilt of the popular idolatry than Terah and Nachor. For why is it said that the fathers of the people served strange gods, and that Abraham was rescued from the country, but just to shew how the free mercy of God was displayed in their very origin? Had Abraham been unlike the rest of his countrymen, his own piety would distinguish him. The opposite, however, is expressly mentioned to shew that he had no peculiar excellence of his own which could diminish the grace bestowed upon him, and that therefore his posterity behoved to acknowledge that when he was lost, he was raised up from death unto life.

It seems almost an incredible and monstrous thing, that while Noah was yet alive, idolatry had not only spread everywhere over the world, but even penetrated into the

[1] One of the fables here alluded to is, that Terah was not only a worshipper but a maker of idols, and that Abraham, convinced of the absurdity of idolatrous worship, destroyed all his father's idols. After doing so he laboured to convince his father of the propriety of his conduct by a series of arguments which are gravely recorded, but not having succeeded in his pious endeavours, was forced to flee, and thus became a wanderer.—*Ed.*

family of Shem, in which at least, a purer religion ought to have flourished. How insane and indomitable human infatuation is in this respect, is proved by the fact that the holy Patriarch, on whom the divine blessing had been specially bestowed, was unable to curb his posterity, and prevent them from abandoning the true God, and prostituting themselves to superstition.

3. *And I took your father Abraham*, &c. This expression gives additional confirmation to what I lately shewed, that Abraham did not emerge from profound ignorance and the abyss of error by his own virtue, but was drawn out by the hand of God. For it is not said that he sought God of his own accord, but that he was taken by God and transported elsewhere. Joshua then enlarges on the divine kindness in miraculously preserving Abraham safe during his long pilgrimage. What follows, however, begets some doubt, namely, that God multiplied the seed of Abraham, and yet gave him only Isaac, because no mention is made of any but him. But this comparison illustrates the singular grace of God towards them in that, while the offspring of Abraham was otherwise numerous, their ancestor alone held the place of lawful heir. In the same sense it is immediately added, that while Esau and Jacob were brothers and twins, one of the two was retained and the other passed over. We see, therefore, why as well in the case of Ishmael and his brother as in that of Esau, he loudly extols the divine mercy and goodness towards Jacob, just as if he were saying, that his race did not excel others in any respect except in that of being specially selected by God.

4. *But Jacob and his children went down*, &c. After mentioning the rejection of Esau, he proceeds to state how Jacob went down into Egypt, and though he confines himself to a single expression, it is one which indicates the large and exuberant and clear manifestation of the paternal favour of God. It cannot be doubted, that although the sacred historian does not speak in lofty terms of each miracle performed, Joshua gave the people such a summary exposition of their deliverance as might suffice. First, he points to the miracles performed in Egypt; next, he celebrates the passage

of the Red Sea, where God gave them the aid of his inestimable power; and thirdly, he reminds them of the period during which they wandered in the desert.

8. *And I brought you into the land*, &c. He at length begins to discourse of the victories which opened a way for the occupation of their settlements. For although the country beyond the Jordan had not been promised as part of the inheritance, yet, as God, by his decree, joined it to the land of Canaan as a cumulative expression of his bounty, Joshua, not without cause, connects it with the other in commending the divine liberality towards the people, and declares, not merely that trusting to divine aid, they had proved superior in arms and strength, but had also been protected from the fatal snares which Balak had laid for them. For although the impostor Balaam was not able to effect anything by his curses and imprecations, it was, however, very profitable to observe the admirable power of God displayed in defeating his malice. For it was just as if he had come to close quarters, and warred with everything that could injure them.

The more firmly to persuade them that they had overcome not merely by the guidance of God, but solely by his power, he repeats what we read in the books of Moses, (Deut. vii. 20,) that hornets were sent to rout the enemy without human hand. This was a more striking miracle than if they had been routed, put to flight, and scattered in any other way. For those who, contrary to expectation, gain a victory without any difficulty, although they confess that the prosperous issue of the war is the gift of God, immediately allow themselves to become blinded by pride, and transfer the praise to their own wisdom, activity, and valour. But when the thing is effected by hornets, the divine agency is indubitably asserted. Accordingly, the conclusion is, that the people did not acquire the land by their own sword or bow, a conclusion repeated in the 44th Psalm, and apparently borrowed from the passage here. Lastly, after reminding them that they ate the fruits provided by other men's labours, he exhorts them to love God as his beneficence deserves.

15. And if it seem evil unto you to serve the Lord, choose you this day whom ye will serve; whether the gods which your fathers served, that *were* on the other side of the flood, or the gods of the Amorites, in whose land ye dwell: but as for me and my house, we will serve the Lord.

15. Quod si molestum est[1] vobis servire Jehovæ, eligite vobis hodie quos colatis: sive deos, quibus servierunt patres vestri, qui fuerunt trans flumen, sive deos Æmorrhæi, in quorum habitatis terra: ego vero, et domus mea colemus Jehovam.

16. And the people answered and said, God forbid that we should forsake the Lord, to serve other gods;

16. Cui respondit populus, dicens, Absit a nobis ut derelinquamus Jehovam, serviendo diis alienis.

17. For the Lord our God, he *it is* that brought us up and our fathers out of the land of Egypt, from the house of bondage, and which did those great signs in our sight, and preserved us in all the way wherein we went, and among all the people through whom we passed:

17. Jehova enim Deus noster ipse est qui eduxit nos et patres nostros e terra Ægypti, e domo servorum,[2] et qui fecit in oculis nostris signa ista magna: servavitque nos in omni via per quam ambulavimus, et in omnibus populis per quorum transivimus medium.

18. And the Lord drave out from before us all the people, even the Amorites which dwelt in the land: *therefore* will we also serve the Lord; for he *is* our God.

18. Expulitque Jehova omnes populos, atque adeo Æmorrhæum habitatorem terræ a facie nostra: etiam nos serviemus Jehovæ, quia ipse est Deus noster.

19. And Joshua said unto the people, Ye cannot serve the Lord: for he *is* an holy God; he *is* a jealous God; he will not forgive your transgressions nor your sins.

19. Dixitque Josue ad populum, Non poteritis servire Jehovæ, quia Deus sanctus est, Deus æmulator est: non parcet sceleribus vestris, atque peccatis vestris.

20. If ye forsake the Lord, and serve strange gods, then he will turn and do you hurt, and consume you, after that he hath done you good.

20. Si dereliqueritis Jehovam, et servieritis deo alieno, convertet se, et malefaciet vobis, consumetque vos, postquam benefecerit vobis.

21. And the people said unto Joshua, Nay; but we will serve the Lord.

21. Cui respondit populus, Nequaquam: sed Jehovæ serviemus.

22. And Joshua said unto the people, Ye *are* witnesses against yourselves, that ye have chosen you the Lord, to serve him. And they said, *We are* witnesses.

22. Dixitque Josue ad populum, Testes estis contra vos quod vos elegeritis vobis Jehovam ut illi serviatis. Et dixerunt, Testes.[3]

23. Now therefore put away (*said he*) the strange gods which *are* among you, and incline your heart unto the Lord God of Israel.

23. Nunc ergo auferte deos alienos, qui sunt in medio vestri, et inclinate cor vestrum ad Jehovam Deum Israel.

[1] Literally, "And if it be evil in your eyes." This differs little from the English version, "And if it seem evil unto you," and is preferable both to Calvin's Latin, "Quod si molestum est," "But if it is irksome;" and to the Septuagint, Εἰ δὲ μὴ ἀρέσκει ὑμῖν, "If it is not pleasing to you." The last is exactly followed by Luther, "Gefällt es euch aber nicht."—*Ed.*

[2] The Septuagint omits the words "from the house of bondage."—*Ed.*

[3] The Septuagint omits the response of the people.—*Ed.*

24. And the people said unto Joshua, The Lord our God will we serve, and his voice will we obey.

24. Cui respondit populus, Jehovæ Deo nostro serviemus, et voci ejus obediemus.

15. *And if it seem evil unto you*, &c. It seems here as if Joshua were paying little regard to what becomes an honest and right-hearted leader. If the people had forsaken God and gone after idols, it was his duty to inflict punishment on their impious and abominable revolt. But now, by giving them the option to serve God or not, just as they choose, he loosens the reins, and gives them license to rush audaciously into sin. What follows is still more absurd, when he tells them that they cannot serve the Lord, as if he were actually desirous of set purpose to impel them to shake off the yoke. But there is no doubt that his tongue was guided by the inspiration of the Spirit, in stirring up and disclosing their feelings. For when the Lord brings men under his authority, they are usually willing enough to profess zeal for piety, though they instantly fall away from it. Thus they build without a foundation. This happens because they neither distrust their own weakness so much as they ought, nor consider how difficult it is to bind themselves wholly to the Lord. There is need, therefore, of serious examination, lest we be carried aloft by some giddy movement, and so fail of success in our very first attempts.[1] With this design, Joshua, by way of probation, emancipates the Jews, making them, as it were, their own masters, and free to choose what God they are willing to serve, not with the view of withdrawing them from the true religion, as they were already too much inclined to do, but to prevent them from making inconsiderate promises, which they would shortly after violate. For the real object of Joshua was, as we shall see, to renew and confirm the covenant which had already been made with God. Not without cause, therefore, does he give them freedom of choice, that they may not afterwards pretend to have been under compulsion, when they bound themselves by their

[1] Latin, "Atque ita inter primos conatus nos successus destituet." French, "Et qu'ainsi entre les premiers efforts nous nous trouvions n'estre pas bien fournis pour rencontrer ainsi qu'il faut, et tenir bon;" "And that thus among the first efforts we may find ourselves not well furnished for encountering as is meet, and standing firm."—*Ed.*

own consent. Meanwhile, to impress them with a feeling of shame, he declares that he and his house will persevere in the worship of God.

16. *And the people answered and said*, &c. Here we see he had no reason to repent of the option given, when the people, not swearing in the words of another, nor obsequiously submitting to extraneous dictation, declare that it would be an impious thing to revolt from God. And thus it tends, in no small degree, to confirm the covenant, when the people voluntarily lay the law upon themselves. The substance of the answer is, that since the Lord has, by a wonderful redemption, purchased them for himself as a peculiar people, has constantly lent them his aid, and shewn that he is among them as their God, it would be detestable ingratitude to reject him and revolt to other gods.

19. *And Joshua said unto the people*, &c. Here Joshua seems to act altogether absurdly in crushing the prompt and alert zeal of the people, by suggesting ground of alarm. For to what end does he insist that they cannot serve the Lord, unless it be to make them, from a sense of their utter powerlessness, to give themselves up to despair, and thus necessarily become estranged from the fear of God. It was necessary, however, to employ this harsh mode of obtestation, in order to rouse a sluggish people, rendered more lethargic by security. And we see that the expedient did not fail to obtain, at least, a momentary success. For they neither despond nor become more slothful, but, surmounting the obstacle, answer intrepidly that they will be constant in the performance of duty.

In short, Joshua does not deter them from serving God, but only explains how refractory and disobedient they are, in order that they may learn to change their temper. So Moses, in his song, (Deut. xxxii.,) when he seems to make a divorce between God and the people, does nothing else than prick and whet them, that they may hasten to change for the better. Joshua, indeed, argues absolutely from the nature of God; but what he specially aims at is the perverse behaviour and untamed obstinacy of the people. He declares that Jehovah is a holy and a jealous God. This, certainly, should not by any means prevent men from worshipping him; but it follows from it that impure, wicked, and profane despisers, who have no religion, provoke his anger, and can have no intercourse with him, for they will feel him to be implacable. And when it is said that he will not spare their wickedness, no general rule is laid down, but the discourse is directed, as often elsewhere, against their disobedient temper. It does not refer to faults in general, or to special faults, but is confined to gross denial of God, as the next verse demonstrates. The people, accordingly, answer the more readily,[1] that they will serve the Lord.

22. *And Joshua said unto the people*, &c. We now understand what the object was at which Joshua had hitherto aimed. It was not to terrify the people and make them fall away from their religion, but to make the obligation more sacred by their having of their own accord chosen his government, and betaken themselves to his guidance, that they might live under his protection. They acknowledge, therefore, that their own conscience will accuse them, and hold them guilty of perfidy, if they prove unfaithful.[2] But although they were not insincere in declaring that they would be witnesses to their own condemnation, still how easily the remembrance of this promise faded away, is obvious from the Book of Judges. For when the more aged among them had died, they quickly turned aside to various superstitions. By this example we are taught how multifarious are the fallacies which occupy the senses of men, and how tortuous the recesses in which they hide their hypocrisy and folly, while they deceive themselves by vain confidence.[3]

23. *Now, therefore, put away the strange gods*, &c. How

[1] Latin, "Liberius." French, "Plus hardiment et franchement;" "More boldly and frankly."—*Ed.*

[2] French, "Leur propre conscience les redarguera comme coulpables et conveincus de desloyauté, et d'avoir faussé leur foy, s'ils ne tiennent leur promesse;" "Their own conscience will condemn them as guilty and convicted of disloyalty, and as having broken their faith, if they do not keep their promise."—*Ed.*

[3] The French adds, "Comme s'il n'y avoit rien a redire en eux;" "As if there was nothing to gainsay in them."—*Ed.*

can it be that those who were lately such stern avengers of superstition, have themselves given admission to idols? Yet the words expressly enjoin that they are to put away strange gods from the midst of them. If we interpret that their own houses were still polluted by idols, we may see, as in a bright mirror, how complacently the greater part of mankind can indulge in vices which they prosecute with inexorable severity in others. But, as I do not think it probable that they dared, after the execution of Achan, to pollute themselves with manifest sacrilege, I am inclined to think that reference is made not to their practice but to their inclinations, and that they are told to put all ideas of false gods far away from them. For he had previously exhorted them in this same chapter to take away the gods whom their fathers had served beyond the river and in Egypt. But nobody will suppose that the idols of Chaldea were treasured up in their repositories, or that they had brought impure deities with them from Egypt, to be a cause of hostility between God and themselves. The meaning, therefore, simply is, that they are to renounce all idols, and clear themselves of all profanity, in order that they may purely worship God alone.[1] This seems to be the purport of the clause, *incline your heart unto the Lord*, which may be taken as equivalent to, *rest in him, and so give up your heart to the love of him, as to delight and be contented only with him.*

25. So Joshua made a covenant with the people that day, and set them a statute and an ordinance in Shechem.	25. Percussit itaque Josue fœdus cum populo in die illa: et proposuit ei præceptum et judicium in Sechem.[2]
26. And Joshua wrote these words in the book of the law of God, and took a great stone, and set it up there under an oak that *was* by the sanctuary of the Lord.	26. Scripsit Josue verba ista in libro Legis Dei: tulit quoque lapidem magnum, statuitque eum ibi subter quercum, quæ erat in sanctuario Jehovæ.

[1] The words meaning literally, "The gods which are in the midst of you,' would rather seem to indicate that even at this time some of the Israelites were addicted to the secret practice of idolatry.—*Ed.*

[2] The Septuagint says, "In Shiloh, before the tabernacle of the God of Israel;" and some expositors, induced by this and other considerations, labour, though with little plausibility, to shew that the whole transaction here recorded took place at Shiloh, and that the name of Shechem is not here given to the town of that name, but to a district so large, that even Shiloh was included in it.—*Ed.*

27. And Joshua said unto all the people, Behold, this stone shall be a witness unto us; for it hath heard all the words of the Lord which he spake unto us: it shall be therefore a witness unto you, lest ye deny your God.	27. Dixitque Josue ad universum populum, En lapis iste erit nobis in testimonium: ipse enim audivit omnia verba Jehovæ quæ loquutus est nobiscum, eritque contra vos in testimonium, ne forte mentiamini contra Deum vestrum.
28. So Joshua let the people depart, every man unto his inheritance.	28. Remisitque Josue populum, quemlibet in hæreditatem suam.
29. And it came to pass after these things, that Joshua the son of Nun, the servant of the Lord, died, *being* an hundred and ten years old.	29. His autem gestis, mortuus est Josue filius Nun servus Jehovæ centum et decem annorum.[1]
30. And they buried him in the border of his inheritance in Timnath-serah, which *is* in mount Ephraim, on the north side of the hill of Gaash.	30. Sepelieruntque eum in termino hæreditatis ejus in Thimnat-serah, quæ est in monte Ephraim ad aquilonem montis Gaas.
31. And Israel served the Lord all the days of Joshua, and all the days of the elders that overlived Joshua, and which had known all the works of the Lord, that he had done for Israel.	31. Servivitque Israel Jehovæ cunctis diebus Josue, cunctisque diebus seniorum qui diu vixerunt post Josue, quique noverant omne opus Jehovæ quod fecerat ipsi Israel.
32. And the bones of Joseph, which the children of Israel brought up out of Egypt, buried they in Shechem, in a parcel of ground which Jacob bought of the sons of Hamor, the father of Shechem, for an hundred pieces of silver: and it became the inheritance of the children of Joseph.	32. Ossa autem Joseph quæ detulerant filii Israel ex Ægypto, sepelierunt in Sechem, in parte agri quam acquisierat Jacob a filiis Hamor patris Sechem centum nummis, et fuerunt filiis Joseph in possessione sua.
33. And Eleazar the son of Aaron died; and they buried him in a hill *that pertained to* Phinehas his son, which was given him in mount Ephraim.	33. Porro Eleazar filius Aharon mortuus est, et sepelierunt eum in Gibeath Phinees filii ejus, qui datus fuit illi in monte Ephraim.

25. *So Joshua made a covenant,* &c. This passage demonstrates the end for which the meeting had been called, namely, to bind the people more completely and more solemnly to God, by the renewal of the covenant. Therefore, in this agreement, Joshua acted as if he had been

[1] The Septuagint here transposes the 29th and 31st verses, and to the end of the 29th verse, thus made its 31st, appends the singular statement that they deposited, within the tomb which they erected for him there, the stone knives with which he circumcised the children of Israel at Gilgal, when he brought them out of Egypt, as the Lord commanded them; and there they are at this day.—*Ed.*

appointed on the part of God to receive in his name the homage and obedience promised by the people. It is accordingly added, exegetically, in the second clause, that he set before them precept and judgment. For the meaning is corrupted and wrested by some expositors, who explain it as referring to some new speech of Joshua, whereas it ought properly to be understood of the Law of Moses, as if it had been said that Joshua made no other paction than that they should remain steadfast in observing the Law, and that no other heads of the covenant were brought forward; they were only confirmed in that doctrine which they had formerly embraced and professed. In the same way, Malachi, to keep them under the yoke of God, demands nothing more than that they should remember the Law of Moses. (Mal. iv. 4.)

26. *And Joshua wrote these words*, &c. Understand that authentic volume which was kept near the ark of the covenant, as if it contained public records deposited for perpetual remembrance. And there is no doubt that when the Law was read, the promulgation of this covenant was also added. But as it often happens, that that which is written remains concealed in unopened books,[1] another aid is given to the memory, one which should always be exposed to the eye, namely, the stone under the ark, near the sanctuary. Not that the perpetual station of the ark was there, but because it had been placed there, in order that they might appear in the presence of God. Therefore, as often as they came into his presence, the testimony or memorial of the covenant which had been struck was in their view, that they might be the better kept in the faith.

Joshua's expression, that the stone heard the words, is indeed hyperbolical, but is not inapt to express the efficacy and power of the divine word, as if it had been said that it pierces inanimate rocks and stones; so that if men are deaf, their condemnation is echoed in all the elements. *To lie* is here used, as it frequently is elsewhere, for acting cunningly and deceitfully, for frustrating and violating a promise that

[1] The French adds, "Et on le laisse là dormir;" "And it is left to sleep there."—*Ed.*

has been given. Who would not suppose that a covenant so well established would be firm and sacred to posterity for many ages? But all that Joshua gained by his very great anxiety was to secure its rigorous observance for a few years.

29. *And it came to pass after these things*, &c. The honour of sepulture was a mark of reverence, which of itself bore testimony to the affectionate regard of the people. But neither this reverence nor affection was deeply rooted. The title by which Joshua is distinguished after his death, when he is called the servant of the Lord, took away all excuse from those miserable and abandoned men who shortly after spurned the Lord, who had worked wonders among them. Accordingly, attention is indirectly drawn to their inconstancy, when it is said that they served the Lord while Joshua survived, and till the more aged had died out. For there is a tacit antithesis, implying lapse and alienation, when they were suddenly seized with a forgetfulness of the Divine favours. It is not strange, therefore, if, in the present day also, when God furnishes any of his servants with distinguished and excellent gifts, their authority protects and preserves the order and state of the Church; but when they are dead, sad havoc instantly commences, and hidden impiety breaks forth with unbridled license.[1]

32. *And the bones of Joseph*, &c. The time when the bones of Joseph were buried is not mentioned; but it is easy to infer that the Israelites had performed this duty after they obtained a peaceful habitation in the city of Shechem. For although he had not designated a particular place for a sepulchre, they thought it a mark of respect to deposit his bones in the field which Jacob had purchased. It may be, however, that this is expressed as a censure on the sluggishness of the people, to which it was owing, that Joseph could not be buried with Abraham, that locality being still in the

[1] When these words were penned, the venerable writer, though it could scarcely be said of him that he was, like Joshua, "old and stricken in age," was, however, like him, visibly "going the way of all the earth." In such circumstances, can we doubt, that these words contain a presentiment of the fearful decline which, after his own death, was to take place in the Church of Geneva?—*Ed.*

power of the enemy. Stephen (Acts vii.) mentions the bones of the twelve patriarchs, and it is not impossible that the other tribes, from feelings of emulation, gathered together the ashes of their progenitors. It is there said that the field was purchased by Abraham ; but obviously an error in the name has crept in. With regard to sepulture, we must hold in general, that the very frequent mention of it in Scripture is owing to its being a symbol of the future Resurrection.

END OF THE COMMENTARY ON THE BOOK OF JOSHUA.

A TRANSLATION OF CALVIN'S VERSION

OF

THE BOOK OF JOSHUA.

CHAPTER I.

1. And it came to pass after the death of Moses, that Jehovah addressed Joshua, saying,—

2. Moses my servant is dead: now therefore rise, pass over this Jordan, thou, and all this people, to the land which I give to them, namely, to the children of Israel.

3. Every place which the sole of your foot shall have trod upon, I have given to you; as I said to Moses,

4. From the desert and that Lebanon, even to the great sea, the river Euphrates, the whole land of the Hittites, even to the great sea toward the setting of the sun, will be your boundary.

5. No one shall stand before thee all the days of thy life; because as I was with Moses, so will I be with thee: I will not desert nor forsake thee.

6. Be firm therefore and strong; for thou shalt divide to this people as an inheritance the land which I swore to their fathers that I would give them.

7. Only be firm and strong exceedingly; that thou mayest keep and do according to the whole law which Moses my servant commanded thee: thou shalt not draw back to the right hand or to the left, that thou mayest act prudently (*or* prosperously) in all things.

8. Let not the book of this law depart from thy mouth; but meditate in it day and night, that thou mayest keep and do according to all which has been written in it. For then shalt thou render thy ways prosperous, and then shalt thou act prudently.

9. Have not I commanded thee to make thyself firm and strong? Fear not, nor be dispirited; since I, Jehovah thy God, am with thee in all the places to which thou goest.

10. Then Joshua commanded the prefects of the people, saying,—

11. Pass through the midst of the camp, and command the people, saying, Make ready provision for yourselves; for after three

days shall ye pass over this Jordan, that ye may enter and possess the land, which Jehovah your God giveth you to possess.

12. And to the Reubenites, and Gadites, and half-tribe of Manasseh, spake Joshua, saying,—

13. Remember the word which Moses, the servant of Jehovah, commanded you, saying, Jehovah your God hath rendered you quiet, and hath given you this land :

14. Your wives, your little ones, and your flocks will remain in the land which Moses has given you beyond the Jordan ; but you, as many of you as are men of war, will pass over armed before your brethren, and assist them,

15. Until Jehovah shall have given rest to your brethren as to you ; and they, too, possess the land which Jehovah your God giveth to them ; and then shall ye return to the land of your inheritance, and possess that which Moses, the servant of Jehovah, gave you beyond Jordan toward the rising of the sun.

16. Then they answered Joshua, saying, All things which thou hast commanded us will we do, and to all places to which thou shalt send us, will we go.

17. As in all things we obeyed Moses, so will we obey thee ; only let Jehovah thy God be with thee as he was with Moses.

18. Whoever he shall be that shall rebel against thy mouth, and shall not acquiesce in thy words in all the things which thou shalt command him, let him be put to death. Only be thou firm and strong.

CHAPTER II.

1. Now, Joshua, the son of Nun, had sent from Sittim two men as spies secretly, saying : Go, examine the land and Jericho. They accordingly set out and entered the house of a woman, a harlot, whose name was Rahab, and slept there.

2. And it was told to the king of Jericho, Behold, men of the children of Israel have come hither to-night to spy out the land.

3. Then the king of Jericho sent to Rahab, saying, Bring out the men who have gone in to thee, who have come to thy house ; for they have come to spy out the whole land.

4. Now the woman had taken the two men and hidden them. Then she says, The men, indeed, came to me, but I knew not whence they were.

5. And it was when the gate was shut in the darkness that the men went out, and I know not whither they went. Follow them quickly, for you shall apprehend them.

6. Now she had caused them to go up upon the roof, and had hidden them under stalks of flax, arranged by her on the roof.

7. And the men pursued them by the way of the Jordan, even to the fords ; they, moreover, shut the gate as soon as those who pursued them went out.

8. But before they were asleep, she herself went up on the roof to them.

9. And she says to the men, I know that Jehovah has given you the land, inasmuch as your terror has fallen upon us, and all the inhabitants of the land have melted at your presence.

10. For we heard how the Lord dried up the waters of the sea of Suph (the Red Sea) from before you when you went out from Egypt; and what things ye did to the two kings of the Amorite, who were beyond Jordan, Sihon and Og, whom ye slew.

11. We heard, and our heart was melted, neither had we any more spirit before you. For Jehovah your God is God in heaven above and on the earth beneath.

12. Now therefore swear unto me, I pray, by Jehovah, (for I have dealt mercifully with you,) that you will also deal mercifully with the house of my father, and give me a true sign,

13. That you will save alive my father, and my mother, and my brothers, and my sisters, and all who are theirs, and will rescue our souls from death.

14. The men said unto her, Our life for you unto death; only you will not betray this our conversation; then it will be that when Jehovah shall have delivered the land to us, we will deal truly and mercifully with you.

15. She therefore let them down through the window by a rope; for her house was in the building of the wall, and she herself dwelt on the wall.

16. And she said to them, Hasten to the mountain, lest perchance those who are pursuing fall in with you, and keep lurking there for three days, till those who are pursuing return, and afterwards you will go on your way.

17. Then the men said to her, We shall be blameless from this your oath by which you have bound us.

18. Behold, when we shall enter the land, you will bind this line of purple thread in the window by which you have let us down; moreover, you will assemble in the house with you, your father, and your mother, and all the family of your father.

19. And it shall be that whoever shall go outside beyond the doors of the house, his blood shall be upon his head, but we shall be blameless; and whoever shall be with you, his blood shall be upon our head, if a hand be laid upon him.

20. But if you shall betray this our conversation, we shall be free from the oath by which you have bound us.

21. She answered, As you have spoken, so be it. Then she sent them away, and they departed; and she bound the scarlet thread in the window.

22. Having set out, they came to the mountain, and remained there three days, till the return of those who had pursued, who searched over the whole way, and did not find them.

23. Those two, therefore, returning after they came down from

the mountain, passed over and came to Joshua the son of Nun, and related to him whatever things had happened to them.

24. And they said to Joshua, Jehovah has delivered the whole land into our hands. For all the inhabitants of the land have become melted before our face.

CHAPTER III.

1. And Joshua rose up very early in the morning, and he and all the children of Israel set out from Sittim, and came as far as the Jordan, and passed the night there before crossing.

2. And it was at the end of three days, and the prefects passed through the midst of the camp,

3. And commanded the people, saying, When you see the ark of the covenant of Jehovah your God, and the priests bearing it, you shall set out from your place, and go after it.

4. Nevertheless, between it and you there will be an interval of about two thousand cubits in length: do not approach it that you may know the way by which you are to go. For you have not passed by that way yesterday or the day before yesterday.

5. Now Joshua had said to the people, Sanctify (*or* Prepare) yourselves: for to-morrow Jehovah will do wonders in the midst of you.

6. And Joshua spake to the priests, saying, Take up the ark of the covenant, and pass before the people. They accordingly bare the ark of the covenant, and walked before the people.

7. Now Jehovah had said to Joshua, To-day will I begin to magnify thee in the eyes of all Israel, that they may know that in the same way as I was with Moses will I be with thee.

8. Thou, therefore, wilt command the priests bearing the ark of the covenant, saying, When ye shall have gone in as far as the extremity (outer edge) of the water of the Jordan, ye shall stand in the Jordan.

9. And Joshua said to the children of Israel, Come hither, and hear the words of Jehovah your God.

10. Joshua likewise said, Hereby shall ye know that there is a living God in the midst of you, and that he will thoroughly drive out before you the Canaanite, the Hittite, and the Hivite, and the Perizzite, and the Girgashite, and the Amorite, and the Jebusite.

11. Behold the ark of the covenant of the ruler of the whole earth will pass before you through the Jordan.

12. Now, therefore, select for you twelve men from the tribes of Israel, one for each tribe.

13. And when the soles of the feet of the priests bearing the ark of Jehovah, the ruler of the whole earth, shall have rested in the waters of the Jordan, the waters of the Jordan will be cut off, and the waters flowing from above shall stand in one heap.

14. And it was that when the people set out to cross the Jordan, the priests who bore the ark of the covenant were before the people.

15. And after those who bare the ark came even to the Jordan, and the feet of the priests bearing the ark were dipped in the extremity of the waters, (now the Jordan was full beyond all his banks the whole time of harvest,)

16. The waters which descended from above stood, and rose up into one heap very far, from the city Adam which is at the side of Sarthan, and those which descended to the sea of the desert, the sea of salt, were consumed, were cut off: and the people crossed over against Jericho.

17. And the priests bearing the ark of the covenant of the Lord stood unencumbered (*or* prepared) on dry ground in the midst of the Jordan, while all Israel crossed through dry ground, until the whole people made an end of passing the Jordan.

CHAPTER IV.

1. And it was after the whole people made an end of passing the Jordan; because Jehovah had spoken to Joshua, saying,

2. Take for you from the people twelve men, one man from each tribe;

3. And command them, saying, Take for you hence out of the midst of the Jordan, from the place where the feet of the unencumbered priests stand, twelve stones which ye shall carry with you, and deposit in the place where you shall remain this night.

4. Then Joshua called the twelve men whom he had appointed out of the children of Israel, one from each tribe.

5. And Joshua said to them, Pass before the ark of Jehovah your God through the midst of the Jordan, and let every one of you take up one stone upon his shoulder, according to the number of the tribes of the children of Israel.

6. That it may be among you, (*Hebrew*, in the midst of you,) when your children shall to-morrow ask their fathers, What are those stones beside you?

7. Then ye may answer them, When the waters of the Jordan were cut off before the ark of the covenant of Jehovah, when, I say, it was crossing the Jordan, and the waters of the Jordan were cut off, then were those stones made to be a memorial to the children of Israel for ever.

8. The children of Israel accordingly did as Joshua had commanded, and took up twelve stones out of the middle of the Jordan, as Jehovah had spoken to Joshua, according to the number of the tribes of the children of Israel, and they brought them with them to the place where they passed the night, and laid them down there.

9. Joshua also erected twelve stones in the middle of the Jordan under the station of the feet of the priests who were carrying the ark of the covenant, and they have remained there even to this day.

10. And the priests, bearing the ark, kept standing in the midst

of the Jordan, till all the speech which Jehovah had commanded Joshua to speak to the people was finished; exactly as Moses had commanded Joshua himself: but the people made haste in passing.

11. And when the whole people had made an end of passing, the ark of Jehovah passed, and the priests in presence of the people.

12. The children of Reuben, and the children of Gad, and the half tribe of Manasseh also passed over armed before the children of Israel; in like manner as Moses had spoken to them.

13. Forty thousand armed men passed over in presence of Jehovah to battle to the plains of Jericho.

14. On that day Jehovah magnified Joshua in the eyes of all Israel, and they feared him just as they had feared Moses all the days of his life.

15. And Jehovah spake unto Joshua, saying,

16. Command the priests bearing the ark of the testimony to ascend from the Jordan.

17. And Joshua commanded the priests, saying, Ascend from the Jordan.

18. Moreover, when the priests, bearing the ark of the covenant of Jehovah, had ascended from the midst of the Jordan, and the soles of the feet of the priests were transferred to the dry land, the waters of the Jordan returned to their place, and they flowed as yesterday and the day before yesterday above all its banks.

19. Now the people ascended from the Jordan on the tenth day of the first month, and encamped in Gilgal in the east district of Jericho.

20. And the twelve stones which they had brought out of the Jordan, Joshua placed in Gilgal.

21. And he spake to the children of Israel, saying, When your sons shall to-morrow ask their sons, saying, What mean those stones?

22. You shall explain to your sons, saying, Israel passed through the dry land across that Jordan:

23. Since Jehovah your God dried the waters of Jordan from before your face until you passed over; in like manner as Jehovah your God did to the Red Sea, which he dried up from before our face till we passed over;

24. That all the nations of the earth may recognise the hand of Jehovah, how mighty he is; that you may, during all days, fear Jehovah your God.

CHAPTER V.

1. And it was when all the Amorite kings who were beyond the Jordan, on the west, and all the Canaanitish kings who were near the sea, had heard that Jehovah had dried up the waters of the Jordan from before the children of Israel till they passed over, their heart was melted, and there was no longer any spirit in them before the children of Israel.

2. At that time Jehovah said to Joshua, Make for thee sharp knives, and again circumcise the children of Israel the second time.

3. And Joshua made himself sharp knives, and circumcised the children of Israel on the hill of foreskins.

4. Now this is the reason why Joshua circumcised them. The whole people who had come out from Egypt, all the males, men of war, had died in the desert on the way after they had come out from Egypt.

5. For the whole people who came out had been circumcised, but the whole people who had been born in the desert on the way, after they had come out from Egypt, they had not circumcised.

6. For the children of Israel walked through the desert till the extinction of the whole race of the men of war, who had come out from Egypt, who had not listened to the voice of Jehovah, to whom Jehovah had sworn that he would not shew the land of which he had sworn to their fathers that he would give them—a land flowing with milk and honey.

7. Their sons accordingly whom he substituted in their place, Joshua circumcised, because they were uncircumcised; for they had not circumcised them by the way.

8. And when the whole people were circumcised, they remained in their place in the camp till they were healed.

9. Jehovah said to Joshua, This day have I rolled off the reproach of Egypt from you. And he called the name of that place Gilgal even to this day.

10. The children of Israel therefore encamped in Gilgal, and they kept the Passover on the fourteenth day of the month at evening in the plains of Jericho.

11. And they ate unfermented bread of the produce of the land, the day after the Passover, and cake on the very same day.

12. And the manna ceased the day after they ate of the corn of the country, nor had the children of Israel manna any longer, but they ate of the fruit of the land of Canaan that year.

13. And it happened when Joshua was at Jericho, that he lifted up his eyes and looked, and behold a man stood over against him, in whose hand was a drawn sword, and Joshua went to him, and said to him, Art thou on our side? or art thou on our enemies' side?

14. And he said, Nay, but I am prince of the army of Jehovah: I have now come. And Joshua fell on his face to the ground, and worshipped, and said to him, What saith my Lord to his servant?

15. And the prince of the army of the Lord said to Joshua, Loose thy shoe from thy feet: for the place on which thou standest is holiness. And Joshua did so.

CHAPTER VI.

1. And Jericho was closed, and was shut up because of the children of Israel, nor could any one go out or come in.

2. And Jehovah said to Joshua, Behold, I have delivered into thy hand Jericho, and its king, and its men of valour.

3. Ye shall therefore compass the city, all the men of war, going round it once: thus shalt thou do six days.

4. Moreover, seven priests shall bear seven rams' horns before the ark: But on the seventh day ye shall compass the city seven times, and let the priests themselves sound with the trumpets.

5. And when they shall have prolonged the sound with the ram's horn, as soon as ye shall have heard the sound of the trumpet, the whole people will shout with a great shout, and the wall of the city will fall to pieces (under itself): and the people will go up every one from his own place.

6. Accordingly Joshua the son of Nun called the priests, and said to them, Take up the ark of the covenant, and let seven priests take seven trumpets of rams' horns in front of the ark of Jehovah.

7. He said also to the people, Pass over, and go round the city, and let every man armed go before the ark of the Lord.

8. And it was after Joshua spake to the people, seven priests bore seven trumpets of rams' horns, and passing over before the ark of Jehovah sounded with the trumpets. And the ark of the covenant of Jehovah followed them.

9. And every man armed went before the priests sounding with the trumpets; and he who brought up the rear followed the ark while going and sounding with the trumpets.

10. And Joshua had commanded the people, saying, Ye shall not shout, neither will ye let your voice be heard, neither will a word proceed from your mouth, until the day when I shall have said to you, Shout: then shall ye shout.

11. The ark of Jehovah therefore compassed the city, going round once, and they returned to the camp; and they remained there.

12. Joshua rose again in the morning, and the priests bore the ark of Jehovah.

13. And seven priests bearing seven trumpets of ram's horn preceded the ark of Jehovah in going; and they sounded with the trumpets. But he that was armed preceded them, and he who brought up the rear followed the ark of Jehovah in going, and in sounding with the trumpets.

14. They accordingly compassed the city on the second day another time, and returned to the camp; thus did they six days.

15. But when the seventh day arrived, they rose up as soon as it was dawn, and they went round the city after the same manner seven times; only on that day they went round the city seven times.

16. And on the seventh time when the priests sounded with the trumpets, Joshua said to the people, Shout, Jehovah has delivered you the city.

17. And the city will be anathema (set apart) to Jehovah, it and

whatever things are in it; only Rahab, the harlot, shall live, she and all who shall be at home with her; because she concealed the messengers whom we sent.

18. Nevertheless, beware ye of the anathema, lest perhaps you touch something of the anathema, and take away of the anathema, and make the camp of Israel anathema, and trouble it.

19. But all the silver and gold, and the iron and brazen vessels, will be holiness to Jehovah; they will go into Jehovah's treasury.

20. The people accordingly shouted after they sounded with the trumpets. For when the people had heard the noise of the trumpets, they shouted with a very great shout, and the wall fell down, and the people went up, every one from his place, and they took it.

21. And they destroyed all things which were in the city, from the man even to the woman, from the boy even to the old man, to the ox, and the sheep, and the ass, by the edge of the sword.

22. But to the two men who had explored the land Joshua said, Go into the house of the woman, the harlot, and thence lead out her and whatever she hath, as ye have sworn to her.

23. The spies, therefore, having gone in, led out Rahab, and her father, and her mother, and her brothers, and whatever she had, and led out her whole kindred, and placed them without the camp of Israel.

24. But they consumed the city with fire, and every thing therein; only the gold and silver, the brazen and iron vessels, they placed in the treasury of the house of Jehovah.

25. Therefore Rahab the harlot, and the house of her father, and whatever she had, Joshua caused to live; and she dwelt in the midst of Israel even to this day, because she had concealed the messengers whom Joshua had sent to spy out Jericho.

26. And Joshua made an adjuration at that time, saying, Cursed before Jehovah be the man who shall rise to build that city Jericho. In his first-born shall he found it, and in his younger son shall he set up its gates.

27. And Jehovah was with Joshua, and his fame was in the whole land.

CHAPTER VII.

1. Now the children of Israel transgressed with transgression (grievously) in the anathema, inasmuch as Achan, son of Charmi, son of Zabdi, son of Zerah, of the tribe of Judah, took of the anathema; and the wrath of Jehovah was kindled against the children of Israel.

2. Moreover, Joshua sent men from Jericho against Hai, which was near Bethaven to the east of Bethel, and he spake with them, saying, Go up and explore the land. The men accordingly went up and explored Hai.

3. And having returned to Joshua, they said to him, Let not the

whole people go up; let about two thousand men, or about three thousand men go up, and they shall smite Hai.

4. About three thousand men therefore went up from the people, and they fled before the men of Hai.

5. And they smote about thirty-six men of them, and pursued them from the gate even to Sebarim, and smote them in the descent; and thus the heart of the people was melted, and was like water.

6. Moreover, Joshua rent his clothes, and fell on his face to the ground before the ark of Jehovah even till evening, himself and the elders of Israel, and they put dust upon their head.

7. And Joshua said, Ah, ah! Sovereign Jehovah, how is it that thou hast brought this people across the Jordan, that thou mightst deliver us into the hand of the Amorite, who will destroy us? Would that it had pleased us to remain in the desert beyond the Jordan!

8. O Lord, what shall I say after Israel turns his back before his enemies?

9. And the Canaanite and all the inhabitants of the land will hear, and will turn against us, and will destroy our name from the earth; and what wilt thou do to thy great name?

10. Then Jehovah said to Joshua, Arise. Why is it that thou thus fallest upon thy face?

11. Israel hath sinned, and they have even transgressed my paction which I enjoined upon them, and they have also taken of the anathema, and they have also stolen, and they have also lied, and they have also deposited it among their vessels.

12. Therefore the children of Israel have not been able to stand before their enemies; they will turn their back before their enemies; because they are in anathema, I will not continue to be with you, unless you destroy the anathema from the midst of you.

13. Arise, sanctify the people, and say, Sanctify yourselves against to-morrow; for thus saith Jehovah, God of Israel, there is anathema in the midst of thee, Israel.

14. You shall therefore come near in the morning by your tribes; and the tribe which Jehovah shall detect will come near by families; and the family which Jehovah shall detect shall come near by houses; and the house which Jehovah shall detect will come near by men.

15. And the man who shall be detected in the anathema, will be burnt with fire, himself and all things which are his, because he has transgressed the paction of Jehovah, and has done iniquity in Israel.

16. Joshua accordingly rose early in the morning, and caused Israel to draw near by their tribes, and the tribe of Judah was taken.

17. Then he put in the kindreds of Judah, and took the kindred of Zera; then he put in the families of Zari by men, and the family of Zabdi was taken.

18. And he took his house by men, and Achan, son of Charmi, son of Zabdi, son of Zera, was taken.

19. Then said Joshua to Achan, My son, now give glory to

Jehovah, God of Israel, and make confession to him, and discover to me what thou hast done; do not conceal it from me.

20. Achan replied to Joshua and says, Truly I have sinned to Jehovah God of Israel, and thus and thus have I done.

21. I saw among the spoils a good Babylonish cloak, and two hundred shekels of silver, and one wedge of gold, whose weight was fifty shekels, which I coveted and carried off; and, behold, they are hidden in the ground, in the midst of my tent, and the silver beneath.

22. Joshua therefore sent messengers, who ran to the tent; behold it was hid in his tent, and the silver under it.

23. And they took them from the midst of the tent, and they brought them to Joshua, and to all the children of Israel, and placed them before Jehovah.

24. Joshua, therefore, taking Achan, the son of Zera, and the silver, and the cloak, and the golden wedge, and his sons, and his daughters, and his oxen, and his asses, and his flocks, and his tent, and all things which were his, and at the same time all Israel with him, led them down into the valley of Achor.

25. And Joshua said, Why hast thou troubled us? Jehovah trouble thee this day. And all Israel overwhelmed him with stones, and burnt them with fire after they stoned them with stones.

26. And they placed over him a great heap of stones, even to this day, and Jehovah was turned from his hot anger; therefore they called the name of that place The valley of Achor, even to this day.

CHAPTER VIII.

1. And Jehovah said to Joshua, Fear not, dread not; take with thee all the men of war, and arise, go up to Hai. See, I have given into thy hand the king of Hai, and his people, his city, and his land.

2. And thou shalt do to Hai and its king, as thou hast done to Jericho and its king; yet its spoil and animals you shall take to yourselves as booty. But place an ambuscade for the city in its rear.

3. Joshua accordingly arose, and all the people of war, that they might go up against Hai; and Joshua selected thirty thousand men of strength and valour, and sent them by night.

4. And he commanded them, saying, Give heed, you shall lay an ambuscade for the city in its rear; do not remove far from it, but be all of you ready.

5. And I, and all the people who are with me, will draw near to the city; and when they will come out to encounter us as formerly, we will flee before them.

6. Then they will come out after us, until we draw them away from the city; for they will say, They flee before us as before; and we will flee before them.

7. But you will rise from the ambush, and will drive out the inhabitants of the city, and Jehovah your God will deliver it into your hand.

8. When ye shall have taken the city, ye shall set it on fire; according to the word of Jehovah shall ye do. See, I have commanded you.

9. Joshua accordingly sent them, and they proceeded to the ambush, and remained between Bethel and Hai, on the west of Hai. But Joshua remained that night in the midst of the people.

10. Afterwards Joshua rose up very early, and reviewed the people, and went up, he and the elders of Israel, before the people toward Hai.

11. And all the men of war who were with him, went up and drew near, and came opposite to the city, and encamped on the north of Hai. And there was a valley between them and Hai.

12. And he brought besides about five thousand men, whom he placed in ambush between Bethel and Hai, on the west of the city.

13. And the people approached nearer to the whole camp which was on the north of the city, and their ambuscade was on the west of the city itself; and Joshua proceeded that night into the midst of the valley.

14. Moreover, when the king of Hai saw, the men of the city hastened, and rose up early, and came out to meet Israel in battle, he and all his people, at the appointed time before the plains; but he knew not that there was an ambuscade for him behind the city.

15. And they routed Joshua and all Israel before them, who fled by the way of the desert.

16. And the whole people who were in the city mustered to pursue them. And they pursued Joshua, and were drawn away from the city.

17. Nor did any one remain of Bethel and Hai who did not go out after Israel; and they left the city open, and pursued Israel.

18. And Jehovah said to Joshua, Lift up the spear which is in thy hand against Hai, for I will give it into thy hand. And Joshua lifted up the spear which was in his hand against the city.

19. Then those in ambush rose suddenly from their place, and ran when he had lifted up his hand, and they came to the city, and took it, and hastened to set fire to the city.

20. And the men of Hai turning, saw, and lo, the smoke of the city was rising up to heaven, and they had no room to flee this way or that. And the people who had fled turned against their pursuers.

21. Joshua, therefore, and all Israel, when they saw that the ambuscade had taken the city, and the smoke of the city had ascended, returned and smote the men of Hai.

22. Those besides came out of the city to encounter them, and they were in the middle between Israel, part of whom were on this side and part on that. And they smote them, till not one remained who had survived and escaped.

23. They also took the king of Hai alive, and placed him before Joshua.

24. And when the men of Israel had made an end of slaying all the inhabitants of Hai in the desert whither they had pursued them, and they had all fallen by the edge of the sword till they were consumed, all Israel returned to Hai, and smote it with the edge of the sword.

25. And the number of all who fell on that day, male and female, was about twelve thousand, all people of Hai.

26. Moreover, Joshua did not draw back his hand which he had raised to the spear, until he slew all the inhabitants of Hai.

27. Only the animals and the spoils of that city the children of Israel took to themselves for booty, according to the word of Jehovah, which Joshua had commanded them.

28. Joshua therefore burnt Hai, and made it an eternal heap, a devastation even to this day.

29. And he hung the king of Hai on a gibbet even until the time of evening; and when the sun had gone down, Joshua commanded, and they took down his corpse from the gibbet, and cast it forth at the entrance of the gate of the city, and placed over it a great heap of stones, even to this day.

30. Then Joshua built an altar to Jehovah the God of Israel in mount Ebal,

31. According as Moses, the servant of Jehovah, had commanded the children of Israel; as it is written in the book of the law of Moses, an altar of entire stones, on which they had lifted an iron, and they sacrificed upon it holocausts to Jehovah, and they sacrificed victims of prosperity.

32. He also wrote there on stones a duplicate law of Moses, which he wrote in presence of the children of Israel.

33. And the whole of Israel, and their elders and prefects, and their judges, stood on this side and on that at the ark before the priests the Levites, bearing the ark of the covenant of Jehovah, as well the stranger as the native, half of them against mount Garizin, and half of them against mount Ebal, as Moses, the servant of Jehovah, had commanded, that he might first bless the people.

34. And after these things he read all the words of the law, blessing and cursing according to all that which is written in the book of the law.

CHAPTER IX.

1. And when all the kings had heard, who were beyond Jordan in the mountain, and in the plain, and in the whole coast of the great sea from the region of Lebanon, the Hittite, Amorite, Canaanite, Perizzite, Hivite, and Jebusite,

2. They assembled together to fight with Joshua and Israel with one consent.

3. But the inhabitants of Gibeon hearing what Joshua had done to the city of Jericho and to Hai,

4. They too acted craftily. For they went away, and pretended
that they were ambassadors, and brought old sacks on their asses,
and wine-bladders, old, and broken, and bound up;
5. And old and patched shoes on their feet, and old clothes
upon them, and the whole bread for their journey was dry and
musty.
6. They proceeded therefore to Joshua to the camp in Gilgal,
and they said to him and to the men of Israel, We have come from
a far country, now therefore make a covenant with us.
7. Then the men of Israel replied to the Hivite, Perhaps thou
dwellest in the midst of me, and how shall I make a league with
thee?
8. But they said to Joshua, We are thy servants. And Joshua
says to them, Who are ye, and whence have ye come?
9. They answered him, From a very far country have thy servants come in the name of Jehovah thy God. For we have heard
his fame, and what things he did in Egypt,
10. Likewise what things he did to the two Amorite kings, who
were beyond Jordan, Sihon, king of Hesbon, and Og, king of Basan in Astaroth.
11. And our elders, and all the inhabitants of our land said to
us, Take in your hand food for the journey, and go to meet them,
and say to them, We are your servants, and now make a league
with us.
12. That is our bread; we brought it warm from our houses
on the day on which we left to come to you, and now it is hard and
dry.
13. And those are the wine-bladders, which we filled when new,
and behold they are burst. And those our clothes, and our shoes
have become worn by reason of the long journey.
14. The men therefore took of their victuals, and did not inquire
at the mouth of Jehovah.
15. And Joshua made peace with them, and entered into a
league with them, that they would permit them to live, and the
princes of the congregation sware to them.
16. But three days after they had entered into covenant with
them, they heard that they were their neighbours, and dwelt in the
midst of them.
17. And the children of Israel set out and came to their cities
on the third day. And their cities were Gibeon, Chephirat, Beeroth, Ciriath-Jearim.
18. And the children of Israel did not smite them, because the
princes of the congregation had sworn to them by Jehovah God of
Israel; and the whole congregation murmured against the princes.
19. Then all the princes said to all the congregation, We have
sworn to them by Jehovah God of Israel, therefore we cannot now
touch them.
20. This we will do to them, we will save them alive, lest wrath
be against us because of the oath which we have sworn to them.

21. Therefore the princes said to them, Let them live, and hew wood, and dig water for the whole congregation, as all the princes have spoken to them.

22. Joshua therefore called them, and spake unto them, saying, How is it that you have deceived us, saying, We are very remote from you, seeing you dwell in the midst of us.

23. Now, therefore, are you cursed, and there shall never cease among you slaves, both hewing wood and digging water for the house of my God.

24. And they answered Joshua and said, When it was distinctly told (by telling it was told) to thy servants how Jehovah thy God had commanded Moses his servant to give you the land, and utterly destroy all the dwellers of the land from before you, we feared greatly for our lives from before you, and did that thing.

25. And now, behold, we are in thy hand; as it pleaseth, and as it is right in thy eyes to do to us, thou shalt do.

26. And he did to them thus, and delivered them in the hand of the children of Israel, and they did not slay them.

27. And Joshua, on that day, appointed them to be hewers of wood and drawers of water for the congregation, and for the altar of Jehovah, even to this day, in the place which he shall have chosen.

CHAPTER X.

1. When Adoni-zedec king of Jerusalem had heard that Joshua had taken Hai and destroyed it, (that as he had done to Jericho and its king, so had he done to Hai and its king,) and that the inhabitants of Gibeon had made peace with Israel, and were among them;

2. Then they feared greatly, because Gibeon was a large city, (citizenship or territory,) as one of the Royal cities, inasmuch as it was greater than Hai, and all its men brave.

3. Therefore Adoni-zedec king of Jerusalem sent to Hoham king of Hebron, and to Piram king of Jarmuth, and to Japhiam king of Lachis, and to Debir king of Eglon, saying,

4. Come up to me, and bring reinforcements to me, that we may smite Gibeon who has made peace with Joshua, and the children of Israel.

5. Accordingly, the five Amorite kings,—the king of Jerusalem, the king of Hebron, the king of Jarmuth, the king of Lachis, the king of Eglon, they and all their armies assembled, and went up and encamped near Gibeon, and fought against it.

6. Therefore the men of Gibeon sent to Joshua to the camp in Gilgal, saying, Do not keep back thy hands from thy servants; come up to us quickly, and save us, and assist us, for all the Amorite kings, dwelling in the mountain, have assembled against us.

7. Joshua therefore came up from Gilgal, he and all the people of war with him, all the men of might.

8. And Jehovah said to Joshua, Be not afraid of them; for I

have delivered them into thy hand, nor shall any one of them stand in thy presence.

9. And Joshua came upon them suddenly; for during the whole night he went up from Gilgal.

10. And Jehovah crushed them before Israel, and smote them with a great overthrow in Gibeon, and pursued them by the way of the ascent of Beth-horon, and smote them even to Azecah, and even to Malzeda.

11. And when they were fleeing from the face of Israel, and were on the descent of Beth-horon, Jehovah sent down upon them great stones from heaven even to Azecah, and they died; more died by the hailstones than those whom the children of Israel slew with the sword.

12. Then Joshua spake to Jehovah on the day on which Jehovah delivered up the Amorite before the children of Israel. And he said in the eyes of Israel, Sun, wait in Gibeon, and Moon, in the valley of Ajalon.

13. And the sun waited, and the moon stood until the people avanged themselves on their enemies. Has this not been written in the book of Jasar? (*or*, of right.) The sun therefore stood in the midst of heaven, and did not hasten to set for about one entire day.

14. And there was no day like that before it or after it, on which Jehovah hearkened to the voice of a man; for Jehovah was fighting for Israel.

15. And Joshua and all Israel with him returned to the camp in Gilgal.

16. But the kings themselves had fled, and hid themselves in a cave in Malzeda.

17. And it was told to Joshua in these words, The five kings have been found hidden in a cave in Malzeda.

18. Then Joshua said, Roll great stones to the mouth of the cave, and set men near it to guard them.

19. But do you follow after your enemies, and cut off their tail, (*or*, rear,) and allow them not to enter their cities; for Jehovah your God hath delivered them into your hand.

20. And when Joshua and the children of Israel had made an end of smiting them with a very great overthrow till they were consumed, and the survivors who had escaped had entered into fortified cities,

21. The whole people returned to the camp to Joshua in Malzeda in peace; no one moved his tongue against the children of Israel.

22. Then said Joshua, Open the mouth of the cave, and bring me those five kings from the cave.

23. And they did so, namely, they brought to him those five kings from the cave, the king of Jerusalem, the king of Hebron, the king of Jarmuth, the king of Lachis, the king of Eglon.

24. And when they had brought out those five kings to Joshua, Joshua called all the men of Israel, and he said to the leaders of the men of war who had accompanied him, Come near, put your feet

upon the necks of those kings. And they came near and put their feet upon their necks.

25. Then Joshua said to them, Fear not and dread not, be strong and of good courage; for Jehovah will do thus to all your enemies against whom you fight.

26. After this Joshua smote them, and slew them, and hung them on five gibbets; and they were suspended on the gibbets till evening.

27. Moreover, at the time when the sun goes down, Joshua commanded, and they took them down from the gibbets, and cast them into the cave in which they had hid themselves, and they placed great stones at the mouth of the cave until this day.

28. But Joshua on that day took Malzeda, and smote it with the edge of the sword, and slew their king along with them, and left no soul which was in it surviving; and did to the king Malzeda as he had done to the king of Jericho.

29. Thereafter, Joshua, and all Israel with him, passed over from Malzeda to Libna, and besieged Libna.

30. And Jehovah delivered it also, and its king, into the hand of Israel, and smote it with the edge of the sword, and did not leave surviving a single soul which was in it; and did to its king in like manner as he had done to the king of Jericho.

31. Joshua afterwards passed, and all Israel with him, from Libna to Lachis, and encamped near it, and besieged it.

32. And Jehovah gave Lachis into the hand of Israel, and he took it on the second day, and struck it with the edge of the sword, and every soul which was in it, exactly as he had done to Libna.

33. And Horam king of Gezer, went up to give assistance to Lachis, and Joshua smote him and his people, so that he did not leave a survivor.

34. Joshua, moreover, and all Israel with him, passed from Lachis to Eglon, and they encamped against it, and besieged it.

35. And they took it on that day and smote it with the edge of the sword; and every soul which was there Joshua slew on that day exactly as he had done to Lachis.

36. Joshua thereafter went up, and all Israel with him, from Eglon to Hebron, and besieged it.

37. And they took it, and smote it with the edge of the sword, and its king, and all its towns, and he did not leave surviving a single soul which was in it, exactly as he had done to Eglon. He accordingly destroyed it, and every soul which was in it.

38. Afterwards Joshua returned, and all Israel with him, to Debir, and besieged it.

39. And they took it, and smote it with the edge of the sword, and its king and all its towns, and they smote them with the edge of the sword, and slew every soul which was there; he did not leave a survivor; as he had done to Hebron, so he did to Debir and its king, as he had done to Libna and its king.

40. And thus Joshua smote all the land of the mountain, and

the south, and the plain, and the slopes, and all their kings; he did not leave a survivor; he slew every soul, as Jehovah the God of Israel had commanded.

41. Wherefore, Joshua smote from Cades-Barne even to Asa, and the whole land of Gosen even to Gibeon.

42. And all those kings and their land Joshua took at the same time, for Jehovah the God of Israel was fighting for Israel.

43. Thence Joshua, and all Israel with him, returned to the camp in Gilgal.

CHAPTER XI.

1. And when Jabin king of Hasor had heard, he sent to Jobab king of Madam, and to the king of Simerom, and to the king of Achsaph,

2. To the kings also who dwelt in the north among the mountains and in the plain to the south of Cineroth, and in the plain in Naphoth-Dor on the west.

3. To the Canaanite on the east and west, and to the Amorite and Hittite, and Perizzite, and Jebusite among the mountains, and to the Hivite under Hermon in the land of Mispah.

4. And they went out, themselves, and all their armies with them, many people, like the sand which is near the sea-shore for multitude, and horses and chariots very many.

5. All those kings assembled, and coming encamped together at the waters of Merom, that they might fight with Israel.

6. And Jehovah said unto Joshua, Fear not before them; for to-morrow, at this time, I will deliver them all up slain before Israel: their horses thou shalt hough, and their chariots thou shalt burn with fire.

7. Joshua therefore came, and all the people of war with him, against them to the waters of Merom suddenly, and they rushed upon them.

8. And Jehovah delivered them into the hand of Israel, and they smote them, and pursued them as far as great Sidon, and even to the boiling springs, and even to the plain of Mispé on the east; and they smote them till he left none of them surviving.

9. And Joshua did to them as Jehovah had said to him; he houghed their horses, and burnt their chariots with fire.

10. And Joshua having returned, at the same time took Hasor, and smote its king with the sword. For Hasor had formerly been the head of all those kingdoms.

11. They also smote every soul which was therein, destroying by the edge of the sword; no soul remained; and he burnt Hasor with fire.

12. All the cities of those kings Joshua took, and smote them with the edge of the sword, destroying them as Moses the servant of Jehovah had commanded.

13. Only all the cities which remained in their state Joshua burned not, except Hasor alone, which Joshua burnt.

14. And all the spoils of those cities, and the cattle, the children of Israel took as booty to themselves; nevertheless all the men they smote with the edge of the sword, they did not leave any soul.

15. As Jehovah had commanded Moses his servant, so Moses commanded Joshua, and Joshua did so, that he might not omit any one of all the things which Jehovah had commanded Moses.

16. And Joshua took all that mountain land, and all the south, and all the land of Goshen, and the plain and level lands, the mountain of Israel also, and its plain.

17. From the mountain of the left, which rises towards Seir, as far as Baal-gad, in the plain of Lebanon under Mount Hermon; also all their kings he took, and smote and slew them.

18. Many days did Joshua carry on war with all those kings.

19. There was no city which made peace with the children of Israel except the Hivites, the inhabitants of Gibeon; they took them all in battle.

20. Because it was from Jehovah to harden their heart to encounter Israel in war, that he might destroy them, and no pity might remain for them; but that he might destroy them, as Jehovah had commanded Moses.

21. And Joshua came at that time and cut off Analzim from the mountains, from Hebron, from Debir, from Anab, and from all the mountains of Juda, and from all the mountains of Israel; Joshua destroyed them along with their cities.

22. There remained not of the Analzim in the land of the children of Israel; only in Gad and in Ashdod was there a residue.

23. Accordingly Joshua took all the land according as Jehovah had said to Moses, and he gave it over as an inheritance to Israel according to their divisions by their tribes; and the land rested from war.

CHAPTER XII.

1. These are the kings of the land whom the children of Israel smote, and whose land they possessed beyond the Jordan, towards the rising of the sun, from the torrent Arnon even to Mount Hermon, and all the eastern plain.

2. Sehon the Amorite king, who dwelt in Hesbon, who ruled from Aroer to the bank of the torrent Arnon, and to the middle of the torrent, and to the middle part of Gilead, even to the torrent Jabbolz, which is the boundary of the children of Ammon.

3. And from the plain even to the sea of Cineroth on the east, and even to the sea of the desert, the sea of salt on the east, by the way of Beth-hagesimoth, and from the south under the outpourings (springs) of Pisgah.

4. The boundary besides of Og king of Basan, of the residue of the Rephaim, who dwelt in Astaroth and Hedrei,

5. Who ruled in mount Hermon, and in Salchah, and in all

Basan, even to the border of Gessuri and Maachathi, and the middle part of Gilead: (such was) the boundary of Sehon king of Basan.

6. Moses, the servant of Jehovah, and the children of Israel, smote them, and Moses, the servant of Jehovah, gave it for a possession to the Reubenites, and Gadites, and the half tribe of Manasseh.

7. Now these are the kings whom Joshua and the children of Israel smote beyond the Jordan on the west, from Baal-gad in the plain of Lebanon even to the mountain Laevis which rises in Seir; and Joshua delivered it to the tribes of Israel for a possession according to their portions.

8. Among the mountains, and in the plain, and in the lowlands, and in Asdoth, and in the desert, and in the south; the Hittite, the Amorite, the Canaanite, the Perizzite, the Hivite, and the Jebusite:

9. The king of Jericho, one; the king of Hai, who was on the side of Bethel, one;

10. The king of Jerusalem, one; the king of Hebron, one;

11. The king of Jarmath, one; the king of Lachis, one;

12. The king of Eglon, one; the king of Jeser, one;

13. The king of Debir, one; the king Jeder, one;

14. The king of Hormah, one; the king of Arad, one;

15. The king of Libna, one; the king of Adulam, one;

16. The king of Makeda, one; the king of Bethel, one;

17. The king of Tapuah, one; the king of Epher, one;

18. The king of Aphek, one; the king of Lasaron, one;

19. The king of Madon, one; the king of Asor, one;

20. The king of Simron Meron, one; the king of Achsaph, one;

21. The king of Taanach, one; the king of Megiddo, one;

22. The king of Kedesch, one; the king of Jocnam at Carmel, one;

23. The king of Dor, at Naphath-dor, one; the king of Grim in Gilgal, one;

24. The king of Thirsa, one; all the kings thirty and one.

CHAPTER XIII.

1. And when Joshua had become old and stricken in years, Jehovah said to him, Thou hast become old and stricken in years, and very much land still remains to be possessed.

2. This is the land which remains: all the limits of the Philistines, and all Gessuri,

3. From the Nile, which is in the direction of Egypt, even to the border of Ekron, which is on the north, which is considered part of Canaan: five princedoms of the Philistines, Azath, Asdod, Askalon, Gittha, Ekron, and Avei.

4. From the south, the whole land of the Canaanite and Meara, which belongs to the Sidonians, even to Paera, even to the border of the Amorite;

5. And the land of Gibli, and all Lebanon toward the sun-rising, from Baal-gad under mount Hermon, until you come to Haemath.

6. All the inhabitants of the mountain, from Lebanon even to the boiling springs, all the Sidonians will I drive out from before the children of Israel; only do thou cast the lot, that it may be for an inheritance to Israel, as I have commanded thee.

7. Now, therefore, divide the land for an inheritance to the nine tribes and the half tribe of Manasseh;

8. Besides it the Reubenites, and Gadites have received their portions, which Moses gave them beyond Jordan on the east, as Moses, the servant of Jehovah, gave them;

9. From Aroer, which is near the bank of the river Arnon, and the city itself, which is in the midst of the valley, and the whole plain of Medeba as far as Debon;

10. And all the cities of Sihon, the Amorite king, who reigned in Hesbon, even to the boundary of the children of Ammon;

11. And Gilead, and the border of Gessuri, and Maachathi, and the whole of mount Hermon, and all Basan as far as Salchah;

12. The whole kingdom of Og in Basan, who reigned in Astaroth, and in Edrei; the remains of the residue of the Rephaim, whom Moses smote and expelled.

13. But the children of Israel did not expel the Geshurites and Maacathites; therefore Geshur and Maachath have dwelt in the midst of Israel even to this day.

14. Only to the tribe of Levi did he not give an inheritance: the sacrifices of Jehovah the God of Israel are their inheritance, as he spake concerning it.

15. Moses therefore gave to the tribe of Reuben by their families:

16. And their border was from Aroer, which is near the bank of the torrent Arnon, and the city which is in the midst of the valley, and the whole plain which is near Medeba.

17. Hesbon and all its cities which were in the plain; Debon and Bamoth-baal, and Beth-baalmeon,

18. And Jahasah, and Cedemoth, and Mephaath.

19. And Ciriathaim, and Sibmah, and Sereth-sahar in the mountain of the valley,

20. And Beth-peor, and Asdoth-Pisgah, and Beth-Jesimoth.

21. And all the cities of the plain, and the whole kingdom of Sihon the Amorite king, who reigned in Hesbon, whom Moses slew: and the princes of Midian, Evi, and Rekem, and Sur, and Hur, and Reba, leaders of Sihon, inhabitants of the land.

22. And Balaam son of Beor, the diviner, the children of Israel slew with the sword among their slain.

23. And the boundary of the children of Israel was the Jordan and its boundary. This is the inheritance of the children of Reuben by their families, cities, and villages.

24. And Moses gave to the tribe of Gad, to the children of Gad by their families:

25. And their boundary was Jazer, and all the cities of Gilead, and the half of the land of the children of Ammon, even to Aroer which is before Rabbah:

26. And from Hesbon even to Ramath of Mispe itself, and Bethonim; and from Mahanaim even to the border of Debir itself;

27. And in the valley of Beth-haran, and Beth-nimrah, and Succoth, and Saphon; a remnant of the kingdom of Sihon king of Hesbon, the Jordan and its confines, even to the extremity of the Sea of Chinnereth, beyond Jordan on the east.

28. This is the inheritance of the children of Gad, by their families, their cities, and their villages.

29. Moses, moreover, gave to the half tribe of Manasse: and there was to the half tribe of the children of Manasse by their families,

30. Their border, I say, was from Mahanaim, all of Basan, the whole kingdom of Og king of Basan, and all of Havoth-Jair which are in Basan, sixty cities:

31. And the half of Gilead, and Astaroth, and Edrei, cities of Og king of Basan, of the sons of Machir, the son of Manasse, to the half part of the sons of Machir by their families.

32. Those are the inheritances which Moses delivered in the plains of Moab, from the passage of Jordan to Jericho itself, on the east.

33. But to the tribe of Levi Moses did not give an inheritance; Jehovah the God of Israel himself is their inheritance, as he said to them (or concerning them.)

CHAPTER XIV.

1. These are the territories which the children of Israel received as an inheritance, in the land of Canaan, which Eleazar the priest and Joshua the son of Nun, and the heads of the tribes of the children of Israel, delivered to them, for an inheritance,

2. By the lot of their inheritance, as Jehovah had commanded by the hand of Moses, to give to the nine tribes and the half tribe.

3. For Moses had given to the two tribes and to the half tribe beyond the Jordan. But he had not given to the Levites an inheritance in the midst of them.

4. For the sons of Joseph were the two tribes of Manasse and Ephraim: accordingly they did not give a portion to the Levites in the land except cities to dwell in, and the suburbs of them for their herds and flocks.

5. As Moses had commanded, so did the children of Israel, and they divided the land.

6. And the children of Judah came near to Joshua in Gilgal, and Caleb the son of Jephunneh the Kenezite said to him, Thou knowest the word which Jehovah spake to Moses the man of God, concerning me and concerning thee in Cades-barnea.

7. I was forty years old when Moses the servant of Jehovah sent

me from Cades-barnea to explore the land, and I reported the matter to him as it was in my heart.

8. And when my brethren who had come down with me melted the heart of the people, I perseveringly followed Jehovah my God.

9. And Moses sware on that day, saying, Surely the land which thy foot has trod shall be thine for an inheritance, and to thy children for ever, because thou hast perseveringly followed Jehovah my God.

10. And now Jehovah has granted me life as he had said. Forty-five years have elapsed since the time when the Lord declared this matter to Moses, and since Israel has walked through the desert: and now, indeed, this day am I eighty-five years of age.

11. And still am I this day vigorous as on that day on which Moses sent me; as great as my vigour was then, so great is my vigour this day for battle, both for going out and coming in.

12. Now, therefore, give me that mountain, as Jehovah spake on that day, For thou didst hear on that day that the Anakim are there, and cities great and fortified: perhaps Jehovah will be with me, and I shall drive them out, as Jehovah said.

13. And Joshua blessed him, and gave Hebron to Caleb himself the son of Jephunneh for an inheritance.

14. Therefore has Hebron belonged to Caleb himself the son of Jephunneh, the Kenezite for an inheritance unto this day, because he perseveringly followed Jehovah, the God of Israel.

15. Now the name of Hebron was formerly Ciriath-arba, which Arba was a great man among the Anakim, and the land rested from war.

CHAPTER XV.

1. And there was a lot to the children of Judah by their families near the border of Edom, and the desert of Sin towards the south, from the extremity of the south.

2. And their south boundary was from the extremity of the salt sea, that is, from the rock which looks towards the south.

3. And it goes out towards the south of Maale-acrabim, and thence passes over into Sin: and proceeding from the south in Cades-barnea, it passes over thence into Esron, and again goes up in Adar, and makes a circuit in Carcaa.

4. Thence it passes into Asmon, and goes out to the torrent of Egypt: and the outgoings of this boundary are toward the west: that will be your boundary toward the south.

5. And the boundary toward the east is the salt sea, even to the extremity of the Jordan; and the boundary of the north corner is from the rock of the sea, from the extremity of the Jordan.

6. And that boundary goeth up into Beth-hoglah, and passes from the north to Beth-araba: and thence that boundary goeth up to the stone of Bohan the son of Reuben.

7. That boundary, moreover, goeth up into Debir from the valley of Achor, and towards the north looks to Gilgal, which is over against the ascent of Adummim, which, indeed, is to the torrent on the south: and that boundary passes to the waters of En-semes, and its outgoings are at En-rogel.

8. And that boundary goeth up to the valley of the son of Hinnom, to the side of the Jebusite on the south; the same is Jerusalem: that boundary, moreover, goeth up to the top of the mountain which is over against the valley of Hinnom on the west, which valley is at the extremity of the valley of Rephaim on the north.

9. And the boundary goes round from the top of the mountain, to the fountain of the water of Nephthoah, and goeth out to the cities of mount Ephron, and that boundary maketh a circuit in Baala, the same is Ciriath-Jearim.

10. And thence that boundary winds round from Baala on the west to mount Seir, and thence passes through to the side of mount Jearim on the north, the same is Chesalon, and it goeth down into Beth-semes, and passeth over into Timna.

11. And the boundary goeth out to the side of Ecron on the north, and that boundary makes a circuit to Sichron, and passes through even to mount Baala: and thence goes out into Jabneel: and the outgoings of this boundary are at the sea.

12. Moreover, the west boundary is at the great sea and its coast: that is the boundary of the children of Judah round about, by their families.

13. And he gave to Caleb the son of Jephunneh in the midst of the children of Judah, according to the word of Jehovah to Joshua, the portion of Ciriath-arba, the father of Anac, the same is Hebron.

14. Caleb drove thence the three sons of Anac, Sezadi, and Haiman, and Thalmai, who were sons of Anac.

15. And he went up from thence to the inhabitants of Debir, whose name was formerly Ciriath-sepher.

16. And Caleb said, To him who shall smite Ciriath-sepher and take it, will I give my daughter Achsa to wife.

17. And Othoniel the son of Cenas, the brother of Caleb, took it, and he gave him Achsa his daughter to wife.

18. And it was when she came, that she persuaded him to ask a field of her father, and she dismounted from the ass, and Caleb said to her, What wouldst thou?

19. She answered, Give me a blessing; since thou hast given me an arid land, give me springs of water. And he gave her upper springs and lower springs.

20. That is the inheritance of the tribe of the children of Judah by their families.

21. And the cities in the extremity of the tribe of Judah, near the border of Edom on the south were Capsee, and Eder, and Jagur,

22. And Cina, and Dimona, and Adada,

23. And Cedes, and Hasor, and Ithnan,

24. Ziph, and Telem, and Bealot,

25. And Hazor, n Hadatha, and Cerioth, Hesron, the same is Hazor.
26. Amam, and Sema, and Molada,
27. And Hasar-Gadda, and Hesmon, and Beth-phelet,
28. And Hasar-sual, and Beerseba, and Biziotheia,
29. Baala, and Jim, and Asem,
30. And Eltholad, and Chesil, and Hormah,
31. And Siclag, and Madmannah, and Sensannah,
32. And Lebaoth, and Silhim, and Ain, and Rimon: all the cities twenty-nine, and their villages.
33. In the plain Esthaol, and Sora, and Asnah,
34. And Zanoah, and En-gannim, and Thaphuah, and Enam,
35. Jarmuth, and Adulam, Sochoch, and Azecah,
36. And Saaraim, and Adithaim, and Gederah, and Gederothaim: fourteen cities and their villages.
37. Senam, and Hadasa, and Migdalgad,
38. And Dilan, and Mispeh, and Jocteel,
39. Lachis, and Boscath, and Eglon,
40. And Chabbon, and Lahmam, and Chithlis,
41. And Gederoth, Beth-dagon, and Naamah, Makeda: sixteen cities and their villages.
42. Liona, and Ether, and Asan,
43. And Jephtha, and Asna, and Nesib,
44. And Cheila, and Achzib, and Marezah: nine cities and their villages.
45. Ecron, and its towns and its villages.
46. From Ecron, and to the sea, all which are on the side of Asdod, and their villages.
47. Asdod, its towns and its villages: Azza, its towns and its villages, even to the torrent of Egypt, and the great sea; and this is its boundary.
48. And in the mountain, Samir and Jathur, and Sochoch,
49. And Dannah, and Ciriath-sannah, the same is Debir,
50. And Anab, and Estemoth, and Anim,
51. And Gosan, and Holon, and Giloh: eleven cities and their villages.
52. Arab, and Dumah, and Esan,
53. And Janum, and Beth-thappuah, and Aphecah,
54. And Humtha, and Ciriath-Arba, the same is Hebron, and Sior: nine cities and their villages.
55. Mahon, Carmel, and Ziph, and Juttah,
56. And Jezreel, and Jocdean, and Zaura,
57. Cain, Giba, and Thimna: ten cities and their villages.
58. Hal-hul, and Beth-sur, and Gedor,
59. And Maarath, and Bethanoth, and Elthecon: six cities and their villages.
60. Ciriath-baal, the same is Ciriath-Jearim, and Rabba: two cities and their villages.
61. In the desert Beth-arabah Middin, and Sech-acha,

62. And Nibsan, and the city of Salt, and En-gedi: six cities and their villages.

63. Moreover, the children of Judah were not able to expel the Jebusites, the inhabitants of Jerusalem; therefore the Jebusite hath dwelt with the children of Judah in Jerusalem even to this day.

CHAPTER XVI.

1. And the lot for the children of Joseph fell out from the Jordan to Jericho, to the waters of Jericho on the east, to the desert which goeth up from Jericho to mount Bethel.

2. And it goeth out from Bethel into Luz, and hence passeth through to the boundary of Archi Atharoth.

3. It afterward goeth up to the sea, to the border of Japhletus, even to the border of lower Beth-horon, and even to Gazer, and its outgoings are at the sea.

4. And thus the children of Joseph, Manasseh, and Ephraim received their inheritance.

5. And this was the boundary of the children of Ephraim by their families; the border of their inheritance was, I say, on the east from Atroh-Addar, even to upper Beth-horon.

6. And that border goes out to the sea, to Michmethath on the north; and the boundary goes round to the east, to Thaanath-Siloh, and crosses it from the east to Janoah.

7. And it descends from Janoah in Atharoth, and Maarath, and reaches to Jericho, and goeth out to Jordan.

8. From Thappuah the boundary proceeds to the sea, to the torrent of reeds, and its outgoings are at the sea; this is the inheritance of the tribe of the children of Ephraim by their families.

9. And cities were set apart for the children of Ephraim in the midst of the inheritance of the children of Manasseh, all the cities and their villages.

10. Nor did they expel the Canaanite dwelling in Gazer; wherefore the Canaanite hath dwelt in the middle of Ephraim to this day, and been tributary to him.

CHAPTER XVII.

1. There was also a lot to the tribe of Manasseh, (for he was the first-born of Joseph,) to Machir himself, the first-born of Manasseh, the father of Gilead, (for he was a man of war,) to him, I say, there was Gilead and Basan.

2. There was likewise to the other children of Manasseh by their families, to the sons of Abiezer, and the sons of Helec, and the sons of Asriel, and the sons of Sechem, and the sons of Hepher, and the sons of Semida. These are the children of Manasseh, the male children by their families.

3. Moreover, to Selophead, the son of Hepher, the son of Gilead, the son of Machir, the son of Manasseh, there were no sons but daughters whose names are these, Mahala, and Noa, Hogla, Milcha, and Thirsa.

4. These came into the presence of Eleazar the priest, and into the presence of Joshua, the son of Nun, and into the presence of the princes, saying, Jehovah commanded Moses to give us an inheritance in the midst of our brethren. He therefore gave them according to the word of Jehovah, an inheritance in the midst of the brethren of their father.

5. And there fell to Manasseh ten inheritances, besides the land of Gilead and Basan, which were beyond Jordan.

6. For the daughters of Manasseh obtained an inheritance in the midst of the sons; and the land of Gilead was to the other children of Manasseh.

7. And the boundary of Manasseh was from Aser to Michmethath, which is before Sechem, and the boundary proceedeth to the right, to the inhabitants of En-thappua.

8. To Manasseh himself belonged the land of Thappua; but the Thappua which was at the border of Manasseh belongs to the children of Ephraim.

9. And the boundary descends to the torrent of reeds, to the south of the torrent itself; these cities in the midst of the cities of Manasseh belong to the tribe of Ephraim; but the boundary of Manasseh is on the north of the torrent itself, and its outgoings are at the sea.

10. On the south it belongs to Ephraim himself, and on the north to Manasseh himself, and the sea is its boundary, and they meet together in Aser on the north, and in Issachar on the east.

11. And it was to Manasseh himself in Issachar, and in Aser, Beth-sean, and its towns; and Ibleam and its towns; and the inhabitants of Dor and its towns; and the inhabitants of Endor and its towns, and the inhabitants of Thaanach, and its towns; and the inhabitants of Megiddo, three districts.

12. And the children of Manasseh were not able to expel the inhabitants of those cities, but the Canaanite began to dwell in the land itself.

13. But when the children of Israel had acquired strength, they made the Canaanite tributary, and did not by expelling expel (completely expel) him.

14. And the children of Joseph spake unto Joshua, saying, Why hast thou given me one lot for an inheritance, and one inheritance, seeing I am a numerous people, so hath Jehovah hitherto blessed me?

15. And Joshua said unto them, If thou art a numerous people, go up into the wood, and cut down for thyself there, in the land of the Perizzite, and the Rephaim, if the mountain of Ephraim is narrow for thee.

16. And the children of Joseph replied to him, That mountain

will not suffice us, and there are iron chariots to every Canaanite who dwelleth in the land of the valley, and to him who dwelleth in Beth-sean and its towns, and to him who dwelleth in the valley of Jezrael.

17. And Joshua spake to the house of Joseph, namely, to Ephraim and Manasseh, saying, Thou art a numerous people, and hast great courage: thou shalt not have (*merely*) a single lot.

18. For the mountain will be thine, inasmuch as it is a wood; thou shalt therefore cut it down, and its outgoing shall be thine; for thou shalt expel the Canaanite, though he have iron chariots, and though he be brave.

CHAPTER XVIII.

1. And the whole multitude of the children of Israel assembled in Silo, and placed there the tabernacle of convention, after the land was subdued before them.

2. And there had remained of the children of Israel, to whom they had not divided their inheritance, seven tribes.

3. And Joshua said unto the children of Israel, How long do ye delay to go in to possess the land which Jehovah the God of your fathers hath given you?

4. Each tribe of you give up three men whom I will send; and they shall rise and walk through the land, and shall describe it according to its inheritance; afterwards they shall return to me.

5. And they shall divide it into seven portions; Judah will stand in his confines on the south, and the families of Joseph will stand in their confines on the north.

6. And do you describe the land in seven portions, and bring it hither to me: then I will cast the lot here before Jehovah our God.

7. For there is no part to the Levites in the midst of you, because the priesthood of Jehovah is their inheritance; and Gad, and Reuben, and the half tribe of Manasseh, have received their inheritance beyond the Jordan on the east, which Moses the servant of Jehovah gave to them.

8. And those men rose up, and went away; and Joshua commanded those who went to describe the land, saying, Go and walk through the land, and describe it; afterwards you will return to me, and I will cast the lot for you here in Silo.

9. The men therefore went away, and passed through the land, and described it by cities in seven parts, in a book: and they returned to Joshua, to the camp in Silo.

10. And Joshua cast a lot for them in Silo before the Lord; and there Joshua divided the land to the children of Israel according to their portions.

11. And the lot of the tribe of the children of Benjamin by their families came up, and the boundary of their lot fell out between the children of Judah and the children of Joseph.

12. And their boundary was on the side of the north by the Jordan; and their boundary went up to the side of Jericho on the north, and went up to the mountain at the sea; and their outgoings are at the desert of Beth-aven.

13. And thence the boundary passes through into Luz to the side of southern Luz, (the same is Bethel,) and the boundary descends into Ateroth-Adar near the mountain which is on the south of lower Beth-horon itself.

14. And the boundary is marked out, and goes round to the side of the sea at the south, from the mountain which is over against Beth-horon on the south; and its outgoings are at Ciriath-Baal, (the same is Ciriath-Jearim,) a city of the sons of Judah, that is, the side of the sea.

15. And the side on the south is from the extremity of Ciriath-Jearim; accordingly the boundary goeth out to the sea, goeth out, I say, to the fountain of the waters of Nephthoah.

16. And the boundary descends to the extremity of the mountain which is over against the valley of Ben-Hinnom, and which is in the valley of the Rephaim on the north, and it descends to the valley of Hinnom to the side of the Jebusite on the south, and thence descends to En-rogel.

17. And it makes a circuit from the north, and goes out to En-semes, and proceeds outwards to Gehloth, which is over against the acclivity of Adummim; and descends to Eben of Bohan, the son of Reuben.

18. Thence it passes through to the side which is over against the plain on the north, and descends into Arabah.

19. Thence the boundary passes through to the side of Beth-hogla on the north; and the outgoings of its boundary are at the limit of the salt sea on the north, at the extremity of the Jordan on the south; that is the south boundary.

20. And the Jordan bounds it on the east side. This is the inheritance of the children of Benjamin, by his boundaries round about by his families.

21. And these were the cities of the tribe of the children of Benjamin by their families, Jericho, and Beth-hoglah, and the valley of Cesis.

22. And Beth-araba, and Semarain, and Bethel,

23. And Avim, and Parah, and Ophrah,

24. And Haamonai, and Ophni, and Gaba; twelve cities and their villages.

25. Gibon, and Raamah, and Beeroth,

26. And Mispeh, and Chephirah, and Mosah,

27. And Recem, and Irpeel, and Tharalah.

28. And Sela Eleph, and Jebusi, (the same is Jerusalem,) Gibath, Ciriath, fourteen cities and their villages; this is the inheritance of the children of Benjamin by their families.

CHAPTER XIX.

1. And the second lot came out to Simeon, the tribe of the children of Simeon by their families; and their inheritance was in the midst of the inheritance of the children of Judah.

2. And they had for their inheritance Beer-seba, and Seba, and Moladah,

3. And Hasar-Sual, and Balah, and Asen,

4. And Eltholad, and Bethul, and Hormah,

5. And Siclag, and Beth-Marcaboth, and Hasarsusa,

6. And Beth-Lebaoth, and Saruhen; thirteen cities and their villages.

7. Ain, Rimmon, and Ether, and Asan; four cities and their villages.

8. And all the villages which were around those cities even to Baalath-beer, southern Ramath. This is the inheritance of the tribe of the children of Simeon by their families.

9. Out of a portion of the children of Judah was made the inheritance of the children of Simeon: for the portion of the children of Judah was too great for them, and thus the children of Simeon received an inheritance in the midst of their inheritance.

10. And the third lot came up for the sons of Zabulon, by their families, and the boundary of their inheritance was even to Sarid.

11. And their boundary goes up to the sea, and Maralah, and reaches to Dabbaseth, and arrives at the river which is over against Jocnea.

12. And returns from Sarid to the east, that is, to the sun-rising, to the border of Chisloth-Thabor, and thence goes out to Dabrath, and goes up to Japhia.

13. Thence, moreover, it passes to the east, at its rising, to Githah-Hepher, and Ihtahcasin: and thence it goes out into Rimmon, and winds round to Neah.

14. The same boundary likewise winds round from the north to Hannathon: and its goings out are to the valley of Iphthael,

15. And Catthath, and Nahalal, and Simron, and Idalah, and Bethlehem: twelve cities and their villages.

16. This is the inheritance of the children of Zabulon by their families: these cities and their villages.

17. The fourth lot came out to Issachar, to the children of Issachar, I say, by their families.

18. And their boundary was Jezrael, and Chesuloth, and Sunem.

19. And Hapharaim, and Sion, and Ana-harat,

20. And Rabbith, and Cision, and Abeth,

21. And Remeth, and Engannim, and Enhaddad, and Bethpasseth.

22. And their boundary reached to Thabor, and Sahasima, and Beth-semes: and the outgoings of their boundary will be at the Jordan: sixteen cities and their villages.

23. This is the inheritance of the tribe of the children of Issachar by their families, their cities and villages.

24. And the fifth lot came out for the tribe of the children of Aser by their families.

25. And their boundary was Helcath, and Hali, and Bethen, and Achsaph,

26. And Alamelech, and Amad, and Misal: and it reached to Carmel at the sea, and to Sihor-libnath.

27. And it returns to the east in Beth-dagon, and reaches to Zabulon, and to the valley of Iphtahel on the north, and to Beth-emec, and Neel, and it goes out to Chabul on the left,

28. And Ebron, and Rehob, and Hammon, and Canah, even to great Sidon:

29. And the boundary returns to Ramah, even to the fortified city of the rock; thence the boundary returns to Hosah, and its outgoings are at the sea by the coast of Achzib;

30. And Ummah, and Aphec, and Rehob: twenty-two cities and their villages.

31. This is the inheritance of the tribe of the children of Aser by their families; those cities and their villages.

32. To the sons of Naphtali the sixth lot came out, to the sons of Naphtali, I say, by their families.

33. And their boundary was by Heleph, and by Elon in Saanannim, and Adami, Neceb, and Jabneel, even to the lake, and its outgoings are at the Jordan.

34. Afterwards the boundary returns to the sea at Aznoth-thabor, and proceeds thence to Huccoc, and reaches to Zabulon on the south, and reaches to Aser on the west, and to Judah on the Jordan on the east.

35. And the fortified cities are Siddim, Ser, and Hammath, Raccath, and Chinnereth,

36. And Adamah, and Ramah, and Hasor,

37. And Cedes, and Hedrei, and En-Hasor,

38. And Iron, and Migdal-el, Horem, and Beth-anath, and Beth-semes: nineteen cities and their villages.

39. This is the inheritance of the tribe of the children of Naphtali, by their families, their cities, and their villages.

40. The seventh lot came out to the tribe of the children of Dan, by their families.

41. And the boundary of their inheritance was Sorah, and Esthaol, and Ir-semes,

42. And Saalabbin, and Ajalon, and Ithlah,

43. And Elon, and Thimnathah, and Ecron,

44. And Elthece, and Gibbethon, and Baalath,

45. And Jehud, and Bene-berac, and Gath-rimon,

46. And Mehaiarcon, and Raccon, with its boundary against Japho.

47. And the boundary of the children of Dan went out from them: and the children of Dan went up and fought with Lesem,

and took it, and smote it with the edge of the sword, and received it with their inheritance, and dwelt in it, and they called Lesem Dan after the name of Dan their father.

48. This is the inheritance of the tribe of the children of Dan, by their families; those cities and their towns.

49. And when they had made an end of dividing the land, assigning each their boundaries, the children of Israel gave an inheritance to Joshua himself the son of Nun, in the midst of them:

50. According to the word of Jehovah, they gave him the city which he asked, Thimnath-serah in mount Ephraim; and he built a city and dwelt in it.

51. Those are the inheritances, possession of which was delivered by Eleazar the priest, and Joshua the son of Nun, and the chiefs of the fathers of the tribes of the children of Israel, by lot, in Silo, before Jehovah, at the door of the tabernacle of convention; and they made an end of dividing the land.

CHAPTER XX.

1. And Jehovah spake to Joshua, saying,

2. Address the children of Israel in these words, Give cities of refuge of which I spake to you by the hand of Moses;

3. That the homicide, who has taken away a life through mistake, not knowingly, may flee thither: and they will be to you for a refuge from the kinsman of blood.

4. And he shall fly to one of those cities, and shall stand at the door of the gate of the city, and speak his words in the ears of the elders of the city itself, and they will receive him into the city, and give him a place, and he shall dwell with them.

5. And when the kinsman of blood shall have pursued him, they shall not deliver up the homicide into his hand; because he smote his neighbour unknowingly, and had no hatred to him in time past, (yesterday and the day before yesterday.)

6. And he will dwell in that city until he stand before the assembly for judgment, even until the high priest, who shall be in those days, shall die: for then the homicide will return, and come to his city, and to his house, to the city whence he had fled.

7. And they assigned Cedes in Galilee, in mount Naphtali, and Sechem in mount Ephraim, and Ciriath-arba (the same is Hebron) in mount Judah.

8. And from beyond the Jordan of Jericho on the east, they gave Beser, in the desert in the plain, of the tribe of Reuben: and Ramoth in Gilead of the tribe of Gad; and Golan in Basan, of the tribe of Manasseh.

9. Those were the cities of convention to all the children of Israel, and to the stranger sojourning in the midst of them, that whosoever had slain any one by mistake might flee thither, and not die by the hand of the kinsman of blood before he had stood before the assembly.

CHAPTER XXI.

1. And the princes of the fathers of the Levites came near to Eleazar the priest, and to Joshua the son of Nun, and to the princes of the fathers of the tribes of the children of Israel.

2. And spake to them in Silo, in the land of Canaan, saying, Jehovah commanded by the hand of Moses, that ye should give us cities to dwell in, and their suburbs for our cattle.

3. Therefore the children of Israel gave to the Levites of their inheritance, according to the word of Jehovah, those cities and their suburbs.

4. And the lot fell out by the families of the Ceathites, and there were to the children of Aaron the priest, of the Levites, of the tribe of Judah, and of the tribe of Simeon, and of the tribe of Benjamin, by lot, thirteen cities.

5. And to the remaining sons of Ceath, of the families of the tribe of Ephraim, and of the tribe of Dan, and of the half tribe of Manasseh, by lot, ten cities.

6. But to the sons of Gerson, of the families of the tribe of Issachar, and of the tribe of Aser, and of the tribe of Naphtali, and of the half tribe of Manasseh in Basan, by lot, thirteen cities.

7. To the children of Merari by their families, of the tribe of Reuben, and of the tribe of Gad, and of the tribe of Zabulon, twelve cities.

8. The children of Israel, I say, gave to the Levites those cities and their suburbs, by lot, as Jehovah had commanded by the hand of Moses.

9. They gave therefore of the tribe of the children of Judah, and of the tribe of the children of Simeon, those cities which he called by name.

10. And they were to the sons of Aaron, of the families of Ceath, of the sons of Levi; for theirs was the first lot:

11. And they gave to them Ciriath-arba of the father of Anac, (the same is Hebron,) in mount Judah, and its suburbs round about it.

12. But the field of that city and its villages they gave to Caleb the son of Jephunneh, for his possession.

13. To the sons of Aaron the priest, I say, they gave the city of refuge, for the homicide, Hebron and its suburbs, and Libna and its suburbs.

14. And Jathir and its suburbs, and Esthemoa and its suburbs,

15. Holon and its suburbs, and Debir and its suburbs,

16. And Ain and its suburbs, and Juttah and its suburbs, and Beth-semes and its suburbs: nine cities of those two tribes.

17. And of the tribe of Benjamin, Gibcon and its suburbs, and Geba and its suburbs,

18. Anathoth and its suburbs, Almon and its suburbs: four cities.

19. All the cities of the sons of Aaron, the priests, were thirteen cities and their suburbs.

20. But to the families of the sons of Cahath, Levites who remained of the sons of Cahath, (now the cities of their lot were of the tribe of Ephraim.)

21. They gave to them, I say, as a city of refuge for the homicide, Sechem and its suburbs, in mount Ephraim, and Geser and its suburbs,

22. And Cibsaim and its suburbs, and Beth-horon and its suburbs: four cities.

23. And of the tribe of Dan, Elthece and its suburbs, and Gibbethon and its suburbs,

24. And Ajalon and its suburbs, and Gath-rimmon and its suburbs: four cities.

25. And of the half tribe of Manasseh, Thaanach and its suburbs, Gath-rimmon and its suburbs: two cities.

26. All the ten cities and their suburbs, to the remaining families of the sons of Cahath.

27. Moreover, to the sons of Gerson of the families of the Levites, from the half tribe of Manasseh, as a city of refuge for the homicide, Golan in Basan and its suburbs, Beesthera and its suburbs: two cities.

28. Of the tribe of Issachar, Cision and its suburbs, Dabrath and its suburbs,

29. Jarmuth and its suburbs, Engannim and its suburbs: four cities.

30. And of the tribe of Aser, Misal and its suburbs, Abdon and its suburbs,

31. Helcath and its suburbs, and Rehob and its suburbs: four cities.

32. And of the tribe of Naphtali, as a city of refuge for the homicide, Cedes in Galilee and its suburbs, and Hamath-Dor and its suburbs, and Carthan and its suburbs: three cities.

33. All the cities of the Gersonites, by their families, were thirteen cities and their suburbs.

34. And to the families of the sons of Merari remaining of the Levites, out of the tribe of Zabulon, Jocnea and its suburbs, Cartha and its suburbs,

35. Dimnah and its suburbs, Nahalal and its suburbs: four cities.

36. And of the tribe of Reuben, Beser and its suburbs, and Jehasa and its suburbs,

37. Cedemoth and its suburbs, Mephaath and its suburbs: four cities.

38. And of the tribe of Gad, as a city of refuge from the homicide, Ramoth in Gileath and its suburbs,

39. Hesbon and its suburbs, Jazer and its suburbs: four cities.

40. All the cities of the sons of Merari by their families which remained of the families of the Levites, as was their lot, were twelve cities.

41. All the cities of the Levites in the midst of the possession of the children of Israel, were eighty-four cities and their suburbs.

42. Those were single cities, and their suburbs were round about them; so was it with all those cities.

43. Jehovah, therefore, gave to Israel the whole land, of which he had sworn that he would give it to their fathers; and they possessed it and dwelt in it.

44. Jehovah also gave them rest round about, exactly as Jehovah had sworn to their fathers; nor was there any one of all their enemies who could resist them; Jehovah delivered all their enemies into their hand.

45. Not a word failed of all the good word which Jehovah had spoken to the house of Israel; all things were fulfilled.

CHAPTER XXII.

1. Then Joshua called the Reubenites and the Gadites, and the half tribe of Manasseh,

2. And said to them, you have kept all things which Moses the servant of Jehovah commanded you, and you have obeyed my voice in all things which I have commanded you.

3. You have not deserted your brethren now for many days, even to this day, but you have carefully observed the command of Jehovah your God.

4. And now Jehovah your God has given rest to your brethren, as he had said to them; now, therefore, return and set out to your tents, to the land of your possession, which Moses the servant of Jehovah gave you beyond the Jordan.

5. Only observe carefully to do the commandment and the law, which Moses the servant of Jehovah commanded you, to love Jehovah your God, and walk in all his ways, and observe his precepts, and adhere to him, and serve him with all your heart and all your soul.

6. And Joshua blessed them, and discharged them, and they went away to their tents.

7. Now, to the half tribe of Manasseh Moses had given (an inheritance) in Basan; and to the other half, Joshua gave (an inheritance) with their brethren beyond Jordan on the west. And also when Joshua was dismissing them to their tents, and had blessed them,

8. Then he spake to them, saying, Return with much riches to your tents, and with very much property, with silver, and gold, and brass, and iron, and very much raiment; divide the spoils of your enemies with your brethren.

9. Accordingly, both the children of Reuben and the children of Gad, and the half tribe of Manasseh returned, and went away from the children of Israel, from Silo, which is in the land of Canaan, to go to the land of Gilead, to the land of their possession, in which

they had received a possession, according to the word of Jehovah, by the hand of Moses.

10. And they came to the limits of the Jordan, which were in the land of Canaan, and the children of Reuben, and the children of Gad, and the half tribe of Manasseh, built there an altar near the Jordan, an altar of conspicuous appearance.

11. And the children of Israel heard it said, Behold, the children of Reuben, and the children of Gad, and the half tribe of Manasseh, have built an altar over against the land of Canaan, on the confines of the Jordan, at the crossing of the children of Israel.

12. The children of Israel, I say, heard, and the whole body of the children of Israel assembled in Silo, to go up against them to battle.

13. And the children of Israel sent to the children of Reuben, and to the children of Gad, and to the half tribe of Manasseh, to the land of Gilead, Phinehas, son of Eleazar the priest,

14. And ten princes with him, a single prince for each house, selected from all the tribes of Israel; for there were single princes of the families of their fathers among the thousands of Israel.

15. They came, therefore, to the children of Reuben, and the children of Gad, and to the half tribe of Manasseh, to the land of Gilead, and spoke with them, saying,

16. Thus saith the whole congregation of Jehovah, What falsehood is this which ye have devised against the God of Israel, in turning away this day from going after Jehovah, by building an altar for yourselves to rebel this day against Jehovah?

17. Is it little for us to have been involved in the iniquity of Peor, from which we are not yet cleansed even at the present day, and yet there was a plague in the congregation of Jehovah?

18. Now you are turning aside this day from going after Jehovah, and it will be that you will rebel this day against Jehovah, and to-morrow he will be wroth against the whole congregation of Israel;

19. And, indeed, if the land of your possession is impure, pass over to the land of the possession of Jehovah, in which the tabernacle of Jehovah dwells, and receive possessions in the midst of us, and rebel not against Jehovah, nor revolt from us by building an altar for yourselves besides the altar of Jehovah our God.

20. Did not Achan, the son of Zerah, sin grossly in the anathema, and was (there not) anger against the whole congregation of Israel? That man did not die alone on account of his iniquity.

21. And the children of Reuben, and the children of Gad, and the half tribe of Manasseh answered and spake with the princes of the thousands of Israel.

22. Jehovah, God of gods, Jehovah, God of gods, himself knoweth, and Israel will know; if it be through rebellion, if it be through falsehood, against Jehovah, save us not this day.

23. If we have thought to build for us an altar, to turn away

from going after Jehovah ; if to sacrifice upon it burnt-offerings and sacrifice; and if to make upon it sacrifices of prosperity, let Jehovah himself inquire :

24. And if we have not rather done it from a fear of this thing, saying, Your children will to-morrow speak unto our children, saying, What have you to do with Jehovah the God of Israel ?

25. For Jehovah has put the Jordan as a boundary between us and you, ye children of Reuben and children of Gad ; ye have no portion in Jehovah; and your children will make our children desist from fearing Jehovah.

26. And we said, Let us now give our endeavour to build an altar, neither for burnt-offerings nor for sacrifice ;

27. But that it may be a witness betwixt us and you, and between our generations after us, that we may diligently serve Jehovah before him in our burnt-offerings, and our sacrifices, and our offerings of prosperity ; and lest your children may to-morrow say to our children, You have no part in Jehovah.

28. We said therefore, And it shall be, if they say to us or to our generations to-morrow, then shall we say, Ye see the likeness of an altar to Jehovah, which our fathers made, not for burnt-offering, nor for sacrifice, but to be a witness between us and you.

29. Far be it from us to rebel against Jehovah, and to turn away this day from going after Jehovah, by building an altar for a burnt-offering, for oblation, and for sacrifice, beyond the altar of Jehovah our God, which is before his tabernacle.

30. Moreover, when Phinehas the priest, and the princes of the congregation, and the heads of the thousands of Israel who were with him, had heard the words which the children of Reuben, and the children of Gad, and the children of Manasseh had spoken, it was pleasing in their eyes.

31. And Phinehas, the son of Eleazar the priest, said to the children of Reuben, and to the children of Gad, and to the children of Manasseh, This day we know that Jehovah is in the midst of us, in that ye have not sinned that sin against Jehovah ; then you have freed the children of Israel from the hand of Jehovah.

32. Therefore Phinehas, the son of Eleazar the priest, and those princes returned from the children of Reuben, and from the children of Gad, from the land of Gilead to the land of Canaan, to the other children of Israel, and reported the matter to them.

33. And the thing was pleasing in the eyes of the children of Israel, and the sons of Israel blessed God, and did not determine to go up against them to battle, to destroy the land in which the children of Reuben and the children of Gad were dwelling.

34. And the children of Reuben and the children of Gad called the altar Hed, saying, For it will be a witness between us that Jehovah is God.

CHAPTER XXIII.

1. And it was after many days, after Jehovah gave rest to Israel from all their enemies round about, that Joshua became old and stricken in years.

2. Then Joshua called all Israel, their elders, their heads, and their judges, and their prefects, and said to them, I am old and stricken in years,

3. And you have seen all that Jehovah your God has given to all those nations in your sight, because Jehovah your God has fought for you.

4. See that those remaining nations have been distributed to you for an inheritance by your tribes, from the Jordan, and all the nations which I have destroyed, even to the great sea towards the setting of the sun.

5. And Jehovah your God will himself drive them before you, and will drive them out from your presence, and you shall possess their land by hereditary right, as Jehovah your God spake to you.

6. Be very strong, therefore, to keep and do whatever is written in the book of the law of Moses, not to recede from it, either to the right hand or the left;

7. Do not become mingled with those nations which remain with you, and do not make mention of the name of their gods, nor swear by them, nor serve them, nor bow yourselves to them;

8. But cleave to Jehovah your God, as you have done even to this day.

9. Therefore he has driven out before you great nations and strong, nor has any one stood in your presence even to this day.

10. One man of you has pursued a thousand, because Jehovah your God is he who fighteth for you, as he had spoken to you.

11. Be very watchful over your souls in loving Jehovah your God.

12. For if you shall turn and turn away, and adhere to those remaining nations, those remaining nations, I say, which are with you, and contract marriages with them, and mingle yourselves with them, and they with you;

13. Then know how that after this Jehovah your God will not drive out all those nations from your face; but they will be to you for a snare, and an offence, and a scourge in your sides, and thorns in your eyes, until you perish from that best land which Jehovah your God has given you.

14. And lo, I am this day entering the way of all the earth; know, therefore, with your whole heart and your whole soul, that not one word hath fallen of all the most excellent words which Jehovah your God spake over you; all things have happened to you; not one word of them hath fallen.

15. Therefore, as every good word which Jehovah your God

spake to you has been fulfilled, so Jehovah will bring upon you every evil word, until he destroy you from that best land which Jehovah your God hath given you.

16. When ye shall have transgressed the covenant of Jehovah your God, which he commanded you, and shall have gone away and served other gods, and bowed yourselves unto them, the wrath of Jehovah will be kindled against you, and you will perish quickly from the most excellent land which he hath given you.

CHAPTER XXIV.

1. And thus Joshua assembled all the tribes of Israel in Sichem, and called the elders of Israel, and their heads, and their judges, and their prefects; and they stood before God.

2. And Joshua said unto the whole people, Thus saith Jehovah the God of Israel, Your fathers dwelt beyond the river at the beginning, as Thare, the father of Abraham and father of Nachor, and they served strange gods.

3. And I brought your father Abraham from the place which was beyond the river, and I led him through the whole land of Canaan, and I multiplied his seed and gave him Isaac.

4. And to Isaac I gave Jacob and Esau; and to Esau I gave mount Seir, that he might possess it; but Jacob and his sons went down into Egypt.

5. And I sent Moses and Aaron, and smote Egypt, as I did in the midst of it, and I afterwards led you out.

6. And I led your fathers out of Egypt, and you came down to the sea, and the Egyptians pursued your fathers with chariots and horses even to the Red Sea.

7. Then they cried to Jehovah, and he placed darkness between you and the Egyptians, and he brought the sea over him and covered him; and your eyes saw what I did in the desert, and ye dwelt in the desert during many days.

8. Afterwards I brought you to the land of the Amorite, dwelling beyond the Jordan; and they fought with you, and I delivered them into your hand; and you possessed their land, and I destroyed them before your face.

9. And Balac the son of Sippor, the king of Moab, rose up and fought with Israel; and he sent and called Bileam, the son of Beor, to curse you.

10. And I refused to hear Bileam; but blessing I blessed you, and freed you from his hand.

11. And ye crossed the Jordan and came to Jericho, and the men of Jericho, the Amorite, and the Perezite, and the Canaanite, and the Hittite, and the Girgashite, and the Hivite, and the Jebusite fought against you, and I delivered them into your hand.

12. And I sent before you hornets, who expelled them before

your face, the two kings of the Amorite, not by thy sword nor by thy bow.

13. And I gave to you a land in which you laboured not, and cities which you built not, and you dwelt in them; of vineyards and oliveyards which ye planted not, ye eat.

14. Now therefore fear Jehovah, and serve him in perfection and truth, and take away the gods which your fathers served beyond the river and in Egypt, and serve Jehovah.

15. But if it is irksome to you to serve Jehovah, choose ye this day whom ye are to worship; whether the gods whom your fathers who were beyond the river served, or the gods of the Amorite, in whose land ye dwell; but I and my house will worship Jehovah.

16. And the people answered him, saying, Far be it from us to forsake Jehovah, by serving strange gods;

17. For Jehovah our God is he who led us and our fathers out of the land of Egypt, from the house of slaves, and who did in our eyes those great signs: and he preserved us in all the way in which we walked, and among all the nations through the midst of whom we passed.

18. And Jehovah drove out all the nations, and also the Amorite, the inhabitant of the land, from our face; even will we serve Jehovah, for he is our God.

19. And Joshua said unto the people, Ye will not be able to serve Jehovah, inasmuch as he is a holy God, he is a jealous God; he will not spare your wickedness and your sins.

20. If ye shall forsake Jehovah, and serve a strange god, he will turn, and do you evil, and consume you, after he hath done you good.

21. And the people answered him, By no means; but we will serve Jehovah.

22. And Joshua said unto the people, Ye are witnesses against yourselves, that ye have chosen Jehovah, to serve him; and they said, (We are) witnesses.

23. Now therefore take away the strange gods which are in the midst of you, and incline your heart to Jehovah the God of Israel.

24. And the people answered, Jehovah our God will we serve, and his voice will we obey.

25. Joshua therefore made a covenant with the people on that day; and held forth to them precept and judgment in Sichem.

26. Joshua wrote those words in the book of the law of God; he also brought a great stone, and placed it there beneath the oak which was in the sanctuary of Jehovah.

27. And Joshua said to all the people, Behold, that stone will be for a testimony to you, for it has heard all the words of Jehovah which he has spoken to us, and it will be for a testimony against you, lest perchance ye lie against your God.

28. And Joshua sent back the people, every one to his own inheritance.

29. And these things having been done, Joshua the son of Nun, the servant of Jehovah, died at the age of a hundred and ten years.

30. And they buried him in the border of his inheritance in Thimnat-serah, which is on mount Ephraim, to the north of mount Gaas.

31. And Israel served Jehovah all the days of Joshua, and all the days of the elders, who lived long after Joshua, and who had known all the work of Jehovah, which he had done to Israel.

32. And the bones of Joseph, which the children of Israel had brought out of Egypt, they buried in Sichem, in a part of the field which Jacob had acquired from the children of Hamor, the father of Sichem, for a hundred pieces of money, and the children of Joseph had them in their possession.

33. Moreover, Eleazar the son of Aaron died, and they buried him in Gibeath, belonging to Phinehas his son, which was given him in mount Ephraim.

THE END OF THE NEW TRANSLATION

OF THE BOOK OF JOSHUA.

INDICES

TO THE

COMMENTARIES ON THE BOOK OF JOSHUA.

INDEX OF HEBREW WORDS EXPLAINED.

INDEX OF PASSAGES REFERRED TO, QUOTED, OR EXPLAINED.

GENERAL INDEX.

A

K

L

T

U

www.ingramcontent.com/pod-product-compliance
Lightning Source LLC
LaVergne TN
LVHW020532100826
845148LV00010B/1428

* 9 7 9 8 3 8 5 2 1 4 9 2 1 *